SELECTED SHORT WRITINGS

The German Library: Volume 56

Volkmar Sander, General Editor

SELECTED SHORT WRITINGS

Karl Kraus
Hermann Broch
Elias Canetti
Robert Walser

Edited by Dirck Linck

continuum

NEW YORK • LONDON

2006

The Continuum International Publishing Group Inc
80 Maiden Lane, New York, NY 10038

The Continuum International Publishing Group Ltd
The Tower Building, 11 York Road, London SE1 7NX

The German Library is published in cooperation with Deutsches Haus,
New York University.

This volume has been supported by Inter Nationes,
and by a grant from the funds of
Stifterverband für die Deutsche Wissenschaft.

Printed in the United States of America

Library of Congress Cataloging-in-Publication Data

Selected short writings / Karl Kraus . . . [et al.] ; edited by Dirck Linck.
   v. cm.—(The German library ; v. 56)
   Contents: Karl Kraus—Hermann Broch—Elias Canetti—Robert Walser.
   ISBN-13: 978-0-8264-1800-5 (hardcover : alk. paper)
   ISBN-10: 0-8264-1800-7 (hardcover : alk. paper)
   ISBN-13: 978-0-8264-1801-2 (pbk. : alk. paper)
   ISBN-10: 0-8264-1801-5 (pbk. : alk. paper)
   1. German literature—20th century—Translations into English.
I. Kraus, Karl, 1874–1936. II. Linck, Dirck, 1961– . III. Series.
PT1113.S45   2006
830.8'0091—dc22

                                      2006010405

Contents

ROBERT WALSER

Introduction

In a series of outstanding works, which thanks to their artistic riches have held their appeal as objects of aesthetic experience, the literature of the *Wiener Moderne* exhibits a notable propensity for social criticism and diagnostics. The editor of this volume of The German Library has taken this propensity as the criterion for his selection. The scope of the material ranges from class conditions under the liberated forces of capitalism, through the phantasmagoria of bourgeois sexuality, to the biopolitics of a state that sought to regulate even the morality of its citizens. As literary texts, the works collected here are not just—like all writings with poetic pretensions—self-presentations; to an immeasurable degree, they also present the thoughts that arose along with them concerning the reduction of the human spirit in the sphere of power. The literary composition of these texts is characterized by an extension into the range of philosophical construction, or theoretical writing, whereby they subscribe to a nonnegotiable idea of humanity to which their authors remain faithful with unfaltering admiration. The organization of the culture-critical text becomes an indispensable form of literary activity.

Important representatives of this trend toward an anthropologically based literature are the satirist and playwright Karl Kraus (1874–1936), and the epic novelists and essayists Hermann Broch (1886–1951), and Elias Canetti (1905–94), all of Jewish origin and all deeply influenced by experiences of marginalization, which honed their sensitivity to the pitfalls and fault lines in the supposedly stable order into which Europe had settled. These authors were qualified to accuse and entitled to complain. Amid a culture intoxicated with progress, they regarded their works as products of the end of time, paradoxical writings for a world without readers. The eschatological texts for which these Viennese writers have become famous are about the termination of life in an onrush of violence and mendacity, and as such they describe an era that was slipping into speechless darkness. The tenor of their writings is religious, insofar as they convey the possibility of unredeemable error as a terrifying reality. One example in the current volume is Karl Kraus's "Reklamefahrten zur Hölle" ("Tourist Trips to Hell"). Like so many of the satirical masterpieces by this astute language-critic, this text illustrates the metaphysical dimension of Kraus's commentaries. In it, he arraigns those who exploit the victims of a war that was itself pursued for business ends, accusing them not of a crime, but of a sin, the scale of which precludes all hope of redemption. He speaks as attorney for the victims, a status that justifies and legitimizes the incisiveness of his language.

Thanks to its alliance of throne and altar, the Habsburg monarchy believed itself well prepared for the 20th century, and while it enjoyed the pomp of its self-presentations, with the delusive promise of future greatness, artists were turning their attentions to the outer surface of this immense state, decoding and analyzing the signs of impending collapse, a calamity that would eventually end with the ruin of European civilization in the Nazi death camps. The texts selected for this volume are indebted to a phenomenological preoccupation with the ways in which everyday language and behavior can betray an otherwise imperceptible current of underlying violence. It was this violence, due to come to light on the battlefields of World War I, destroying everything in its path, sparing nothing, which justified Kraus to speak of "the last days of mankind."

Hermann Broch's novels *Die Schlafwandler* ("The Sleepwalkers") and *Die Schuldlosen* ("The Guiltless") bring together character types and voices from German and Austrian history, which Broch uses to illustrate his historical and philosophical reflections on the transformation of the bourgeois order into barbarism. Figures like the commercial clerk August Esch in *"Esch oder die Anarchie"* ("The Anarchist") from the trilogy *Die Schlafwandler,* who loses himself in an irrational cult of sex, the maid Zerline in *"Die Erzählung der Magd Zerline"* ("Zerline's Tale"), who abandons herself to her unbridled passions, or the unprincipled social democrat Zacharias in *"Die vier Reden des Studienrats Zacharias"* ("Studienrats Zacharias's Four Speeches"), whose proto-Fascist opinions weave the slogans and catchphrases of the age into a single betrayal of language—such figures are all characters from a post-character period. By means of such figures, Broch wanted to depict the "decay of values" that would, he believed, permit the ruthless logic of capitalism to subject all aspects of life to an economic efficiency of benefit only to those who cling to money, while at the same time allowing the most elementary and insidious emotional urges to break free from the control of a capacity for reason that had fallen into disrepute. During his exile in the United States, Broch wrote a series of theoretical texts describing various international legal mechanisms intended to restrain instrumental reason. In his narrative collages, his characters speak as if wanting to warn us about themselves, as if aware that, unless restrained, they would constitute the recruits of the Third Reich.

Elias Canetti moved to Vienna in 1924 and wrote his first works after the fall of the monarchy. In the self-assertive struggles of the Republic, he witnessed the socio-psychological phenomenon of the violent masses, a theme to which he devoted his attention in his monumental study *Masse und Macht* (*Crowds and Power*), and in numerous lesser works. It was something he perceived as the ecstasy of communal experience, whereby the dynamic of the crowd overrode the *principium individuationis,* drawing its deadly energy from the mechanical continuation of violent actions that targeted outsiders and minorities as their first victims. *Die Blendung (Auto-da-Fe),* the novel that Canetti wrote in 1930–31, was from the outset interpreted as a parable for the hopeless position of the human spirit in confrontation with this new violence—a violence fed by an atavistic drive in which the consciousness of death was only productive as the will to survive at any cost. In the chapter *"Der Überlebende"* ("The Survivor") in *Masse und Macht,* Canetti describes—albeit without great conviction—the praxis of the artist as a taming of the will to survive. Kien, the protagonist of *Die Blendung* however, sees himself as an anachronism. To an accompaniment of shrill laughter, he allows himself, together with the books that have been his world substitute, to be consumed by fire, which for Canetti is a symbol for the new destructive force that is perfecting total annihilation. In the later tales of the volume *"Die Stimmen von Marrakesch"* ("The Voices of Marrakech"), Canetti contrasts—not without a certain exotic whimsicality—the European morbidity with images of an alternative history of development, which allows the subject to open up emphatically to others, trusting in their similarity.

What Kraus, Broch, and Canetti present in their works is a symptomatology of the epochal violence that was clearing the ground for the terrors of National Socialism. It is no coincidence, therefore, that both Broch and Canetti backed up their literary works with significant theoretical reflections on mass psychology, jurisprudence, and politics, all aimed at the totalitarian disposition of the century. When violence outstrips the human dimension, which provides the measure for all aesthetics, art loses its voice. At that point, the theoretician may take the floor. The texts of this collection are aligned with violence and death. The works themselves are infected with the violence against which they are pitted. They are violent in their incessant efforts to uphold against the demise of life and crimes against the dignity of the creature the eternal moral law in which the will of the Creator can be seen, and which is betrayed by power.

Above and beyond their various ideological and personal differences, these authors are united by the conviction—somewhat remote for contemporary readers—that, even during a crisis, the complex vicissitudes of history can be translated into symmetrical relations between guilt and responsibility, executioners and victims, virtues and vices. In the works presented here, the criteria of intelligibility, of criticism and its truth, of proof and differentiation, remain largely unquestioned. Ideological critique is achieved by means of a cathartic language critique, in which the linguistic idiosyncrasies of the period are artfully turned into a depressing experience for the reader, the intellectual penetration of which facilitates the redeeming distinction between truth and falsity.

The enduring fame of these texts in Germany has to do with the established view that they embody the lofty voice of a truth that is all the more brilliantly vindicated insofar as it was left to great but solitary figures to secure it against the totalitarian power that was imposing form and order. The ethos of these texts is corroborated by the biographies of their authors, people repeatedly abused by state authority, deformed by anti-Semitic persecution and the travails of exile. Against the trend toward collectivization, these men mustered the pathos of the freethinker. In the reception of these works, there was never anything controversial about relating the insights conveyed through their form to the specific historic realities that they both describe and criticize. In these works, aesthetic experience and moral reflection are conceived as interrelated. The enjoyment in reading Kraus, Broch, and Canetti has invariably consisted not least in being witness to a symbolic victory over indubitable evil, the Protean guises of which always point ultimately to the essence of a single metaphysical evil opposed to the human spirit and to Nature, and that found embodiment in the armies of World War I no less than in those who reported on that war, as well as in the Storm Troopers of fascism. The artwork stood up to this evil as a creation of life and human spirit. The world of the *Wiener Moderne* was Manichean, and at its center stood Karl Kraus.

For 37 years, in 23,000 pages and 415 editions of his periodical *Die Fackel* ("The Torch") Kraus paraded his age before the jury of his language critique in the name of the eternal law. And he passed judgment. Kraus's fame was immense. His social criticism held sway throughout the intellectual circles of Vienna. His admirers included the young and befriended writers Broch and Canetti, who in their reminiscences of Kraus's public appearances evoke the image of an Old Testament prophet liberating the word from enslavement and privileged to address his remarks to the Creator in person.

Kraus left behind an unparalleled—and superhuman—corpus of work. No writer since Goethe had enriched the German language with comparable beauty, complexity, and power. No one remained more faithful to the ideal of language, and no one defended it with greater subtlety or polemic skill against those who treated it as a means to an end, forcing it into the Procrustean bed of communication. Kraus wrestled with powerful opponents: the state, the military, the press. He fought them by repeating what they said. He accused them with their own words. In his satires, of which selected extracts appear in this collection, he lifted individual figures of speech out of the bewildering torrent of social discourse—yet not at random. He made those idioms audible by forcing their deceptive intonations into consciousness, by allowing the age in which he lived to speak against itself. In his finished products, constructed from pathos-laden formulae and expressions, Kraus discovered the defects of thought. The presentation of quotations induced the reader to shift the expectation of revelations away from the author and onto the quoted material. Kraus delegated the satirical work to the reader, whom he guided by means of his choice of quotations. His play *Die letzten Tage der Menschheit (The Last Days of Mankind)*, in which he himself appears in the mask of the "Grumbler," is to this day an antidote to seduction by the *Vaterland*. In the estimation of its readers, this work retains an undiminished vitality as the most incisive condemnation of war in German literature. Despite massive obstruction by the censor, Kraus's play defends life and honor against the military, and amid the universal euphoria of violence he follows the blood trail of patriotic lies in the press and politics through to the remotest field hospital in Herzegovina. The monologue of the "Grumbler" included in this collection binds together the various intentions of this play, and delivers them as a bill of indictment, composed by the "Grumbler" as the spokesman of a creation soiled in blood and printer's ink, which Karl Kraus avenges with the devastating pen of the satirist.

In the course of the modern period, the greatness of this literature also became its burden. Along with the criteria of great literature written by a self-confident subject, the criterion of greatness itself succumbed to questioning, as something measured according to the patriarchal order that this literature itself opposed. For this reason, the collection concludes with a text by the Swiss writer Robert Walser (1878–1956). As a contemporary of Kraus, Broch, and Canetti, Walser cultivated a "small" literature, which overcame the stable relations between repression and revolt that constituted the literature of the *Wiener Moderne*. As ethical reflections, the writings of Kraus, Canetti, and Broch confront their age with the hardened certainties of moral principles, thus producing a trait of violence in themselves. Robert Walser, who in 1929 finally sought refuge in a sanatorium, employed a more modest literary form to describe a social *object* that seeks and finds its scandalous pleasures in being moved by society. Typical of this perspective is the novel *Jakob von Gunten* (1909), which is set in a school for servants. For Walser this is a paradise. He depicts the servants' desire to serve as a subversive strategy adopted by the object. It is a strategy that undermines the order of the male economy, which presupposes that everyone longs to be master and no one a servant. Walser's works celebrate this longing to be an automaton served by others and deriving pleasure from passivity, a pleasure that blunts the violent edge of power relations. In this way, Walser turns his back on the field of tyranny and places himself in opposition to the heroism of the era, which even an artist-priest like Kraus facilitated by refining their forms of self-presentation. By means of thematic devices that invert subjectivity to objectivity, Walser offends not only against the image of the artist intervening in time, but also against the norms of his own gender, which sanction the desire for passivity. In his prose sketches and novellas, now counted among the most important works of 20th century German literature, Robert Walser undermines the hero's delusion of omnipotence, parrying the martial body of the master with the body of the servant, which owes its form not to close encounters with death, but to the cunning of the slave to exploit the freedoms available. The servant settles into his place in the hierarchy, repeating and accumulating the experiences of his marginality, until ultimately the process releases a joy of existence that makes him master of his life. By opting for the modest and radically unbelligerent life, a form of life well served by the smaller literary form in which it is presented, Walser brings about shifts in the symbolic order, thereby altering it in accordance with the very law to which the Viennese social critics felt themselves committed. It may well be that among the works presented here those of Robert Walser are the most courageous.

D.L.
Translated by Peter Cripps

Karl Kraus

The Cross of Honor
[1909]

I n Austria there is a graduated scale of culpability for young girls
who embrace a life of vice. A distinction is made between girls
who are guilty of engaging in prostitution without authorization,
girls who falsely declare that they are under the supervision of the
police morals division and, finally, girls who are licensed to practice
prostitution but not to wear a cross of honor. This classification is
confusing at first sight, yet it is in complete accord with the facts of
the situation.

A girl who looked suspicious to a detective (nothing looks more
suspicious to a detective than a girl) declared that she was under
the supervision of the police morals division. She had only allowed
herself the license of a joke, but the matter was investigated. Since
her declaration turned out to be false, the police investigated her
for unlawfully practicing prostitution. But when this suspicion also
proved to be unfounded and it turned out consequently that she
was not practicing prostitution at all, the public prosecutor brought
charges of misrepresentation against her. The girl had, so the accusation read, "arrogated to herself in talking to a detective a social
position to which she was not entitled." She was practicing neither
lawful nor unlawful prostitution and was therefore an imposter;
and she escaped being sentenced only because during the hearing,
in reply to the magistrate's question as to what had been in the back
of her mind at the time, she replied, "Nothing."

To recapitulate: She had asserted that she was under the supervision of the police morals division. Because this was untrue, she was investigated by the police on suspicion of immoral conduct. She could prove all right that she was not immoral enough to lead an immoral life but, on the other hand, she could not prove that she was moral enough to be under the supervision of the police morals division. There was nothing left to do except charge her with making false statements, for which, after all, murderers are also sentenced in Austria in those cases where murder cannot be proved.

Now let us go a step further. It is possible that a girl who is licensed to practice prostitution might conceal the fact and fraudulently declare that she was not licensed to practice prostitution. She would then arrogate to herself an immoral life which she was not leading because she was licensed to do so but leading despite not being licensed to do so, being in fact licensed only to lead the immoral life for which she was licensed. Such cases rarely occur in practice, and the opinions of the Supreme Court vary considerably. But the most difficult case was one that recently occurred in Wiener-Neustadt. In a brothel in that suburb lives a girl who is licensed to practice prostitution, a girl who has never been in any trouble. She has never arrogated to herself an immoral life which she does not lead, and it has never been proved that she has falsely declared she does not practice any form of prostitution for which she is not licensed. But the devil pursued that hitherto unblemished girl, and one evening she walked about the salon of the house wearing a military cross of honor on her breast. "She thereby aroused in the guests . . ." well, what do you imagine she aroused in the guests? Not what you think, but the opposite: indignation. And when a daughter of joy arouses indignation in the guests of a house of joy, it is high time for the public prosecutor to step in.

In actual fact, the girl was charged with arousing an emotion for which she was not licensed. The first magistrate acquitted her. He said that the cross of honor was not an authorized military decoration and that the indignation aroused was merely the kind that the police could handle. To be sure, he thus acknowledged that the girl would have been guilty if she had worn, say, the order of Takowa. Now it is obvious that the unauthorized wearing of a military decoration might make a journalist culpable, but never a prostitute. In Wiener-Neustadt, however, the feminist movement seems to have made such strides that both sexes are considered equally capable of lusting after medals. At any rate, the lower court declared that a cross of honor does not constitute a military decoration.

The public prosecutor, however, was of a different opinion. He appealed, and the higher court imposed a fine of twenty crowns on the defendant. A cross of honor, the higher court held, was a badge of honor equivalent to any military decoration. And the court characterized "the wearing of a medal in a brothel" as a particularly aggravating circumstance. When the defendant was asked what had been in the back of her mind, she replied, "Nothing." But this time the answer availed her nothing. For a respectable girl could sooner presume to prostitution than a prostitute to a cross of honor. What excuse did she have? A civilian, she said, had given it to her as a gift. He was generous and had given her the cross of honor as her wages of shame. But then she should have slipped it into her stocking. Only the guests of a brothel are entitled to wear a cross of honor, and if they thereby incur the indignation of the girls, the girls would then be guilty of a culpable act. But if a guest gives a girl a cross of honor instead of twenty crowns, she may not wear the cross of honor, or else she must give twenty crowns to the court. For justice is a whore that will not be gypped and exacts the wages of shame even from the poor!

Translated by Frederick Ungar

Tourist Trips to Hell

[1920]

I have in my hands a document* that surpasses and seals the shame of this age, and would warrant assigning a place of honor in a cosmic boneyard to this money-hungry mess that calls itself mankind. If ever a newspaper clipping meant a clipping of creation—here we face the utter certainty that a generation to which such solicitations could be directed no longer has any better instincts to be violated.

After the enormous collapse of the pretense of culture, and after the nations have proved by their actions that their relationship to anything in the realm of the spirit is of the most shameless deception—perhaps good enough to further the tourist trade but never sufficient to raise the moral level of this mankind—nothing is left but the naked truth of mankind's condition, which has almost reached a point where it is no longer able to lie. In no portrait could it recognize itself as well as in this one.

But what does it mean, this picture of horror and frightfulness revealed by one day at Verdun—what does it mean, this most gruesome spectacle of bloody delirium through which the nations let themselves be dragged to no purpose whatsoever, compared with the enormity of this ad! Is the mission of the press not revealed here—first to lead mankind to the battlefields, and then the survivors?

- You receive a newspaper in the morning.
- You will read how comfortable survival is made for you.

---

*An advertisement in the Basel (Switzerland) newspaper *Basler Nachrichten,* the bulk of which is quoted on the following pages.

- You will learn that 1,500,000 bled to death exactly at the spot where wine and coffee—and everything else—are included.
- You have the decided advantage over the martyrs and the dead of first-class meals in Ville Martyre and at the Ravin de la Mort.
- You ride to the battlefield in a comfortable car, but they got there only in cattle cars.
- You learn about all that is offered as compensation to you for their sufferings and for an experience whose purpose, sense, and cause you have been unable to grasp to this day.
- You understand that all this came about so that some day, when nothing was left of the glory except moral bankruptcy, at least a battlefield par excellence would still be available.
- You learn that there is still something new at the battlefront, and that one can live better there now than before on the home front.
- You realize that what the competition can offer—the Argonne and Somme battles, the boneyards of Rheims and St. Mihiel—is a mere trifle compared with the first-class offering of the *Basler Nachrichten.* They will doubtless succeed to fatten their list of subscribers using the casualties of Verdun.
- You understand that the goal is to make the tourist trip pay, and the tourist trip was worth the World War.
- You receive an ample breakfast, even if Russia starves to death, as soon as you make up your mind to take in the battlefields of 1870–71 as well—all in one package.
- You still have time after lunch to see the remains of the unidentified dead brought in, and after completion of this program event you still have an appetite for dinner.
- You learn that the nations whose victim you are in war and in peace will even spare you passport formalities—no minor matter—if the trip goes to the battlefield and if you get your ticket through the newspaper by the deadline.
- You realize that these nations have criminal laws to protect the life and even the honor of these press scoundrels who make a mockery of death and a profit out of catastrophe, and who particularly recommend this side trip to hell as an autumn special.

BATTLEFIELD EXCURSION

Arranged by the *Basler Nachrichten*

Tourist trips from September 25 to October 25 at the reduced price of 117 francs

Unforgettable impressions

No passport necessary

To register just fill out the questionnaire.

Especially recommended as a Fall trip!

". . . the trip through the battlefield of Verdun conveys to the visitor the quintessence of the horror of modern warfare. It is not only the French who consider this a battlefield par excellence, on which the gigantic struggle between France and Germany was ultimately decided. No other battlefield of the West will make as deep an impression on anyone who sees this part of the front, with Fort Vaux and Fort Douamont in the center. If the entire war cost France 1,400,000 dead, almost one third of them were killed in that sector of Verdun comprising a few square kilometers, and the German losses were more than double. In that small sector where perhaps more than 1,500,000 bled to death, there is no square centimeter not rutted by shells. Afterward one drive through the area of the Argonne and Somme battles, walks through the ruins of Reims, and returns via St. Mihiel and through the Priester Woods; all this is only a mere run-through of details which at Verdun, combine to create an unbelievably impressive picture of horror and frightfulness . . ."

Everyone who inquires receives a printed guide listing the detailed itinerary for the trip and all necessary information. Trips depart every day. Comfortable seating is guaranteed to every participant.

TRIPS BY CAR!

600 kilometers by rail, second class. An entire day through the battle-fields in a comfortable car, overnight stay, first-class meals, wine, coffee, tips, passport formalities and visas from Basel round trip, all included in the price of 117 Swiss francs.

- You leave Basel in the evening in an express train, second class.
- You are picked up at the Metz railway station and taken by car to the hotel.
- You stay overnight at a first-class hotel, service and tips included.
- You receive an ample breakfast in the morning.
- You leave Metz in a comfortable car and ride through the battlefield area of 1870–71 (Gravelotte).
- You have a guided tour of the highly interesting blockhouse in Etain (quarters of the Crown Prince and site of a large German headquarters).
- You ride through the destroyed villages in the fortress area of Vaux with its gigantic cemeteries holding hundreds of thousands of dead.
- You inspect, with a guide, the subterranean casemates of Fort Vaux.
- You visit the Ossuaire (boneyards) of Thiamont where the remains of the unidentified dead are constantly deposited.
- You drive along the Ravin de la Mort past the Carrières d'Haudromont at the foot of the Côte du Poivre to Verdun.
- You have lunch in the best hotel in Verdun, with wine and coffee, tips included.
- You have time after lunch to visit destroyed Verdun and Ville Martyre, and passing through the battlefields of 1870–71 you return to Gravelotte and Metz.
- You have dinner in your hotel in Metz with wine and coffee, tips included.
- You are taken to the station by car after dinner.
- You return to Basel on a night express second class.

**Everything included in the price of 117 francs,
with ample meals at first-rate restaurants**

A large number of letters of praise and appreciation from people who have taken the trip is available at our office.

- You will have difficulty not violating these laws, but afterward you will be expected to send a letter of appreciation and thanks to the *Basler Nachrichten.*
- You will have unforgettable impressions of a world in which there is no single square centimeter not rutted by shells and advertisements.
- And if, even then, you have not recognized that your very birth has brought you into a murderers' pit and that a mankind which profanes even the blood it shed is shot through and through with evil, and that there is no escaping it and no help—then the devil take you to a battlefield par excellence!

The Last Days of Mankind

Scene 53

A deserted street. It is getting dark. Suddenly, from all sides, figures rush into the street, each with a bundle of newsprint, breathless. Corybants and Mænads rage the length and breadth of the street, they roar and seem to call out a murder. The cries are incomprehensible. Many seem to literally groan out the news. It sounds as if the agony of mankind was being drawn from a deep well.

——stra-a-a——! extra-a-a——! fi-i-i——na-a-a-l——edi-i-i ——na-a-a-l——edi-i-i-i——shu-u-u-un!   ——edi-i-i—— fi-i-i-i——na-a-a-l——shu-u-u-un——!

(They disappear. The street is empty.)

(Scene change.)

Scene 54

The Grumbler at his desk. He reads:

"The wish to establish the exact time that a tree standing in the forest needs in order to be converted into a newspaper has given the owner of a Harz paper mill the occasion to conduct an interesting experiment. At 7:35 he had three trees felled in the forest neighboring the factory, which, after their bark was scaled off, were hauled into the pulp mill. The transformation of the three tree trunks into liquid wood pulp proceeded so quickly that as early as 9:39 the first roll of newsprint left the machine. This roll was immediately taken by car to the printing plant of a daily newspaper four kilometers away; and no later than 11:00 A.M. the newspaper was being sold on the street. Accordingly, a time span of only three hours and twenty-five minutes was required in order that the public could read the latest news report on the material that stemmed from trees on whose branches the birds had sung their songs that very morning."

(Outside, from quite far off, the cry: "E-e-xtra—")

GRUMBLER: So it is five o'clock. The answer is here, the echo of my blood-haunted madness. And no longer does anything resound to me out of ruined creation except this one sound, out of which ten millions who are dying accuse me of still being alive, I who had eyes so to see the world, and whose stare struck it in such a fashion that it became as I saw it. If heaven was just in letting this come about, then it was unjust in not having annihilated me. Have I deserved this fulfillment of my deathly fear of life? What's looming there, invading all my nights? Why was I not given the physical strength to smash the sin of this planet with one ax blow? Why was I not given the mental power to force an outcry out of desecrated mankind? Why is my shout of protest not stronger than this tinny command that has dominion over the souls of a whole globe?

I preserve documents for a time that will no longer comprehend them or will be so far removed from today that it will say I was a forger. But no, the time to say that will not come. For such time will not be. I have written a tragedy, whose perishing hero is mankind, whose tragic conflict, the conflict between the world and nature, has a fatal ending. Alas, because this drama has no actor other than all mankind, it has no audience!

So you would have to continue to die for something, which you call Honor or the Bucovina province. For what have you died? Why this scorn of death? Why should you scorn that which you know not? To be sure, one scorns life, which one knows not. You first come to know it when the shrapnel has not quite killed you, or when the beast, acting on orders, foaming at the mouth, not long ago a man like yourself, throws himself on you, and you have a flash of consciousness on the threshold. And now the beast who commands you dares to say of you, you scorn death? And you have not used this moment to shout to your superior that he was not God's superior who could order Him to uncreate what was created? Oh, had you known, at the moment of sacrifice, about the profit that grows despite—no, with—the sacrifice, fattening itself on it! For never, until this indecisive war of the machines, has there been such godless war profit, and you, winning or losing, lost the war, from which only your murderers profited.

You, faithful companion of my words, turning your pure faith upward to the heaven of art, laying your ear in tranquil scholarship to its bosom—why did you have to pass into the beyond? I saw you on the day when you marched out. The rain and the mud of this fatherland and its infamous music were the farewell, as they herded you into the cattle car! I see your pale face in this orgy of filth and lies in this frightful farewell at a freight station, from which the human material is dispatched. Why could you not have died just from experiencing this initiation, one that makes Wallenstein's camp seem truly like the lobby of a palatial hotel! For technological man becomes dirty before he gets bloody. This is how your Italian journey began, you quester after art.

And you, noble poet's heart who, between the voices of the mortars and the murderers, attended to the secret of a vowel—have you spent four years of your springtime beneath the earth in order to test your future abode? What had you to seek there? Lice for the fatherland? To wait, until the grenade splinter came? To prove that your body can better resist the effectiveness of the Schneider-Creuzot works than the body of a man from Torino can that of the Skoda works? What, are we the traveling salesmen of arms factories who are to testify to the superiority of our firms, and to the inferiority of the competition, not with our mouths but with our bodies?

Where there are many who travel, there will be many who limp. So let them turn their sales areas into battlefields. But that they also had the power to coerce higher natures into the service of wickedness—the devil never would have dared to imagine such a consolidation of his dominion. And had one whispered to him that in the first year of the war, the war into which he had chased people, hornbook in hand, in order that they transact his business with more soul, if one had whispered to him that in that first year an oil refinery would reap a one hundred and thirty-seven percent net profit, David Fanto, seventy-three percent, Kreditanstalt Bank, twenty million, and that the profiteers in meat and sugar and alcohol and fruit and potatoes and butter and leather and rubber and coal and iron and wool and soap and oil and ink and weapons would be indemnified a hundredfold for the depreciation of other people's blood—the devil himself would have advocated a peace treaty that renounced all war aims.

And for that, you lay four years in dirt and damp, for that, the letter that wanted to reach you was obstructed, the book that wanted to comfort you was stopped. They wanted you to stay alive, for they had not yet stolen enough on their stock exchanges, had not yet lied enough in their newspapers, had not yet harassed people enough in their governmental offices, had not yet sufficiently whipped mankind into confusion, had not yet sufficiently made the war the excuse, in all their doings and circumstances, for their ineffectuality and their maliciousness—they had not yet danced this whole tragic carnival through to its end, this carnival in which men died before the eyes of female war reporters, and butchers became doctors of philosophy *honoris causa*!

You have lain weeks on end under the assault of mine throwers; you have been threatened by avalanches; you have hung by a rope, three thousand meters high, between the enemy barrage and the machine-gun fire of your own lines; you have been exposed to the ordeal, prolonged a hundredfold, of the condemned; you had to live through the whole variety of death in the collision of organism and machine, death by mines, barbed wire, dumdum bullets, bombs, flames, gas and all the hells of curtain fire—all this because madness and profiteering had not vented on you enough of their cowardly spite. And you out there, and we here, are we supposed to stare still longer into the graves that we had to dig for ourselves by orders from highest quarters—as the old Serbian men were ordered to do, and for no other reason than that they were Serbs and still alive and therefore suspect!

Alas, if one were only—having got out of this adventure unscathed, although careworn, impoverished, aged—if one were only, by the magic of some divine retribution, granted the power to hold accountable, one by one, the ringleaders of this world crime, the ringleaders who always survive, to lock them up in their churches, and there, just as they did with the old Serbian men, to let each tenth one draw his death lot! But then not to kill them—no, to slap their faces! And to address them thus: What, you scoundrels, you did not know, you had no idea, that among the millions of possibilities of horror and shame, the consequences of a declaration of war, if it was so decided in the profiteers' war plans, would also be these: that children have no milk, horses no oats, and that even one far from the battlefield can go blind from methyl alcohol, if it has been so decided in the war plans of the profiteers? What, did you not conceive of the misery of one hour of a captivity that was to last for many years? Of one sigh of longing and of sullied, torn, murdered love? Were you not even capable of imagining what hells are opened up by one tortured minute of a mother's harkening into the distance, through nights and days of this years-long waiting for a hero's death? And you did not notice how the tragedy became a farce, became, through the simultaneousness of a new and hateful nuisance and a mania for fossilized forms, an operetta, one of those loathsome modern operettas, whose libretto is an indignity and whose music is torture?

What, and you there, you who have been murdered, you did not rise up against this order? Against this system of murder. Against an economic system that for all the future had to condemn life to sticking it out, to drop the curtain on all hope, and to relinquish to the hatred of nations the snatching of even the smallest bit of happiness? Outrages in war senselessly committed and outrages committed against everybody because there was a war on. Poverty, hunger, and shame piled up on those fleeing and those who could still stay in their homes, and all mankind shackled, within and without.

And statesmen in precipitous times called upon to their one duty, to curb mankind's bestial impulse—they have unleashed it!

Cowardly hatred of life, inclined even in peacetime to kill animals and children, turned to the machine to ravish all that grows! Hysteria, protected by technology, overpowers nature; paper commands weapon. We were disabled by the rotary presses before there were victims of cannons. Were not all realms of imagination vacated when that manifesto declared war on all the inhabited globe?

In the end was the word. For the word that killed the spirit, nothing remained but to give birth to the deed. Weaklings became strong to force us under the wheel of progress. And that was the press's doing, the press alone, which with its whoring corrupted the world! Not that the press set the machinery of death into motion—but that it eviscerated our hearts, so we could no longer imagine what was in store for us: that is its war guilt! And from the lascivious wine of its debauchery all peoples have drunk, and the kings of the earth fornicated with the press. And the horseman of the apocalypse drank to it, he whom I saw galloping through the German Reich, long before he actually did so.

A decade has passed since I knew that his task was achieved. He is rushing ahead at full speed in all the streets. His moustache stretches from sunrise to sunset and from south to north. "And power was given to him that sat thereon to take peace from the earth, and that they should kill one another." And I saw him as the beast with the ten horns and the seven heads and a mouth like the mouth of a lion. "They worshipped the beast, saying, Who is like unto the beast? Who is able to make war with him? And there was given unto him a mouth speaking great things." And we fell through him and through the whore of Babylon, who, in all tongues of the world, persuaded us that we were each other's enemy, and there should be war!

And you who were sacrificed did not rise up against this scheme? Did not resist the coercion to die, did not resist the last liberty—to murder? All human rights and values traded for the idea of the material; the child in his mother's womb pledged to the imperative of hatred; and the image of this fighting manhood, yes, even of this nursing womanhood, armored bodies with gas masks, like those of a horde of mythical beasts, handed down to the horror of posterity. With church bells you fired on the devout, and before altars of shrapnel, you did not repent.

And in all that, glory and fatherland? Yes, you have experienced this fatherland, before you died for it. This fatherland, from that moment when you had to wait undressed in the sweaty and beery air of the entrance hall to the hero's death, while they inspected human flesh and forced human souls to take the most godless oaths. Naked you were, as only before God and your beloved, before a board of tyrannical martinets and swine! Shame, shame for body and soul should have made you deny yourself to this fatherland!

We have all seen this fatherland, and the luckier ones among us, who could escape it, saw it in the figure of the impudent border guard. We saw it in all shapes of the greed for power of the freed slaves, in the accommodativeness of the tip-greedy extorter. Only we others did not have to experience the fatherland in the shape of the enemy, the real enemy, who with machine guns drove you in front of the enemies' machine guns. But had we seen it only in the likenesses of these hideous generals, who, all through this time of greatness, publicized themselves in fan magazines, as expensive ladies do in peacetime, to show that people are not always only whoring, but are also killing—truly we longed for this blood brothel's closing hour!

What, you there, who were murdered, who were cheated, you did not rise up against this system? You endured the license and luxury of the press strategists, parasites, and buffoons, just as you endured your misfortune and your coercion? And you knew, that for your martyrdom they received medals of honor? And you did not spit this glory in their faces? You were lying in trains that carried the wounded, which the rabble were permitted to write up for their papers? You did not break out, did not desert for a holy war, to liberate us at home from the archenemy who daily bombarded our brains with lies? And you died for this business? Lived through all this horror, only to prolong our own, while we here groaned in the midst of profiteering and misery and the harrowing contrasts of bloated impudence and the voicelessness of tuberculosis.

Oh, you had less feeling for us than we had for you, we who wanted to demand back a hundredfold each hour of these years that they tore out of your lives, we who always had only one question to ask you: what will you look like when you have survived this! When you have escaped glory's ultimate goal—that the hyenas become tourist guides, offering the site of your graves as sightseeing attractions! To be ill, impoverished, dissolute, full of lice, famished, killed in battle in order for the tourist trade to increase—this is the lot of all of us! They have carried your hide to market—but even out of ours their practicality lined their money purse.

But you had weapons—and did not march against this home front? And did not turn around from that field of dishonor to take up the most honorable war, to rescue us and yourselves? And you, the dead, do not rise up out of your trenches to take these vipers to account, to appear to them in their sleep with the twisted countenances that you wore in your dying hour, with the lusterless eyes of your heroic waiting, with the unforgettable masks to which your youth was condemned by this regime of madness! So, rise up, and confront them as the personification of a hero's death, so that the cowardice of the living, empowered to command, might finally come to know death's features and look death in the eye for the rest of their lives. Wake their sleep with your death cry! Interrupt their lust by the image of your sufferings! They were able to embrace women the night after the day on which they strangled you.

Save us from them, from a peace that brings us the pestilence of their nearness. Save us from the calamity of shaking hands with army prosecutors who have returned home and of meeting executioners in their civilian occupations.

Help me, you who have been murdered! Come to my aid, so that I do not have to live among men who, out of ambition or self-preservation, gave orders that hearts should stop beating and that the heads of mothers turn white! As sure as there is a God, without a miracle there can be no salvation! Come back! Ask them what they have done with you! What they did, as you suffered through them, before you died through them! What they did during your Galician winters! What they did that night when telephoning command posts got no answer from your positions. For all was quiet on the front.

And only later they saw how bravely you stood there, man by man, rifle ready to fire. For you did not belong to those who went over to the enemy or to those who went behind the lines and who, because they were freezing, had to be warmed up with machine-gun fire by a fatherly superior officer. You held your positions and were not killed while stepping backward into the murderous pit of your fatherland. Before you the enemy, behind you the fatherland, and above you, the eternal stars! And you did not flee into suicide. You died, neither for, nor through, the fatherland, neither through the ammunition of the enemy, nor through ours—you stood there and died through nature!

What a picture of perseverance! What a Capuchins' Crypt! Arms-bearing corpses, protagonists of Hapsburgian death-life, close your ranks and appear to your oppressors in their sleep. Awaken from this rigor! Step forth, step forth, you beloved believer in the spirit, and demand your precious head back from them! And where are you, you who died in the hospital? From there they sent back my last greeting, stamped: "No longer here. Address unknown." Step forth to tell them where you are, and how it is there, and that you never again will let yourself be used for such a thing.

And you there, with the face to which you were condemned in your last minute, when the beast, acting upon orders, frothing at the mouth, maybe once a man like you, plunged into your trench—step forth! Not that you had to die—no, that you had to experience this is what henceforth makes all sleep and all dying in bed a sin. It is not your dying, but what you have lived through that I want to avenge on those who have inflicted this on you. I have formed them into shadows. I have stripped off their flesh! But to their stupid thoughts, to their malicious sentiments and the frightful rhythm of their nothingness, I have given body and now make them move.

Had one preserved the voice of this era on a phonograph, the outer truth would have been in conflict with the inner truth and the ear would not have recognized either of them. Thus, time makes the essential truth unrecognizable and would grant amnesty to the greatest crime ever perpetrated under the sun, under the stars. I have preserved this truth, and my ear had detected the sound of their deeds, my eyes the gestures of their speaking, and my voice, when it only quoted, did so in such a way that the fundamental tone remains for all time.

> And let me speak to the yet unknowing world
> How these things came about: so shall you hear
> Of carnal, bloody, and unnatural acts,
> Of accidental judgments, casual slaughters,
> Of deaths put on by cunning and forced cause
> And in this upshot, purposes mistook
> Fall'n on the inventors' heads. All this can I
> Truly deliver.

And should the times hear no more, so surely will hear a being above them! I have done nothing but abridge this deadly quantity, which, in its immeasurability, may try to exonerate itself by pointing to the fickleness of time and the press. All their blood after all was only ink—now the writing will be done in blood! This is the war. This is my manifesto. *I have considered everything carefully.* I have taken it upon myself to tell the tragedy, which breaks down into the scenes of mankind breaking down, so that the Spirit, which has compassion for the victims, would hear it, even had he renounced for all future time any connection with a human ear. May he receive this era's fundamental tone, the echo of my madness haunted by blood through which I, too, am guilty of these sounds. May he accept it as redemption!

(From outside, quite far off, the cry: "E-e-xtra, E-e-xtra!")

(Scene change.)

Self-Admiration
[1908]

"... thus he has so long to subsist on his own approval until that of the world follows it. Until then even his own approval is spoiled for him in that he is expected to be nicely modest. It is, however, as impossible for someone who has merit and knows its cost to be blind to it himself as for a man six feet tall not to notice that he towers above the others ..."

Schopenhauer, *The World as Will and Idea*

"Self-admiration is permissible if the self is beautiful. It becomes an obligation if the reflecting mirror is a good one."

Kraus, *Sprüche und Widersprüche*

That I accept the reproach of self-admiration as the observation of a character trait well known to me and that I respond, not with contrition, but by continuing the provocation—this my readers should know by now. Naturally, I do not do this in defiance, nor even for my own benefit. In speaking about myself, I aim neither to offend nor to please anyone. Rather, as a representative of Austrian intellectual life I simply wish to guard against the danger of its being said some day that no one here in Austria ever talked about me. Viennese intellectuals ought to be grateful to me for having taken the trouble off their shoulders and preserved their reputation. Why should I not admit that delight at a word of appreciation makes me want to repeat it? Whoever gladly dispenses with praise from the multitude, will not deny himself the chance to be his own partisan. Imagination has the right to revel in the paltriest shade of the tree out of which it makes a forest. There exists no reproach more ridiculous than that of vanity, if it is conscious of itself. I take the liberty of giving to myself all the pleasures of the cliques. Not even the most malicious idiot will believe I set great store on being the darling of the Viennese critics and am complaining because I am not. But to assert that they are hiding their respect for me, which grows greater by the day, behind the cowardly mask of convention, and that they do not open their mouths even when they would like to speak, is a task incumbent on me just then when I am considered to be merely a watchdog for the corrupt machinations of a city. What would I gain from this silence if I did not make it audible? It would be a poor retort not to talk about it.

The citing of opinions from outside Austria, however, also confirms a universal aesthetic insight. Such opinions indicate the distance foreign readers have toward a work that grows from current or accidental, almost always insignificant incidents into an artistic structure with a distinct perspective. In the city in which the works were written, the incidents are too well known for the readers to appreciate their artistic presentation. This distinction seems to suggest that here also enhanced comprehension will depend on diminished topicality and that distance in time will have the same effect on local readers as distance in space already has on foreign readers and that my writings need only go out of date in order to become up to date also in Vienna.

Such hopes are justified above all by the headshaking with which many greeted my "personal" publications, even on the part of such readers who concede the right to surprises once and for all to an author who publishes his diary as a periodical. Of course, from one who looks only for the actual target of aphoristic remarks I expect only the question "who" is the target. I answer: I myself, nobody but me!

Readers who take a love poem for an address and the satirical portrayal of a type for an attack I cannot please and do not want to. Others again know the accidental target for my self-laceration—in that case their interest in the specific subject matter is satisfied to such an extent that they become blind to the perspective, even if they might otherwise be capable of appreciating it. They concede, at least in principle, that a dramatist has the right to overrate the most insignificant real-life person and make use of his peculiarities if they seem fruitful for the artistic portrayal of the typical.

But in practice such readers still respond as if it were a play *à clef*. They see only the portrait of the person familiar to them, misjudge the artistic achievement that ought to obliterate all memory of an indifferent model, and believe that "too much honor" has been done it.

Only those readers who neither seek nor know the incident can fully appreciate the expression of anger or love. They do not demand that one sing the praises of a queen or that blame be meted out to a king; they judge the poem itself, whether a fool, male or female, be its subject. After all, no sensitive person must be denied the right to be inspired by the most insignificant stimulus; and analyzing the stimulus, if the inspiration was good, is a method that kills any artistic venture. Whoever takes aphorisms for mere polemics may take for a play *à clef* any drama in which he happens to know the concrete allusions. Polemics presuppose notoriety of the evil and demand congruity of fictitious character and real person. But I have never let the fear of making the target well known or popular deprive me of my pleasure in the satirical portrayal of experiences that, objectively speaking, mean only little. I have always done too much honor to the most trivial incident.

Whoever does not like such subjective arbitrariness may avoid the author, but he does not have the right in every single case to chide him for his consistency. It should altogether surprise no one that I give personal matters a personal form; and to blame me for putting myself in the center of my own experiences is an impropriety I do not deserve. The long-eared faithful reader who adds up for me how many times "I" and "my" occur in a publication—and I am not such a jackass as to want to justify its appearance in print—is, of course, correct from his point of view. I just fail to comprehend why he is indiscreet enough to stick his nose into someone else's diary. That I am arrogant enough to have it printed does not by any means justify such curiosity. Reflections about current affairs are not to be found in it, and the useful activity of cleaning imperial façades cannot be expected from me. To be sure, no "I" would be involved in that kind of work. Yet people who are not involved with me and those who live abroad do not measure the merit of my literary creations by their subject matter, which here constitutes the sole justification of my existence, but recognize literary merit exactly because they are far removed from the subject matter.

No writer has ever made vanity easier for his reader to discover than I have. For even if he did not notice himself that I am vain, he learned it from my repeated admissions of vanity and from the unrestrained approval I lavished on this vice. The informed smile at the finding out of an Achilles heel is frustrated by a consciousness that voluntarily bared it, before it could be discovered. But I capitulate. If the most fruitless objection is still raised in the tenth year of my incorrigibility, any reply becomes useless. I simply cannot infuse into hearts made of parchment a feeling for the state of self-defense in which I live, for the special rights of a new form of writing and for the harmony between this seeming self-interest and the general goals of my work. They cannot understand that whoever totally identifies with some matter always talks to the point of that matter, and most of all when he talks about himself. They cannot understand that what they term vanity is actually that modesty which can never be quieted, which measures itself by its own standard, and that standard of mine is that humble striving for enhancement which always subjects itself to the most pitiless of judgments, which is always its own. Vain is the contentedness that never returns to the work. Vain is the woman who never looks into a mirror. Looking at oneself is essential for beauty and also for the mind. The world, however, has only one psychological noun for the two sexes and mistakes the vanity of a head finding inspiration and fulfillment in artistic creativity for the preening fussiness of working up a new coiffure. The world demands that one be responsible to it, not to oneself. The world considers it more important for someone not to regard his work as great than that it be great. The world wants an author's modesty; it would be prepared to overlook that of the achievement.

And in order once and for all to dispose of the idiocy that grows less modest every day, that resents my preoccupation with myself, my position, my books, and my enemies, and demonstrates admonishingly or derisively that this preoccupation takes up "half of my literary activity," when in fact it takes up all of my literary activity; and because this riffraff, for whom you can never be an authority as long as you are alive, will only leave you in peace if you cite "authorities;" in order to liquidate all the anonymous advisers and to complete the education of those worldly-wise nobodies who like to look things up in books, I welcome these words of Schopenhauer: "That one can be a great mind without noticing anything of it is an absurdity of which only hopeless incompetence can persuade itself, in order that it may regard the feeling of its own nothingness as modesty . . . I always have the suspicion about modest celebrities that they may well be right . . . Goethe has said it bluntly: 'Only good-for-nothings are modest.' But even more incontestable would be the assertion that those who so eagerly demand modesty from others, urge modesty, and unceasingly cry, 'Only be modest, for God's sake, only be modest!' *are assuredly good-for-nothings*, i.e., wretches entirely without merit, standard products of nature, ordinary members of the great pack of humanity."

Translated by Helene Scher

Aphorisms

An aphorism need not be true, but it should surpass the truth. It must go beyond it with one leap.

You cannot dictate an aphorism into a typewriter. It would take too long.

One who can write aphorisms should not waste his time writing essays. Aphorisms call for the longest breath.

It is often difficult to write an aphorism if one knows how to do it. It is much easier if one does not.

*   *   *

I speak of myself and mean the cause. They speak of the cause and mean themselves.

Why is it that so many people find fault with me? Because they praise me and I find fault with them nevertheless.

My public and I understand each other very well: it does not hear what I say, and I do not say what it would like to hear.

You wouldn't believe how hard it is to transform an action into a thought!

Through my satire I make unimportant people so big that later they are worthy targets of my satire, and no one can reproach me any longer.

I am already so popular that anyone who vilifies me becomes more popular than I.

The world wants one to be responsible to it, not to oneself.

It happened so often that one who shared my opinions kept the larger share for himself that I have learned my lesson, and now offer people merely thoughts.

To me it still is a greater miracle that a fly flies than that a human being flies.

I hear noises which others don't hear and which disturb for me the music of the spheres, which others don't hear either.

I have often been begged to be just and to view a situation from all sides. I have done this in the hope that a situation might be better looked at from all sides. But I came to the same conclusion about it. So I persist in viewing a situation from only one side, whereby I save myself much labor and disappointment.

If I knew for a fact that I might have to share immortality with certain people, I would prefer a separate oblivion.

My readers believe that I write just for the day because I write about the day. So I must wait until my writings are outdated. Then they may possibly achieve timeliness.

*   *   *

Erotics is to sexuality what gain is to loss.

Eroticism is the overcoming of obstacles. The most tempting and most popular obstacle is morality.

Eroticism transforms a despite into a because.

It is not the beloved who is distant but distance is the beloved.

Love and art embrace not what is beautiful but what by that embrace becomes beautiful.

Woman's sensuality is the primary source in which man's mind finds renewal.

Man has channeled the torrent of woman's sexuality. It no longer inundates the land but neither does it fertilize it.

The seducer who boasts of initiating women into the mystery of sex is like a stranger who arrives at the railway station and offers to show the tourist guide the beautiful sights of a town.

There is no provision in law against a man who marries a young, innocent girl on the promise of seduction and when the victim consents has no further interest.

They treat a woman like a cordial. They do not want to accept the fact that women thirst.

Moral responsibility is what man is lacking when he demands it from women.

"That hateful man," she cried, "has given me a love child."

An unscrupulous painter who, on the pretext that he wanted to seduce a woman, lures her into his studio to paint her picture.

If a connoisseur of women falls in love, he is like a doctor who gets infected at the patient's bed. A vocational risk.

Man's superiority in love relations is a paltry advantage by which nothing is gained and only violence is done to woman's nature.

For her perfection only a flaw is missing.

She entered into marriage with a lie. She was a virgin and did not tell him.

If a man has not married a virgin, he is a fallen man; he is ruined for life and at the very least has a claim for alimony.

The ideal of virginity is the ideal of those who would ravish.

Jealousy is a dog's barking that attracts thieves.

If one does not derive pleasure from making gifts to a woman one should not do it. There are women compared with whom the filling of the Danaides' sieve is the merest money box.

There is no more unfortunate being under the sun than a fetishist, who longs for a woman's shoe and has to make do with a whole woman.

Cosmetics is the science of woman's cosmos.

He forced her to do her bidding.

It is the true relationship between the sexes when the man affirms: I think of nothing else but you and therefore always have new thoughts.

In man's love life complete disorder has come about. One finds mixed forms, the potentiality of which one had hitherto no idea. A Berlin female sadist was recently said to have let slip the words: "Wretched slave, I command you to slap my face at once!" Whereupon the young lawyer in question fled in terror.

The highest position of trust: to be a father confessor of uncommitted sins.

No boundary is so conducive to smuggling as the age boundary.

Vienna has beautiful surroundings to which Beethoven often fled.

*   *   *

Come on, don't be a bore, says the Viennese to anyone who is bored in his company.

Suggestions as to how to lure me back to this city: change the dialect and prohibit procreation.

When someone has behaved like an animal, he says: "I am only human." But when he is treated like an animal, he says: "I, too, am a human being."

That we all are only human, is no excuse but a presumption.

I found somewhere the notice "It is requested that you leave this place as you would wish to find it." If only philosophers would speak half so impressively to mankind as hotel owners!

Often even I sense something like a presentiment of love for mankind. The sun smiles, the world is young again, and if on this day someone asked me for a light, I would be tempted, I almost think, I wouldn't let him ask long, and would give him one.

A cigar, said the altruist, a cigar, my dear fellow, I cannot give you. But if you ever need a light, just come round; mine is always lit.

A country horse will sooner get accustomed to a motor car than a passer-by on the Ringstrasse. There have already been many accidents through shying.

I know a country where the slot machines rest on Sunday, and do not work during the week.

Nationalism is the love that ties me to the fatheads of my country, the insulters of my moral sense, the profaners of my language.

Curses on the law! Most of my fellow citizens are the sorry consequences of uncommitted abortions.

The devil is an optimist if he thinks he can make people worse.

*　　*　　*

Psychotherapy: When one is in good health, he can best be cured of that condition by being told what illness he has.

Psychoanalysis is that mental illness for which it regards itself as therapy.

One of the most common illnesses is the diagnosis.

The psychoanalyst is a father confessor who lusts to listen also to the sins of the father.

Medicine: Your money and your life!

He died from the bite of the Aesculapian serpent.

*   *   *

Christian morality prefers remorse to precede lust, and then lust not to follow.

Christianity has enriched the erotic meal with the hors d'oeuvre of curiosity and spoiled it with the dessert of remorse.

It puzzles me how a theologian can be praised because after long struggles he has made up his mind not to believe in dogma. True recognition, as for a heroic deed, always seemed to me due the achievement of those who have struggled to the conclusion to believe in dogma.

*   *   *

Language is the mother of thought, not its handmaiden.

Language the mother of thought? Thought not the merit of the one who thinks: Oh, surely he must impregnate language.

What lives of subject matter, dies of subject matter. What lives in language, lives by language.

My language is the common prostitute that I turn into a virgin.

I master only the language of others. Mine does with me what it will.

The closer one looks at a word, the farther away it moves.

Why do some people write? Because they do not have enough character not to write.

Word and essence—the only connection I ever sought in my life.

A love affair that did not remain without consequences. He presented a work to the world.

The dog sniffs first, then he lifts his leg. One cannot well object to this lack of originality. But that the writer reads first, before he writes, is pitiful.

Despise people who have no time. Have compassion for those who have no work. But those who have no time for work, they are worthy of our envy!

It is a pitiful sort of mockery that expends itself in punctuation—employing exclamation marks, question marks, and dashes as if they were whips, snares, and goads.

The most dangerous writers are those whom a good memory relieves of all responsibility. They cannot help having things come flying to them. I would prefer an honest plagiarist.

Many talents preserve their precocity right into their old age.

Young Jean Paul's plan was to write books so that he could buy books. The plan of our young writers is to get books as gifts so that they can write books.

If Mr. Shaw attacks Shakespeare he acts in justified self-defense.

Today's literature is prescriptions written by patients.

No ideas and the ability to express them—that's a journalist.

Journalists would like to be writers. Collections of columns are published at which one looks with nothing more than astonishment that the work has not fallen apart in the hands of the bookbinder.

Bread is baked from crumbs. What is it that leads them to hope for permanence? The on-going interest in the subject which they "choose" for themselves. When one prattles about eternity, should he not be heard for as long as eternity lasts? Journalism lives on this fallacy. It always has the greatest themes, and in its hands eternity can become topical; but it must also become obsolete again with equal ease. The great writer fashions the day, the hour, the minute. However limited and conditioned in time and place his cause may be, his work grows the more boundless and free the further it is removed from the incident; don't worry about its going out of date now; it will become current again in decades to come.

*   *   *

That a work is artistic need not necessarily prejudice the public against it. One overestimates the public in thinking that they resent stylistic excellence. They pay no attention whatsoever to style and unhesitatingly accept what is of lasting value provided that the subject happens to appeal to a vulgar interest.

You must read all writers twice, the good and the bad. You will recognize the former and unmask the latter.

I know of no heavier reading than light reading. Fantasy strikes against matter and dissipates too soon to keep on working spontaneously. One rushes through the lines, in which a garden wall is described, and the mind lingers on an ocean. How enjoyable the spontaneous voyage would be if at not just the wrong time the rudderless ship is once more dashed to pieces against the garden wall. Heavy reading presents dangers one can overlook. It strains one's own energy, while the other releases energy and leaves it to itself. Heavy reading can be a danger to weak energy. Strong energy is a danger to light reading. The mind must be a match for the former; the latter is no match for the mind.

How is it that I have all the time not to read so much?

Writing a novel may be pure pleasure. Experiencing a novel is not without difficulty. But reading a novel I guard against as best I can.

I haven't tried it yet, but I believe I would first have to coax myself and then close my eyes fast to read a novel.

*   *   *

Much knowledge has room in an empty head.

An illusion of depth often occurs if a blockhead is a muddlehead at the same time.

One shouldn't learn more than what one absolutely needs against life.

I saw a terrible apparition: An encyclopedia walked toward a polyhistor and looked him up.

The value of education is most clearly revealed when educated people begin to speak on a problem that lies outside the sphere of their competence.

Education is what most receive, many pass on, and few possess.

*   *   *

It has been said that I had tried to reduce him to a nonentity. That's not true. I only succeeded.

I once knew a hero who reminded you of Siegfried because of the thickness of his skin and of Achilles because of the peculiarity of his heel.

After he had made his position among the Anarchists untenable, there remained no alternative for him other than to become a useful member of bourgeois society and join the ranks of the Social Democrats.

What are all the orgies of Bacchus compared to the intoxications of one who surrenders himself to unbridled abstinence!

My son is not doing well. He is a mystic.

The words "family ties" have a flavor of truth.

Thoughts are duty-free. But they do cause you trouble.

Progress celebrates Pyrrhic victories over nature.

There is no gratitude to technology; it has to invent.

The secret of the demagogue is to appear as stupid as his audience so that it can believe itself to be as smart as he.

War is at first the hope that things will get better for oneself; after that the expectation that things will get worse for the other; then satisfaction that things are no better for the other; and after that astonishment that things are going badly for both.

Social policy is the despairing decision to undertake a corn operation on a cancer patient.

Hermann Broch

The Anarchist
[1903]

I

The 2nd of March 1903 was a bad day for August Esch, who was thirty years old and a clerk; he had had a row with his chief and found himself dismissed before he had time to think of giving notice. He was irritated, therefore, but less by the fact of his dismissal than by his own lack of resourcefulness. There were so many things that he could have flung in the man's face: a man who didn't know what was happening under his very nose, a man who believed the insinuations of a fellow like Nentwig and had no idea that the said Nentwig was pocketing commissions right and left—unless, indeed, he was shutting his eyes deliberately because Nentwig knew something shady about him. And what a fool Esch had been to let the pair of them catch him out like that: they had fallen foul of him over an alleged mistake in the books that wasn't a mistake at all, now that he came to think of it. But they had bullied him so insolently that it had simply turned into a shouting match, in the middle of which he suddenly found himself dismissed. At the time, of course, he hadn't been able to think of anything but gutter-snipe abuse, whereas now he knew exactly how he could have scored. "Sir," yes, "Sir," he should have said, drawing himself up to his full height, and Esch now said "Sir" to himself in a sarcastic voice, "have you the slightest idea of the state your business is in . . . ?" yes, that's what he should have said, but now it was too late, and although he had gone and got drunk and slept with a girl he hadn't got rid of his irritation, and Esch swore to himself as he walked along beside the Rhine towards the town.

He heard steps behind him and, turning, caught sight of Martin, who was swinging along between his crutches with the foot of his game leg braced against one of them. If that wasn't the last straw! Esch would gladly have hurried on, at the risk of getting a wallop over the head from one of the crutches—serve him right too if he did get one over the head—but he felt it would be a low-down trick to play on a cripple, and so he stood waiting. Besides, he would have to look round for another job, and Martin, who knew everybody, might have heard of something. The cripple hobbled up, let his crooked leg swing free, and said bluntly: "Got the sack?" So he had heard of it already? Esch replied with bitterness: "Got the sack." "Have you any money left?" Esch shrugged his shoulders: "Enough for a day or two." Martin reflected: "I know of a job that might suit you." "No, you won't get me into your union." "I know, I know; you're too high and mighty for that. . . . Well, you'll join some day. Where shall we go?" Esch was going nowhere in particular, so they proceeded to Mother Hentjen's. In the Kastellgasse Martin stopped: "Have they given you a decent reference?" "I'll have to call for it to-day." "The Central Rhine people in Mannheim need a shipping clerk, or something in that line . . . if you don't mind leaving Cologne," and they went in. It was a fairly large, dingy room that had been a resort of the Rhine sailors probably for hundreds of years; though except for the vaulted roof, blackened with smoke, no sign now indicated its antiquity. The walls behind the tables were wainscoted in brown wood half-way up, to which was fixed a long bench that ran round the room. Upon the mantel-piece was an array of Munich quart-jugs, among which stood an Eiffel Tower in bronze. It was embellished with a red-and-black-and-white flag, and when one looked more closely the words "Table reserved" could be deciphered on it in faded gold-lettering. Between the two windows stood an orchestrion with its folding-doors open, showing its internal works and the roll of music. Actually the doors should have remained closed, and anyone who wished to enjoy the music should have inserted a coin in the slot.

But Mother Hentjen did nothing shabbily, and so the customer had merely to thrust his hand into the machinery and pull the lever; all Mother Hentjen's customers knew how to work the apparatus. Facing the orchestrion the whole of the shorter back wall was taken up by the buffet, and behind the buffet was a huge mirror flanked on either side by two glass cabinets containing brightly hued liqueur bottles. When in the evening Mother Hentjen took her post behind the buffet, she had a habit of turning round to the mirror every now and then to pat her blond coiffure, which was perched on her round, heavy skull like a hard little sugar-loaf. On the counter itself stood rows of large wine and Schnapps bottles, for the gay liqueur bottles in the cabinet were seldom called for. And finally, between the buffet and the glass cabinet, a zinc washing-basin with a tap was discreetly let into the wall.

The room was unheated, and its coldness stank. The two men chafed their hands, and while Esch sat down dully on a bench Martin put his hand into the works of the orchestrion, which blared out *The March of the Gladiators* into the cold atmosphere of the room. In spite of the din they could presently hear a wooden stair creaking under someone's footsteps, and the swing door beside the buffet was flung open by Frau Hentjen. She was still in her morning working-garb, an ample blue-cotton apron was tied over her dress, and she had not yet donned her evening corset, so that her breasts lay like two sacks in her broad-checked dimity blouse. Her hair, however, was still as stiff and correct as ever, crowning like a sugar-loaf her pale, expressionless face, which gave no indication of her age. But everybody knew that Frau Gertrud Hentjen had thirty-six years to her credit, and that for a long, long time—they had reckoned a little while ago that it must certainly be fourteen years—she had been the relict of Herr Hentjen, whose photograph, yellow with age, gazed out over the Eiffel Tower between the restaurant licence and a moonlit landscape, all three in fine black frames with gold scroll-work. And although with his little goat's beard Herr Hentjen looked like a snippet of a tailor, his widow had remained faithful to him; at least nobody could say anything against her, and whenever anyone dared to approach her with an honourable proposal she would remark with disdain: "Yes, the business would suit him to a T, no doubt. No, I'd rather carry on alone, thank you."

"Morning, Herr Geyring. Morning, Herr Esch," she said. "You're early birds to-day." "We've been long enough on our legs, though, Mother Hentjen," replied Martin, "if one works one must eat," and he ordered wine and bread and cheese; Esch, whose mouth and stomach were still wry with the wine he had drunk yesterday, took Schnapps. Frau Hentjen sat down with the men and asked after their news. Esch was monosyllabic, and although he was not in the least ashamed of his dismissal, it annoyed him that Geyring should publish the fact so openly. "Yes, another victim of capitalism," the trade-union organizer concluded, "but now I must get to work again; of course the Duke here can spread himself at his ease now." He paid and insisted on settling for Esch's Schnapps at the same time—"One must support the unemployed"—grasped his crutches, which he had propped beside him, braced his left foot against the wood, and swung himself out through the door between his two supports with a great clatter.

After he had gone the two of them remained silent for a little; then Esch jerked his chin towards the door: "An anarchist," he said. Frau Hentjen shrugged her plump shoulders: "And what if he is? He's a decent man." "He's a decent man, right enough," Esch corroborated, and Frau Hentjen went on: "but they'll lay him by the heels again sooner or later: he's done time for six months already . . ." then: "Well, it's all in his day's work." Once more they became silent. Esch was wondering whether Martin had been a cripple since his childhood; misbegotten, he thought to himself, and said: "He would like to land me among his socialist friends. But I'm not having any." "Why not?" asked Frau Hentjen without interest. "It doesn't suit my plans. I want to get to the top of the tree; law and order are necessary if you want to get to the top." Frau Hentjen could not but agree with that: "Yes, that's true, you must have law and order. But now I must go to the kitchen. Will you be having dinner with us to-day, Herr Esch?" Esch might as well dine here as anywhere else, and after all why should he wander about in the icy wind? "Strange that the snow hasn't come yet," he said, "the dust fairly blinds you." "Yes, it's dismal outside," said Frau Hentjen. "Then you'll just stay here?" She disappeared into the kitchen, the swing door vibrated for a little longer, and Esch dully followed its vibrations until it finally came to rest. Then he tried to sleep. But now the coldness of the room began to strike into him; he walked up and down with a heavy and rather unsteady tread and took up the newspaper that lay on the buffet; but he could not turn the pages with his stiff fingers; his eyes too were painful. So he resolved to seek out the warm kitchen; with the newspaper in his hand he walked in. "I suppose you've come to have a sniff at the saucepans?" said Frau Hentjen, suddenly remembering that it was cold in the eating-room, and as it was her custom not to put on a fire there until the afternoon she suffered him to bear her company. Esch watched her bustling about the hearth and had a longing to seize her beneath the breasts, but her reputation for inaccessibility checked his desire at once. When the kitchenmaid who helped Frau Hentjen with her work went out he said: "I can't understand your liking to live alone." "Aha!" she replied, "you're beginning that song too, are you?" "No," said Esch, "it isn't that. I was just wondering." Frau Hentjen's face had taken on a strangely frozen expression; it was as though she were disgusted at some thought, for she shook herself so violently that her breasts quivered, and then went about her work with the bored and empty face with which she always confronted her customers. Esch, sitting at the window, read his newspaper and afterwards looked out into the yard, where the wind was raising little cyclones of dust.

Later the two girls who acted as waitresses in the evening arrived, unwashed and unslept. Frau Hentjen, the two waitresses and the little kitchenmaid and Esch took their places round the kitchen table, stuck out their elbows, hunched themselves over their plates, and ate their dinner.

Esch had drawn up his application for the Mannheim post; he now needed only the reference to enclose with it. Actually he was glad that things had turned out as they had. It wasn't good for a man to vegetate all the time in one place. He felt he must get out of Cologne, and the farther the better. A fellow must keep his eyes open; as a matter of fact he had always done that.

In the afternoon he went to the office of Stemberg & Company, wholesale wine merchants, to get his reference. Nentwig kept him waiting at the counter, and sat at his desk, fat and slouching, totting up columns. Esch tapped impatiently with his strong finger-nails on the counter. Nentwig got up: "Patience, patience, Herr Esch," and he stepped to the barrier and said condescendingly: "Oh, about your reference?—that can't be so very urgent. Well? Date of birth? Date of employment here?" With his head averted Esch supplied this information and Nentwig took it down. Then Nentwig dictated to the stenographer and brought the reference. Esch read it through. "This isn't a reference," he said, handing the paper back. "Oh! Then what is it?" "You must certify to my ability as a book-keeper." "You—a book-keeper! You've shown us what you can do in that line." Now the moment of reckoning had come: "It's a very special kind of book-keeper that's needed for the inventories you draw up, I happen to know." Nentwig was taken aback: "What do you mean?" "I mean what I say." Nentwig changed his tune, became friendly: "You only harm yourself with your obstreperousness; here you had a good post, and you had to get into a row with the chief!" Esch tasted victory and began to roll it on his tongue: "I mean to have a talk with the chief later." "For all I care you can say what you like to the chief," Nentwig countered. "Well, what do you want me to put in your reference?" Esch decreed that he should be described as "conscientious, reliable and thoroughly versed in all matters relating to book-keeping." Nentwig wanted to be rid of him. "It isn't true, of course, but as far as I'm concerned——" He turned again to the stenographer to dictate the new version. Esch grew red in the face: "Oh, so it isn't true? . . . then please add: 'We heartily recommend him to any employer who may be in need of his services.' Have you got that?" Nentwig bowed elaborately: "Delighted, I'm sure, Herr Esch." Esch read the new copy through and was appeased. "The chief's signature," he commanded. But this was too much for Nentwig, who shouted: "So mine isn't good enough for you?" "If the firm authorizes you I'll let that pass," was Esch's large and magnanimous reply, and Nentwig signed.

Esch stepped out into the street and made for the nearest pillar-box. He whistled to himself; he felt rehabilitated. He had his reference, good; it was in the envelope with his application to the Central Rhine Company. The fact that Nentwig had given in showed that he had a bad conscience. So the inventories were faked then, and the man should be handed over to the police. Yes, it was simply one's duty as a citizen to give him in charge straight away. The letter dropped into the postbox with a soft, muffled thud, and Esch, his fingers still in the aperture, considered whether he should go at once to the police headquarters. He wandered on irresolutely. It had been a mistake to send off the reference, he should have given it back to Nentwig; to force a reference out of a man and then give him in charge wasn't decent. But now it was done, and besides, without a reference he had little chance of getting a post with the Central Rhine Shipping Company—there would be absolutely nothing left for him but to go back to his old job in Stemberg's again. And he saw a vision of the chief discovering the fraud, and Nentwig languishing in prison. Yes, but what if the chief himself was involved in the swindle? Then of course the public interrogation would bring the whole concern toppling down. And then there would be another bankruptcy, but no post for a book-keeper. And in the newspapers people would read: "Revenge of a dismissed clerk." And finally he would be suspected of collusion. And then he would be left without a reference and without a job, for nobody would take him on. Esch congratulated himself on the shrewdness with which he drew all the consequences, but he was furious. "A fine bloody firm!" he swore under his breath. He stood in the Ring in front of the Opera House, cursing and swearing into the cold wind which blew the dust into his eyes, and could not come to any decision, but finally resolved to postpone the affair; if he didn't get the post with the Central Rhine there would still be time left to act the part of Nemesis. He went through the darkening evening, his hands buried in the pockets of his shabby overcoat, actually went, indeed, as a matter of form, as far as the police headquarters. There he stood looking at the policemen on guard, and when a police wagon drove up he waited until all the prisoners had got out, and felt disappointed when the policeman finally slammed to the door without Nentwig's having put in an appearance. He remained standing for a few moments, then he turned resolutely and made for the Alt Markt. The two faint vertical lines on his cheeks had deepened. "Wine faker," he muttered in a fury, "vinegar tout." And morose and disillusioned over his poisoned victory, he ended the day by getting drunk again and sleeping with another girl.

In her brown-silk dress, which she was accustomed usually to don only in the evening, Frau Hentjen had been spending the afternoon with a woman friend, and now, as always on her return, she was put into a bad temper by the sight of the house and the restaurant in which for so long she had been compelled to pass her life. Certainly the business allowed her to lay by a little now and then, and when she was praised and flattered by her women friends for her capability she experienced a faintly pleasant sensation which made up for a good deal. But why wasn't she the owner of a linen-draper's shop, or a ladies' hairdressing saloon, instead of having to deal every evening with a pack of drunken louts? If her corset had not prevented her she would have shaken herself with loathing when she caught sight of her restaurant; so intensely did she hate the men who frequented it, these men that she had to serve. Though perhaps she hated still more the women who were always such fools as to run after them. Not a single one of her women friends belonged to the kind that took up with men, that trafficked with these creatures and like animals lusted for their embraces. Yesterday she had caught the kitchenmaid in the yard with a young lad, and the hand which had dealt the buffet still tingled pleasantly; she felt she would like to have it out with the girl again. No, women were probably still worse than men. She could put up only with her waitresses and all the other prostitutes who despised men even though they had to go to bed with them; she liked to talk to these women, she encouraged them to tell her their stories in detail, and comforted and pampered them to indemnify them for their sufferings. And so a post in Mother Hentjen's restaurant was highly prized, and her girls looked upon it as well worth the best they could give in return and did all they could to retain it. And Mother Hentjen was delighted with such devotion and love.

Her best room was up on the first floor; really too big, with its three windows on the narrow street it took up the full breadth of the house above the restaurant; in the back wall, corresponding to the buffet downstairs, there was an alcove shut off by a light curtain which was always drawn. If one drew aside the curtain and let one's eyes get used to the darkness, one could make out the twin marriage-beds. But Frau Hentjen never used this room, and nobody knew whether it had ever been used. For a room of such a size was difficult to heat except at a considerable cost, and so Frau Hentjen could not be blamed for choosing the smaller room above the kitchen as her bed- and sitting-room, employing the chill and gloomy parlour only for storing food that might go bad. Also the walnuts which she was accustomed to buy in autumn were stored here and lay strewn in heaps about the floor, upon which two broad green strips of linoleum were laid crosswise.

Still feeling angry, Frau Hentjen went up to the parlour to fetch sausage for her customers' suppers, and as anger makes one careless she stumbled into some of the nuts, which rolled before her feet with an exasperatingly loud clatter. It exasperated her still more when one cracked beneath her foot, and while she picked up the nut so that it might not be altogether wasted, and carefully detached the kernel from the splintered pieces of shell, and stuck the white fragments with the bitter pale-brown skin into her mouth, she kept meanwhile screaming for the kitchenmaid; at last the brazen trollop heard her, came stumbling up the stairs, and was received with a torrent of incoherent abuse: of course a girl that flirted with half-grown louts would be stealing nuts too—the nuts had been stored beside the window and now they were just inside the door, and nuts didn't walk across a floor of their own accord—and Frau Hentjen was preparing to raise her fist, and the girl had ducked and put up her arm, when a piece of shell caught in her mistress's teeth, who contented herself with spitting it out contemptuously; then, followed by the sobbing maid, she descended to the kitchen.

When she entered the restaurant, where already a thick cloud of tobacco smoke was hanging, she was overcome again, as almost every evening, by that apprehensive torpor which was so incomprehensible to her and yet so difficult to overcome. She went up to the mirror and mechanically patted the blond sugar-loaf on her head and pulled her dress straight, and only when she had assured herself that her appearance was satisfactory did her composure return. Now she looked round and saw the familiar faces among her customers, and although there was more profit on the drinks than on the food, she prized the eaters among her customers above the drinkers, and she stepped out from behind the buffet and went from table to table asking whether the food was to their liking. And she summoned the waitress almost with elation when a customer demanded a second helping. Yes, Mother Hentjen's cooking had no need to fear examination.

Geyring was already there; his crutches were leaning beside him; he had cut the meat on his plate into small pieces and now ate mechanically while in his left hand he held one of his Socialist papers, a whole bundle of which were always sticking out of his pocket.

Frau Hentjen liked him, partly because, being a cripple, he did not count as a man, partly because it was not to shout and drink and make up to the waitresses that he came, but simply because his post demanded that he should keep in touch with the sailors and dock workers; but above all she liked him because evening after evening he had his supper at her restaurant and praised up her food. She sat down at his table. "Has Esch been here yet?" asked Geyring. "He's got the job with the Central Rhine, starts work on Monday." "And it's you that got it for him, I'm sure, Herr Geyring," said Frau Hentjen. "No, Mother Hentjen, we haven't got the length yet of filling posts through the union . . . no, not by a long way . . . well, that'll come too in time. But I put Esch on the track of it. Why shouldn't one help a nice lad, even if he isn't one of ourselves?" Mother Hentjen showed little sympathy with this sentiment: "You just eat that up, Herr Geyring, and you'll have an extra titbit from myself as well," and she went over to the buffet and brought on a plate a moderate-sized slice of sausage which she had garnished with a sprig of parsley. Geyring's wrinkled face of a boy of fourteen smiled at her in gratitude, showing a mouthful of bad teeth, and he patted her white, plump hand, which she immediately drew back with a slight return of her frozen manner.

Later Esch arrived. Geyring looked up from his paper and said: "Congratulations, August." "Thanks," said Esch. "So you know already?—there was no difficulty, a reply by return engaging me. Well, I must thank you for putting me on to it." But his face beneath the short, dark, cropped hair had the wooden empty look of a disappointed man. "A pleasure," said Martin, then he shouted over to the buffet: "Here's our new paymaster." "Good luck, Herr Esch," replied Frau Hentjen dryly, yet she came forward after all and gave him her hand. Esch, who wished to show that all the credit was not due to Martin, pulled his reference out of his breastpocket: "It wouldn't have gone so smoothly, I can tell you, if I hadn't made Stemberg's give me such a good reference." He heavily emphasized the "made," and then added: "A measly firm." Frau Hentjen read the reference absently: "A splendid reference." Geyring too read it and nodded: "Yes, the Central Rhine must be glad they've got hold of such a first-class fellow. . . . I'll really have to get the Chairman, Bertrand, to fork out a commission for my services."

"An excellent book-keeper, excellent, what?" Esch preened himself. "Well, it's nice when anyone can have such things said about him," Frau Hentjen agreed. "You may feel very proud of yourself, Herr Esch; you've every right to: do you want anything to eat?" Of course he did, and while Frau Hentjen looked on complacently to see that he enjoyed his food, he said that now he was going farther up the Rhine he hoped to get one of the travelling jobs; that would mean going as far as Kehl and Basel. Meanwhile several of his other acquaintances had come up, the new paymaster ordered wine for them all, and Frau Hentjen withdrew. With disgust she noticed that every time Hede, the waitress, passed the table, Esch could not help fondling her, and that finally he ordered her to sit down beside him, so that they might drink to each other. But the score was a high one, and when the gentlemen broke up after midnight, taking Hede with them, Frau Hentjen pushed a mark into her hand.

Nevertheless Esch could not feel elated over his new post. It was as though he had purchased it at the cost of his soul's welfare, or at least of his decency. Now that things had gone so far and he had already drawn an advance for his travelling expenses from the Cologne branch of the Central Rhine, he was overcome anew by the doubt whether he shouldn't give Nentwig in charge. Of course in that case he would have to be present at the official inquiry, could not therefore leave the town, and would almost certainly lose his new job. For a moment he thought of solving the problem by writing an anonymous letter to the police, but he rejected this plan: one couldn't wipe out one piece of rascality by committing another. And on top of it all he was beginning to resent his own twinges of conscience; after all he wasn't a child, he didn't give a damn for the parsons and their morality; he had read all sorts of books, and when Geyring had recently begged him yet again to join the Social Democratic Party he had replied: "No, I don't have anything to do with you anarchists, but I'll go with you this far: I'll turn Freethinker." The thankless fool had replied that that didn't matter a damn to him. That was what people were like: well, Esch wouldn't give a damn either.

Finally he did the most reasonable thing: he set off for Mannheim at the appointed time. But he felt violently uprooted, he had none of his accustomed pleasure in travelling, and as a safeguard he left part of his belongings in Cologne: he even left his bicycle behind. Nevertheless his travelling allowance put him in a generous mood. And standing with his beer-glass in his hand and his ticket stuck in his hat on Mainz platform, he thought of the people whom he had left, felt he wanted to show them a kindness, and, a newspaper man happening to push his barrow past at that moment, he bought two picture postcards. Martin in particular deserved a line from him; yet one did not send picture postcards to a man. So first he scribbled one to Hede: the second was destined for Frau Hentjen. Then he reflected that it might seem insulting to Frau Hentjen, who was a proud woman, to receive a postcard by the same post as one of her employees, and as he was in a reckless mood he tore up the first one and posted only the one to Frau Hentjen, containing his warmest greetings to her and all his kind friends and acquaintances and Fräulein Hede and Fräulein Thusnelda from the beautiful town of Mainz. After that he felt again a little lonely, drank a second glass of beer, and let the train carry him on to Mannheim.

He had been instructed to report to the head office. The Central Rhine Shipping Company Limited occupied a building of its own not far from the Mühlau Dock, a massive stone edifice with pillars in front of the door. The street in which it stood was asphalted, good for cycling; it was a new street. The heavy door of wrought-iron and glass—it would certainly swing smoothly and noiselessly on its hinges—stood ajar, and Esch entered. The marble vestibule pleased him; over the stair hung a glass sign-plate on whose transparent surface he read the words: "Board Room" in gold letters. He made straight for it. When his foot was on the first stair he heard a voice behind him: "Where are you going, please?" He turned round and saw a commissionaire in grey livery; silver buttons glittered on it and the cap had a strip of silver braid. It was all very elegant, but Esch felt annoyed—what business was it of this fellow's?—and he said curtly: "I was asked to report here," and made to go on. The other did not weaken: "To see the Chairman?" "Why, who else, do you think?" replied Esch rudely. The stair led up to a large, gloomy waiting-room on the first floor. In the middle of it stood a great oaken table, round which were ranged a few upholstered chairs. It was certainly very splendid. Once more a man with silver buttons appeared and asked what he wanted. "The Chairman's office," said Esch. "The gentlemen are at a board meeting," said the attendant.

"Is it important?" Driven to the wall, Esch had to tell his business; he drew out his papers, the letter engaging him, the receipt for his travelling allowance. "I've some references with me too," he said, and made to hand over Nentwig's reference. He was somewhat taken aback when the fellow did not even look at it: "You've no business with this up here . . . ground floor, through the corridor, then the second stair—inquire down below."

Esch remained standing where he was for a moment; he grudged the attendant his triumph and asked once more: "So this isn't the place?" The attendant had already turned away indifferently: "No, this is the Chairman's waiting-room." Esch felt anger rising up in him; they made too much of a blow with their Chairman, their up-holstered furnishings and their silver-buttoned attendants; Nentwig too would no doubt like to play this game; well, their fine Chair-man was probably not so very different from Nentwig. But, willy-nilly, Esch had to go back the same road again. Down below the commissionaire was still at his post. Esch looked at him to see whether he was angry; but as the commissionaire merely gazed at him indifferently he said: "I want the engagement bureau," and asked to be shown the way. After taking a couple of steps he turned round, jerked his thumb towards the staircase, and asked: "What's the name of your boss up there, the Chairman?" "Herr von Ber-trand," said the commissionaire, and there was almost a respectful ring in his voice. And Esch repeated, also somewhat respectfully: "Herr von Bertrand": he must have heard the name at some time or other.

In the engagement bureau he learned that he was to be employed as stores clerk in the docks. As he stepped out into the street again a carriage halted before the building. It was a cold day; the powdery snow, drifted by the wind, lay on the kerb and against the corners of the wall; the horse kept striking a hoof against the smooth as-phalt. It was obviously impatient and with reason. "A carriage, no less, for the Chairman," Esch said to himself, "but as for us, we have to walk." Yet all the same he liked all this elegance, and he was glad that he belonged to it. After all, it was one in the eye for Nentwig.

In the warehouse of the Central Rhine Shipping Company the office was a glass-partitioned box at the end of a long line of sheds. His desk stood beside that of the customs officer, and at the back glowed a little iron stove. When one was bored with one's work, or felt lonely and forsaken, one could always watch the trucks being loaded and unloaded. The sailings were to begin in a few days, and on all the boats there was a great bustle. There were cranes which revolved and lowered their hooks as though to pick something or other cautiously out of the ships' entrails, and there were others which projected over the water like bridges that had been begun but never completed. Of course these sights were not new to Esch, for he had seen exactly the same in Cologne, but there he had been so used to the long row of storage sheds that he had never thought of them, and if he had forced himself to consider them, the buildings, the cranes and the landing-stages would have appeared almost meaningless, put there to serve human needs that were inexplicable. But now that he himself was concerned in these things they had grown into natural and purposive structures, and this gladdened him. While formerly he had at the most been surprised, occasionally indeed even irritated, that there should be so many export firms, and that the sheds, all alike, on the quays, should bear so many separate names, now the different businesses took on an individuality which one could recognize from the appearance of their stout or lean storekeepers, their gruff or pleasant stevedores. Also the insignia of His Majesty the Emperor of Germany's customs officers at the gates of the closed dock quarter flattered him: they made him vaguely conscious that here one lived and moved on foreign soil. It was both a constricted and a free life that one led in this sanctuary where wares could lie untaxed; it was frontier air that one breathed behind the iron gratings of the customs barriers. And even although he had no uniform to wear, and was, so to speak, only a private official, yet by virtue of his association with these customs and railway officials Esch had himself become almost an official figure, particularly as he carried in his pocket an official pass allowing him to wander at liberty through this exclusive province, and was already greeted with a welcoming salute by the watchman at the main gate. When he returned that salute he threw his cigarette away with a lordly sweep in obedience to the prohibition against smoking that was stuck up everywhere, and proceeded with long and important strides—a strict non-smoker himself, ready at any moment to come down upon any too familiar civilian for an infringement of the rule—to the office, where the storekeeper had already laid his list upon the desk. Then he drew on his grey-woollen mittens that left the finger-tips free, for without them his hands would have frozen in the musty coldness of the shed, looked over the lists, and checked the piled-up packing-cases and bales. Should a packing-case be in the wrong place he did not fail to throw the storekeeper, whose province it was to supervise the deliveries, a severe or at least an impatient look, so that he might give the docker responsible for it a proper talking-to. And when later the customs officer in his round stepped into the glass partition and said how warm it was in here, unfastening the collar of his tunic and pleasantly yawning in his chair, by that time the lists were checked and the contents copied into the books, and there was no difficulty about the rest; the two men sat at the table and lazily went over the papers. Then the customs officer, rapidly as ever, endorsed the lists with his blue pencil, took up the duplicates and locked them in his desk, and if there was nothing more to be done they proceeded together to the canteen.

Yes, Esch had made a good exchange, even if justice had suffered in the process. Still, he could not help wondering—and it was the only thing that disturbed his contentment—whether there mightn't be some way after all of duly giving Nentwig in charge; for only then would everything be in order.

Customs Inspector Balthasar Korn came from a very matter-of-fact part of Germany. He was born on the frontier-line between Bavaria and Saxony, and had received his earliest impressions from the hilly town of Hof. His mind was divided between a matter-of-fact desire for coarse amusements and a matter-of-fact parsimony, and after he had worked his way up to a sergeant's rank in active military service, he had seized the opportunity offered by a paternal Government to its faithful soldiers, and had obtained his transfer to the customs. A bachelor, he lived in Mannheim with his sister Erna, also unmarried, and as the empty best bedroom in his house was a standing offence in his eyes, he prevailed upon August Esch to give up his expensive room in the hotel and accept cheaper lodgings with him. And although he did not entirely approve of Esch, seeing that Esch as a Luxemburger could not boast of military service, yet he would not have been displeased to find in Esch a husband for his sister as well as an occupant for the spare bedroom; he was not sparing in unequivocal hints, and his sister, who was no longer young, accompanied them with bashful and tittering signs of protest. Indeed he actually went so far as to jeopardize his sister's good name, for he did not scruple to address Esch before the others in the canteen as "Herr Brother-in-Law," so that everybody must think that his friend already shared his sister's bed. Yet Korn did this not exclusively for the sake of having his joke; rather his intention was to compel Esch, partly by constantly accustoming him to the idea, partly through the pressure of public opinion, to transform into solid actuality the fictitious part which he was thus called on to play.

Esch had not been unwilling to move into Korn's house. Though he had knocked about so much he felt lonely. Perhaps the numbered streets of Mannheim were to blame, perhaps he missed the smells of Mother Hentjen's restaurant, perhaps it was that scoundrel Nentwig that still troubled him; at any rate he felt lonely and stayed on with the brother and sister, stayed on although he was quick to observe how the wind blew, stayed on although he had no intention of having anything to do with that elderly virgin; he was not impressed in the least by the great display of lingerie which Erna had gathered together in the course of the years, and which she showed him with considerable pride, nor did even the savings-bank book which she once let him see, showing a balance of over two thousand marks, attract him. But Korn's efforts to lure him into the trap were so amusing that they were worth taking some risk for; of course one had to be wary and not let oneself be caught. As for example: Korn would rarely let him pay for their drinks when they forgathered in the canteen before they went home together; and after they had heartily cursed the quality of the Mannheim beer Korn was not to be dissuaded from turning in for Munich beer at the Spatenbräu cellar. Then, if Herr Esch hastily put his hand into his pocket, Korn would again refuse to let him pay: "You'll have your revenge yet, Herr Brother-in-law." But when they were sauntering down Rheinstrasse the customs inspector would punctually halt before certain of the lighted shop-windows and clap Esch on the shoulder with his great paw: "My sister has been wanting an umbrella like that for a long time: I'll have to buy it for her birthday," or: "Every house should have a gas-iron like that," or: "If my sister had a wringer she would be happy." And when Esch made no reply to all these hints Korn would become as furiously angry as he had once been at recruits who refused to understand how to handle their rifles, and the more silent Esch was as they walked on, the more furious grew his burly companion's rage at the impudently knowing expression on Esch's face.

But it was by no means parsimony that made Esch dumb on those occasions. For although he was thrifty and fond of picking up small gains, yet the thorough and righteous book-keeping which in his soul he believed in did not allow him to accept goods without payment; service demanded counter-service, and goods must be paid for; nevertheless he thought it unnecessary to have a purchase forced on him in too great a hurry; indeed it would have seemed to him almost clumsy and inconsiderate to crown Korn's breezy demands with actual success. So for the time being he had hit upon a curious kind of revenge which allowed him to repay his obligations to Korn and at the same time show that he was in no hurry to marry; after dinner he would invite Korn out for a little evening's entertainment which took them to those beer-shops where there were barmaids, and unavoidably ended for them both in the so-called disreputable streets of the town. It sometimes cost a good deal of money to foot the bill for both of them—even if Korn could not get out of tipping his girl himself—yet the sight of Korn on the way home afterwards, walking along morosely, chewing at his black, bushy moustache, which was now limp and dejected, growling that this loose life Esch was leading him into must be put an end to: that was well worth all the expense. And besides, Korn was always in such a bad temper with his sister next morning that he went out of his way to wound her in her tenderest feelings, accusing her of never having been able to catch a man. And when thereupon she maintained hotly that she had had hosts of admirers, he would remind her contemptuously of her single estate.

One day Esch managed to wipe off his debt to a considerable extent. While he was on his way through the company's stores his vigilant eye was caught by the curiously shaped packing-cases and properties of a theatrical outfit, which were just being unloaded. A clean-shaven gentleman was standing by in great agitation, shouting that his valuable property, which represented untold wealth, was being handled as roughly as if it were firewood, and when

Esch, who had been looking on gravely with the air of a connoisseur, threw a few pieces of superfluous advice to the labourers, and
in this unmistakable fashion gave the gentleman to know that he
was in the presence of a man of knowledge and authority, the for-
midable volubility of the stranger was turned upon him and they
soon found themselves engaged in a friendly conversation, in the
course of which the clean-shaven gentleman, raising his hat slightly,
introduced himself as Herr Gernerth, the new lessee of the Thalia
Theatre, who would be particularly flattered—in the meanwhile the
work of unloading had been completed—if the Shipping Inspector
and his esteemed family would attend the opening performance,
and begged to present him with the necessary tickets at reduced
prices. And when Esch agreed with alacrity, the manager put his
hand in his pocket and actually wrote out three free tickets for him
on the spot.

Now Esch was sitting with the Korns in the variety theatre at a
table covered with a white cloth. The programme opened with a
novel attraction, the moving pictures or, as they were called, the
cinematograph. These pictures, however, did not meet with much
applause from the audience, or indeed from the public in general at
that time, not being regarded as serious and genuine entertainment,
but merely as a prelude to it; nevertheless this modern art-form
really held one's attention when a comedy was put on showing the
comic effects of laxative pills, the critical moments being emphasized with a ruffle of drums. Korn roared with mirth and brought
down the flat of his hand on the table; Fräulein Korn put her hand
over her mouth and giggled, throwing stolen coquettish glances at
Esch through her fingers, and Esch was as proud as though he himself were the inventor and producer of this highly successful entertainment. The smoke from their cigars ascended and melted into
the cloud of tobacco smoke which very soon floated under the low
roof of the hall traversed by the silvery beam of the limelight which
lit up the screen. During the interval, which came after an act imitating the whistling of birds, Esch ordered three glasses of beer,
though it cost considerably more here in the theatre than anywhere
else, but he was relieved when it proved to be flat and stale and they
decided to give no further orders, but to have a drink in the Spatenbräu after the performance. He felt once more in a generous mood,
and while the prima donna was being passionate and despairing to

the best of her ability he said significantly: "Ah, love, Fräulein Erna, love." But when, after the vociferous applause which greeted the singer from all sides, the curtain rose again, the whole stage glittered as with silver, and little nickel-plated tables stood about, and all the other glittering apparatus of a juggler. On the red-velvet cloths with which the various stands were either hung or completely draped stood balls and flasks, little flags and banners, and also a great pile of white plates. On a ladder running up to a point—it too shone with nickel-plating—hung some two dozen daggers whose long blades glittered no less brilliantly than all the shining metal round them. The juggler in his black dress-suit was supported by a female assistant, whom he brought on, it was clear, simply to display her striking beauty to the public, and also the spangled tights she wore must have been designed merely to that end, for all that she had to do was to hand the juggler the plates and the flags, or to fling them to him in the midst of his performance whenever, as a signal, he clapped his hands. She discharged this task with a gracious smile, and when she threw him the hammer she emitted a short cry in some foreign tongue, perhaps to draw the attention of her master to her, perhaps also to beg for a little affection, which her austere tyrant, however, sternly denied her. And although he must certainly have known that he ran the risk of losing the audience's sympathy by his hard-heartedness, he did not accord his beautiful helper even a single glance, and only when he had to acknowledge the applause with a bow did he indicate by a casual wave of his hand in her direction that he allowed her a certain percentage of it. But then he walked to the back of the stage, and quite amicably, as though the affront which he had just put upon her had never happened, they lifted up together a great black board which, noticed by nobody, had been waiting there all the time, brought it forward to the waiting array of shining paraphernalia, set it up on end, and fastened it securely to the ladder. Thereupon, mutually encouraging each other with short cries and smiles, they pushed the black board, now set up vertically, to the front of the stage, and secured it to the floor and the wings with cords which suddenly appeared from nowhere. After they had seen to this with profound solemnity, the beautiful assistant once more emitted her short cry and skipped over to the board, which was so high that, stretching her arms upwards, she could scarcely touch the top edge. And now one saw that two handles were fixed into the board near the top, and the assistant, who stood with her back against the board, seized hold of those handles, and this somewhat constrained and artificial posture gave her, as she stood sharply outlined in her glittering and flimsy attire against the black board, the look of someone being crucified. Yet all the same she still went on smiling her gracious smile, even when the man, after regarding her with sharp half-shut eyes, went up to her and altered her position, altered it so slightly as to be unnoticcable, it is true, yet in such a way that the spectators became aware that everything depended on that fraction of an inch. All this was done to the subdued strains of a waltz, which immediately broke off at a slight sign from the juggler. The theatre became quite still; an extraordinary isolation, divested even of music, lay on the stage up there, and the waiters did not dare to walk up to the tables with the beer and food they were carrying, but stood, themselves tense with excitement, by the yellow-lighted doors at the back; guests who were on the point of eating put back their forks, on which they had already spitted some morsel, on their plates, and only the limelight, which the operator had directed full on the crucified girl, went on whirring. But the juggler was already testing one of the long daggers in his murderous hand; he bent his body back and now it was he who sent out the discordant exotic cry, while the dagger flew whistling from his hand, whizzed straight across the stage, and quivered in the black wood with a dull impact beside the body of the crucified girl. And now, faster than one could follow him, he had both hands full of glittering daggers, and while his cries became more rapid and more brutal, indeed, veritably bestial, the daggers whizzed in more and more rapid succession through the quivering air, struck with ever more rapid impact on the wood, and framed the girl's face, which still smiled, numb and yet confident, appealing and yet challenging, brave and yet apprehensive. Esch could almost have wished that it was himself who was standing up there with his arms raised to heaven, that it was himself being crucified, could almost have wished to station himself in front of that gentle girl and receive in his own breast the menacing blades; and had the juggler, as often happened, asked whether any gentleman in the audience would deign to step on to the stage and place himself against the black board, in sober truth Esch would have accepted the offer. Indeed the thought of standing up there alone and forsaken, where the long blades might pin one against the board like a beetle, filled him with almost voluptuous pleasure; but in that case, he thought, correcting himself, he would have to stand with his face to the board, for a beetle was never spitted from the under side: and the thought of standing with his face to the darkness of the board, not knowing when the deadly daggers might fly, transfixing his heart and pinning it to the board, had so extraordinary and mysterious a fascination for him, grew into a desire so novel, so powerful and satisfying, that he started as out of a dream of bliss when with a flourish of drums and fanfares the orchestra greeted the juggler, who had triumphantly dispatched the last of the daggers, and the girl skipped out of her frame, which was now complete, and both of them with a graceful pirouette, holding hands and executing spacious gestures with their free arms, bowed to the audience, now released from its ordeal. It was the fanfare of the Last Judgment, when the guilty were to be trodden underfoot like worms; why shouldn't they be spitted like beetles? Why, instead of a sickle, shouldn't Death carry a long darning-needle, or at least a lance? One always lived in fear of being awakened to the Last Judgment, for even if one had once upon a time almost thought of joining the Freethinkers, yet one had a conscience. He heard Korn saying: "That was great," and it sounded like blasphemy: and when Fräulein Erna remarked that, if they asked her, she would take good care not to be set up there almost naked and have knives thrown at her before the whole audience, it was too much for Esch, and in the most ungentle manner he flung away her knee, which was leaning against his; one shouldn't take people like these to see a superior entertainment; interlopers without a conscience, that's what they were; and he was not in the least impressed by the fact that Fräulein Erna was always running to her confessor; indeed the life of his Cologne friends seemed to him by far more secure and respectable.

In the Spatenbräu Esch drank his dark beer in silence. He was still in the grip of an emotion that could only be called yearning. Especially when it took shape as a need to send a picture postcard to Mother Hentjen. It was of course only natural that Erna should add a line: "Kind regards from Erna Korn," but when Balthasar too insisted on contributing and beneath his, "Regards, Korn, Customs Inspector," scored in his firm hand a black definitively conclusive flourish, it was like a sort of homage to Frau Hentjen, and it softened Esch so much that he became unsure of himself: had he really quite fulfilled his obligation to give an honest return for the Korns' kindness? Actually, to round off the evening, he should steal across to Erna's door, and if he had not thrust her away so ungently just now the door would certainly have been left unbarred. Yes, properly regarded, that was the right and fitting conclusion to the evening, yet he did nothing to bring it about. A sort of paralysis had fallen on him; he paid no further attention to Erna, did not seek her knee with his, and nothing happened either on the way home or afterwards. For some reason or other his conscience was troubling him, but finally he decided in his mind that he had done enough after all, and that it might even lead to trouble if he showed too much attention to Fräulein Korn; he felt a fate hovering over his head with threateningly upraised lance ready to strike if he should go on behaving like a swine, and he felt that he must remain true to someone, even though he did not know who it was.

While Esch was still feeling the stab of conscience in his back so palpably that he declared he must have sat in a cold draught, and every night rubbed himself as far as he could reach with a pungent embrocation, Mother Hentjen was rejoicing over the two picture postcards which he had sent her, and stuck them, before they should go for final preservation into her picture-postcard album, in the mirror frame behind the buffet. Then in the evening she took them out and showed them to the regular customers. Perhaps she did this also lest anybody might say of her that she was carrying on a secret correspondence with a man; for if she let the postcards go the round of the restaurant then they were no longer directed merely to her, but to the establishment, which was only incidentally personified in her. For this reason too she was glad that Geyring undertook the task of replying; yet she would not hear of Herr Geyring going to any expense, so she herself procured next day a particularly beautiful panorama card, as it was called, three times the length of an ordinary postcard, showing the whole of Cologne stretching along the dark-blue banks of the Rhine, and leaving space for a great number of signatures. At the top she wrote: "Many thanks for the beautiful postcards from Mother Hentjen." Then Geyring gave the command: "Ladies first," and Hede and Thusnelda signed their names. And then followed the names of Wilhelm Lassmann, Bruno May, Hoelst, Wrobek, Hülsenschmitt, John, the English mechanic Andrew, the sailor Wingast, and finally, after several more, all of which were not decipherable, the name of Martin Geyring. Then Geyring wrote out the address: "Herr August Esch, Head Book-keeper, Shipping Depot, Central Rhine Shipping Company Limited, Mannheim," and handed the finished product to Frau Hentjen, who, after reading it through carefully, opened the cash drawer to take from the large wire basket in which the bank-notes lay the necessary postage stamp. To her now the enormous card, with the long list of signatures, seemed almost too marked an honour for Esch, who had not been after all among the best patrons of the restaurant. But as everything she did she liked to do thoroughly, and as on the huge card there still remained, in spite of all the names, enough empty space not only to offend her sense of proportion, but also to provide the desired chance of putting Esch in his place by filling it in with a name of more humble rank, Mother Hentjen bore the card to the kitchen for the maid to sign her name, doubly pleased that in this way she could give pleasure to the poor girl without its costing anything.

When she returned to the restaurant Martin was sitting at his usual place in the corner near the buffet, buried in one of the Socialist journals. Frau Hentjen sat down beside him and said jestingly, as she often did: "Herr Geyring, you'll get my restaurant a bad name yet if you use it all the time for reading your seditious papers." "I'm disgusted enough myself with these scribblers," was the answer, "fellows like us do all the work, and these chaps only scribble a lot of nonsense." Once more Frau Hentjen felt a little disappointed in Geyring, for she had never given up the hope that he would yet come out with something revolutionary and full of hatred on which she might feed her own resentment against the world. She had often glanced into the Socialist papers, but really what she found there had seemed to her pretty tame, and so she hoped that Geyring's living speech would have more to give her than the printed word. So to a certain extent she was pleased that Geyring too did not think much of the newspaper writers, for she was always pleased when anyone did not think much of anyone else; yet, on the other hand, he still continued to disappoint her expectations. No, these anarchists didn't get you very far, there wasn't much help in a man like Geyring who sat in his trade-union bureau just like a police sergeant in his office, and Frau Hentjen was once more firmly convinced that the whole structure of society was simply a put-up job among the men, who laid their heads together to injure and disappoint women. She made one more attempt: "What is it that you don't like in your papers, Herr Geyring?" "They write such stuff," growled Martin, "turn the people's heads with their revolutionary rant, and then we've got to pay for it." Frau Hentjen did not quite understand this; besides, she was no longer interested. Mainly out of politeness she sighed: "Yes, life isn't easy." Geyring turned over a page and said absently: "No, life isn't easy, Mother Hentjen." "And a man like you, always on the go, always at it from early morning till late at night. . . ." Geyring said almost with satisfaction: "There won't be any eight-hour day for men like me for a long time yet: everybody else will get it first. . . ." "And to think that they try to make it harder for you!" said Frau Hentjen in amazement, shaking her head and throwing a glance at her coiffure in the mirror behind the buffet. "Yes, they can make a fine noise in the Reichstag and the newspaper, our friends the Jews," said Geyring, "but when it comes to the real work of organization they turn tail." Frau Hentjen could understand this: she agreed indignantly: "They're everywhere, these Jews; they have all the money and no woman is safe from them, they're just like bulls." The old expression of petrified loathing overspread her face. Martin looked up from his paper and could not help smiling: "It isn't as bad as all that, surely, Mother Hentjen." "So now you're sticking up for the Jews next?" there was a hint of hysterical aggressiveness in her voice, "but you always stick up for one another, you men," and then quite unexpectedly: "a girl in every port." "That may be, Mother Hentjen," laughed Martin, "but you won't find such good cooking as Mother Hentjen's anywhere in a hurry." Frau Hentjen was appeased: "Not even in Mannheim, maybe," she said, heading Geyring the picture postcard that he was to send off to Esch.

Gernerth, the theatre manager, now belonged to Esch's intimate circle of friends. For Esch, an impetuous man, had bought another ticket the very day after the first performance, not merely because he wanted to see that brave girl again, but also that he might look up a somewhat astonished Gernerth after the performance and introduce himself as a paying client; while doing this he once more thanked the manager for a lovely evening's enjoyment, and Gernerth, who saw a request for more free tickets in the offing, and was already preparing to refuse them, could not but feel touched. And heartened by his cordial reception Esch simply remained sitting; thus achieving his second object, for he was presented to the juggler Herr Teltscher and also to his brave companion Ilona, who, it turned out, were both of them of Hungarian birth, at least Ilona was, and she had very little command over German, while Herr Teltscher, whose professional name was Teltini, and who employed English on the stage, came from Pressburg.

Herr Gernerth, on the other hand, was an Egerlander, and this was a matter for great joy to Korn, the first time that the two men met; for the towns of Eger and Hof were close neighbours, and Korn could not but regard it as an extraordinary coincidence that two men who were almost landsmen should meet in Mannheim of all places. Still his expressions of joy and surprise were more or less rhetorical, for in less desirable circumstances the fact that he was meeting almost a landsman would have left him quite indifferent. He invited Gernerth to visit his sister and himself, partly perhaps because he could not bear the idea of his presumptive brother-in-law having private acquaintanceships of his own, and Herr Teltscher too was presently invited to a repast of coffee and cakes.

So now on a dull Sunday afternoon they all sat at the round table, on which beside the bulging coffee-pot the cakes, contributed by Esch, were piled up artistically in a pyramid, while outside the rain poured down the window-panes. Herr Gernerth began, trying to set the conversation going: "You've a very nice place here, Herr Customs Inspector, roomy, lots of light. . . ." And he looked out through the window at the dreary suburban street, in which lay great puddles of rain. Fräulein Erna remarked that it was really too small for their circumstances, yet a fireside of one's own was the only thing that could make life sweet. Herr Gernerth became elegiac: no place like home, yes, she might well say that, but for an artist it was an unfulfillable dream; no, for him there could be no home; he had a flat, it was true, a pleasant and comfortable flat in Munich, where his wife lived with the children, but he was almost a stranger to his family by this time. Why didn't he take them with him? It was no life for children, on tour all the time. And besides—— No, his children would never be artists, *his* children wouldn't. He was obviously an affectionate father, and Esch as well as Fräulein Erna felt touched by his goodness of heart. And perhaps because he felt lonely Esch said: "I'm an orphan, I can scarcely remember my mother." "Poor fellow!" said Fräulein Erna. But Herr Teltscher, who did not seem to relish this lugubrious talk, now made a coffee-cup revolve on the tip of his finger so that they could not help laughing, all but Ilona who sat impassively on her chair, recuperating, it seemed, from the perpetual smiles with which she had to embellish her evenings. At close quarters she was by no means so lovely and fragile as she had been on the stage, but might even have been called plump; her face was slightly puffy, there were heavy pouches covered with freckles under her eyes, and Esch, now become mistrustful, began to suspect that her beautiful blond hair, too, might not be genuine, but only a wig; yet his suspicions faded whenever he looked at her body, for he could not help seeing the knives whizzing past it. Then he noticed that Korn's eyes too were caressing that body, and so he tried to attract Ilona's attention, asked her whether she liked Mannheim, whether she had seen the Rhine before, with similar geographical inquiries. Unfortunately his attempts were unsuccessful, for Ilona only replied now and then and at the wrong point: "Yes, very nice," and wished, it seemed, to have nothing to do either with him or with Korn; she drank her coffee heavily and seriously, and even when Teltscher spluttered something at her in their sibilant native idiom, obviously something disagreeable, she scarcely listened. Meanwhile Fräulein Erna was telling Gernerth that a happy family life was the most beautiful thing in the world, and she gave Esch a little nudge with her toe, either to encourage him to follow Gernerth's example, or perhaps merely to withdraw his attention from the Hungarian girl, whose beauty, however, she praised none the less; for the greedy longing with which her brother was regarding the girl had not escaped her vigilant glance, and she considered it preferable that the lovely charmer should fall to her brother rather than to Esch. So she stroked Ilona's hands and praised their whiteness, rolled up the girl's sleeve and said that she had a lovely fine skin, Balthasar should only look at it. Balthasar put out his hairy paw to feel it. Teltscher laughed and said that every Hungarian woman had a skin like silk, whereupon Erna, who also had a skin of her own, replied that it was all a matter of tending one's complexion, and that she washed her face every day in milk. Certainly, said Gernerth, she had a marvellous, indeed an international, complexion, and Fräulein Erna's withered face parted in a smile, showing her yellow teeth and the gap where one tooth was missing in her left upper jaw, and blushed to the roots of the hair at her temples, which hung down thin and brown and a little faded, from her coiffure.

Twilight had fallen; Korn's fist grasped Ilona's hand more and more firmly, and Fräulein Erna was waiting until Esch, or Gernerth at least, should do the same with hers. She hesitated to light the lamp, chiefly because Balthasar would have radically disapproved of the disturbance, but at last she was forced to get up so as to fetch the blue carafe of home-brewed liqueur which stood ostentatiously on the sideboard. Proudly announcing that the recipe was her own secret she served out the brew, which tasted like flat beer, but was applauded as delicious by Gernerth; in his admiration he even kissed her hand. Esch remembered that Mother Hentjen did not like Schnapps drinkers, and it filled him with particular satisfaction to think that she would have had all sorts of hard things to say of Korn, for he was tossing down one glass after another, smacking his lips each time, and sucking the drops from his dark, bushy moustache. Korn poured out a glass for Ilona too, and it may have been her imperturbable indifference and impassivity that made her allow him to lift the glass to her mouth and raise no objection even when he took a sip from it himself, dipping his moustache into it, and declaring that it was a kiss. Evidently Ilona did not understand what he had said, but on the other hand Teltscher must know what was happening. Incomprehensible that he should look on so calmly. Perhaps he was suffering inwardly, and was simply too well-bred to create a scene. Esch had a strong desire to do it for him, but then he remembered the rough tone in which Teltscher had ordered the brave girl to hand him things on the stage; perhaps he was deliberately trying to humiliate her? Something or other should be done, somebody ought to shield Ilona! But Teltscher merely clapped him jovially on the shoulder, calling him colleague and brother, and when Esch looked at him questioningly pointed to the two couples and said: "We must stick together, we young bachelors." "I'll have to take pity on you, I see," said Fräulein Erna, changing places so that she sat now between Gernerth and Esch, but Herr Gernerth said in an offended tone: "That's how we poor artists are always being slighted . . . for these commercial fellows." Teltscher declared that Esch shouldn't allow this, for it was only in the commercial class that solidity and breadth of vision were still to be found. The theatrical industry itself might even be regarded as a branch of commerce, and indeed as the most difficult of the lot with all respect to Herr Gernerth, who was not only his manager, but in a sense his partner, besides being in his own way a very capable man of business, even if he didn't exploit possible avenues of success as he might. He, Teltscher-Teltini, could see that very well, for before he felt drawn to an artist's life he had been in commerce himself. "And what's been the end of it all? Here I sit, when I might have lots of first-class engagements in America. . . . And I ask you, is my turn a first-class one, or isn't it?" A vague memory rose up rebelliously in Esch; what reason had they to praise up the commercial classes so much? The precious solidity they talked of wasn't so solid as they thought. He said so frankly, and ended: "Of course there's a great difference, for instance, between Nentwig and von Bertrand, the Chairman of our company; they're both in commerce, but the one is a swine and the other . . . well, he's something different, something better." Korn growled contemptuously that Bertrand was a renegade officer, everybody knew that, he needn't give himself airs. Esch was not displeased to hear this; so the difference between them wasn't so very great after all! But that didn't alter matters; Bertrand was something better, and in any case these were speculations which he had no desire to pursue too far. Meanwhile Teltscher went on talking about America; over there one could soon come to the top, over there one didn't need to work oneself to skin and bone for nothing as one did here. And he quoted: "America, you lucky land." Gernerth sighed: yes, if he had only had enough of the commercial spirit things would be different now; he had been very rich once himself, but in spite of all his business acumen he had kept the childlike trustfulness of the artist and had been cheated out of all his capital, almost a million marks, by pure fraud. Yes, Herr Esch might well look at him, Gernerth had once been a rich man! *Tempi passati.* Well, he would make his pile again. He had the idea of a theatrical trust, a huge limited liability company for whose shares people would yet be falling over one another. One had simply to march with the times and get hold of capital. And once more kissing Fräulein Erna's hand he asked his glass to be filled again, and said with the air of a connoisseur: "Delicious," still clasping her hand, which remained willingly and contentedly surrendered to him. But Esch, overwhelmed by all that he had heard, and now sunk in thought, scarcely noticed that Fräulein Erna's shoe was pressing against his, and saw only as from a distance and in the darkness Korn's yellow hand which lay on Ilona's shoulder and made it easy to guess that Balthasar Korn had put his powerful arm round Ilona's neck.

But then finally the lamp had to be lit, and now the conversation became general, only Ilona remaining silent. And as it was time to leave for the theatre, and they did not want to break up, Gernerth invited his hosts to attend the performance. So they got ready and took a tram to the theatre. The two ladies went inside and the men smoked their cigars on the platform at the back. Cold drops of rain spattered now and then into their heated faces, refreshing them pleasantly.

The name of the tobacconist from whom August Esch usually bought his cheap cigars was Fritz Lohberg. He was a young man about the same age as Esch, and this may have been the reason why Esch, who was always in the company of people older than himself, treated him as if he were a fool. Nevertheless the fool must have had some slight importance for him, and really it should have given Esch himself matter for thought that just in this shop he should feel so much at home as to become a regular customer. True, the shop lay on the way to his work, yet that was no reason why he should feel at home in it so immediately. Certainly it was very spick-and-span, a pleasant place to dawdle in: the light, pure fragrance of tobacco that filled it gave one an agreeable titillation in the nose, and it was nice to run one's hand over the polished counter, at one end of which, beside the glittering nickel-plated automatic cash register, invariably stood several open sample boxes of light-brown cigars and a little stand containing matches. If one made a purchase one received a box of matches free, a stylishly ample one. Further, there was a huge cigar-cutter which Herr Lohberg always had at hand, and if one wanted to light one's cigar on the spot, then with a sharp little click he snipped off the end that one held out to him. It was a good place to spend one's time in, bright and sunny and hospitable behind its plate-glass windows, and during these cold days full of a sort of pleasant smooth warmth that lay on the white floor-tiles and was a welcome change from the dusty, overheated atmosphere of the glass cage in the warehouse. But while that was sufficient reason for liking to come here after one's work or during the lunch-hour, it had no further significance. At these times one was full of praise for neatness and order, and grumbled at the filth one had to slave among; yet one did not intend this quite seriously, for Esch knew quite well that the perfect orderliness which he kept in his books and his goods lists couldn't be imposed on piles of packing-cases and bales and barrels, no matter how good the foreman might be at his job. But here in this shop, on the other hand, a curiously satisfying sense of order, an almost feminine precision, ruled, and this seemed all the stranger to Esch because he could scarcely picture to himself, or only with discomfort, girls selling cigars; in spite of all its cleanliness it was a job for men, a thing suggesting good-fellowship; yes, this was what friendship between men should be like, and not careless and perfunctory like the casual helpfulness of a trade-union secretary. But these were things which Esch really did not bother his mind about; they occurred to him only by the way. On the other hand, it was both funny and curious that Lohberg shouldn't be content with a job that suited him so well and in which he might have been happy, and still funnier were the grounds that he offered for his dissatisfaction, and in advancing which he showed so clearly that he was a fool. For although he had hung over the automatic cash register a board with the inscription: "Smoking has never harmed anybody"; although his boxes of cigars were accompanied by neat cards which displayed not only his business address and the names of the different brands, but also a little couplet: "Smoke good and pure tobacco every day, And you will have no doctors' bills to pay," yet he himself did not believe in these sentiments; indeed he smoked his own cigarettes simply from a sense of duty and because his conscience pricked him, and, in perpetual dread of so-called smoker's cancer, constantly felt in his stomach, his heart, his throat, all the evil symptoms of nicotine-poisoning. He was a lank little man with a dark shadow of a moustache and lifeless eyes which showed a great deal of white, and his somewhat coy charm and bearing were just as incompatible with his general principles as the business which he carried on and had no thought of exchanging for another; for he was not content to regard tobacco as a popular poison undermining the national well-being, perpetually reiterating that the people must be saved from this virus; no, he was also an advocate of a spacious, natural, genuinely German way of life, and it was a great disappointment to him that he could not live in the open air, a deep-chested, blond giant. For this deprivation, however, he partly compensated himself by subscribing to anti-alcoholic and vegetarian associations, and so beside the cash register there was always lying a pile of pamphlets on such subjects, most of them sent to him from Switzerland. No doubt about it, he was a pure fool.

Now Esch, who smoked cigars and drank wine and treated himself to huge portions of meat whenever he had the chance, might not have been so deeply impressed by Herr Lohberg's arguments, in spite of the persuasive phrases about saving the people which always recurred in them, if he had not been struck by a curious parallelism between them and the principles of Mother Hentjen. Of course Mother Hentjen was a sensible woman, even an unusually sensible woman, and so her opinions had nothing in common with Lohberg's jargon. Yet when Lohberg, true to the Calvinistic convictions which reached him from Switzerland along with his pamphlets, inveighed like a priest against sensual indulgence and in the same breath pleaded like a Socialist orator addressing a Freethinking audience for a free and simple life in the bosom of nature; when in his own modest way he let it be understood that there was something amiss with the world, a glaring error in the books which could only be put right by a wonderful new entry, in all this confusion only one thing was absolutely clear, that Mother Hentjen's restaurant was in the same case as Lohberg's tobacconist shop: she had to depend for her living on the men who boozed at her tables, and she too hated her business and her customers. No doubt about it, it was a queer coincidence, and Esch half thought of writing to Frau Hentjen to tell her about it, it would interest her. But he dropped the idea when he reflected that Frau Hentjen might think it odd, perhaps even feel insulted, to be compared with a man who, in spite of all his virtues, was an idiot. So he saved it up until he should see her; in any case he would soon have to go to Cologne on business.

All the same the case of Lohberg was well worth mentioning; and one evening, while Esch was sitting at dinner with Korn and Fräulein Erna, he gave way to his desire to talk about it.

Of course the two Korns knew of Lohberg. Korn had already been in his shop several times, but he had observed none of the man's peculiarities. "One wouldn't think it to see him," he said, after an interval of silent thought, and agreed with Esch that the man was a fool. But Fräulein Erna seemed to be seized with a violent aversion to this spiritual double of Frau Hentjen, and inquired sharply whether Frau Hentjen perchance was Herr Esch's long and carefully concealed lady-love. She must be a very virtuous lady, no doubt, but Fräulein Erna thought all the same that she herself was just as good. And as for Herr Lohberg's virtuous scruples, of course it wasn't nice when a man made the curtains stink with his perpetual smoking as her brother did. Yet on the other hand one knew at least that there was a man about the house. "A man that does nothing but drink water . . ." she searched for words, "would sicken me." And then she inquired, did Herr Lohberg even know what it was to have a woman? "He's still an innocent, I suppose, the fool," said Esch, and Korn, foreseeing that there was sport to be had out of him yet, exclaimed: "A pure Joseph!"

Whether for this purpose, or because he wished to keep an eye on his lodger, or simply by pure chance, Korn too now became a regular customer of Lohberg's, and Lohberg shrank every time that the Herr Customs Inspector noisily entered his shop. His fear was not without cause. A few evenings later the blow fell; shortly before closing time Korn appeared with Esch and commanded: "Make yourself ready, my lad; to-night you're going to lose your innocence." Lohberg rolled his eyes helplessly and pointed to a man in the uniform of the Salvation Army who was standing in the shop. "Fancy dress?" said Korn, and Lohberg stammeringly introduced the man: "A friend of mine." "We're friends too," replied Korn, holding out his paw to the Salvation Army soldier. He was a freckled, somewhat pimply, red-haired youth, who had learned that one must be friendly to every soul one meets; he smiled in Korn's face and rescued Lohberg: "Brother Lohberg has promised to testify in our ranks to-night. I've come to fetch him." "So, you're going out to testify? Then we'll come too." Korn was enthusiastic. "We're all friends." "Every friend is welcome," said the joyful Salvation Army man. Lohberg was not consulted; he had the look of a thief caught in the act, and closed up the shop with a guilty air. Esch had followed the proceedings with great amusement, yet as Korn's high-handedness annoyed him he clapped Lohberg jovially on the shoulder, reproducing the very gesture that Teltscher had often expended on him.

They made for the Neckar quarter. In Käfertalerstrasse they could already hear the beating of the drums and tambourines, and Korn's feet, as if remembering their time in the army, fell into step. Whey they came to the end of the street they saw the Salvation Army group standing at the corner of the park in the dying twilight. Watery sleet had fallen, and where the group was gathered the snow had melted into black slush which soaked through one's boots. The Lieutenant was standing on a wooden bench and cried into the falling darkness: "Come to us and be saved, poor wandering sinners, the Saviour is near!" But only a few had answered his call, and when his soldiers, with drums and tambourines beating, sang of the redeeming love and made their chorus resound: "Lord God of Sabaoth save, Oh, save our souls from Hell," hardly anybody in the crowd standing round joined in, and it was obvious that the majority were merely looking on out of curiosity. And although the honest soldiers sang on lustily, and the two girls struck their tambourines with all their might, the crowd grew thinner and thinner as the light faded, and soon they were left alone with their Lieutenant, their only audience now being Lohberg, Korn and Esch. Yet even now Lohberg was probably ready to join in the hymn, and indeed he would certainly have done so without feeling either embarrassed or intimidated by Esch and Korn if Korn had not kept on digging him in the ribs and saying: "Sing, Lohberg!" It wasn't a very pleasant situation for Lohberg, and he was glad when a policeman arrived and ordered them to move on. They all set out for the Thomasbräu cellar. And yet it was almost a pity that Lohberg hadn't joined in the singing, yes, then perhaps a minor miracle might have happened, for it wouldn't have taken much to make Esch too lift up his voice in praise of the Saviour and His redeeming love; indeed only a slight impetus would have been required, and perhaps the sound of Lohberg's voice would have provided it. But one can never be sure of those things afterwards.

Esch himself could not make out what had happened to him at the open-air meeting: the two girls had beaten their tambourines when the officer standing on the bench gave the signal, and that had reminded him strangely of the commands which Teltscher gave

Ilona on the stage. Perhaps it was the sudden dead silence of the evening that had affected him, for there at the outskirts of the city the sounds of the evening broke off as abruptly as the music in the theatre; perhaps it was the motionlessness of the black trees that gazed up into the darkening sky; and then behind him in the square the arc-lamps had flared out. It was all incomprehensible. The biting coldness of the wet snow had pierced through his shoes; but that was not the only reason why Esch would have liked to be standing up there on the bench pointing out the way of salvation, for his old strange feeling of orphaned isolation had returned again, and suddenly it had become dreadfully clear to him that some time he would have to die in utter and complete loneliness. A vague and yet unforeseen hope had risen in him that things would go better, far better, with him if he could but stand up there on the bench; and he saw Ilona, Ilona in the Salvation Army uniform, gazing up at him and waiting for his redeeming signal to strike the tambourine and cry "Hallelujah!" But Korn was standing beside him, grinning out from between the great upturned collars of his damp customs cloak, and at the sight of him Esch's hopes had ignominiously melted away. Esch's mouth twisted wryly, his expression became contemptuous, and all at once he was almost glad to be orphaned and alone. In any case he too was relieved that the policeman had moved them on.

Lohberg was walking in front with the pimply Salvation Army man and one of the girls. Esch trudged behind. Yes, whether a girl like that beat a tambourine or threw plates, one only had to order her to do it, it was just the same, only the clothes were different. They sang about love in the Salvation Army as in the theatre. "Perfect redeeming love," Esch had to laugh, and he decided to sound the good Salvation Army girl on this question. When they were nearing the Thomasbräu cellar the girl stopped, planted her foot on a ledge projecting from the wall, bent down, and began to tie the laces of her wet, shapeless boots. As she stood there bent double, her black hat almost touching her knee, she looked lumpish and hardly human, a monstrosity, yet with a certain, as it were, mechanical effectiveness of structure, and Esch, who in other circumstances would have requited such a posture with a clap on the part most saliently exposed, was a little alarmed that no desire to do so awoke in him, and it almost seemed as though another bridge between him

and his fellow-creatures had been broken, and he felt homesick for
Cologne. That day in the kitchen he had wanted to take hold of
Mother Hentjen under the breasts; yes, he would not have been put
off had Mother Hentjen bent down and laced her shoes. But as all
men have the same thoughts, Korn, who felt on good terms with all
the world, now pointed to the girl: "Any chance with her, do you
think?" Esch threw him a furious glance, but Korn did not stop:
"Among themselves they're probably hot enough, the soldiers."
Meanwhile they had reached the Thomasbräu cellar, and they
walked into the bright, noisy room, which smelt pleasantly of roast
beef, onions and beer.

Here, at any rate, Korn met with a disappointment. For the Salvation Army people were not to be prevailed upon to sit down at
the same table; they said good-bye and gathered at one end of the
room to distribute the *War Cry.* Esch too would have preferred not
to be left alone with Korn; some remnant of hope still fluttered in
his soul that these people might be able to bring back to him what
he had felt under the darkening trees and yet had not been able to
grasp. But it was a good thing, on the other hand, that they were
now beyond the reach of Korn's raillery, and it would have been
still better if they had taken Lohberg with them, for Korn was now
anxious to get his own back and was beginning his joke at Lohberg's expense by trying to make the helpless fellow violate his principles with the aid of a portion of steak and onions and a great jug
of beer. But the ninny stood his ground, merely saying in a quiet
voice: "You shouldn't joke with a fellow's convictions," and
touched neither the meat nor the beer, and Korn, once more disappointed, had to be content with morosely devouring them himself,
so that they might not be wasted. Esch contemplated the dark resi-
due of beer at the bottom of his jug; absurd to think that one's salvation could depend on whether one drank that up or not. All the
same he felt almost grateful to the mild and obstinate fool. Lohberg
sat there smiling meekly, and sometimes one almost expected tears
to start to his great eyes with the exposed whites. Yet when the Salvation Army people in their round of the tables drew near again he
stood up and it looked as though he were about to shout something
to them. Against Esch's expectations he did not do so, but simply
remained standing where he was. Then suddenly he uttered without
warning or reason a single word, a word quite incomprehensible to

everyone who heard it; he uttered loudly and distinctly the word "Redemption," and then sat down again. Korn looked at Esch and Esch looked at Korn. But when Korn put his finger to his brow and twirled it to indicate that Lohberg was weak in the head, the whole situation changed in the most extraordinary and terrifying manner, for it was as though the word of redemption, now set free, hovered over the table maintained in its detachment by an invisibly revolving mechanism, detached even from the mouth that had uttered it. And although Esch's contempt for Lohberg remained undiminished, yet it seemed now that the kingdom of salvation did exist, could exist, must exist, if only because Korn, that dead lump of flesh, was sitting on his broad hindquarters in the Thomasbräu cellar, quite incapable of sending his thoughts even as far as the next street corner, far less of losing them in the infinite spaces of freedom. And although, in spite of these ideas, Esch refused to act the prig, but instead rapped with his jug on the table and ordered another beer, yet he too became silent like Lohberg; and when on rising to leave Korn proposed that they should take the pure Joseph to visit the girls, Esch refused to second him, left a completely disappointed Balthasar Korn standing on the pavement, and escorted the tobacconist home, quite pleased that Korn should shout insults after them. It had stopped snowing, and in the warm wind that had risen Korn's rude words fluttered past like light spring blossoms.

Driven by that extraordinary oppression which falls on every human being when, childhood over, he begins to divine that he is fated to go on in isolation and unaided towards his own death; driven by this extraordinary oppression, which may with justice be called a fear of God, man looks round him for a companion hand in hand with whom he may tread the road to the dark portal, and if he has learned by experience how pleasurable it undoubtedly is to lie with another fellow-creature in bed, then he is ready to believe that this extremely intimate association of two bodies may last until these bodies are coffined: and even if at the same time it has its disgusting aspects, because it takes place under coarse and badly aired sheets, or because he is convinced that all a girl cares for is to get a husband who will support her in later life, yet it must not be forgotten that every fellow-creature, even if she has a sallow complexion, sharp, thin features and an obviously missing tooth in her left upper jaw, yearns, in spite of her missing tooth, for that love which she thinks will for ever shield her from death, from that fear of death which sinks with falling of every night upon the human being who sleeps alone, a fear that already licks her as with a tongue of flame when she begins to take off her clothes, As Fräulein Erna was doing now; she laid aside her faded red-velvet blouse and took off her dark-green skirt and her petticoat. Then she drew off her shoes; but her stockings, on the other hand, as well as her white, starched under-petticoat, she kept on; indeed she could not even summon the resolution to undo her corsets. She was afraid, but she concealed her fear behind a knowing smile, and by the light of the flickering candle-flame on the bedside-table she slipped, without undressing further, into bed.

Now it came to pass that she heard Esch walking several times through the lobby, in doing which he made a greater noise than the necessary arrangements he was engaged in should have required. Perhaps these arrangements themselves were not indeed altogether necessary, for what need could there be to fetch water to his room twice? And the water-jug was surely not so heavy that he had to set it down with a bang in the passage immediately outside Erna's door. But every time that Fräulein Erna heard anything she resolved not to be outdone and made a noise too; stretched herself till the bed creaked, even pushed deliberately with her toes against the foot of it and sighed an audible "This is nice," as if she were sleepy; also she coughed and cleared her throat in pursuit of her purpose. Now Esch was an impetuous man, and after they had telegraphed to each other in this way for a little while he walked resolutely into her room.

There lay Fräulein Erna in bed and smiled knowingly and slyly and yet a little invitingly at him with her missing tooth, and really she did not attract him very much. All the same he paid no attention to her protest: "But Herr Esch, you mustn't stay here," but remained calmly where he was; and he did this not merely because he was a man of coarse appetites, like most men, he did it not merely because two people of different sexes living on intimate terms in the same house can scarcely escape the automatic functioning of physical attraction, and with the reflection "Why not, after all," will eventually yield casually to it, he did it not only because he divined that her feelings were much the same as his and so discounted her words, he did it therefore not simply in obedience to a low impulse, even if we add jealousy to it, the jealousy which any man might feel on seeing a woman flirting with Herr Gernerth; no, Esch did it because he was a man for whom it was essential that this pleasure, which people imagine one seeks for its own sake, should serve also a higher purpose, a purpose which he could scarcely name and yet felt bound to obey, but which nevertheless was nothing but the compulsion to put an end to a tremendous fear that extended far beyond himself, even if sometimes it might seem to be merely the fear that befalls the commercial traveller when, far from his wife and children, he lies down in his lonely hotel bed; the fear and desire of the traveller who resorts to the plain and elderly chambermaid, sometimes heartbroken by the squalor of the affair, and generally filled with remorse of conscience. Of course when Esch banged down his water-jug hard on the floor he was no longer thinking of the loneliness which had descended upon him since he had left Cologne, nor was he thinking of the isolation that had lain on the stage before Teltscher let fly the whistling, glittering daggers. Yet now that he sat on the edge of Fräulein Erna's bed and bent over her in desire, he wanted more from her than is currently construed as the satisfaction of an average sensual man's lust, for behind the very palpable, indeed banal, immediate object of desire, yearning was hidden, the yearning of the captive soul for redemption from its loneliness, for a salvation which should embrace himself and her, yes, perhaps all mankind, and most certainly Ilona, a salvation which Erna could not vouchsafe him, because neither she nor he knew what he wanted. So the rage which seized him when she refused him the final favour and gently said: "When we're man and wife," was neither merely the rage of the thwarted male, nor simple fury at the discovery of the trick she had played him in only half-undressing; it was more, it was despair, even if the words with which, sobered now, he rudely replied, were by no means highsounding: "Well, it's all off, then." And although her refusal seemed to him a sign from God warning him to be chaste, he left the house immediately and went to a more willing lady. And that deeply wounded Erna.

From that evening there was open war between Esch and Fräulein Erna. She let no opportunity pass of provoking his desire, and he no less eagerly seized every pretext to renew his attempt and to lure the recalcitrant one into his bed without promise of marriage. The battle began in the morning when she brought his breakfast into his room before he was properly dressed, a lascivious kind of mothering that maddened him; and it ended in the evening in indifference, whether she had barred her door or let him in. Neither of them ever mentioned the word love, and the fact that open hatred did not break out between them, but was dissembled in spiteful jests, was due simply to the other fact that they had not yet possessed each other.

Often he thought that with Ilona things must be different and better, but strangely enough his thoughts did not dare to rise to her. She was something better, much in the same way as the Chairman of the company, Bertrand, was something better. And Esch did not even mind very much that one of Erna's tricks was to frustrate any chance of his meeting Ilona, indeed he was even glad of this, bitterly as he resented all her silly fuss and her tittering facetiousness. Meanwhile Ilona was about the place almost every day, and between her and Erna a sort of friendship had grown up, yet what they could find in each other was incomprehensible to Esch; if when he got home he smelt the cheap and powerful scent which Ilona used, and which always excited him, he was sure to find the two ladies in an extraordinary dumb dialogue; for Ilona knew scarcely a word of German and Fräulein Erna was forced to fall back on fondling her friend, stationing her before the mirror and admiringly patting and rearranging her coiffure and her dress. But generally Esch found himself excluded. For Erna now set herself to conceal from him even the presence of her friend in the house. So one evening he happened to be sitting quite innocently in his room when the door-bell rang. He heard Erna opening the door and would not have thought anything further about the matter if he had not suddenly heard the key of his door being turned. Esch made a spring for the door; he was locked it! The trollop had locked him in! And although he should simply have ignored the stupid joke, it was too much for him, and he began to bawl and bang on the door, until at last Fräulein Erna opened it and slipped into the room with a giggle. "Well," she said, "now I can attend to you . . . we have a visitor, I may say, but Balthasar is looking after her all right." Esch rushed out of the house in a rage.

When he returned late at night the lobby again reeked of Ilona's perfume. So she must have come back again, or rather she must still be here, for now he saw her hat hanging on the hat-rack. But where could she be? The parlour was dark. Korn was snoring next door. She simply couldn't have gone away without her hat! Esch listened at Erna's door; the agitating and oppressive thought came into his mind that the two women were lying in there side by side. He cautiously tried the door-handle; the door did not yield, it was barred as always when Fräulein Erna really wanted to sleep. Esch shrugged his shoulders and walked noisily to his room. But he could not rest in bed; he peered out into the passage; the perfume still hung in the air and the hat was still there. Something wasn't in order, one could feel that, and Esch stole through the house. It seemed to him that he could hear whispering in Korn's room; Korn wasn't the man to speak in a whisper, and Esch listened more intently: then suddenly Korn groaned, unmistakably he groaned, and Esch, a fellow who had no occasion to fear a man like Korn, fled back to his room in his bare feet as though something dreadful were pursuing him. He even felt he wanted to put his hands to his ears.

Next morning Erna awakened him out of a leaden sleep, and before he could bring out his question she said: "Hsh! I've a surprise for you. Get up at once!" He hastily put on his clothes, and when he walked into the kitchen, were Erna was busy, she took him by the hand and led him on tiptoe to her room, opened the door slightly and asked him to look in. There he saw Ilona; her round white arm, which still did not show any dagger wounds, was hanging over the edge of the bed, the heavy pouches under her eyes showed distinctly on her somewhat puffy face, and she was asleep.

Now Ilona frequently arrived at a late hour at the flat, and this lasted for a comparatively long time before Esch grasped the fact that she spent the night with Balthasar Korn and that Erna was shielding her brother's love affair, in a sense, with her own body.

Martin called on him at his work. It was extraordinary, the ease with which this pariah, whom every gate-keeper had orders to keep out, always managed to get himself admitted everywhere quite openly and swung at his ease on his crutches through places of business, nobody stopping him, many saluting him affectionately, partly no doubt because one was shy of appearing unkind to a cripple. Esch was not particularly pleased to receive a visit from a trade-union secretary at his work; Martin could just as well have waited for him outside, but on the other hand one could rely on his discretion; he knew the right time to come and the right time to go; he was a decent fellow. "'Morning, August," he said. "I just wanted to see how you were getting on. You've a nice job here, made a good exchange." Did the cripple want to remind him that he had him to thank for being in this accursed Mannheim? All the same Martin could not be held responsible for the affair between Ilona and Korn, and so Esch simply replied in a morose voice: "Yes, a good exchange." And somehow it rang true. For now that Martin reminded him of his former job and Nentwig, Esch was jolly glad that he had nothing more to do with Cologne. Like a thief he still kept Nentwig's misdemeanour concealed, and the fact that one might come across the man's ugly mug at any street corner in Cologne took away all pleasure at the thought of returning there. Cologne or Mannheim, there was nothing to choose between them. Was there really any place where one could be rid of all this rottenness? Nevertheless he asked how things were in Cologne. "Later," said Martin, "I haven't time just now; where are you having your dinner?" And as soon as Esch told him he swung himself hastily away.

By now Esch really felt glad at meeting Martin again, and as he was an impatient fellow he could scarcely wait for the dinner-hour to come. Spring had arrived overnight, and Esch left his greatcoat in the office; the flagstones between the sheds were bright with the cool sunshine, and in the corners of the buildings young tender grass had suddenly appeared between the cobbles. As he passed the unloading stage he laid his hand on the iron bands with which the clumsy grey wooden erection was clamped together, and the iron too felt warm. If he shouldn't be transferred to Cologne he must arrange to have his bicycle sent on soon. He breathed in the air deeply and easily, and the food had quite a different taste; perhaps because the windows of the restaurant were open. Martin related that he had come to Mannheim on strike business; otherwise he would have taken his time. But something was happening in the South German and Alsatian factories, and such things soon spread: "For all I care they can strike as much as they like, only we can't afford any nonsense just now. A strike of the transport workers would be pure madness at the moment . . . we're a poor union and there's no money to be had from the central office . . . it would be a complete wash-out. Of course it's no use talking to a docker: if a donkey like that makes up his mind to go on strike nothing will stop him. But sooner or later they'll have my blood yet." He said all this indulgently, without bitterness. "Now they're raising the cry again that I'm being paid by the shipping companies." "By Bertrand?" asked Esch with interest. Geyring nodded: "By Bertrand, too, of course." "A proper swine," Esch could not help saying. Martin laughed. "Bertrand? He's a very decent fellow." "Oho, so he's a decent fellow? Is it true that he's a renegade officer?" "Yes, he's supposed to have quit the service—but that only speaks in the man's favour." Oho, that spoke in the man's favour, did it? Nothing was clear and simple, thought Esch in anger, nothing was clear and simple, even on a lovely spring day like this: "All I would like to know is why you stick to this job of yours." "Everybody must stay where God has put him," said Martin, and his old-young face took on a pious look. Then he told Esch that Mother Hentjen sent her greetings and that everybody was looking forward to seeing him soon.

After dinner they went along to Lohberg's shop. They were in no hurry, and so Martin rested in the massive oaken chair that stood beside the counter and was as bright and solid as everything else in the shop. Accustomed to pick up anything in print that came within his reach, Martin glanced through the anti-alcoholic and vegetarian journals from Switzerland. "Dear, dear!" he said, "here's almost a comrade of mine." Lohberg felt flattered, but Esch spoilt his pleasure for him: "Oh, he's one of the teetotal wash-outs," and to crush him completely he added: "Geyring has a big meeting to-night, but a real one—not a meeting of the Salvation Army!" "Unfortunately," said Martin. Lohberg, who had a great weakness for public demonstrations and oratorical performances, proposed immediately to go. "I advise you not to," said Martin. "Esch at least mustn't go, it might go badly with him if he were seen there. Besides, there's bound to be trouble." Esch really had no anxiety about endangering his post, yet strangely enough to attend the meeting seemed to him an act of treachery towards Bertrand. Lohberg, on the other hand, said boldly: "I'll go in any case," and Esch felt shamed by the teetotal ninny; no, it would never do to leave a friend in the lurch; if he did he would never dare to face Mother

Hentjen again. But meanwhile he said nothing about his decision. Martin explained: "I fancy that the shipping companies will send an *agent provocateur* or two; it's all to their interest that the strike should be as violent as possible." And although Nentwig was not a shipper, but only the greasy head clerk in a firm of wine merchants, to Esch it seemed that the rascal had his greasy fingers in this piece of perfidy too.

The meeting took place, as was usual in such cases, in the public room of a small tavern. A few policemen were standing before the entrance keeping an eye on those who went in, who on their side pretended not to notice the policemen. Each arrived late; as he was about to enter someone tapped him on the shoulder, and when he turned round he saw it was the inspector of the dock police squad: "Why, what takes you here, Herr Esch?" Esch thought quickly. Actually simple curiosity; he had learned that Geyring, the trade-union secretary, whom he had known in Cologne, was to speak, and as in a way he was connected with shipping he felt interested in the whole business. "I advise you against it, Herr Esch," said the inspector, "and just because you're in a shipping firm; it will look fishy, and it can't do you any good." "I'll just look in for a minute," Esch decided, and went in.

The low room, adorned with portraits of the Kaiser, the Grand Duke of Baden, and the King of Württemberg, was crammed full. On the raised platform stood a table covered with a white cloth, behind which four men were sitting; Martin was one of them. Esch, at first a little envious because he too was not sitting in such a prominent position, was surprised next moment that he had noticed the table at all, so great was the uproar and disorder in the room. Indeed it was some time before he noticed that a man had mounted on a chair in the middle of the hall and was shouting out an incomprehensible rigmarole, emphasizing every word—he seemed to love particularly the word "demagogue"—with a sweeping gesture, as though to fling it at the table on the platform. It was a sort of unequal dialogue, for the only reply from the table was the thin tinkle of a bell which did not pierce the din; yet it finally had the last say when Martin, supporting himself on his crutches and the back of his chair, got up, and the noise ebbed. True, it wasn't very easy to grasp what Martin, with the somewhat weary and ironical fluency of a practised speaker, was saying, but that he was worth twice all these people bawling at him Esch could see. It almost looked as though Martin had no wish to get a hearing, for with a faint smile he stopped and let the shouts of "Capitalist pimp!" "Twister!" and "Kaiser's Socialist!" pass over him, until suddenly, amid the whistling and catcalls, a sharper whistle was heard. In the sudden silence a police officer appeared on the platform and said curtly: "In the name of the law I declare this meeting closed; the hall must be cleared." And while Esch was being borne through the door by the crush he had time to see the police officer turning to Martin.

As if by arrangement the most of the audience had made for the side-door of the tavern. But that did not help them much, for meanwhile the whole place had been encircled by the police, and every one of them had either to explain his presence or go to the police station. At the front entrance the crush was not so great; Esch had the good luck to encounter the dock inspector again and said hastily: "You were right, never again," and so he escaped interrogation. But the affair was not yet ended. The crowd now stood before the place quite quietly, contenting themselves with swearing softly at the committee, the union and Geyring. But all at once the rumour flew round that Geyring and the committee were arrested and that the police were only waiting for the crowd to disperse to lead them away. Then suddenly the feeling of the crowd swung round; whistles and cat-calls rose again, and the crowd made ready to rush the police. The friendly police inspector gave Esch a push: "You'd better disappear now, Herr Esch," and Esch, who saw that there was nothing else he could do, withdrew to the nearest street corner, hoping at least to run up against Lohberg.

Before the hall the noise still went on for a good while. Then six mounted police arrived at a sharp trot, and because horses, who although docile are yet somewhat insane creatures, exert on many human beings a sort of magical influence, this little equestrian reinforcement was decisive. Esch looked on while a number of workers in handcuffs were led away amid the terrified silence of their comrades, and then the street emptied. Wherever the police, now become rough and impatient, saw two men standing together, they drove them harshly away, and Esch, considering with good reason that he would be handled just as ruthlessly, vacated the field.

He went to Lohberg's house. Lohberg had not yet returned, and Esch remained waiting before his door in the warm spring night.

He hoped that they hadn't led Lohberg away too in handcuffs. Although really that would have been a good joke. Lord! what would Erna say if she saw this paragon of virtue before her in handcuffs? Just when Esch was about to give up his watch Lohberg arrived in a terribly excited state, and almost weeping. Bit by bit, and very disconnectedly, Esch managed to discover that at first the meeting had proceeded quite quietly, even if the audience had shouted all sorts of abuse at Herr Geyring, who had spoken very well. But then a man had got up, obviously one of those *agents provocateurs* whom Herr Geyring himself had mentioned at dinner-time, and had made a furious speech against the rich classes, the State and even the Kaiser himself, until the police officer threatened to close the meeting if anything else of that nature was said. Quite incomprehensibly Herr Geyring, who must have known quite well what sort of a bird he had to deal with, had not unmasked the man as an *agent provocateur*, but had actually come to his assistance and demanded freedom of speech for him. Well, after that it grew worse and worse, and finally the meeting was broken up. The committee and Herr Geyring were under arrest; he could vouch for that, for he had been among the last to leave the hall.

Esch felt upset, indeed more upset than he would admit. All that he knew was that he must have some wine if he was to bring order into the world again; Martin, who was against the strike, was arrested by police who were in with the shipping companies and a renegade officer, police who, in the most infamous manner, had seized an innocent man—perhaps because Esch himself had not handed Nentwig over to them! Yet the inspector had acted in a very friendly way towards him, actually had shielded him. Sudden anger at Lohberg overcame him; the confounded fool was probably so taken aback simply because he had expected harmless and uplifting twaddle about brotherhood and did not understand that things could turn to deadly earnest. Suddenly all this brotherhood twaddle seemed disgusting to Esch; what was the use of all these brotherhoods and associations? They only made the confusion greater and probably they were the cause of it; he brutally let fly at Lohberg: "For God's sake put away that cursed lemonade of yours, or I'll sweep it off the table . . . if only you drank honest wine you would be able at least to give a sensible answer to a plain question." But Lohberg only looked at him with his great uncomprehending eyes,

in whose whites little red veins now appeared, and was in no state
to resolve Esch's doubts, doubts which next day became much
worse when he heard that as a protest against the arrest of their
union secretary the transport and dock workers had gone on strike.
Meanwhile Geyring was sentenced to await his trial for the crime
of sedition.

During the performance Esch sat with Gernerth in the so-called
manager's office, which always reminded him of his glass cage in
the bonded warehouse. On the stage Teltscher and Ilona were going
through their act, and he heard the whizzing knives striking against
the black board. Above the writing-table was fixed a little white
box marked with a red cross, supposed to contain bandages. For a
long time it had certainly contained none, and for decades nobody
had even opened it, yet Esch was convinced that at any moment
Ilona might be carried in to have her bleeding wounds bound. But
instead Teltscher appeared, slightly perspiring and slightly proud of
himself, and wiping his hands on his handkerchief said: "Real
work, good honest work . . . must be paid for." Gernerth made
some calculations in his notebook: "theatre rent, 22 marks; tax, 16
marks; lighting, 4 marks; salaries . . ." "Oh, stow that!" said Teltscher. "I know it all by heart already. I've put four thousand crowns
into this business and I'll never see them again . . . I'll just have to
grin and bear it. . . . Herr Esch, don't you know anybody who
would buy me out? He can have a twenty-per-cent rebate, and I'll
give you ten-per-cent commission over and above." Esch had already heard these outbursts and these offers and no longer paid any
attention to them, although he would gladly have bought out Teltscher to get rid both of him and Ilona.

Esch was in an ill humour. Since Martin's imprisonment life had
become radically darker: the fact that his skirmishing with Erna
had grown burdensome and intolerable was really secondary; but
that Bertrand had bribed the police, and that the police had behaved abominably, was more than exasperating, and Ilona's relations with Korn, no longer concealed either by them or by Erna,
were repulsive in his sight. It was disgusting. The very thought of it
repelled him: Ilona, after all, was something superior. Yes, better
that he should know nothing about her, and that she should disappear out of his life for ever. And Bertrand as well, along with his

Central Rhine Shipping Company. This became quite clear to Esch for the first time now that Ilona came in in her outdoor clothes and silently and seriously sat down without being accorded a glance by the two men. Korn would presently appear to take her away; lately he had been going in and out here quite at his ease.

Ilona had been overcome by a genuine passion for Balthasar Korn, perhaps because he reminded her of some sergeant whom she had loved in her youth, perhaps simply because he was such a complete contrast to the adroit, sickly, blasé Teltscher, who in spite of his sickliness was so essentially brutal. Frankly, Esch did not waste any thought on such things; enough that a woman whom he himself had renounced, because she was destined for a better fate, was now being degraded by a man like Korn. But Teltscher's attitude was quite inexplicable. The fellow was clearly a pimp, and yet that wasn't a thing to trouble one's head about. Besides, the whole business could not bring him in very much; Korn certainly was generous enough, and in the new clothes which he had given her Ilona really looked superb, so superb that Fräulein Erna no longer regarded her brother's expensive love affair with by any means the same favour as at first; but in spite of all this Ilona would accept no money from Korn, and he had literally to force his presents on her; so deeply did she love him.

Korn appeared at the door and Ilona flung herself on his uniformed breast with Eastern words of endearment. No, it was past endurance! Teltscher laughed: "See that you enjoy yourself," and as they went out together he shouted after her in Hungarian a few words, obviously spiteful, which earned him not only a glance full of hatred from Ilona, but also a half-joking, half-serious threat from Korn that he would give the Jewish knife-thrower a beating yet. Teltscher paid no attention to this, but returned to his beloved business speculations: "We must provide something that isn't too expensive and that will draw the crowd." "Oh, what an epoch-making discovery, Herr Teltscher-Teltini," said Gernerth, making calculations in his notebook again. Then he looked up: "What do you say to wrestling matches for women?" Teltscher whistled reflectively through his teeth: "Might be considered: of course that can't be done either without money." Gernerth scribbled in his notebook. "We'll need some money, but not so very much; women don't cost much. Then tights . . . we'll have to get someone inter-

ested in it." "I'm willing to teach them," said Teltscher, "and I can
be the referee too. But here in Mannheim?" he made a contemptuous gesture, "there's no closing one's eyes to the fact that business
is bad here. What do you say, Esch?" Esch had formed no definite
opinion, but the hope rose within him that with a change of scene
Ilona might be saved from Korn's clutches. And as it lay nearest to
his heart, he replied that Cologne seemed to him a splendid place
for staging wrestling matches; in the previous year wrestling
matches had been given there in the circus, serious ones of course,
and the place had been packed. "Ours will be serious too," Teltscher decided. They talked it over from all sides for a while longer,
and finally Esch was empowered to discuss the matter, on his approaching visit to Cologne, with the theatrical agent, Oppenheimer,
whom Gernerth would have written to in the interval. And if Esch
should succeed in hunting up some money for the undertaking, it
would not only be a friendly service, but he might get a percentage
on it himself.

Esch knew at the moment of nobody likely to invest money. But
in secret he thought of Lohberg, who might almost be regarded as
a rich man. But would a pure Joseph have any interest in wrestling
matches for women?

The arrests that had been made in advance of the strike had deprived the dock labourers of all their leaders, yet after ten days the
strike was still lingering on. There were indeed some blacklegs, but
they were too few to handle the railway freights, and since shipping
in any case was partially paralysed, they were employed only on the
most urgent work. In the bonded warehouses a Sabbath quiet
reigned. Esch was annoyed, because it was unlikely that he could
get away until the strike was over, and he lounged idly round the
sheds, leaned against the door-posts, and finally sat down to write
to Mother Hentjen. He gave her the details of Martin's arrest and
told her about Lohberg, but he did not even mention Erna and
Korn, for the mere thought of doing so disgusted him. Then he procured a fresh batch of picture postcards and addressed them to all
the girls he had slept with in recent years, and whose names he
could remember. Outside in the shadow the foremen and stevedores
stood in a group, and behind the half-open sliding doors of an
empty goods truck some men were playing cards. Esch wondered

whom he should write to next, and tried to count in his head all the women he had ever had. He could not be sure of the total, and it was as if a column in his books would not balance properly, so to get it right he began to make a list of the names on a piece of paper, entering the month and year after each. Then he added them up and was satisfied, more especially as Korn came in boasting, as usual, what a fine woman Ilona was, and what a fiery Hungarian. Esch pocketed his list and let Korn go on talking; he would not be able to talk like that for much longer. Only let the strike once come to an end, and the Herr Customs Inspector would have to run all the way to Cologne for his Ilona, perhaps even farther still, to the end of the world. And he was almost sorry for the man because he did not know what was in store for him. Balthasar Korn went on boasting happily of his conquest, and when he had said his say about Ilona he drew out a pack of cards. In brotherly amity they sought out a third man and settled down to play for the rest of the day.

In the evening Esch looked in on Lohberg, who was sitting in his shop with a cigarette in his mouth before a pile of vegetarian journals. He laid these aside when Esch came in and began to talk about Martin. "The world," he said, "is poisoned, not only with nicotine and alcohol and animal food, but with a still worse poison that we can hardly even recognize . . . it's just like boils breaking out." His eyes were moist and looked feverish; he gave one an unhealthy impression; it seemed possible that there really was some poison working within him. Esch stood, lean and robust, in front of him, but his head was empty after so much card-playing and he did not catch the sense of these idiotic remarks, he hardly realized that they referred to Martin's imprisonment; everything was wrapped in a fog of idiocy, and his only definite wish was to have the affair of the theatre partnership cleared up once and for all. Esch didn't like hole-and-corner methods: "Will you go shares in Gernerth's theatre?" The question took Lohberg quite by surprise, and opening his eyes wide he merely said: "Eh?" "I'm asking you, are you willing to go shares in the theatre business?" "But I have a tobacco business." "You've been lamenting all this time that you don't like it, and so I thought you might want a change." Lohberg shook his head: "So long as my mother's alive I'll have to keep on the shop; the half of it's hers." "Pity," said Esch, "Teltscher thinks that putting on women wrestlers would bring in a hundred-per-cent profit."

Lohberg did not even ask what the theatre had to do with wrestling, but merely said in his turn: "Pity." Esch went on: "I'm as tired of my trade as you are of yours. They're on strike now and there's nothing to do but sit about, it's enough to make one sick." "What do you want to do, then? Are you going into the theatre business too?" Esch thought it over; that meant simply being tied to a stool in some dusty manager's office beside Gernerth and Teltscher. The artists didn't appeal to him now that he had been behind the scenes; they weren't much better than Hede or Thusnelda. He had really no idea what he wanted to do; the day had been so stale. He said: "Clear out, to America." In an illustrated journal he had seen pictures of New York; these now came into his head; there had been also a photograph of an American boxing match and that brought him back to the wrestling. "If I could make enough money out of it to pay my fare I'd go to America." He was himself astonished to find that he meant it seriously, and now began seriously counting up his resources: he had nearly three hundred marks; if he put them into the wrestling business he could certainly increase them, and why shouldn't he, a strong, capable man with book-keeping experience, try his luck in America as well as here? At the very least he would have seen a bit of the world. Perhaps Teltscher and Ilona might actually come to New York on that engagement Teltscher was always talking about. Lohberg interrupted his train of thought: "You have some knowledge of languages, but I haven't, unfortunately." Esch nodded complacently; yes, with his French he could manage somehow, and English couldn't be so very much of a mystery; but Lohberg didn't need to know languages in order to go shares in promoting wrestling bouts. "No, not for that, but for going to America," Lohberg replied. And although to Lohberg it was almost inconceivable that any man, let alone himself, should live in any town but Mannheim, both Esch and he felt almost like fellow-travellers as they discussed the cost of the voyage and how the money could be raised. This discussion brought them back, by a natural concatenation of thought, to the chances of making money through women wrestlers, and after much hesitation Lohberg came to the conclusion that he could quite well abstract a thousand marks from his business and invest them with Gernerth. Of course that wouldn't be enough to buy out Teltscher, but it was quite good for a start, especially when Esch's three hundred were counted in.

The day had ended better than it began. As he went home Esch brooded over the problem of raising the rest of the money, and Fräulein Erna came into his mind.

Strong as was Erna's temptation to bind Esch to her by financial obligations, she remained firm even here to her principle of parting with nothing except to her affianced husband. When she archly intimated this resolve Esch was indignant: what kind of a man did she think he was? Did she imagine he wanted the money for himself? But even as he said this he felt that it was beside the point; that it was not really the money that was in question, and that Fräulein Erna was much more in the wrong than she could ever be made to understand; of course the money was only a means of ransoming Ilona, of shielding defenceless girls from ever having knives hurled at them again; of course he didn't want it for himself. But even that was by no means all, for over and above that he wanted nothing from Ilona herself—not he, not at the cost of other people's money—and he was quite glad, too, to be in that position; he didn't give a fig for Ilona, he was thinking of more important things, and he had every right to be angry when Erna supposed him to be self-seeking, every right to tell her rudely: well, she could keep her money, then. Erna, however, took his rudeness as an admission of guilt, exulted in having unmasked him, and giggled that she knew all about that, thinking meanwhile of a commercial traveller in Hof, who had not only enjoyed her favours, but had involved her in the more serious loss of fifty marks.

It was altogether a good day for Fräulein Erna. Esch had asked her for something which she could refuse him, and besides she was wearing a pair of new shoes that made her feel gay and looked well on her feet. She was ensconced on the sofa, and as a saucy and slightly mocking gesture she let her feet peep from under her skirt, and swung them to and fro; she liked the faint creaking of the leather and the pleasant tension across her instep. She had no desire to abandon this delightful conversation, and in spite of the rude end that Esch had put to it she asked again what he wanted so much money for. Esch once more remarked that she could keep it; Lohberg had been glad enough to get a share in the business. "Oh, Herr Lohberg," said Fräulein Erna, "he has plenty, he can afford it." And with that waywardness which characterizes many phases of love, and in virtue of which Fräulein Erna would have given herself to any chance comer rather than to Herr Esch, who was to be granted nothing except in wedlock, she was very eager now to infuriate him by giving the money to Lohberg instead of to him. She swung her feet to and fro. "Oh, well, in partnership with Herr Lohberg, that's a different story. He's a good business man." "He's an idiot!" said Esch, partly from conviction and partly from jealousy, a jealousy that pleased Fräulein Erna, for she had reckoned on it. She turned the knife in the wound: "I wouldn't give it to *you*." But her remark was strangely ineffective. What did it matter to him? He had given up Ilona, and it was really Korn's business to redeem her from those knives. Esch looked at Erna's swinging feet. She would open her eyes if she were told that her money was really to be applied in helping her brother's affair. Of course even that wouldn't do what was needed. Perhaps it was really Nentwig who should be made to pay. For if the world was to be redeemed one must attack the virus at its source, as Lohberg said; but that source was Nentwig, or perhaps even something hiding behind Nentwig, something greater—perhaps as great and as securely hidden in his inaccessibility as the chairman of a company—something one knew nothing about. It was enough to make a man angry, and Esch, who was a strong fellow and not in the least afflicted with nerves, felt inclined to stamp on Fräulein Erna's swinging feet to make her quiet. She said: "Do you like my shoes?" "No," retorted Esch. Fräulein Erna was taken aback. "Herr Lohberg would like them . . . when are you going to bring him here? You've simply been hiding him . . . out of jealousy, I suppose, Herr Esch?" Oh, he could bring the man round at once if she was so anxious to see him, remarked Esch, hoping privately that they would come to an understanding about the theatre business. "No need for him to come at once," said Fräulein Erna, "but why not this evening for coffee?" All right, he'd arrange that, said Esch, and took himself off.

Lohberg came. He held his coffee-cup with one hand and stirred in it mechanically with the other. He left his spoon in the cup even while he was drinking, so that it hit him on the nose. Esch spread himself insolently, asking if Balthasar and Ilona were coming, and making all kinds of tactless remarks. Fräulein Erna took no notice of him. She regarded with interest Herr Lohberg's rachitic head and his large white eyeballs; truly, he looked as if it would not take much to make him cry. And she wondered if, in the heat and ardour of love, he would be moved to tears; it annoyed her to think that her brother had pushed her into an unsatisfactory relation with Esch, a brute of a man who upset her, while only two or three houses farther away there was a well-established tradesman who blushed whenever she looked at him. Had he ever had a woman, she wondered, and to satisfy these speculations and to provoke Esch she skilfully piloted the conversation towards the subject of love. "Are you another of these born bachelors, Herr Lohberg? You'll repent it when you're old and done and have nobody to look after you."

Lohberg blushed. "I'm only waiting for the right girl, Fräulein Korn."

"And she hasn't turned up yet?" Fräulein Korn smiled encouragingly and pointed her toe under the hem of her skirt. Lohberg set down his cup and looked helpless.

Esch said tartly: "He hasn't tried yet, that's all."

Lohberg's convictions came to his support: "One can only love once, Fräulein Korn."

"Oh!" said Fräulein Korn.

That was clear and unambiguous. Esch was almost ashamed of his unchaste life, and it seemed to him not improbable that this great and unique love was what Frau Hentjen had felt for her husband, and perhaps that was why she now expected chastity and restraint from her customers. All the same it must be dreadful for Frau Hentjen to have to pay for her brief wedded bliss by renouncing love for ever afterwards, and so he said: "Well, but what about widows, then" At that rate, a widow shouldn't go on living . . . especially if she has no children . . ." and because he was observant of what he read in the illustrated papers he added: "Widows ought in that case really to be burned, so that . . . so that they might be redeemed, in a manner of speaking."

"You're a brute, Herr Esch," said Fräulein Erna. "Herr Lohberg would never say such things."

"Redemption is in God's hands," said Herr Lohberg, "if He grants anyone the great gift of love it will last for all eternity."

"You're a clever man, Herr Lohberg, and lots of people would be the better of taking your words to heart," said Fräulein Erna, "the very idea of letting oneself be burned for any man! The impudence . . ."

Esch said "If the world was as it should be it could be redeemed without any of your silly organizations . . . yes, you can both look incredulous," he almost shouted, "but there would be no need for a Salvation Army if the police locked up all the people who deserved to be locked up . . . instead of the ones that are innocent."

"I wouldn't marry any man unless he had a pension, or could leave something for his widow, some kind of security," said Fräulein Erna, "that's only what one is entitled to expect from a good man."

Esch despised her. Mother Hentjen would never think of talking in such a way. But Lohberg said: "It's a bad provider who doesn't set his house in order."

"You'll make your wife a happy woman," said Fräulein Erna.

Lohberg went on: "If God blesses me with a wife, I hope I can say with confidence that we shall live in true Christian unity. We shall renounce the world and live for each other."

Esch jeered: "Just like Balthasar and Ilona . . . and every evening she gets knives chucked at her."

Lohberg was indignant: "A man who drinks cheap spirits can't appreciate crystal-clear water, Fräulein Korn. A passion of that kind isn't love."

Fräulein Erna took the crystalline purity as a reference to herself and was flattered: "That dress he gave her cost thirty-eight marks. I found that out in the shop. To fleece a man like that . . . I could never bring myself to do it."

Esch said: "Things need to be set right. An innocent man sits in jail, and another runs around as he pleases; one ought either to do *him* in or do oneself in."

Lohberg soothed him down: "Human life isn't to be lightly taken."

"No," said Fräulein Erna, "if anyone should be done in it's a woman who has no feelings where men are concerned . . . as for me, when I have a man to look after I'm a woman of feeling."

Lohberg said: "A genuine Christian love is founded on mutual respect."

"And you would respect your wife even if she weren't as educated as yourself . . . but more a creature of feeling, as a woman should be."

"Only a person of feeling is capable of receiving the redeeming grace and ready for it."

Fräulein Erna said: "I'm sure you're a good son, Herr Lohberg, one that is capable of feeling gratitude for all his mother has done for him."

That made Esch angry, angrier than he knew: "Good son or no . . . I don't give *that* for gratitude; as long as people look on while injustice is being done there's no grace in the world . . . why has Martin sacrificed himself and been put in jail?"

Lohberg answered: "Herr Geyring is a victim of the poison that's destroying the world. Only when they get back to nature will people stop hurting each other."

Fräulein Erna said that she too was a lover of nature and often went for long walks.

Lohberg went on "Only in God's good air, that lifts our hearts up, are men's nobler feelings awakened."

Esch said "That kind of thing has never got a single man out of jail yet."

Fräulein Erna remarked: "That's what you say . . . but I say, a man with no feelings is no man at all. A man as faithless as you are, Herr Esch, has no right to put in his word. . . . And men are all the same."

"How can you think so badly of the world, Fräulein Korn?"

She sighed: "The disappointments of life, Herr Lohberg."

"But hope keeps our hearts up, Fräulein Korn."

Fräulein Erna gazed thoughtfully into space: "Yes, if it weren't for hope . . ." then she shook her head: "Men have no feelings, and too much brains is just as bad."

Esch wondered if Frau Hentjen and her husband had spoken in that strain when they got engaged. But Lohberg said: "In God and in God's divine Nature is hope for all of us."

Erna did not want to be outdone: "I go regularly to church and confession, thank God . . ." and with triumph she added: "Our holy Catholic faith has more feeling in a way than the Protestant religion—if I were a man I would never marry a Protestant."

Lohberg was too polite to contradict her:

"All ways to God are equally worthy of respect. And those whom God has joined will learn from Him to live peaceably together . . . all that is needed is good will."

Lohberg's virtue once more disgusted Esch, although he had often compared him with Mother Hentjen because of that same virtue. He burst out: "Any idiot can talk."

Fräulein Erna said with disdain: "Herr Esch, of course, would take anybody he came across, he doesn't bother about such things as feelings or religion; all he asks is that she should have money."

He simply couldn't believe that, said Herr Lohberg.

"Oh, you can take my word for it, I know him, he has no feelings, and he never thinks about anything . . . the kind of thoughts you have, Herr Lohberg, aren't to be found in everybody."

But if that were so he was sorry for Herr Esch, remarked Lohberg, for that meant he would never find happiness in this world.

Esch shrugged his shoulders. What did this fellow know about the new world? He said contemptuously: "First set the world right."

But Fräulein Erna had found the solution: "If two people worked together, if your wife, for instance, were to help you in your business, then everything else would be all right, even if the man was a Protestant and the wife a Catholic."

"Of course," said Lohberg.

"Or if two people should have something in common, a common interest, as they say . . . then they must stand by each other, mustn't they?"

"Of course," said Lohberg.

Fräulein Erna's lizard eye glanced at Esch as she said: "Would you have any objections, Herr Lohberg, if I joined you in the theatre business that Herr Esch was speaking of? Now that my brother has lost his senses I at least must try to bring in some money."

How could Herr Lohberg have any objection! And when Fräulein Erna said that she would invest the half of her savings, say about a thousand marks, he cried, and she was delighted to hear it: "Oh! Then we'll be partners."

In spite of this Esch was dissatisfied. The fact that he had got his own way had all at once ceased to matter, maybe because in any case he had renounced Ilona, maybe because there were more important aims at stake, but perhaps only because—and this was the sole reason of which he was conscious—he suddenly had serious misgivings.

"Talk it over first with Gernerth, the manager of the theatre. I've only told you about it, I don't accept any responsibility."

"Oh yes," said Fräulein Erna, she knew well enough that he was an irresponsible man, and he didn't need to be afraid that he would be called to account. He wasn't much of a Christian, and she thought more of Herr Lohberg's little finger than of Herr Esch's whole body. And wouldn't Herr Lohberg come in now and then for a cup of coffee? Yes? And since it was getting late, and they had already got to their feet, she took Lohberg by the arm. The lamp above them shed a mild light upon their heads, and they stood before Esch like a newly engaged couple.

Esch had taken off his coat and hung it on the stand. Then he began to brush and beat it and examined its worn collar. Again he was conscious of some discrepancy in his calculations. He had given up Ilona, yet he was supposed to look on while Erna turned away from him and set her cap at that idiot. It was against all the laws of book-keeping, which demanded that every debit entry should be balanced by a credit one. Of course—and he shook the coat speculatively—if he chose he could keep a Lohberg from getting the better of *him*; he was easily a match for the man; no, August Esch was far from being such an ugly monstrosity, and he actually took a step or two towards the door, but paused before he opened it; tut, he didn't choose to, that was all. The creature across the passage might think he had come crawling to her out of gratitude for her measly thousand marks. He turned and sat down on his bed, where he unlaced his shoes. The balance was all right, so far. And the fact that he was at bottom resentful because he couldn't sleep with Erna, that was all right, too. One cut one's losses. Yet there was an obscure miscalculation somewhere that he couldn't put his finger on: granted that he wasn't going across the passage to that woman, granted that he was giving up his bit of fun, what was his real reason for doing so? Was it perhaps to escape marriage? Was he making the smaller sacrifice to escape the greater, to avoid paying in person? Esch said: "I'm a swine." Yes, he was a swine, not a whit better than Nentwig, who also shuffled off responsibility. His accounts were in a disorder which it would take the devil and all to clear up.

But disorderly accounts meant a disorderly world, and a disorderly world meant that Ilona would go on being a target for knives, that Nentwig would continue with brazen hypocrisy to evade punishment, and that Martin would sit in jail for ever. He thought it all over, and as he slipped off his drawers the answer came spontaneously: the others had given their money for the wrestling business, and so he, who had no money, must give himself, not in marriage, certainly, but in personal service, to the new undertaking. And since that, unfortunately, did not fit in with his job in Mannheim, he must simply give notice. That was the way he could pay his debt. And as if in corroboration of this conclusion, he suddenly realized that he ought not to remain any longer with a company that had been the means of putting Martin in jail. No one could accuse him of disloyalty; even the Herr Chairman would have to admit that Esch was a decent fellow. This new idea drove Erna out of his head, and he lay down in bed relieved and comforted. Going back to Cologne and to Mother Hentjen's would, of course, be pleasant, and that diminished his sacrifice a little, but so little that it hardly counted; after all, Mother Hentjen hadn't even answered his letter. And there were restaurants a-plenty in Mannheim. No, the return to Cologne, that unjust town, was a very negligible offset to his sacrifice; it was at most an entry in the petty-cash account, and a man could always credit himself with petty cash. His eagerness to report his success drove him to see Gernerth early next morning: it was no small feat to have raised two thousand marks so quickly! Gernerth clapped him on the shoulder and called him the devil of a fellow. That did Esch good. Yet his decision to give up his job and take service in the theatre astounded Gernerth; he could not, however, produce any valid objection. "We'll manage it somehow, Herr Esch," he said, and Esch went off to the head office of the Central Rhine Shipping Company.

In the upper floors of the head office buildings there were long, hushed corridors laid with brown linoleum. On the doors were stylish plates bearing the names of the occupants, and at one end of each corridor, behind a table lit by a standard lamp, sat a man in uniform who asked what one wanted and wrote down one's name and business on a duplicate block. Esch traversed one of the corridors, and since it was for the last time he took good note of everything. He read every name on the doors, and when to his surprise he came on a woman's name, he paused and tried to imagine what she would be like: was she an ordinary clerk casting up accounts at a sloping desk with black cuffs over her sleeves, and would she be cool and offhand with visitors like all the others? He felt a sudden desire for the unknown woman behind the door, and there arose in him the conception of a new kind of love, a simple, one might almost say a business-like and official kind of love, a love that would run as smoothly, as calmly, and yet as spaciously and never-endingly, as these corridors with their polished linoleum. But then he saw the long series of doors with men's names, and he could not help thinking that a lone woman in that masculine environment must be as disgusted with it as Mother Hentjen was with her business. A hatred of commercial methods stirred again within him, hatred of an organization that, behind its apparent orderliness, its smooth corridors, its smooth and flawless book-keeping, concealed all manner of infamies. And that was called respectability! Whether head clerk or chairman of a company, there was nothing to choose between one man of business and another. And if for a moment Esch had regretted that he was no longer a unit in the smoothly running organization, no longer privileged to go out and in without being stopped or questioned or announced, his regret now vanished, and he saw only a row of Nentwigs sitting behind these doors, all of them pledged and concerned to keep Martin languishing in confinement. He would have liked to go straight down to the counting-house and tell the blind fools there that they too should break out of their prison of hypocritical ciphers and columns and like him set themselves free; yes, that was what they should do, even at the risk of having to join him in emigrating to America.

"But it's a pretty short star turn you've given us here," the staff manager said when he gave in his notice and asked for a testimonial, and Esch felt tempted to divulge the real reasons for his departure from such a despicable firm. But he had to leave them unsaid, for the friendly staff manager immediately bent his attention to other matters, although he repeated once or twice: "A short star turn . . . a short star turn," in an unctuous voice, as if he liked the phrase and as if he were hinting that theatrical life wasn't so very different from or even superior to the business that Esch was relinquishing. What could the staff manager know about it? Was he really reproaching Esch with disloyalty and planning to catch him unawares? To trip him up in his new job? Esch followed his movements with a suspicious eye and with a suspicious eye ran over the document that was handed to him, although he knew very well that in his new profession nobody would ask to see a testimonial. And since the thought of his work in the theatre obsessed him, even as he was striding over the brown linoleum of the corridor towards the staircase he no longer remarked the quiet orderliness of the building, nor speculated about the woman's name on the door he passed by, nor saw even the notice-board marked "Counting House"; the very pomp of the board-room and the Chairman's private office in the front part of the main building meant nothing to him. Only when he was out in the street did he cast a glance back, a farewell glance, as he said to himself, and was vaguely disappointed because there was no equipage waiting at the main entrance. He would really have liked to set eyes on Bertrand for once. Of course, like Nentwig, the man kept himself well out of the way. And of course it would be better not to see him, not to set eyes on him at all, or on Mannheim for that matter and all that it stood for. Goodbye for ever, said Esch; yet he was incapable of departing so quickly and found himself lingering and blinking in the midday sunlight that streamed evenly over the asphalt of the new street, lingering and waiting for the glass doors to turn noiselessly on their hinges, perhaps, and let the Chairman out. But even though in the shimmering light it looked as if the two wings of the door were trembling, so that one was reminded of the swing doors behind Mother Hentjen's buffet, yet that was only a so-called optical illusion and the two halves of the door were immobile in their marble framework. They did not open and no one came out. Esch felt insulted: there he had to stand in the glaring sun simply because the Central Rhine Shipping Company had established itself in a flashy new asphalt road instead of a cool and cellar-like street; he turned round, crossed the street with long, rather awkward strides, rounded the next corner, and as he swung himself on to the footboard of a tram that rattled past, he had finally decided to leave Mannheim the very next day and go to Cologne to start negotiations with Oppenheimer, the theatrical agent.

Zerline's Tale

The bells of the town churches had just sounded two in jumbled medley—only the baroque chimes of the Schlosskirche on the gently sloping hill stood out in a clearer line. The summer Sunday was sinking from its zenith, more tediously and no doubt more slowly than any weekday. Lying on his living room sofa, A. reflected: the tedium of Sundays is atmospheric; the cessation of mass bustle has communicated itself to the air, and the only way to avoid being submerged is to fill up your Sunday with more and more work. On weekdays, you don't hear the church bells, not even if you are totally inactive.

Work? A. thought of the office he had set up in the business section of town; sometimes, when he was in it, he flung himself into feverish activity, but more often he spent his days doing nothing, though his thoughts persisted in revolving around money and possibilities of making it. That irritated him. There was something uncanny about his flair for moneymaking. True, he liked to eat and drink; he liked to live in relative comfort. But he did not love money as such; on the contrary, he loved to give it away. Why then this uncanny ease with which he gathered in money far in excess of his needs? He had always found the problem of investing his money soundly and safely more difficult than that of making it. At the moment he was buying up land and houses; he paid for them with depreciated marks and they cost him next to nothing. But the operation gave him no pleasure; it was no more than a burdensome duty.

The morning sun had made him pull down the blinds, but now that it was gone he was too lazy to pull them up again. Of course it was just as well; thus darkened, the room would probably keep cooler, and in the evening he would open the windows. Time and again, his laziness turned to his advantage. Still, he was not really lazy; he merely shied away from decision. He was incapable of forcing the hand of fate; no, he expected fate to do the deciding for him, and he submitted, though not without a certain vigilance, nay, guile, necessitated by the fact that this organ of decision had worked out a strange system for his guidance: it confronted him with dangers, which he had to run away from, and invariably his flight brought in money. His panic fear of his final high-school examination, his fear of the lynx-eyed examiners whom fate had endowed with an instrument of terror, namely, insight into the candidate's deepest secrets, which enabled them to drain him of all knowledge, as though he had never learned anything—fifteen years before, this panic fear had driven him to Africa. Without a cent to his name—infuriated by his son's behavior, his father had given him the price of the trip and nothing more—he had landed on the coast of the Congo, a penniless young man who shied away from decisions, yet happy because in the unforeseen there are no examiners, but in all probability a propitious fate. In those days he had developed a belief in fate; it took the form of a wakeful somnolence, and for that very reason, perhaps because of the wakefulness and perhaps because of the somnolence, he had never since wanted for money. Whether as gardener's helper, as waiter or as clerk—he had many such jobs at first—he did the job to his employer's satisfaction only so long as no one asked him about his qualifications; when asked, he left the job at once, each time, to be sure, with a little more money in his pocket because, as usual in the colonies, he always found an opportunity for some sideline, and soon the sidelines became his main occupation. He drifted to Cape Town, he drifted to Kimberley, he drifted into a diamond syndicate in which he became a partner. It was always his fate that drove him hither and thither, his tendency to evade unpleasantness, to sidestep the reckoning that would have been demanded of him if he had stayed in one place. He could not remember that his will had ever driven him to do anything; the substance of his reliance on fate had always been an indecision hardly distinguishable from inertia, a busy laziness, and that had been the key to his success. "Lazy digestion of life, lazy digestion of fate," said a voice within him. That brought him contentedly back to the present: let the Sunday trickle away, let the blinds stay down, it will all turn out for the best.

At that point—perhaps after a timid knocking—the door was opened ever so slightly, and Zerline, the aged servant, thrust her head birdlike through the opening:

"Are you asleep?"

"No, no . . . come in."

"She's asleep."

"Who?" A stupid question. Whom could she mean but the baroness?

A look of sly contempt passed over her wrinkles:

"In there . . . she's sound asleep." This was immediately followed, partly as an explanation for the quietness of the afternoon and partly as an announcement of the first point on the program: "Hildegard has gone out . . . the bastard."

"What?"

By then she was wholly inside the room. She kept a respectful distance, but to favor her gouty knee rested one hand on the dressing table: "She got her by another man," she revealed. "Hildegard is a bastard."

Gladly as he would have heard more, it would have been wrong to encourage her: "Look, Zerline, I'm only a roomer here, such things are none of my business. . . . I won't even listen."

Shaking her head, she looked down at him: "You think about them, though . . . what are you thinking about?"

Her look of scrutiny irritated and troubled him. Were his trousers not buttoned properly? He had an unpleasant feeling that he had been caught in the act and would have liked to reply that he was thinking of his business. But what had got into her? What made her think he owed her an account of his thoughts? He said nothing.

Sensing his embarrassment, she pressed her advantage:

"It will be your business when she crawls into bed with you."

"See here, Zerline, what's got into you?"

Inexorably, she went on:

"She's always running away. If she had a regular lover she slept with, it would be all right; then she'd be a real woman . . . but she's only putting on, she hasn't her equal for that . . . she only pretends to be sneaking off to her lover like a real woman. She can't do any better, so she hides behind clumsy lies . . . but even her clumsiness is an act; she takes her prayer book as if she were going to church, and do you know why? Because everybody knows when the services are really held, so everybody can see through her flimsy pretense, and that's just what she wants. . . . Even her lies are a fake; they're double lies, and there's something horrible behind them . . . what she does in that bed she's running off to with her prayer book I don't even want to know, but I'll find out. . . . I find everything out."

She waited a moment and when A., who had closed his eyes as though in token of dismissal, made no reply, she glided a few steps closer, with one hand on the edge of the dressing table and the other hanging down stiffly:

"I find everything out, didn't I even find out how the old . . . how the baroness got the child. . . . It didn't take me long. I wasn't all that young and stupid, though it was a long time ago, more than thirty years. I was with the Frau Generalin then . . . she was the baroness's mother, God rest her soul. That was a fine household. I was the first maid, the second was my lieutenant, so to speak, and we had a cook and a kitchen maid besides. And as long as his Excellency, the general, lived, there was an orderly for the heavy work, and he helped wait on table. But by that time his Excellency was dead and one fine day, it was February—I remember like it was yesterday the way the damp snow stuck to the windowpanes, her Excellency rings and when I came she says: 'Zerline, you know, we've got to cut down on the household, but I don't want to lose you entirely.' . . . Yes, that's what she said. . . . 'Wouldn't you like to go to work for my daughter? She's expecting a child, and I'd rather have you in the house with my grandchild than some strange nursemaid.' Yes, that's what she said to me, and I did what I was told. With a heavy heart, though. I wasn't so young any more, and God knows I'd sooner have had children of my own and taken care of them. But when a girl goes into service, she has to get such ideas out of her head; a girl that goes into service can't do as she pleases, and she'd better not have a child if she knows what's good for her. The more's the pity; I could have had a dozen. When I went to work for her Excellency, young as I was"—she flung up an arm in a way that was probably supposed to suggest girlish exuberance, but made an almost Goya-like impression—"you should have seen me then; all firm and hard; the way my breasts stuck out they all wanted to grab them. Even the baron, he wasn't chief justice yet, only a judge of the county court; he couldn't control himself. I suppose you think he hadn't have ought to, because he was a young husband and it wasn't the right thing. Fiddlesticks, that wasn't it. He was one of those men that are way above desire; it's for the good of their souls, they can't let themselves desire any woman. I don't think he ever desired *her*"—here she waved her thumb behind her in the direction of the door. "Well, she wasn't the kind to give him much fun. Me, well, yes, I could have given him his fun, but I didn't want to, though he was a handsome man; it would have been bad for his soul. I made love with his Excellency's orderlies instead. I most always enjoyed it, but that was no good either. Never properly in bed, always with my clothes on and one-two-three in the dark, in the drawing room when the masters went to the theater. That's how it is when a country girl goes into service. The men have their girls at home in their villages. Maybe they had more fun with me, maybe I was prettier than the one at home, but that didn't mean a thing; the one that's waiting has all the rights. That's the way it was. 'The years of youthful bloom'"—obviously a quotation—"passed away. I was with her Excellency for more than twelve years, and then *she*"—another backward wave of the thumb—"got pregnant, not me. And I was still a lot better looking than she was. She won. And I accepted the position with her and her bastard."

She paused to sigh her fill. Then, taking little notice of her listener who had sat up, she continued:

"By the time the child—Hildegard—was born, the baron was getting on toward fifty. He had just been appointed chief justice. Maybe he didn't like having me in the house, he probably hadn't forgotten any more than I had the way he used to go after my breasts; those things are timeless, they stay with you. Of course he wasn't interested in me anymore, though I was still a fine figure of a woman. He had become what he was meant to be, the kind of man who has stopped desiring women. It wasn't just because he couldn't; there are plenty of men who want it all the more, just because they can't. Those are the ugliest. But if he couldn't, it was because he didn't want to, and that made him handsomer and handsomer. If Hildegard had been his, she'd be a beautiful woman."

Here A. had to contradict: "She is a beautiful woman. The first time I saw the judge's portrait in the dining room, I was struck by the resemblance between them."

Zerline giggled:

"Resemblance. I made that resemblance, and nobody else. I used to take the child in to look at the picture, I taught her to put that same expression in her eyes . . . it's all in the eyes."

That was a startling turn; A. couldn't deny it. "She must have acquired his soul along with his eyes," he said thoughtfully.

"That's exactly what I wanted . . . but she's a woman, and she has another man's blood in her veins."

"Who was this other man?" He had said that involuntarily, driven by something far more compelling than mere curiosity.

"The other man?" Zerline smiled. "I'll tell you. He used to drop in for tea with her Excellency now and then. At first I didn't notice how often the baroness was there too, and always without her husband. But one thing that I noticed right off was that this other man, Herr von Juna, was very good-looking too; he had a rust-brown goatee and rust-brown curls, his skin was like weathered meerschaum, and he carried himself with a slight bend at the waist as if he were going to ask you for the next dance. Oh yes, to give the devil her due, she knew how to pick them. Except that if you took a good look at him you could see the ugliness behind his pretty goatee, even behind his pretty mouth, you could see that he couldn't and kept on wanting to, the ugly lust that comes of weakness. That kind of man is easy to get. If I had wanted him"—she pinched an imaginary flea between two fingers—"I'd have had him just like that. Her Excellency said he was a traveling kind of man, in the diplomatic service she called it, a diplomat. So far so good. He set up house at the Old Hunting Lodge out there in the woods"—her arm pointed to a distant Somewhere—"but not for the hunting, on account of the women he always had in tow. Nobody knew much about him, but of course people gossiped; he did all he could to arouse their curiosity, what with all his women and the way he'd disappear and suddenly turn up again. I was curious myself. But I couldn't get anything out of the Forester's wife, who kept house for him. She held her tongue, and I'd be very much surprised if he passed her up; she wasn't bad. Well, that was his way, and the child looked like him from the start. But how would she manage to show him the child? That's what I was waiting to see. Well, she worked it out very nicely; it was arranged for the child to visit her grandma on her two months' birthday. Aha, so that was it. We rode out to her Excellency's; the child was put to bed in the guest room, and wild horses couldn't have dragged me out of that room, because I knew he'd just happen to come by. And I was dead sure she'd give herself away. I didn't have long to wait. It was all I could do to keep from laughing when she led him in right on the dot, and I really had to bite my lips when Daddy bent down over the bed and she was too moved to hide it and took hold of his hand. Her feeling was sincere, but it was false, too. He was slyer; he saw I was watching them, so on his way out he looked at me in a certain way, meaning that I, and not the baroness, was the right one for him, as if that would clear him of his paternity. I didn't hang back; quick as a flash I gave him a sign that I'd understood."

Her answering smile returned to her face as though by enchantment, and there it hovered, a wrinkled, faded, senile echo of itself, dried and everlasting, an everlasting answer:

"I let him know and I knew it myself, I knew that desire had shot into him and shaken him, that he'd know no peace until he had slept with me. That was all right with me. It had taken hold of me too, though it wasn't what either of us had intended. People are cheap. Not just a poor servant girl from the country; no, everybody; only a saint has wisdom and strength enough that he doesn't need to be cheap. And even if desire is cheap, it takes strength, and the worst people are the ones who try to disown their cheapness because they're incapable of desire. They put on airs and that only makes them cheaper, they lie because they're so refined, they lie because they're so weak, they try to drown out desire with soul-noise, because it's not refined enough for them, or more often because they haven't got any desire, and they think the noise will make some and keep it up. They try to conjure up desire by fraud, with soul-noise, but at the same time they want to drown it out. And the baroness? Not a loud word by day, but I'll bet you, plenty of soul-noise at night. Of course you've got to forgive her, because she was never a real woman and it's not the baron's straitlaced holiness that could have taught her to be one. So it was only natural that she'd end up with the other, the lecher. She got the child by him on her last trip to the baths; it works out to the day. And then? Why didn't she run away with him? Why didn't she go and live with him at the Hunting Lodge? Oh no! For that, her desire was too small, her fear too great, she was much too weak and full of lies. You could just as well have asked her to lie down with him in the market place. All the same I wanted to help her, at the expense of my own desire, so to speak, without regard for my jealousy, but she couldn't learn. Finally, one time when the judge went to Berlin, I came right to the point. 'Frau Baronin,' I said. 'You ought to have company now and then.' She gives me a stupid look and asks: 'Company? Who?' And like I was pulling a name out of the air, I said: 'Well, Herr von Juna, for instance.' She gave me a suspicious look out of the corner of her eye and said: 'Oh no, not him.' Forget it, I said to myself. But she didn't forget it, and a few days later she invited him to dinner. In those days we still had our fine villa. The drawing rooms and dining room were on the ground floor; there was no such jumble of furniture as in this place, where you can't move without bumping into things and there's no end of work, especially with Hildegard never lifting a finger. Well, it was a real dining room, and there they sat, a good way apart. I served dinner, I didn't answer his glances, and afterward I asked leave to retire. I don't have to tell you that my room in the attic was a lot nicer than my room here. But later when I crept down to see how it was going, they were just the same, sitting quietly side by side, except that they'd moved to the drawing room; his lovely languishing eyes looked bored, and even when she stood up to pour him a fresh cup of coffee he didn't try to stroke her hand, or even to touch it. So she's lost him too, I thought to myself; it's no good, when you're in bed, harping on love all the time instead of pleasure. She was hopeless. Deep down I felt sorry for them both, especially for him, because after all the child was a tie between them. Still deeper down, I've got to admit, I was tickled. So I waited for him in the bushes out in front, and no sooner had he stepped out of the house than without a moment's hesitation, without a single word, we were swept into a kiss. I fastened onto his mouth so hard, with my lips, my teeth, my tongue, that I almost fainted, but all the same I resisted. I couldn't make out why I didn't just roll over in the grass with him, still less why, when his voice went husky and he begged me to take him up to my room, I didn't do it. Why did I have to say: 'At the Hunting Lodge'? But when a look of horror, an animal look of madness, came into his eyes, and he gave me to understand that I was asking the impossible because he had a woman out there, it dawned on me that this impossibility and the need to shatter it had been the reason for my resistance, and that a cold, merciless curiosity about the Hunting Lodge had itched me more than my desire, though it was also a bitter, necessary part of my desire."

The lingering agitation of that moment obliged her to sit down. Propping her elbows on the table, holding her head between her fists, she was silent for a time. When she resumed her story, it was in an entirely different voice, a whispered chant, as though someone were speaking in her stead:

"People are cheap and their memories are full of holes they can never mend. How many things must be done that we forget forever, to sustain the little we remember forever. We all forget our everyday lives. In my case it was all the furniture I've dusted, day in day out, all the dishes that had to be washed. Like everyone else I sat down to eat every day, and like everyone else I know all this without really remembering it, as if it had happened in a space without weather, either good or bad. Even the pleasure I've had became a space without weather, and though my gratitude for what was alive is still with me, the names and features that once meant pleasure and even love to me have faded more and more, vanished into a glass gratitude that has lost its content. Empty glasses, empty glasses. And yet, if not for the emptiness and all that I've forgotten, the unforgettable could not have come into being. Empty-handed, the forgotten sustains the unforgettable, and we are sustained by the unforgettable. With the forgotten we feed time, we feed death, but the unforgettable is death's gift to us. In the moment of receiving it we are still here where we happen to be, but at the same time we are there, where the world falls headlong into darkness. For the unforgettable is a piece of the future, a piece of timelessness given to us in advance, which sustains us and makes our fall into darkness gentle, a gentle gliding. Everything that passed between me and Herr Juna was such a darkly gentle, timeless gift of death, and one day it will help to carry me gently down, itself carried by the full-ness of memory. Anyone would say it was love, love to the death. No, it had nothing to do with love, not to speak of soul-noise. Many things can become unforgettable, helping friends and friendly helpers, without being love, without so much as a possibility of becoming love. The unforgettable is a moment of ripening, issued from infinitely many preparatory moments and preparatory similarities, and sustained by them; it is the moment in which we sense that in giving form we are formed and have been formed. It is dangerous to mistake that for love."

This was what A. had heard, but there is no certainty that it was what Zerline had said. Many old people have a way of breaking into a mumbling chant, into which the imagination can easily read one thing and another, especially on a hot Sunday afternoon behind lowered blinds. Wanting to make sure, A. waited to see if the singsong would resume, but when Zerline spoke again it was in her usual old woman's voice:

"Of course he could have overcome my resistance out there in the bushes in the middle of the night. If he had, I'd probably have forgotten him like the rest. But he didn't. Weak men are usually calculating. Anyway, what difference does it make whether it was weakness or calculation that made him leave me when I told him to? One way or another, it drove me wild. The minute he went, I started to wait. I wanted to write and tell him to come right back up to my room and into me. It's a wonder I was able to control myself. A merciful wonder. Because before the week was out, there was a letter from him. I couldn't help laughing. He'd written the address in block letters on a business envelope, so the baroness wouldn't see he was corresponding with me too, and inside it said he'd pick me up with the trap the very next evening at the end of the streetcar line. Even if the baroness had a letter from him too, even if she was reading it at that very moment, it was a kind of victory for me. He didn't mention the Hunting Lodge in his letter to me, meaning that he still had his hussy out there, but that was all the more reason for me to meet him. Before I'd even climbed up on the box with him, I put it to him straight. He had nothing to say, but that in itself was a kind of confession, so I kissed him and said: 'Let's go. Wherever you like, but too bad it can't be the Hunting Lodge.' 'It will be the Hunting Lodge next time,' he said. I asked him if that was a promise, and he said Yes. 'Will you really send her away?' I asked, and again he said Yes. To make really sure, I asked if her hands were manicured. That kind of surprised him. 'Yes,' he said. 'Why?' I took off my gloves and I laid my two red hands on the fine woolen blanket he had spread over our knees, and I said:

'Washerwoman's hands.' He looks down at my hands and I can't
tell if he's shocked. 'Every man,' he says, 'needs a good strong hand
to wash him clean of guilt.' Then he takes my hands and kisses
them, but close to the wrist, not the red part, and then I knew it had
hit him hard, and all I could say was: 'Let's go,' or else I'd have
burst into tears. We drove down the narrow road through the har-
vested fields. I looked across them and then I looked down at the
narrow grassy strip between the dusty wheel tracks where our
horses were putting down new hoof prints and now and then a ball
or two of fresh horse dung. It was just like back home. The only
part I didn't like was the blacks he was driving; a black is no farm
horse, you don't plow with a black, a black is for riding off into the
darkness. When I told him that, he laughed. 'You're my field and
my darkness,' he said, and that made me feel so good that I snuggled up to him. Right now, old as I am, I can feel the heat of the
longing that rose up in me then, my longing for the child he ought
to have made me, and then some, lots and lots of children. Don't
say I loved him. I wanted to take him into me, but not to love him;
he was dark and strange and unholy. And there at the cool edge of
the woods, where you could already feel the night though it still
lurked unseen amid the tree trunks, I didn't give in to my desire; he
stopped the trap, but I didn't get out, and to hurt us both I reminded him that the child was waiting for me and I couldn't stay
any longer. 'Nonsense!' he shouted, but it wasn't nonsense so I
rubbed it in without mercy. 'Make me some children of my own
and I won't need this one any more.' He stared at me helplessly,
again with terror in his eyes, this time, I suppose, because it dawned
on him that he'd saddled himself with a third woman, a new
woman with new claims, even if a servant girl had no call to make
claims. Well, to put Herr von Juna and the servant girl back on an
equal footing, and because his terror was so out of keeping with his
desire, I kissed him with almighty passion, as if this were the parting
of the ways. He didn't argue, he was meek as could be. He drove
me back to the streetcar stop. Our agreement that he would call me
to the Hunting Lodge in his next letter still stood, and I burned and
lusted for it, but I didn't believe it anymore."

Obviously this was the moment for another breather, after which
her tongue moistened her weary lips for further speech:

"I'd given up hope of that letter and that made me doubly vexed that the baroness—who had no desire to visit the Hunting Lodge; the thought of it gave her the horrors—was getting letters from him. I was so jealous and vexed that I just had to lay hands on those letters. Of course she picked them up at the General Delivery under some made-up name, but I thought I could find an envelope with the name on it. Well, believe it or not, I went through the baroness's wastepaper basket every day, and pretty soon I had the name. She was scared, but not very careful. You didn't even need an identification. As if they wanted to make it as obvious as possible, they just turned Elvire, that was the baroness's first name, into Ilvere; that was the post-office name. So from then on, whenever I went shopping or taking the baby out for air, I stopped into the post office for the letters. I steamed them open very carefully, and after reading them I'd drop them back into the box with a fresh stamp. I stole a few. But with that hogwash you couldn't call it theft. And what hogwash! Soul-noise. Queen Elvire was the Elf-Queen; they were crawling with holiness and chaste motherhood and elf-child and love child, and to top it all the elfin love child was bellowing in my ears to be changed! The worst of it was the sniveling drivel about the woman out there at the Hunting Lodge. I made a good note of all that and, well, I stole the wildest ones. This woman 'clung like a leech,' she was a 'burden of destiny,' the kind that 'refuses to admit defeat,' a 'blackmailer who battens on my sinful weakness.' He would find means to 'exterminate the evil, root and branch'; oh yes, he wrote all that, and ended up with the wish: 'if only you, my love, could do likewise with your tyrannical husband.' Of course there was method in his madness; with soul-noise like that he was doing his duty toward a woman like the baroness and at the same time keeping her at arm's length. Even so, I was only too ready to believe that he wished the other one, the lady at the Hunting Lodge, at the bottom of the ocean, especially now that she was preventing him from sleeping with me. All the same it made me sick. Oh, wash me please but don't get me wet, that's what he was saying. I was only a village girl, nobody had ever taught me anything, but it made me ashamed to the bottom of my soul that an educated gentleman could be so false, especially when every inch of me was atremble for him. I was almost glad that I wasn't lady enough to write such lying letters to, and didn't get any. The letter came, though. All of a sudden there it was, only two lines, asking when I wished to arrive at the Hunting Lodge. God knows I was happy. He'd kept his word. What with the slop he'd been writing and I'd been reading all these weeks, that meant a lot to me. I was wild with impatience, but it meant so much to me to be able to respect him again and not to have another disappointment that I gritted my teeth and made myself wait three whole days. You see, I wanted to intercept his next letter to the baroness. If he'd boasted of sending the woman away on her account, I wouldn't have wanted to see him again. I trembled as I picked up the letter at the post office; it almost fell into the boiling water when I was opening it. When there wasn't a word about sending the woman away . . . I couldn't believe my eyes. But after a while I believed it. I ran up to the baroness. I said I hadn't been home in a long while, could I have four weeks off? She allowed me three."

Suddenly she emerged from the past and saw where she was. She began to smooth out the cretonne table cover with the utmost vigor, as though there were a hidden wrinkle which she by some magic must make visible in order to lend meaning to her meaningless activity. But her dreams of the past had not wholly released her: "It carries me through the years, the years go by and it sticks. Even if I tell the story a thousand times, I can't get rid of it; I can't." A. tried to say something, but she stopped him with a laugh: "Who said I wanted to get rid of it?" And she began again:

"You won't believe me, my boy, but I felt sorry for the baroness. I'd been sorry for her ever since the times I listened at the bedroom door and there wasn't so much as a peep out of the bedspring. I was glad the baron was so strict and that was how he wanted it, but all the same she owed it to herself and him, and I felt how wretched and indecent it was, and I was sorry about that. Then when I saw those lying letters, of course it hurt me to see him writing to her like that, but I felt even sorrier for her, because she didn't know any better and especially because her answers—by that time, naturally, I'd have been very glad to read them—were sure to be full of even uglier lies. Wasn't I rich compared to her?"

She looked at A. triumphantly, and A. knew that she was reporting the biggest victory of her life. But he also knew that Herr von Juna's letters were not quite so hypocritical as Zerline thought. For the demon of lust by which he was possessed has two aspects: on the one hand, and this is its better part, the unmingled gravity of the lust itself, its unmistakable honesty, and on the other hand, the consciousness of guilt, the self-vilification inseparable from all possession by a demon. The consequence is that though a devotee of lust may shrink back with full right and sincerity from a lustless woman, her absence of lust, especially when this blemish has been transmuted into motherhood, may appear to him as something nobler, something beyond his understanding, something mysterious and magical and elfin, to which his earthliness must pay homage. Every man, and not only the debauchee, has an intimation of this, hence the understanding, the sympathy one might say, which A. felt for Herr von Juna. Without in any way doubting the truth of Zerline's story, he too wove an elfin mantle around the figure of the baroness. Be that as it may, the victory communiqué proceeded:

"He kept his word, and I was in riches, though all I had with me was my little servant girl's suitcase. I could have gone in the morning, but I wanted to get there at night, so by then it was fairly dark. There he was again with his blacks at the end of the streetcar line. We were both very grave. Riches make you grave. It was riches for me and I hoped in my heart for him, too. Of course you can never tell what makes somebody else grave. I was so distrustful that when I sat down beside him on the box I told him I had only ten days off. If it's nice, I thought to myself, I can own up to the other ten days, and if God is good to me, it can be the eternity of a lifetime. He expressed no regret at my having only ten days, but he was so silent and grave that I swallowed my disappointment. 'Don't take the shortest way,' I begged him. So we rode into the woods and up the hill at a walk; it was a woodcutters' road, the woods were cool-black and dark, and he didn't reach out for me, nor I for him. Up on the knoll there was just a tail end of twilight; for a few moments we could make out the harebells in the clearing, and then only the sky was light, and then we saw the first stars together. Soon the piles of cordwood at the edge of the clearing disappeared in the darkness, leaving only their smell, as if the chirping of the crickets had captured it. Because all those things—the chirping crickets, the harebells, the stars—carried each other, though they never touched. We stood there with the team, I've remembered everything and I'll remember it forever, because it carried me and has never stopped carrying me. Everything there was a part of our desire; mine hung on his and his on mine, and his hand never touched mine, nor mine his. Then I said: 'Drive on home.' It was even darker going down the hill. The blacks were cautious in putting down their hooves, and when they struck a rock there were sparks. The brake was on hard; the wheels scraped; now and then there was a stony squeak; now and then a branch hit me in the face with its wet leaves; I can't forget any part of it. Suddenly he released the brake and we were on level ground, in front of the house. There wasn't a single light on; it hung there in the blackness of night with its own blackness. But in me the heavy light of riches was burning. He helped me down, then he led the team away to the stable; it was so dark out there I'd have thought he wasn't coming back if I hadn't heard the hoofbeats on the stable floor. He came back. We didn't put the light on in the house. We were so grave that we didn't say a word."

Her voice had grown hoarse with emotion, and then she fell back into her chanting singsong:

"He was the best lover I ever had; the others couldn't compare to him. He wanted my pleasure and he looked for it ever so cautiously, like a man seeking his way. He was all impatience for me; he was shivering with impatience, but it didn't overpower him and he didn't overpower me; he waited for me to be carried to the edge of the abyss, ready for the final plunge. If it was a stream that carried me, he heard it, he listened and measured its flow. I was naked and he made me more naked, as if even nakedness had clothes that could be taken off. For shame is a kind of clothing. He took the last trace of shame off me so carefully that I was no longer alone in my most secret depths and we were two. He was as careful with me as a doctor, and he was a teacher to my pleasure; he taught my body to express desires and give orders, some tender, some brutal, for pleasure has many shadings and they all have their rights. He was my doctor and teacher, and at the same time the servant of my pleasure. For his only pleasure was mine; when I cried out in my pleasure, that was the praise he needed, the goad he needed for his desire. His weakness gave him strength. Higher and higher we soared, until we were one being. During those days and nights we were one being at the edge of the abyss. Yet I knew it was no good. For a woman must serve a man's pleasure, not the other way round. The orderlies who had rolled me over and taken their own pleasure without asking about mine had been more in the right way. Even their talk about loving me had been more real; his words needed my crude naked clamor for pleasure to be real; the cruder my words, the more real it became. I discovered why women grew attached to him and wouldn't let him go, but I also discovered that I wasn't one of them, that for all my desire I would have to leave him.

"I was smart." She nodded to herself and to her listener, but she did not wait for his response; the story drove her forward:

"I never laid eyes on the Forester's wife. But I'm a light sleeper when I want to be; she came to clean the house at five in the morning and she left the day's provisions for me on the kitchen table. What bothered me more was that the second we went out for a walk she was back in the house; I could tell she cleaned up after me because I did the bedroom myself. How did he let her know? It was all too smooth, with all those women that came around she was too well drilled. In a place like that any woman gets to be a spy. It wasn't hard. The house was old and the furniture was old; it was easy to pry open the flimsy locks on the cupboards and writing desks. Besides, a man who lets himself be pumped so mercilessly dry sleeps heavily. And by that time I was really merciless. The only trouble was that I hated to leave him then; when he was asleep, the lust was gone from his face, it was flawless and beautiful. Many times I sat on the edge of the bed, taking a long look at his face, before I started in with my spying. It was a sad, angry business. To show that this was her permanent home, the hussy had left all her clothes in the cupboards, and I was sure that when she came back to demand her pleasure, his rage wouldn't prevent him from obliging; maybe it would even spur him on. I'd been mighty curious about the baroness's letters, but now they only sickened me. The drawers were full of them mixed pell-mell with letters from his other women. I knew he wouldn't miss them, and I took as many as I could find. Wait, I'll read you one."

Rummaging her glasses and a few crumpled letters from the pocket of her smock, she went over to the window:

"Listen now. This will show you the kind of soul-noise people fill their empty, boring lives with; you'll see how poor the baroness is. You'll see what wretched, empty wickedness is. You just listen!

My sweet love, with each day of your absence our love is enriched. In our darling child you are always with me. I look upon her as a pledge of our eternal life together, which, as you write, must now begin, regardless of the obstacles. Have faith. Heaven smiles on lovers; heaven will help you to free yourself from that infamous woman who has thrust her claws into you so painfully. I hope and pray I may obtain the same release from my marriage! All in all, my husband is a noble man, but he has never had the least inkling of my sore heart. I must have it out with him. It will be painful, but I shall have the strength; your love for me and mine for you, which is my constant companion, fill me with confidence. In confident certainty I kiss your dear lovely eyes.

Your elfin Elvire

"Well, what do you think of it? The empty-headed mudhen! She poured out that drivel by the barrel, and he put up with it, probably with anger and disgust, but he put up with it. I should have hated him for that. But why did he put up with it? Because he was the kind of man whose opinion of women is too high and too low and who, for that reason, can only serve them with his body, while his soul pays no attention to them at all. That kind of man can't love; he can only serve. In every woman he meets he serves one who doesn't exist, whom he could love if she did exist, but who is actually an evil spirit that enslaves him. I knew I hadn't the strength to save him from the hell he was in, I knew I'd have to run away. That made my hate dissolve in tenderness and I went back to bed with him, to clasp him in my arms and legs, mercilessly out of hatred, mercilessly out of tenderness, but perhaps also in the hope that exhaustion would make our parting easier for both of us. Even so, when the ten days were over I asked if I could stay longer; I said I could manage it. When he heard that, the same sudden terror came into his eyes as in the garden, and he stammered: 'Better make it later, when I get back from my trip.' That was a lie. I was furious and I screamed at him: 'You won't see me here again until you get that woman's clothes out of the house.' Then for the first time he acted like a man, though again there was cowardice behind it. He threw me down and took me without bothering about my pleasure, he was so wild that I kissed him the way I had in the garden. Of course it didn't do any good; the hatred was still there. And that evening we drove down to the streetcar line in silence with my servant girl's suitcase in the back of the trap."

Was that the end of the story? No, apparently it had just begun, for now Zerline's voice became very firm and clear:

"Maybe the hatred was only on my side. Maybe when I threatened never to come back he took it to heart because he sensed that it wasn't soul-noise. Maybe he really wanted to get rid of that woman, who probably came back to her clothes the very next day and cooked the provisions that had been left in the kitchen for me. To make a long story short: a few weeks later the whole town was breathless with excitement because Herr von Juna's mysterious mistress had suddenly died in the Hunting Lodge. Well, those things happen all the time, but all the same a rumor sprang up that he had poisoned her. I didn't start the rumor, of course not; I was only too glad to be out of it and not to have to say anything about the letters or all the little tubes and bottles he had around the house that seemed kind of suspicious to me. But when there's talk, it's easy to add a little something to it, and it's easy to pass it on. Naturally I didn't deny myself the pleasure of telling the baroness what people were saying. She went white as snow; all she could say was: 'It's not possible.' I shrugged my shoulders and hit her with an 'Anything is possible.' The thought that Hildegard had a murderer's blood in her veins brought out something wild and fierce in me. In the meantime there was more and more talk of Herr von Juna's being put on trial, and a few days later he actually was arrested. The more I thought about it, the surer I was that he had killed her; yes, and today I'm surer than ever. He'd done it for my sake, and I didn't want him to be executed. So I was very glad when I heard that the case for the prosecution was too weak to get a conviction. You see, they'd found out that this woman—she was an actress from Munich—was a morphine addict and that she'd practically lived on injections and sleeping pills; a constitution like that can't stand very much. If she'd taken an overdose of sleeping pills, it could have been an accident or it could have been suicide, so there wasn't much chance of proving it was murder. The only really damaging evidence against him was the letters, and I'd stolen those. What luck for him! What luck for the baroness! For a while I was pleased as Punch about what I'd done, until it suddenly dawned on me that I hadn't helped him at all, because he had probably burned all his correspondence before they came to arrest him and he must have eaten his heart out with worry because the most dangerous letters

of all had been missing. I saw the terror in his eyes so plainly that
the same terror took hold of me. So I did what I should have done
before; I took the letters to his lawyers—one of them had come specially from Berlin—so they could relieve him of his worry and torment. They offered me a lot of money for them, but I refused
because I had started dreaming; my dream was that when he was
acquitted he'd be so grateful that he'd have to marry me. God
knows it would have been a blow to his vanity, and even worse for
the baroness, who would have had to congratulate her maid. So just
for that I kept a few of the letters, the most incriminating. Nobody
had any way of knowing whether they were all there, least of all
Herr von Juna himself. The ones I turned over were enough to quiet
his fears, and I needed the rest for my marriage dreams. If you want
to marry somebody, a little something to put on pressure with can
come in very handy, and it wouldn't have been so bad in our marriage, either."

"It was fine of you to save Herr von Juna," A. interposed, "but
you shouldn't always be so hard on the baroness." Zerline disliked
interruptions. "The main part is still to come," she said, overriding
him, and she was right to do so. For transformed into lamentation,
accusation and self-accusation, her story now transcended itself:

"Even my dreams of marriage were wicked; but they were only
put on, to blind myself to a greater wickedness that I needed the
letters for. I was damned, and I didn't know it. Who had brought
me to it? Juna, because he was in my blood and I didn't love him?
The baroness with her bastard that was his child? Or the judge himself, because I couldn't bear his being a cuckold and too holy to see
it? I was the only one who could open his eyes to it, and when after
everything else the news went round that the judge himself would
be trying the Juna case, I was really damned. Was he with his own
lips to acquit the man who had crept into his house to deposit a
bastard? I couldn't bear it, I couldn't bear to know what I knew; it
was almost complicity, and behind the complicity there was something worse; there was wickedness. I wanted to cry out, but what I
wanted to cry out was not my knowledge or my complicity; it was
my wickedness, because that was my only escape from damnation.
I had to go still deeper into my wickedness before I could come out
into the light of day and be whole again, wickedness and all. Even
so, there was more to it than I could understand. All of a sudden, as

if somebody had commanded me to do it, I bundled up all the letters
I had, the ones from him and the ones from the baroness—they'd
both threatened murder—and sent them anonymously to the judge,
addressed in block letters. I had to do it, and I knew just what I was
doing; actually the letters were intended for the public prosecutor;
my idea was that if only because of his wife's disgrace the judge
would have to resign from his post and that Juna, well, he'd have
his head cut off. Or maybe I hoped the judge in his despair would
kill himself and the baroness and the bastard. I wanted to confess
everything, my complicity, and the way I'd stolen the letters at the
Hunting Lodge and in the baroness's bedroom, so I wouldn't have
minded if he'd killed me too. That would have been real justice, because the hussy at the Hunting Lodge was murdered for me and not
for the baroness, and I wanted to admire the judge for this higher
justice. I put the judge to a terrible test, and I wanted him to come
through it in the name of justice; that would redouble my faith in
his greatness and holiness. For that I was willing to pay with my life,
but it was wickedness all the same, and I still don't understand it."

She breathed a deep sigh. This was clearly the heart of the matter; it was the greatest confession of her life, and obviously the
whole story had been told as a confession and not because of her
victory over the baroness, though that too played an indispensable
part in it. And indeed, Zerline seemed relieved. Since reading the
letter she had remained standing at the window, for a good reason
as was soon to be seen. With ceremonious fuss she put her spectacles back on her nose and drew another paper from her pocket. She
drew a long breath, and again her voice became strong and firm:

"The packet of letters had been sent off to the judge, and I
waited in hope and fear for terrible things to happen. The days
went by and nothing happened. He didn't even rake me over the
coals, though the anonymous sender could hardly have been anyone else. I was feeling disappointed, because even the judge was
turning out to be a coward, to whom justice meant less than position and good name, and who for their sake was even willing to
have a murderer's bastard in his house. But my mind was changed
for me, and very thoroughly. One day while I'm waiting on table so
I couldn't help hearing it all, the judge, who usually spoke so little,
suddenly starts talking good and loud about crime and punishment.
I remembered every word faithfully and I wrote it down right after-

ward. I'm going to read it now, so you'll remember it too. Pay close attention!

"'Our criminal courts with their jury system are an important institution but a dangerous one, dangerous because the presiding judge can very easily let himself be guided by emotional motives. In the grave cases where the decision rests with the jury, murder trials in particular, the sentiment of revenge—and no man who metes out punishment can be entirely free from it—may creep imperceptibly into his mind and gain the upper hand. Once this happens, he tends to lose sight of the fact that a judicial error can be murder; he loses sight of the horror of the death sentence, or rather, his scruples are submerged by the desire for revenge. In such a state, judges have often been led to evaluate evidence falsely. To prevent this a judge must be doubly and trebly on his guard in deciding what evidence is to be admitted and how it is to be treated. Even documents written and signed by the accused are subject to misinterpretation. If, for example, a man writes that he would like to have someone "eliminated" or that he would like to "get rid of him," this is not by any means conclusive evidence of intent to murder. But that is just what will be read into such a document by the thirst for vengeance that cries out for the guillotine and for the victim's blood.'

"That's what he said, and I understood him. I understood him so well that my hands began to shake and I almost dropped the roast. He was even greater, even holier than a silly thing like me could ever have imagined. He guessed that I had wanted to drive him to revenge, an executioner's revenge, and he wouldn't have it. He knew everything. But did the baroness understand it? Or was she too empty? If she even half remembered the letters she had received, words like 'eliminate' and 'get rid of' must have struck her. And the judge looked at her, his look was almost kindly, and it wouldn't have surprised me if she had fallen down on her knees before him. But she didn't budge, no, she didn't budge; maybe her lips went a little pale, nothing more. 'Oh, the guillotine,' she says, 'the death penalty, a dreadful institution.' That was all. The judge was looking down at his plate when I brought in the dessert. That's the way she was, so empty. I wasn't the least surprised at what happened after that. The trial was held just before Christmas, and the defense had an easy time of it, because the judge helped them and held the prosecutor down. Not one letter was produced. The jury acquitted him almost unanimously, eleven to one, and the one vote against him could have been mine. All the same I was glad when Herr von Juna was acquitted, and I was even gladder when he left town without thanking me or saying good-bye and went abroad to live, in Spain, I think."

That was the end of the story and Zerline heaved a sigh of relief: "Well, that's the story about me and Herr von Juna, and I'll never forget it. He escaped the guillotine and he escaped from me, which was even luckier for him. Because if he'd been noble and married me, I'd have made his life a hell on earth, and if he were still alive, he'd still have me on his hands, an old woman; just look at me." But before A. could reply to that, she started on the epilogue:

"There was a big stir about the acquittal. The newspapers attacked the judge, especially the red ones, they called it class justice. Naturally he crawled more and more into his shell. He hardly ever came out of his study, and pretty soon I had to make up his bed there. A year later he handed in his resignation, for reasons of health. Actually it was for reasons of death; he wasn't even sixty when it struck, and whatever the doctors may have said, he died of a broken heart. But she went on living with her bastard. That was an injustice, and that's what made me bring Hildegard up as I did. I wanted her to become the judge's real daughter; then he'd have dignity around him and his house wouldn't be sheltering a murderer's bastard. Of course I couldn't cure her of her murderer's blood, but that was one more reason why she had to learn to be a worthy daughter. If she'd been a Catholic, I'd have put her in a convent; as it was, the best I could do was make her look at the chaste holiness of the departed and teach her to imitate him. The more like him I made her, the more she atoned for her guilt and the more her mother's guilt was atoned for, though hers is forever unatonable. Her daughter has taken it over. Because, you see, the more she entered into her father's spirit, the more she was filled with the thirst for revenge, for the revenge that his saintly severity toward her had prevented him from taking. In imitating him she enslaves herself. That's what I enslaved her for, but no one could teach her holiness, and without holiness she can only pass her servitude on. She enslaves her mother with loving care—that is her quiet, mealy-mouthed revenge—and makes her do penance. It all hangs together, and that's how I wanted it; I brought her up to atone for guilt. Of course her lecherous murderer's blood doesn't want to atone; she rebels, but it doesn't help her any."

"But, my God," A. cried out, "what has she got to atone for? Where is her guilt? She can't be held responsible for her parents, and besides there's no good reason for calling the baroness's love for Herr von Juna a crime!" A withering look struck him, less perhaps because of what he said, though that too must have gone against Zerline's grain, than because he had interrupted her epilogue:

"What! Are you succumbing to her lust? I'm warning you. Get yourself a real girl, one you like to sleep with and who likes to sleep with you. Even if her hands are a little red, that's better than soulnoise with a manicure. Do you know why she didn't want you for a roomer? Well, every roomer we ever had, she stood outside his door"—she pointed at the door of the room—"night after night, and night after night an order from her father who's not her father stopped her in her traces; she never got beyond the threshold. If you don't believe me, I'll strew flour on the vestibule floor tonight—I've done it often enough—and you'll see her pussyfooting footprints in the morning. That's how her guilt tortures her; don't get tangled up in it. Because our responsibility like our wickedness is always bigger than ourselves, and the deeper we have to plunge into our wickedness to find ourselves, the more responsibility we have to take for crimes we didn't commit; that goes for everybody, for you and me and Hildegard, and her responsibility is to atone for the crime for her parents. The baroness is our prisoner; she wants to escape from servitude, and she begs every roomer to help her. Mother and daughter—they're both full of soul-noise, and I've fanned it up to a hellish din to make their ears ring with it: this house with its refined quietness is a hell. The saint and the devil, the judge and Herr von Juna, who's probably dead himself by now, are two ghosts that never stir from their sides and are tearing them apart. Maybe I'm being torn apart, too. It didn't help me any that after Herr von Juna I took other lovers, if only because I didn't want to be faithful to him of all people; and to make matters worse I saw pretty soon that I was having to pick them younger and younger. In the end they were practically children; I rocked them in my bosom to make them lose their fear of women and learn pleasure and peace. When I saw that, I gave up for good. Was that the only reason? No. I should have given up long before that, and if it hadn't been for the baroness, I mightn't even have got mixed up with Herr von Juna. The judge's image was in me, ineradicable from the first, and it has grown and grown. . . . Who was his widow after he died? Who, if not me? It's more than forty years since he reached for my breasts, and I've loved him all my life, with all my soul."

That was indeed the natural end of the story, and A. was rather surprised that he hadn't known it all along. Zerline, however, pretty well exhausted as was only natural at her age, looked into the void for a time before saying with her usual lady's maid politeness and in her usual lady's maid voice: "Now I've spoiled your afternoon nap with my chatter, Herr A. I do hope you'll be able to catch up on it now." Stooped and bent, she hobbled out of the room, closing the door ever so gently as though there were already a sleeper within.

A. had sunk down on the sofa. Yes, she was right, he had better sleep a bit. It wasn't so late after all; the church clocks had just struck four. It was only natural that the sleep-muddled thoughts interrupted by Zerline's entrance should resume. But again, to his irritation, the topic of money thrust itself to the fore. Again he was obliged to tell himself how he had started making money on the Cape, and how ever since, with little effort on his part, money had led him from stock exchange to stock exchange, from continent to continent—six in fifteen years if South America was reckoned as a continent, or two-and-a-half years to a continent. And it was all pure chance. As a boy stamp collector he had longed for the triangular Cape of Good Hope series, and his vain longing had left him with his longing for South Africa. Stamps wouldn't have been a bad investment, but he lost interest. What actually did he want? A home, a wife, children? Actually, only grandmothers really enjoy children. If you want to live in ease and comfort, children are a nuisance. And love entanglements are worse; they defy understanding. The baroness was just plain stupid; if he had known her then—but at that time he had scarcely been born—he would have sent for her, she'd have joined him in Cape Town and he'd have saved her from that man and his mistreatment. True, women are not greatly attracted to the place; that accounted for the shortage of women in the diamond fields and the resultant melodramas. Herr von Juna could never have built up a collection of women there. He'd had a very uncomfortable life. Was the judge to be envied? If the two of them had at least given the cuckold a son. But then the son would have run out on him, too, and escaped to Africa, despite the futility of trying to escape; for the widow stays at home, a captive. A man should always be his own son. Hadn't he, after his father's death, wanted to send for his mother, hadn't he wanted to build her a house in Cape Town? If she had gone, she would probably still be alive; in any case she'd have grandchildren. He'd have to start a stamp collection, and he'd get them the triangular Cape of Good Hope series. Let his Sunday trickle away; that was a good plan.

Yes, that was the way to plan his life, that much A. definitely knew. What he did not know was that he had fallen asleep over it.

Studienrat Zacharias's Four Speeches

After Studienrat Zacharias, decorated with the Iron Cross Second Class, had returned from the eventful boredom of the World War to the eventless but more familiar boredom of his daily life at home and in school, and after the Kaiser had fled to Holland, the Social Democrats, who had acceded to power, managed to preserve the life-structure of Imperial Germany, the good with the bad. In this they were motivated in part by a feeling for a still-living tradition, in still greater part by a petty-bourgeois love of petrifacts, a love that was ashamed of itself and therefore required a pretext, in the present case an allegedly Machiavellian desire to please the victor powers, and most of all by distaste for Russian barbarism, a feeling of revulsion for the Bolshevik murder mill whose mechanical, unheroic methods conflicted with all romantic hopes for the revolution. But they had nothing better to oppose to Communism than a hypertrophically unpolitical humanism, unaware that hypertrophies become empty and tend to shift into their opposites, so that hypertrophic humanism would resolve itself into a no less empty but no less hypertrophic barbarism, which would go even the Russians one better. True, in the first postwar years it was not possible to foresee all this.

Zacharias, who was accustomed to culling his opinions uncritically from those who happened to be in power and who consequently was animated by a truly democratic confidence in the wisdom of the majority, joined the Social Democratic Party and accordingly was promoted to the rank of Studienrat while still relatively young. He already had visions of himself as principal. As such he would maintain an iron regime, ruthlessly exclude holders of divergent opinions from his faculty, safeguard his school against dangerous innovations, and by strict discipline teach his students to be staunch democrats. With his own children, a girl of nine and two boys, one eight, the other five—the last the fruit of a wartime leave—his educational principles, which his wife also supported, had achieved admirable success; one word and the children obeyed. Under his model guidance the whole family wore soft felt slippers in the house to protect the well-waxed linoleum flooring, and all looked up with veneration at the portraits—in the center the oleograph triumvirate Wilhelm II, Hindenburg and Ludendorff, flanked by enlarged photographs of the Social Democratic leaders Bebel and Scheidemann—which graced the wall over the carved buffet.

Throughout Germany at that time meetings were beginning to be held in protest against Einstein's theory of relativity which, at least in the view of nationalist circles, had too long been suffered in silence. Zacharias was well aware that Einstein had many supporters in the Social Democratic Party and even that its leaders, if the matter had been put to a vote, would probably have come out unanimously in his favor. It was with a feeling akin to rebelliousness—mingled with a certain professional pride—that he nonetheless attended these meetings, proclaiming that as a mathematician and educator he had not only a right but even an obligation to do so. The theory repelled him by being so hard to understand, though it scarcely affected him personally, for it had not been included in the curriculum of the secondary schools. But just that must be prevented at all costs, regardless of whether the theory was sound or not. How could a man exercise his profession if he had to keep assimilating new material? Wouldn't that give the students a pretext for importunate questions pregnant with embarrassment? Wasn't a teacher justified in insisting that the boundaries of knowledge must be definitive? If not, what was the good of the teacher's examination? Could anyone doubt that this great trial was a milestone separating the period of learning from the period of teaching? Consequently it was an outrage to keep harassing teachers with new theories, especially with theories like Einstein's that were still controversial! These were the views he stated at the meeting, and though his moderately violent speech was too moderate and not violent enough for certain hotheads—here and there a cry of "Jew lover!" was heard—his rejection of unhealthy innovations in the schools—"Let us be progressive but not modish!"—met with general approval, and in the ensuing debate, which was animated to stormy because the supporters of Einstein demanded an objective discussion and objective arguments, he was permitted to stand up again and ask in tones of indignation whether his remarks had been unobjective.

Nevertheless he was not satisfied with the outcome. Apparently it was felt that his membership in the Social Democratic Party gave him an ambivalent attitude toward the theory of relativity, and when the meeting was over he was ignored by both groups. He had pushed his way into the aisle, and as he looked around at the departing contestants, he noted with some satisfaction that their numbers had not been sufficient to fill the hall. A shabby meeting. He was sorry he had come. Party discipline is party discipline, even if one has justified objections to Einstein. It was a small hall, meant for chamber music, and they had been unable to fill it. Opposite the six damask-curtained windows there were six wall niches, housing the heroes of music, Mozart, Haydn, Beethoven, Schubert, Brahms, and Wagner—the last-named in a slanting beret—all gazing inanimate into an even more inanimate space, and Zacharias, who had never in his life attended a serious concert, thought of the brilliant audiences which thronged to this place in the music season and which—dwelling in the light measures of a world of serene enjoyment—would surely have had no more than a smile for him, the outcast whom chance had brought to their hall. Well, he would take it out on their children; he, the stern examiner, would give them nothing to smile about. That cheered him; the satisfactions that were denied him in one quarter would be made good in another. Compensatory injustice.

His spirits rose still further when he reached the shadowy compartments in the cloakroom, unused because it was summer, and saw a man lighting one match after another and looking for something behind the broad counters. He stopped complacently to watch him.

"I give up," said the man, who had noticed him.

"Lost something?"

"I put my hat down here; somebody must have taken it by mistake."

"Not by mistake," said Zacharias.

They went down the stairs together; Zacharias removed his own hat, wiped it on his sleeve and blew on it. "Was it a good hat?" he asked, not exactly out of sympathy.

"Fairly new," said the bareheaded young man. "It happens all the time; I have bad luck with my hats."

"Bad luck? You must learn to take care of your belongings."

"I never will."

They were standing under a street lamp. Zacharias observed the young man who took the loss of a new hat so lightly, not to say frivolously: along his ears he had a narrow strip of close-cropped side-whiskers reminiscent of the Biedermeier period, and he seemed to belong to the better classes, probably those who attended concerts here. None of this was to Zacharias's liking.

"Are you a physicist?"

The young man shook his head.

"A mathematician?"

Another shake of the head, as though the question had been unreasonable.

"An anti-Semite?"

"Not that I know of. . . . I haven't tried it yet."

"It's not something you can try," Zacharias corrected him. "Anti-Semitism is a state of mind."

Looking up at him out of the corners of his eyes—for Zacharias was taller than he—the young man smiled: "Are you going to examine me for my state of mind?"

Zacharias was shaken with wild, unmotivated laughter. "It's only a professional habit, a good one, I might say . . . you see, I'm a high-school teacher and known as a severe examiner."

An almost imperceptible shimmer of anxious defiance, mingled with sardonic distaste, brushed the young man's features. "I'm afraid you'll have no luck with me, because—in the strictest confidence—I don't like to be examined."

"No one does, no one . . ." the young man's fear of examination brought new nourishment to Zacharias's laughter—"yes, no one. . . . Nevertheless, or for that very reason, I must inquire into your motives for attending this anti-Einstein meeting."

The young man seemed amused: "You might get it out of me over a glass of wine, certainly not otherwise. . . . I'm dying of thirst. . . . Will you join me?" And without waiting for an answer, he led the way.

Nearby there was a tavern, a good place for loving couples or quiet boozing, since the whole of it was split up into small booths equipped with pseudo-oriental curtains that could be drawn when privacy was desired, yet not suitable for lovemaking since their sole furnishings were a table and two hard narrow benches. Zacharias and the young man seated themselves in one of these boozing booths and, leaving no doubt that he was the host, the young man ordered a bottle of excellent Burgundy.

Arriving in its wicker cradle, the cellar-dusty bottle was formally presented and uncorked. The wine, a noble, full-bodied vintage, was poured into the glasses, and the young man, with the hesitation of a connoisseur wishing to savor the last moments of thirsty anticipation, raised his glass to eye level and contemplated its deep red, while Zacharias said *"Prost"* and set his to his lips.

"Prost," said the young man, letting the first swallow dissolve in his mouth.

Zacharias tasted the wine in his turn: "Fine stuff. We drank plenty of it in Frogland."

"Ah, you were in France?"

"Yes, sir. . . . I made lieutenant and they gave me the Iron Cross . . . for a leg wound. I still limp a little and I feel it when the weather changes. . . . What about you? Were you in France or in Russia?"

"Neither; I was in Africa."

"I see. Lettow-Vorbeck."

"No, I'm a Dutchman."

"Oh, a neutral . . . well, their so-called neutrality didn't do the Belgians any good; a man has to know where he stands, right or left."

"True enough," said the young man. "We've been punished too. Now we've got your Kaiser on our hands."

Silly neutrality jokes. It was unworthy of a German man to take any note of them: "Left or right; some are for Einstein, some are against, you can't be neutral . . . why did you go to the meeting?"

"Are you against him? Your remarks gave me that impression."

Why couldn't the fellow give a plain answer to a plain question? Zacharias was on the point of administering a sharp and well-deserved censure, but since he was hungry for praise he controlled himself in the hope of belated applause: "My views were clear enough. I assume you agree with them."

"No," said the young man. "Not at all."

With a movement habitual to him on the occasion of grave schoolboy offenses Zacharias removed his spectacles and, blinking nearsightedly, stared at his opposite: "Repeat that."

"I don't agree with you. It's not right to keep new scientific achievements away from the students; that's all . . . here's to relativity; you can't kill it by silence, so why not wish it long life? . . . *Prost*!"

"Did I say anything about killing it by silence?" Zacharias countered sternly. "You weren't paying close attention . . . didn't I make it very clear that I was opposed only to modishness, not to progress? I make bold to state that I am a man of progress. I am a member of the Social Democratic Party, which stands foursquare behind the theory of relativity. But progress must not be allowed to confuse the schoolboy's undeveloped mind. Now do you understand?"

"Of course. Politically you're for Einstein and scientifically you're against him. And altogether you don't like him very much."

An obstinate pupil, Zacharias thought, and with insidious mildness he asked: "Is it customary in the circles you frequent to question the blessings of progress?"

"I don't know what circles you're referring to, my friend; but as for myself, don't tell anybody; I prefer not to think about progress."

"That's intellectual laziness."

"Exactly. What fate gives me, I accept, even progress and its blessings. Since I can't defend myself against fate, I try to take pleasure in it. No one can stop progress. So we've got to promote it."

Zacharias looked at him distrustfully: "Just a minute. Don't try to make a fool out of me. It won't go down."

"Because I believe in fate? Because I accept the unavoidable blessings of progress without a murmur and am even willing to promote it?"

"Don't talk nonsense!" Zacharias blustered. He had drunk the heavy wine too quickly and had reached the belligerent stage.

"Alas," said the young man sadly. "We never succeed in talking nonsense."

"That's more nonsense," said Zacharias. "Obviously you don't see what nonsense you're talking." And when the young man, thus disposed of, did not contradict him, he continued: "Or do you think it makes sense to call the theory of relativity an unavoidable evil?"

"An unavoidable blessing!"

"Will you stop talking rubbish! What do you mean by that?"

The young man replied politely.

"The blessing of progressive knowledge is paid for in suffering."

"Empty words. You must learn to express yourself more precisely."

"No," said the young man. "When I drink I can't be precise."

"I'm glad you admit it," Zacharias triumphed. But his triumph was shortlived, for the other completed his remark:

"All precision brings misfortune."

"That's too much. I shall have to break off this conversation if . . ."

"Just a moment," said the young man, who had discovered that the bottle was empty. Then, having called the waitress and ordered another, he turned back to Zacharias: "What were you saying?"

"Illustrate what you just said with a concrete example."

"My ordering another bottle? That's concrete enough."

"Good God! That bilge about precision bringing misfortune."

"Oh. The Germans are the most precise people in Europe; consequently they have brought all manner of misfortune on themselves and on Europe."

"There we have it!" Zacharias's accumulated truculence exploded into an offensive. "You neutrals with your anti-German sentiment! Germany brings misfortune. Why? Because it's a threat to your shopkeeping, money-grubbing mentality. . . . Will you never learn? Are you incapable of learning?"

"Definitely," said the young man. "Besides, I fail to see what you want me to learn."

"I've had as much as I can take," Zacharias fumed into his face, "but before I go, I'm going to tell you what you and all your neutral countries, the whole world in fact, will have to learn." He took a good swallow and with a disdainful look at the young man let loose:

"To start with a concrete example, which is the only way, I, speaking as a teacher and educator but also as a well-disposed friend, find myself obliged to castigate your contemptible hypocrisy. Because your wallet is well filled and you can afford to order expensive wine, you think you can make a fool of me, but instead of admitting it you hide behind a lot of silly, cowardly evasions. And what do they add up to? The same arrogant, hypocritical moralizing that we Germans have been subjected to for years. We hear it from all over Europe. Well, we've shown Europe what we are.

I've drunk the exact same wine in Laon and Soissons, and I paid for it out of my own pocket"—he gave a short laugh—"with requisitioned francs, I admit. Naturally the French didn't care for that requisitioned money, and they cared still less for us. But they didn't want to make us a present of the wine, so like it or not, they had to put up with our francs, and, never fear, they had to put up with us. We weren't very fond of them either, though in a way we liked them. But one thing we couldn't tolerate: their backtalk. Why? Because they were too short and too dark and their mouths were too big. We don't stand for empty chatter . . . kindly make a note of that. And then the Americans were stupid enough to help them and they started puffing themselves up as victors. That made them doubly detestable. One thing we will not tolerate is hypocrisy, pretense, and they pretend to be something they're not. It's the same with the Jews; we'd like them well enough if they didn't swagger around like big blonds and take themselves for God-knows-what. And another thing that doesn't appeal to us is when they make such a to-do about modernizing our physical world view and bother us with premature, unsubstantiated and therefore futile theories; it's our world view and if we want it made over, we'll do it ourselves and we'll set up something better and solider than they ever could, and without making a big fuss about it. That's our precision, the precision of German science; we'll handle it alone, and never fear, without any help from them. The student has no call to teach the teacher, and if megalomania, hypocrisy and presumption drive him to do it, he'll have to take the consequences. We are a nation of teachers, of world teachers, and it's only natural that other peoples, like bad pupils, often regard our strict precision as injustice and rebel against it. Why, sometimes we can't even understand ourselves, we regard ourselves as unjust and evil, we hesitate and shrink back from our hardness and its applications. But that is our destiny and we can't evade it; time and again we must pass through injustice to achieve justice, world justice; time and again we must sink into evil in order to raise ourselves and the rest of the world to a state of higher perfection, and time and again in our hands injustice has been transformed into justice, to our own surprise. Because we are the nation of the infinite and hence of death, while the other peoples are bogged down in the finite, in shopkeeping and money-grubbing, confined to the measurable world because they know only life and not death and consequently, though they may seem to rise so easily and so far above themselves, they are unable to break through the finite. It is incumbent on us, for their own salvation, to subject them to the punishment of death-pregnant infinity. A hard, a colossal course of instruction, forsooth! A hard course to follow, and an even harder one to give, all the harder because not only the dignity of the judge, but also the indignity of the executioner has been imposed upon us, the teachers. For in the infinite all exist side by side, dignity and indignity, sanctity and the need for salvation, goodwill and ill will, hence the curse and the blessing that are our destiny, the dual role in which we become objects of terror to ourselves and others: every shot we are compelled to fire against them strikes our own hearts as well, every punishment we are obliged to mete out to them is our own punishment as well. Our mission as world teacher is a curse and a blessing, and nevertheless we have taken it upon ourselves for the sake of the truth which is in infinity and therefore in ourselves: as Germans we have taken it upon ourselves; we did not shrink back from it, because we knew that we, alone of all peoples, are free from hypocrisy."

He had stood up and with an unsteady hand emptied what was left in the bottle into the two glasses. Draining his own at one gulp, he announced: "Now I'm going."

"Why?" asked the young man.

"I believe I have made that clear enough."

"No," said the young man. "I feel like drinking some more."

That struck Studienrat Zacharias as almost more illuminating than his own speech. He pondered intensely: should he or should he not sit down again? At length he decided:

"All the same I'm going."

"Where to?" the young man asked, not without interest.

And that inspired Studienrat Zacharias to a second significant speech:

"In your face I read lewd insinuations. You believe I am headed straight for one of those female persons that I make no bones about calling whores. No, nothing of the kind. What deters me is not the mere fear of meeting one or more of my older students, who in a spirit of base vengeance against the strict examiner might ruin my career and family life forever. Not at all. I say not at all, because driven by dark cravings, I have overcome such fear more than once.

And it might almost be wiser to overcome it again tonight. Because if I do as I should like to and hurry home to my faithful wife Philippine, my slight drunkenness may easily provide the occasion for a fourth child, from which statement you may infer that we already have three. Nevertheless, obvious as it is that my fear of this fourth child, which is beyond our means, is greater than my fear of a meeting with my older students, it is not the fact that the child is beyond our means, not our dismal inflationary situation, which may yet be overcome, that makes me reluctant to go home. Far be it from me to underestimate financial insecurity, but in this case the insecurity lies deeper. If I am not mistaken, it is the insecurity of the infinite in which we Germans live and its consequence is that copulation invariably hurls us into the darkness of the infinite. I say 'copulation' with intent, I intentionally avoid the word 'love'; other peoples may still talk of love, we do no longer. Precisely because we, my good wife and I, once partook of the infinite in our embrace, or in more intelligible terms, because on that occasion my knowledge rose to the most distant suns, so that our kiss seemed to hover in the cosmos—precisely for that reason I venture to conclude that at that time I was not present to her nor she to me, that we were both extinguished, each for himself and far more so for each other, extinguished by something bigger than our own being, bigger than any love, infinitely greater than the human person, which is at the center of love and without which love cannot be. Had she, in that moment, any knowledge of my face, or I of hers? No; I can safely say that not even our bodies had any knowledge of each other. Extinction is darkness, is infinite darkness. True, man, especially the breed of man who has succumbed to the infinite, always strives for such infinity and for the darkness that unsouls his soul and disembodies his body. Not only is he prepared to persuade himself that the yearning for darkness is love; no, if I may trust my own experience, he is also prepared to take the unsouling and disembodying seriously and commit suicide, as confirming the infiniteness of his love; but in reality he is only confirming his despair of his love; he kills himself to prevent the hypocrisy of this pretended love from emerging, or if you prefer a somewhat more paradoxical formulation, to prevent the darkness from bringing his hypocrisy to light, to escape the shame which, I tend to believe, is the inevitable aftermath of hypocrisy. We too, my Philippine and I, were so ashamed of what happened to us then that we have never mentioned it since, all the less so because the fruit of our ecstatic extinction, our eldest daughter, whom we named Wilhelmina in honor of the monarch, has been vegetating along with a somewhat extinguished mind or, to put it unkindly, is inclined to idiocy. If I were not slightly drunk, with all due emphasis on the adverb 'slightly,' I would not be remembering all this so shamelessly, let alone voicing it so openly, but would betake myself in silence to my Philippine, who is waiting for me faithfully and patiently and who will not take umbrage at my slight drunkenness, for she has long known that I am obliged to attend political and scientific meetings; ah, she would receive me as a streetwalker receives a visitor, and I would take her as I would take a streetwalker, ah, that's how we'd do it, simply because it was once bigger than ourselves and now it is smaller, but has never never been love. Ah, we Germans are incapable of hypocrisy; when we want love it becomes suicide and murder, for us everything becomes suicide and murder, and if we can't make up our minds to that, we are left with nothing but the darkness of the infinite, the uncertainty and shame of the infinite. Oh, it's so sad, oh so sad. . . ."

Overwhelmed by sadness, sniveling and blubbering with sadness, he sank down on his bench and his blubbering became a loud sobbing when his trembling hand found the bottle empty. But when guided by the sympathy that inebriates have for each other, his companion patted him gently and comfortingly on the shoulder, Zacharias turned on him: "Inattentiveness has brought many a pupil to an early grave. Behold . . . empty nothingness." And to prove it he raised the bottle high.

Suddenly, with equal vehemence and without transition, his sadness turned to joy: as though by magic two filled glasses were on the table. In their surprise both men had to laugh aloud, for neither had noticed that the quick-eyed waitress had taken Zacharias's manipulation of the empty bottle as a sign that a new one was desired. Zacharias nodded: "Instant obedience; that's what I like to see . . . it will be noted in your report card."

"Stop," said the young man with the authority of one well versed in the techniques of sound drinking. "Before you swill any more, you're having something to eat, something substantial, or we won't get out of here on our own legs." Thereupon he ordered sausages with sauerkraut, black bread and Swiss cheese. It was all right with

Zacharias; though he clutched his glass in both hands, he did not drink and waited obediently for the food.

But when it was served he arose and, dominating his trembling legs, assuming in fact a military attitude, he made a reasonably correct bow, all the while holding his glass in his left hand: "Zacharias, Studienrat," he introduced himself. "Let's drink to us." The young man, who had also stood up, seized his outstretched hand and shook it mightily. "That's it. To us." After clinking glasses they hooked arms and in that position drained their glasses at one draught. But then, as they again sat facing one another, Zacharias observed mournfully: "I don't even know your name." The young man put his finger to his lips: "Sh, no examining, I said; I won't even let my name be examined out of me." At that Zacharias became very sad again. "But I told you mine. It's not fair."—"You're Z. and I'm A. We're brothers, aren't we? So now we own all names between us, the whole lot from A to Z." That appealed extraordinarily to Zacharias and to the mathematical educator in him. "All names from A to Z," he chuckled. "That's it," said the young man, raising his glass joyfully. "Here's to our names, and an extra *Prost* to the love that has no name!" Zacharias shook his head: "Love? No, it doesn't exist."—"Then what will we drink to?" That was a very difficult question and Zacharias had to think strenuously before he found the answer: "To brotherhood."—"Does that exist?"—"It will." When they had drunk to brotherhood, Zacharias started on his sausages, packing each mouthful in sauerkraut that hung like hay from a pitchfork, and washing it down with a good swallow of wine.

"Save your wine for your cheese," A. advised. "Sauerkraut isn't worthy of it."

"You've got something there," Zacharias agreed. "Wine and cheese, that's what we did in France. But now we're in Germany."

"The rules of eating and drinking know no national boundaries; they are international, and with them begins the brotherhood of man."

Zacharias smirked knowingly: "International is un-German. Brotherhood is German."

"I thought you were a Social Democrat."

"So I am. A loyal German Social Democrat."

"Then you ought to be international-minded."

"So I am. Loyally one hundred percent international. But the International will have to be led by us Germans; not by the Russians, let alone the French, not to mention the rest of them. The democratic International will be based on brotherhood, not on any phony League of Nations, and it's our mission to drum that into the world, especially the allegedly victorious Western democracies."

"The question is: will they let you?"

Zacharias made a contemptuous grimace: "The victors are the defeated; the world's future and the character of its democracy are determined by the nonvictors. . . . If we don't do it, the Russians will."

"They're democrats?"

"Maybe not. That's why we've got to hurry. All the Western powers do is talk; they talk democracy to mask their business deals. That's why they make so much noise about Einstein. Empty noise. All they really care about is business. That's what we've got to knock out of them."

"Too good to be true."

What kind of argument was that? Instantly Zacharias gave vent to his disapproval. "You're just another neutral yourself, a shop-keeper. You'll be amazed when you see how we do it—we German Social Democrats, and the whole German nation with us. We've put General von Seeckt in command of our Reichswehr."

"Fine," said A. "Setting aside all theories of relativity, we shall strive for world brotherhood . . . is that right?"

"Yes." Zacharias had finished his sausages and sauerkraut. He wiped his plate neatly with bread and cut his cheese into cubes. "I'm not drunk any more," he announced with satisfaction; "we can order another bottle."

"Good idea. But to prolong our recovered well-being, I beg leave to excuse myself."

"A shrewdly weighed suggestion," Zacharias agreed. "We'll take it together. I'll go with you."

Thus the two of them betook themselves to the men's toilet in the rear of the establishment. And there, standing at the urinal, Zacharias was suddenly ravished into a higher sphere, a sphere which, oddly enough, man shares with his faithful and loving four-legged friend, the dog. For man's first rituals were born of tree and stone worship, and to this day he embodies ceremonial rune-covered cornerstones in his buildings of state; to this day he cannot help incising the runes of his love into the bark of trees—and are not tree and stone, and most eminently the cornerstone, sacred also to the dog? Is not the business of bladder relief, for which the dog, alone among animals, requires trees and cornerstones, not always a prelude to a higher ritual, the ritual of aspersion, which is closely related to love? Both are rituals of renewal. In the dog, to be sure, they are primitive, so much so that the profane and the sacred need are indistinguishable and literally merge; yet this strange connection survives in man as well, for by a noteworthy kinship between the human and the canine constitution, between the human and the canine psyche, he too from time immemorial has required tree and wall for his profane as well as his sacred business, and is indeed almost inevitably stimulated by the former to the latter. This truth was clearly attested by the wall on which Zacharias kept his eyes fixed in the course of his profane bodily action, marveling at the laconically sublime eloquence of man. Himself a man among men, he drew a pencil from his vest pocket and after selecting a free place among the more or less imperative, more or less obscene, more or less symbolic runic inscriptions and drawings, drew a handsome heart on the wall, within which he placed the significantly intertwined letters A. and Z. The young man, who had been paying close attention, praised him.

Afterwards they sat with their fourth bottle between them. The waitress had brought them several boxes of cigars to choose from, and Zacharias, who had unbuttoned his vest and loosened his tie because of the stifling heat, wiped his spectacles with care to be sure of selecting the right siesta weed. His efforts were successful. He smelled the cigar and let his companion smell it with a view to consensus. After a second cigar, similar in color and aroma, had been found, he hid both under his napkin and asked slyly: "Left or right?" "Left," said A. To which Zacharias replied triumphantly: "Wrong! I am the man of the left, you will always be on the right: I get the one on the left." The right-hand cigar was handed to the young man and they savored the astute political joke. The conversation lagged. Preoccupied with the glimmer of their cigars, they sat quietly, sipping the noble liquid, turning it over on their tongues, relishing the aftertaste as though in leavetaking, all very slowly and circumspectly since this was really to be the last bottle.

Seemingly without outside provocation, but probably spurred by recollection of the pungent urine smell, which, if only in traces, his nose had carried back from the toilet and which even managed to assert itself against the acrid billows of tobacco smoke as though there were a foreordained necessity in this mixture of smells—in this tobacco haze seasoned with disgust, Zacharias launched into his third speech, first with quiet composure, then as his drunkenness burgeoned anew, with rising passion:

"Brotherhood is both like and unlike love. It is like love in so far as both strive for the extinction of man. But whereas love extinguishes itself in the extinction for which it strives, so revealing and demonstrating its nonexistence, true brotherhood begins with this extinction. For love is a mere playing with extinction and the death in which the extinction should by right culminate; it can be no more than a playing because the beautiful double suicide that love dreams of would inevitably be murder of the just-begotten and -conceived child. Actually lovers fear death, and their pleasure is nondeath, an overcoming of death, an overcoming of death disgust. Indeed, I call this performance of lovers an irresponsible playing with death, a game calculated to increase pleasure, to overcome disgust, for the source of all pleasure is an overcoming of disgust, a playing with the idea of extinction in animality and cosmic oneness, for in animality or cosmic oneness there is no room for disgust. But death is not deceived by any playing; breaking off their game, it hurls lovers back from their play extinction into sober reality, into the hell of extinguished desire, the hell of disgust. Lovers—or, more correctly, would-be lovers—are punished with a twofold and three-fold torment of disgust; each with his nose keeps watch on the other, intent on surprising the smell of death, the smell of aging toward death, the mouth smell that announces the beginning of decay. Death erupts with twofold and threefold force, inflicting the punishments of hell, and under its rule a man loses all certainty of this world and the other; disillusioned in play, he become disillusioned with everything under the sun, not last with the names of things. He is reduced to approaching things through ever-changing constructions and theories and in the end abandons these too in disgust, killed not by pleasure but by self-hatred and self-disgust. Such is love, its nonexistence, its playful dream of twoness, of *Liebestod* and miraculous suicide, its game of pseudoextinction! Brotherhood is a very different matter! In contrast to the wretched creatures who exploit their sexual difference to dream up new heights of pleasure, it is the dream of the great male community, the sublime primordial dream, which through multitude attains to the greatness of reality; it is the dream of mankind, which time and time again achieves reality by making reality subservient to itself. Brotherhood does not try to spirit away death and death disgust by means of a pseudoextinction; no, it achieves a true extinction by boldly taking death and death disgust upon itself. Let the women stay home and bear the child they have conceived; the men bear death into the world and are borne by it, extinguished in the multitude that is the echo of the infinite, the echo of totality. But where is such brotherhood to be found today? Answer me; I'm waiting for your answer. Has no one got the answer? In that case I'll have to supply it myself. I call your attention to the institution of the modern army, and eminently the German army, which is the principal, perhaps the only true community of males and home of true brotherhood. But can you conceive of such a community without a guiding idea, revolutionary in its severity? The first requirement is to kill all thought of rebellion, and to this end all feeling not only of pain but also of disgust must be killed. If love ends in disgust, brotherhood begins with disgust. Army brotherhood does precisely that. It begins with stench, the stench of the barracks and their latrines, the stench of marching columns, the stench of hospitals, the stench of ubiquitous death. Pleasure forgives nothing; brotherhood forgives in advance, the foulest stinking fart can't make a dent in comradeship. Before he even knows it, the recruit, chastised by disgust, forced to overcome it, is on his way to self-discipline and self-extinction; soon he begins to cast off his fear of the smell of decay, hence of death, and is prepared for total self-sacrifice. The army is an instrument of death; the man who enters it is from that moment on unsouled, rid of his individual soul, but inspired by a new soul, for inseparably joined with countless other bodies, his body becomes disembodied and fearless. Here begins true extinction, not the play extinction in vapid infinity that is the goal, the pseudogame of love; no, here begins extinction in the totality, an extinction grounded not in another world but in this, but which in its greatness is equivalent to the infinite and like the infinite eternal. Here there is absolute certainty, and the harder the chastisement that the novice takes on himself in the beginning, the deeper his initial disgust, the more certain he will be of the cosmos-like totality in which he is destined, freed from disgust and freed from fear, to merge into extinction. Without resistance he receives the commands of the totality, and for him each command guarantees the certainty of words, things and names; he is saved from all doubt of reality. Freed from all useless theorems and vacillation, the death-oriented life of the totality—in other words brotherhood—irradiates the life of the individual. That is his extinction and his happiness. That is what we define as German brotherhood."

During the last sentences Zacharias had arisen and started tapping out the rhythm of his words with his knuckles on the table top, as though lecturing in his schoolroom. When he had finished, he seemed unaware that he had only his companion and not a whole class before him; he stared at the young man vacantly, and the young man stared back out of befuddled lusterless eyes. And since it was not quite clear to Zacharias which of them was sitting and which standing, he commanded: "Sit down."

More under the effect of the wine than of the speech, the young man carefully examined his bent knees, felt the junction of his posterior with the wooden bench beneath it, and came to the conclusion that it was he who was sitting—a conclusion which he expressed without hesitation: "Won't you sit down too, Herr Studienrat?"

With a glare of disapproval Zacharias snapped: "No backtalk!"

At this the young man was sufficiently sobered to see that something had to be done: "I believe, Herr Studienrat, that we could both do with a cup of coffee."

Zacharias's mind had slowed down and he was busy with the wine bottle. After a while he muttered: "A student inviting himself to drink coffee with me . . . what gall! What gall!" But without waiting for an answer, A. had made his way flabby-legged to the bar and ordered coffee. When he came back, Zacharias had thought up a new reproof. Still standing stiffly with his hand on his desk, he said: "You've been leaving the room a little too often during the last hour; if you're up to some mischief in the toilet, you'll regret it." Organizing his legs, A. came to attention: "I am not up to any mischief, Herr Studienrat."—"Besides, as you ought to know, you have no business leaving the classroom without permission."—"Beg your pardon, Herr Studienrat, it won't happen again."—Unlike the young man, Zacharias took the matter very seriously: "I shall enter the incident in the class book."—"Couldn't you put mercy before justice, Herr Studienrat?"—"Mercy is effeminate, mercy is unbrotherly. The offender must be chastised." But the coffee had arrived in the meantime, the aroma rose to his nostrils and he asked amiably: "Where did you get the coffee?"—From the janitor, Herr Studienrat."—"Very good; let us fall to." And they both sat down.

When they had chatted a while over their coffee cups, it occurred to them almost simultaneously that the tone of their conversation had relapsed into a certain formality though they had just drunk to brotherhood. And amid the laughter occasioned by their discovery the younger man remarked: "Well, maybe we ought to drink to brotherhood again."—"By all means. Order another bottle." But that struck A. as a little too much. He explained at considerable length that coffee cannot and must not be followed by wine, and in the end they agreed to seal their new blood-brotherhood with kirsch, for, as they were both pleased to recognize, only spirits could set a worthy alcoholic crown to so successful an evening.

Kirsch it was. Again they both stood up; again they hooked elbows to ingurgitate the brotherhood-pledging alcohol, and again they shook hands vigorously. When this had been done and the check paid. Studienrat Zacharias commanded: "Columns of two. Fall in. Forward, march."

On the street a new controversy arose, for once more it became manifest that the young man had no hat. Zacharias tried to clap his own on A.'s head, and A.'s resistance struck him as insulting, nay disdainful: "I suppose it's not stylish enough for you?"—"It's too small." After trying several times to get the hat into a proper position by force, Zacharias commanded: "Stop inflating your skull." Then when A.'s head refused to shrink he hit on the Solomonic solution: the hat must be divided in two. Taking out his pocketknife, he pierced the crown in the middle, intending to cut the hat in two lengthwise. A. stopped him: "That's silly," he said. "Then neither of us will have anything. If you want to divide it, you keep the crown and I'll take the brim." That was simple. Zacharias donned the crown but was very much disappointed when the brim proved to be too big and slid down over the young man's nose. "Idiot," he fumed. "You did it on purpose. Now you've shrunk your skull."— "It's not my fault. The blood rose to my head, and now in the night air it's flowing off again." The young man was seriously troubled; he kept trying to make the brim stay in place and it kept sliding down past his nose to his neck. At last he resigned himself: "I'll wear it as a collar; it will be lovely."

That appealed to Zacharias: "If you want to lift it to somebody, you can slip it over your head. Perfect."

Here and there a passerby glanced with amusement at the strangely adjusted pair, but most of the rare night owls who came their way took no notice. The summer night was tired but could find no rest for its weariness. Blown from somewhere, a few strands of morning freshness wove themselves into the lingering sultry night; as though in self-defense the sultriness hovered like great swarms of gnats in the tremulous white glow of the streetlamps, communicating its sober restlessness to the deadness roundabout and defeating the invading freshness. It was an hour of contradiction, all the more so because the night's emptiness was filled with a restless hammering as of scythe blades being pounded on an anvil, and this too was sober; taking advantage of the hours when the streetcar was not running, some men were mending the tracks. In the midst of this sober deadness, the two of them—Zacharias limping a little—strode staunchly forward; arm in arm but with military bearing they marched through the sober world, by virtue of their motion sobering a little with each step. When in the tree-lined chasm of the dark street the restless hammering became more audible, A. said:

"The city is hammering its scythes."

And Zacharias replied: "Rubbish."

A few minutes later they reached the scene of the hammering. Partly to spare the eyes of the passersby, partly for shelter against the wind, the work site was surrounded by a kind of canvas tent. The flaps were poorly joined at the corners; through the openings welding arcs shot their white glare often tinged with green, and under the intermittent flashes the streetlamps paled to lusterless still moons. About a dozen men were at work. The actual welders wore great black masks and communicated with each other in raucous shouts to make themselves heard over the hammering and the sound of their own arcs.

There was not much to see. Nevertheless, Zacharias was fascinated. He stood there, watching the men with interest. This, as a Studienrat, he should not have done. For as he stood there tall and gaunt, with his spectacles on his nose and his brimless hat on his head, every inch a shy-domineering schoolmaster, he discovered to his consternation that he was arousing a lively counterinterest among the men; one remarked to another that he was worth looking at; they pointed thick fingers at him, and finally united in a chorus of laughter which, amid thigh-clapping and belly-holding, swelled to a mighty roar when he called out to them with schoolmasterly severity: "Stop that clowning at once!"

The laughers spared A., first because he himself was grinning and second because the hat brim around his neck was less conspicuous; all the same, he considered it his duty to call Zacharias's attention to his merriment-inspiring headdress. The outcome, however, was rather startling, for now the Studienrat's anger, though tinged with sorrow, turned against him: "*Et tu, Brute.* I sacrifice my good hat to you and you deliver me up to the mockery of the plebs; *non libet* . . . what ingratitude!" But then the young man had an opportunity to show his loyalty and friendship and devotion: carrying out Zacharias's previous instructions, he slipped the brim over his head, and with a sweeping gesture saluted the howling mob, so provoking applause from which Zacharias also benefited.

Nevertheless, mockery always leaves its barb in a human soul, and so it did in the soul of the wounded Zacharias. No sooner were they out of sight of the hostile levity than he stopped again and said: "I am indignant, profoundly and shamefully indignant." "My goodness," said the young man soothingly, "the poor fellows work so hard; they need a bit of fun once in a while." At this the Studienrat grew very angry. "I'll teach them to have fun, fun at other people's expense. . . . Do you call that brotherhood?"—"No, freedom and equality."—"Aha, so that's the lay of the land . . . freedom and equality; I prefer to call it insolent clowning." And angrily he went a few steps further.

But the cue had been dropped, and stopping once more, he, Studienrat Zacharias, launched into his fourth speech, which may be regarded as a testamentary summation of his three preceding speeches. The unpleasant incident had evidently brought home to him the necessity of developing their social implications.

"Clowning is and remains clowning. I, a friend of the working class, I, a Social Democrat, I, a leading member of the teachers' union, do not hesitate for one moment to declare that clowning is and remains clowning. Those men—men, mind you, not boys, not children—have behaved most clownishly. This irresponsible clowning was directed against me, but I mention that as a mere footnote. The essential lies in the terrifying irresponsibility, yes terrifying, truly terrifying to anyone concerned with the development of our people. For how, we must ask, can this people become the schoolmaster of the world if such irresponsibility is at work in its most basic class, namely, the working class? And here I shall even go one step further and ask: can we apply the term 'responsible' to a trade union which obtains higher wages for the workers and demands only one thing in return: that they vote Socialist? *Panem et circenses!* I have no doubt that those men are perfectly satisfied! All they want is their bread and their fun and their women to sleep with. That's the freedom and equality they dream of. But what then becomes of the infinite to which they as Germans are or ought to be committed? What becomes of the true democracy rooted in the infinite grandeur of death? They want to be softened, not hardened, they want life, the comfort of blindness to death; they want to go on living in this-worldliness. And that has made them fearful of death and un-German, an easy prey for the degenerate Western democracies and their doctrines which seek to overcome disgust through soft living rather than by death-oriented discipline. Are we to be condemned to such unfitness and hence failure? No, a thousand times no! Only the totality is truly free, not the individual. The individual, to put it concisely, is subject to the command of freedom, a higher freedom; his only freedom in his share in the freedom of the totality, and never, never will it be possible or permissible for him to claim personal freedom. We must make a clean break with shopkeeper's freedom, and it is incumbent upon the unions to carry on the indispensable educational groundwork. We need planned freedom; the shallow, chaotic, clownish freedom of the West must be replaced by a freedom that is directed and planned. Here I stand; in self-discipline I am wearing a brimless hat that strikes them as ridiculous; I am wearing it to express my brotherly sentiment, and

I defy the laughter of the West. An equality in the face of commands, an equality of discipline and self-discipline will be ours, a hierarchical equality according to the age, rank and achievement of our citizens, a well-balanced pyramid, and the most excellent will be called to the head, a wise and severe disciplinarian and leader, himself subject to discipline, the guarantor of our brotherhood. How else can it be done? All brotherhood needs a father, needs grandfathers, needs a long line of ancestors to guarantee the unity of the whole and the doubt-dispelling solidity of things. Through chastisement to love, that is our way; it leads to the love which transcends death because it is at all times prepared for death, the love in which, beyond death disgust, animality and infinity are timelessly united. That is the way, and it is the duty of German democracy to travel it, striding forward in self-discipline and so achieving the leadership of the new International."

Soft thunder had become audible while the speech was still in progress, and the distant storm was no doubt responsible for the trickles of coolness which had been infiltrating the sultry air and were now becoming more and more frequent and perceptible. At the sound of the distant rumbling, Zacharias became almost ecstatic: "The All, angrily prepared to chastise in its infinity—the maternal All agrees with me . . . can you hear it? Or have you again failed to understand?"

"Of course not," said the younger man. "I understand; the Germans will be very busy."

"That is their destiny. They cannot and shall not elude it."

"No, but I'm going to elude the storm . . . come on, we'll take a cab; I'll drop you off at your home."

"No, I want to walk; I always walk home from school, for the fresh air. Anyway, it's not far."

"But I'm tired."

"Soldiers must march. Don't be lazy; the faster you march, the more surely you'll escape the storm." And Zacharias set himself in motion.

They strode through a park. It was a place of many statues, some seated, some standing, each framed in picturesquely ordered shrubbery, their marble even whiter, their bronze more scintillant in the lamplight than by day. The professions of most of the individuals portrayed were indicated by the usual accessories, book, scroll, sword, brush and palette. Then the marchers sighted a likeness characterized by none of these, but by Indian clubs and dumbbells; bronze, they nestled against might bronze top boots, out of which, standing on supporting leg and free-moving leg, arose a long-bearded bronze man, hair waving in the still air, plumes waving on the soft hat in his hand. Before the statue Zacharias stopped and barked a command: "Attention! Brim off!" And this was as it should be, for when A., brim in hand, approached the stone pedestal with its crotchety Gothic inscription, he deciphered these words: "Friedrich Ludwig Jahn, Father of German Gymnastics, 1778–1852. He Made the Nation Fit." Yes, indeed, a salute was in order, and Zacharias laughed: "He will be standing here long after Einstein is dead and gone."

They left the park. Again the thunder rumbled, again the young man wanted to look for a cab. And again the older man dragged him onward: "Come on, come on, we'll be home in a minute."—"That's just it," said the younger. "Maybe it won't be possible to find a cab later on; besides, you really don't need me any more."—"Dead wrong and on the contrary, this is just when I do need you," said Zacharias. And then with a guile born of anxiety: "I need you all right, those stairs are hard for a wounded war veteran to take; my good wife Philippine will be grateful if you help me up."—"At this time of night your esteemed wife will be sound asleep."—"Dead wrong and on the contrary, she is waiting for me with tender trepidation."—"In that case she won't be very happy about your bringing a visitor."—Zacharias clung to his phrase: "Dead wrong and on the contrary, you're not a visitor, you're a protector, and as a guest you will be under my protection. A savage would offer you his wife for the night. The least Philippine can do is give you a friendly welcome." At that moment the storm wind sent out a none too violent but menacing gust, a sample, as it were, of what it could do. "Is it really so near?"—"Only a few steps more . . . and if it really starts coming down we'll just keep you overnight."

And indeed, two blocks further on, in a typical red-brick middle-class street—apartment houses, each with a strip of iron-fenced, tree-dotted lawn in front of it—they came to Zacharias's door. As he rummaged in his trousers pocket for his key, the pressure on his abdomen released a great peal of thunder—"Forgive me, brother, it purifies the air!"—And when he had managed to find the key, he switched on the light in the stairwell.

Whether by design, to prove that he needed help, or because his liquor consumption had actually impaired his stair-climbing ability, the higher Zacharias climbed on the squeaking, groaning wooden steps, the more slowly he moved, the more deeply he sighed, the more pitiful became his mien, and the more often A. had to seize him under the arms. Upstairs they found the apartment door wide open; no doubt of it, the Frau Studienrat had observed their coming, and, to be sure, she was waiting in the doorway.

She was a woman in her thirties, whose small stature made her look somewhat older; despite its excessive cushions of fat and malignantly-energetically pursed lips, her face was by no means unattractive, and her hair, though sparse and disorderly, was a pure, vigorous blond. Her rather too stout but well-shaped legs ended in felt slippers. Over her pink dress she wore a loose-fitting, cotton flower-printed housecoat, and in her hand she held a feather duster, motley-bright cock feathers on a thin cane, an instrument of housework with which regardless of the late hour—it was long past midnight—she had apparently been whiling away her wait. Yet though she had waited, the reception was by no means as friendly as Zacharias had predicted. Her greeting was terse: "Two drunks."

An understandable observation in view of the picture the two climbers offered her. For her husband was still wearing the brimless crown of his hat and his companion still had the brim around his neck. With clenched fists, one holding the feather duster, the other propped on her hip, she let the two of them in without another word and silently, with a toss of her chin, directed them to the living room, whither after resolutely slamming the outer door she followed them.

Here under the eyes of Bebel, Scheidemann and Wilhelm II, she measured the two with a cold gaze. The Studienrat, who had been standing with bowed head, ventured to look up: "Philip- . . ." But he got no further. "Into the corner!" she snapped, and apparently in observance of an old custom, he went immediately into one of the corners. Then Philippine, paying no further attention to him, turned to the young man: "I take it you've been having a rather liquid discussion. Am I right? And you'd like to continue it here? I suppose I should be glad that it's just you and he hasn't brought ten more companions of science."—"Philippine," came a lamentable voice from the corner. Philippine was unmoved. "You be still. Face to the wall!" And having made sure that her command had been carried out, she returned to the visitor: "What should I do with you? Should I put you in the corner, too? Is that what he brought you here for? Maybe you'd better just get on home." Again the voice from the corner was heard: "Philippine, my sweet!"—"You be still!"—"I'll be good; let's go to bed."—"You heard me!" Philippine had turned round abruptly. Seizing the duster by the feather end, she snapped the cane through the air. It descended on her husband's posterior, instantly followed by another blow that sent the dust flying. Zacharias, his face turned to the wall, moaned but did not move. On the contrary, he bent slightly forward and seemed to be waiting for the performance to continue.

"Well," said Philippine to the young man. "I hardly think you'll want to try it"—she indicated the handle of the feather duster—"so you'd better run along."

"Don't send him away," said the pleading voice in the corner. "Let him stay with me. Please."

The stern expression of Philippine's face turned to naked rage, and she lost all control. "Shut up, shut up!" she screamed. Her voice cracked. "Not another word! Not a blessed word! Understand?" And with the swing of a golf player if not of a professional executioner, she lashed so hard that the cane bent, scarcely noticing what she was hitting, back or rear end, but striking again and again without letup.

At first silent and immobile, his posterior slightly protruding for the executioner's benefit, Zacharias moaned: "Yes, yes . . . oh, yes . . . more, more, more . . . drive the disgust out of my body . . . make me strong, my angel . . . whip the disgust out of my body . . . yes, yes . . . oh, Philippine, my sweet, I love you . . . more . . . more . . ." But when he started undoing his suspenders, the execution was suddenly interrupted. He turned around in surprise, and glassy-eyed, still with the crown of his hat on his head, staggered toward his wife: "Philippine, I love you."

With the feather duster she knocked the crown off his head and at the same time held him at a distance. With the other hand she took the young man by the shoulder. "Maybe you meant well in coming here; he probably pleaded and whined, and you wanted to help him. And maybe you even want to help me now. But you can't help someone who's living in hell. When a house is hell, it can only get worse and worse. And believe me, it will get worse. We haven't reached our last hell; far from it. Yes, young man, you've had a glimpse of hell, and now the best thing you can do is wipe it out of your memory. Forget it!" All this was said in a quiet tone; but when the young man did not budge, she bellowed in his face: "Out!"

When he opened the street door, big angry raindrops lashed his face; one more step and he would have been wet to the skin. The storm was at its height. Flash followed flash, the water flowed over the black asphalt in long flat waves, swelled into brooks in the gutters, and gurgled around the sewer gratings before hurtling downward as though driven by some inner rage. The streetlamps and the houses across the way were reflected in the black flood, their images reaching down to motionless depths, and every lightning flash brought underwater fireworks. A. pressed close to the house door, and it was a good half-hour before the lightning flashes became paler and less frequent, the thunder died down, and the rain dwindled and finally stopped. The air was peacefully cool. Leaving his shelter, A. looked up at the Studienrat's apartment; the two living-room windows were still brightly lit and so were the two adjoining windows, which presumably belonged to the bedroom; but here the curtains had been drawn.

Up there was hell, yes, the heart of hell. Not the only one, but one of the many scattered about the world, in Germany perhaps a little more densely than elsewhere, and everywhere embedded in the innocuous. Everywhere the menace of hell was enclosed and hidden. The city lay shrouded in the innocuous tranquility of night, and A. had an easy walk home. He sensed the breath of the hills, the breath of the countryside spread out around the city, the vast expanse of inhabited nature. Out there lie fields and the German forest, where trees and game are protected, where the deer still browse, the wild boar still grub, and in its season the rutting cry of the stag still resounds through the shady dampness. The tinkling of cowbells traverses the mountains and the peasant does his hard day's work regardless of the regime that has been set over him, but also regardless of the diabolical cravings that may rage in his own heart; neither the one nor the other deters him from his work. The Germans are more reasonable, more circumspect than other peoples, but at the same time more diabolical, more greedy, more at the mercy of their instincts. The Germans are less sanctimonious than other peoples, but at the same time more fraudulent. For the German seems to have an innate craving for the absolute, which makes him disdain the easy, goodhumored taming of instinct which Western man, though his instincts are often the stronger, looks upon as a principle worth striving for. Humor comes hard to the German, and when he has it, it is a different, a twisted kind of humor, the humor of the circumspect alternative. That is what characterizes his way of life and makes it so ponderous, a fluctuation between total asceticism and unrestrained eruption of the instincts. The German despises in-between solutions; he regards them as sanctimonious and fraudulent, unaware that in taking this attitude he falls into a worse fraudulence, that though he does not assume a false halo, the artificial halo of the West, he instead—and that is surely worse—misrepresents wrong as right by calling his unrestrained bestiality reason, playing it off against the superior right of humanity, and so doing violence to right as such. His honesty is that of the violent man who, in his determination to drive the falsehood out of the world's peace-loving swindlers, regards himself as a bringer of salvation and yet is inevitably a bringer of disaster, because his doctrine is murder. On both sides untruth, and in between, ever so narrow, the path of truth, the path between two worlds, visible to be sure to German man but evidently—because of his incessant stumbling and staggering—closed to him. Was this the path of German virtue? No, dead wrong and on the contrary, as Zacharias would say, though he was blind to the truth, namely, that it is a path of fear and torment.

Whey was that? A. knew no answer. And after all, what business was it of his? Why worry his head? He had reached home and went straight to bed; he had earned his rest.

Elias Canetti

The Morning Walk

'What are you doing here, my little man?'
      'Nothing.'
'Then why are you standing here?'
'Just because.'
'Can you read?'
'Oh, yes.'
'How old are you?'
'Nine and a bit.'
'Which would you prefer, a piece of chocolate or a book?'
'A book.'
'Indeed? Splendid! So that's your reason for standing here?'
'Yes.'
'Why didn't you say so before?'
'Father scolds me.'
'Oh. And who is your father?'
'Franz Metzger.'
'Would you like to travel to a foreign country?'
'Yes. To India. They have tigers there.'
'And where else?'
'To China. They've got a huge wall there.'
'You'd like to scramble over it, wouldn't you?'
'It's much too thick and too high. Nobody can get over it. That's why they built it.'
'What a lot you know! You must have read a great deal already?'

'Yes. I read all the time. Father takes my books away. I'd like to go to a Chinese school. They have forty thousand letters in their alphabet. You couldn't get them all into one book.'

'That's only what you think.'

'I've worked it out.'

'All the same it isn't true. Never mind the books in the window. They're of no value. I've got something much better here. Wait. I'll show you. Do you know what kind of writing that is?'

'Chinese! Chinese!'

'Well, you're a clever little fellow. Had you seen a Chinese book before?'

'No, I guessed it.'

'These two characters stand for Meng Tse, the philosopher Mencius. He was a great man in China. He lived 2250 years ago and his works are still being read. Will you remember that?

'Yes. I must go to school now.'

'Aha, so you look into the bookshop windows on your way to school? What is your name?'

'Franz Metzger, like my father.'

'And where do you live?'

'Twenty-four Ehrlich Strasse.'

'I live there too. I don't remember you.'

'You always look the other way when anyone passes you on the stairs. I've known you for ages. You're Professor Kien, but you haven't a school. Mother says you aren't a real Professor. But I think you are—you've got a library. Our Marie says, you wouldn't believe your eyes. She's our maid. When I'm grown up I'm going to have a library. With all the books there are, in every language. A Chinese one too, like yours. Now I must run.'

'Who wrote this book? Can you remember?'

'Meng Tse, the philosopher Mencius. Exactly 2250 years ago.'

'Excellent. You shall come and see my library one day. Tell my housekeeper I've given you permission. I can show you pictures from India and China.'

'Oh good! I'll come! Of course I'll come! This afternoon?'

'No, no, little man. I must work this afternoon. In a week at the earliest.'

Professor Peter Kien, a tall, emaciated figure, man of learning and specialist in sinology, replaced the Chinese book in the tightly packed brief case which he carried under his arm, carefully closed it and watched the clever little boy out of sight. By nature morose and sparing of his words, he was already reproaching himself for a conversation into which he had entered for no compelling reason.

It was his custom on his morning walk, between seven and eight o'clock, to look into the windows of every book shop which he passed. He was thus able to assure himself, with a kind of pleasure, that smut and trash were daily gaining ground. He himself was the owner of the most important private library in the whole of this great city. He carried a minute portion of it with him wherever he went. His passion for it, the only one which he had permitted himself during a life of austere and exacting study, moved him to take special precautions. Books, even bad ones, tempted him easily into making a purchase. Fortunately the greater number of the book shops did not open until after eight o'clock. Sometimes an apprentice, anxious to earn his chief's approbation, would come earlier and wait on the doorstep for the first employee whom he would ceremoniously relieve of the latch key. 'I've been waiting since seven o'clock,' he would exclaim, or 'I can't get in!' So much zeal communicated itself all too easily to Kien; with an effort he would master the impulse to follow the apprentice immediately into the shop. Among the proprietors of smaller shops there were one or two early risers, who might be seen busying themselves behind their open doors from half past seven onwards. Defying these temptations, Kien tapped his own well-filled brief-case. He clasped it tightly to him, in a very particular manner which he had himself thought out, so that the greatest possible area of his body was always in contact with it. Even his ribs could feel its presence through his cheap, thin suit. His upper arm covered the whole side elevation; it fitted exactly. The lower portion of his arm supported the case from below. His outstretched fingers splayed out over every part of the flat surface to which they yearned. He privately excused himself for this exaggerated care because of the value of the contents. Should the brief case by any mischance fall to the ground, or should the lock, which he tested every morning before setting out, spring open at precisely that perilous moment, ruin would come to his priceless volumes. There was nothing he loathed more intensely than battered books.

To-day, when he was standing in front of a bookshop on his way home, a little boy had stepped suddenly between him and the window. Kien felt affronted by the impertinence. True, there was room enough between him and the window. He always stood about three feet away from the glass; but he could easily read every letter behind it. His eyes functioned to his entire satisfaction: a fact notable enough in a man of forty who sat, day in day out, over books and manuscripts. Morning after morning his eyes informed him how well they did. By keeping his distance from these venal and common books, he showed his contempt for them, contempt which, when he compared them with the dry and ponderous tomes of his library, they richly deserved. The boy was quite small, Kien exceptionally tall. He could easily see over his head. All the same he felt he had a right to greater respect. Before administering a reprimand, however, he drew to one side in order to observe him further. The child stared hard at the titles of the books and moved his lips slowly and in silence. Without a stop his eyes slipped from one volume to the next. Every minute or two he looked back over his shoulder. On the opposite side of the street, over a watchmaker's shop, hung a gigantic clock. It was twenty minutes to eight. Evidently the little fellow was afraid of missing something important. He took no notice whatever of the gentleman standing behind him. Perhaps he was practising his reading. Perhaps he was learning the names of the books by heart. He devoted equal attention to each in turn. You could see at once when anything held up his reading for a second.

Kien felt sorry for him. Here was he, spoiling with this depraved fare an eager spiritual appetite, perhaps already hungry for the written word. How many a worthless book might he not come to read in later life for no better reason than an early familiarity with its title? By what means is the suggestibility of these early years to be reduced? No sooner can a child walk and make out his letters than he is surrendered at mercy to the hard pavement of any ill-built street, and to the wares of any wretched tradesman who, the devil knows why, has set himself up as a dealer in books. Young children ought to be brought up in some important private library. Daily conversation with none but serious minds, an atmosphere at once dim, hushed and intellectual, a relentless training in the most careful ordering both of time and of space,—what surroundings could be more suitable to assist these delicate creatures through the years of childhood? But the only person in this town who possessed a library which could be taken at all seriously was he, Kien, himself. He could not admit children. His work allowed him no such diversions. Children make a noise. They have to be constantly looked after. Their welfare demands the services of a woman. For cooking, an ordinary housekeeper is good enough. For children, it would be necessary to engage a mother. If a mother could be content to be nothing but a mother: but where would you find one who would be satisfied with that particular part alone? Each is a specialist first and foremost as a woman, and would make demands which an honest man of learning would not even dream of fulfilling. Kien repudiated the idea of a wife. Women had been a matter of indifference to him until this moment; a matter of indifference they would remain. The boy with the fixed eyes and the moving head would be the loser.

Pity had moved him to break his usual custom and speak to him. He would gladly have bought himself free of the prickings of his pedagogic conscience with the gift of a piece of chocolate. Then it appeared that there are nine-year-old children who prefer a book to a piece of chocolate. What followed surprised him even more. The child was interested in China. He read against his father's will. The stories of the difficulties of the Chinese alphabet fascinated instead of frightening him. He recognized the language at first sight, without having seen it before. He had passed an intelligence test with distinction. When shown the book, he had not tried to touch it. Perhaps he was ashamed of his dirty hands. Kien had looked at them: they were clean. Another boy would have snatched the book, even with dirty ones. He was in a hurry—school began at eight— yet he had stayed until the last possible minute. He had fallen upon that invitation like one starving; his father must be a great torment to him. He would have liked best to come on that very afternoon, in the middle of the working day. After all, he lived in the same house.

Kien forgave himself for the conversation. The exception which he had permitted seemed worth while. In his thoughts he saluted the child—now already out of sight—as a rising sinologist. Who indeed took an interest in these remote branches of knowledge? Boys played football, adults went to work; they wasted their leisure hours in love. So as to sleep for eight hours and waste eight hours, they were willing to devote themselves for the rest of their time to hateful work. Not only their bellies, their whole bodies had become

their gods. The sky God of the Chinese was sterner and more dignified. Even if the little fellow did not come next week, unlikely
though that was, he would have a name in his head which he would
not easily forget: the philosopher Mong. Occasional collisions unexpectedly encountered determine the direction of a lifetime.

Smiling, Kien continued on his way home. He smiled rarely.
Rarely, after all, is it the dearest wish of a man to be the owner of
a library. As a child of nine he had longed for a book shop. Yet the
idea that he would walk up and down in it as its proprietor had
seemed to him even then blasphemous. A bookseller is a king, and
a king cannot be a bookseller. But he was still too little to be a sales-
man. As for an errand boy—errand boys were always being sent
out of the shop. What pleasure would he have of the books, if he
was only allowed to carry them as parcels under his arm? For a long
while he sought for some way out of the difficulty. One day he did
not come home after school. He went into the biggest bookstore in
the town, six great show windows all full of books, and began to
howl at the top of his voice. 'I want to leave the room, quick, I'm
going to have an accident!' he blubbered. They showed him the way
at once. He took careful note of it. When he came out again he
thanked them and asked if he could not do something to help. His
beaming face made them laugh. Only a few moments before it had
been screwed up into such comic anguish. They drew him out in
conversation; he knew a great deal about books. They thought him
sharp for his age. Towards the evening they sent him away with a
heavy parcel. He travelled there and back on the tram. He had
saved enough pocket money to afford it. Just as the shop was closing—it was already growing dark—he announced that he had completed his errand and put down the receipt on the counter. Someone
gave him an acid drop for a reward. While the staff were pulling on
their coats he glided noiselessly into the back regions to his lavatory
hide-out and bolted himself in. Nobody noticed it; they were all
thinking of the free evening before them. He waited a long time.
Only after many hours, late at night, did he dare to come out. It was
dark in the shop. He felt about for a switch. He had not thought of
that by daylight. But when he found it and his hand had already
closed over it, he was afraid to turn on the light. Perhaps someone
would see him from the street and haul him off home.

His eyes grew accustomed to the darkness. But he could not read; that was a great pity. He pulled down one volume after another, turned over the pages, contrived to make out many of the names. Later on he scrambled up on to the ladder. He wanted to know if the upper shelves had any secrets to hide. He tumbled off it and said: I haven't hurt myself! The floor is hard. The books are soft. In a book shop one falls on books. He could have made a castle of books, but he regarded disorder as vulgar and, as he took out each new volume, he replaced the one before. His back hurt. Perhaps he was only tired. At home he would have been asleep long ago. Not here, excitement kept him awake. But his eyes could not even make out the largest titles any more and that annoyed him. He worked out how many years he would be able to spend reading in this shop without ever going out into the street or to that silly school. Why could he not stay here always? He could easily save up to buy himself a small bed. His mother would be afraid. So was he, but only a little, because it was so very quiet. The gas lamps in the street went out. Shadows crept along the walls. So there *were* ghosts. During the night they came flying here and crouched over the books. Then they read. They needed no light, they had such big eyes. Now he would not touch a single book on the upper shelves, nor on the lower ones either. He crept under the counter and his teeth chattered. Ten thousand books and a ghost crouching over each one. That was why it was so quiet. Sometimes he heard them turn over a page. They read as fast as he did himself. He might have grown used to them, but there were ten thousand of them and perhaps one of them would bite. Ghosts get cross if you brush against them, they think you are making fun of them. He made himself as small as possible; they flew over him without touching him. Morning came only after many long nights. Then he fell asleep. He did not hear the assistants opening up the shop. They found him under the counter and shook him awake. First he pretended that he was still asleep, then he suddenly burst out howling. They had locked him in last night, he was afraid of his mother, she must have been looking for him everywhere. The proprietor cross-questioned him and as soon as he had found out his name, sent him off home with one of the shopwalkers. He sent his sincerest apologies to the lady. The little boy had been locked in by mistake, but he seemed to be safe and sound. He assured her of his respectful attention. His mother believed it all and was delighted to have him safely home again. To-day the little liar of yesterday was the owner of a famous library and a name no less famous.

Kien abhorred falsehood; from his earliest childhood he had held fast to the truth. He could remember no other falsehood except this. And even this one was hateful to him. Only the conversation with the schoolboy, who had seemed to him the image of his own childhood, had recalled it to him. Forget it, he thought, it is nearly eight o'clock. Punctually at eight his work began, his service for truth. Knowledge and truth were for him identical terms. You draw closer to truth by shutting yourself off from mankind. Daily life was a superficial clatter of lies. Every passer-by was a liar. For that reason he never looked at them. Who among all these bad actors, who made up the mob, had a face to arrest his attention. They changed their faces with every moment; not for one single day did they stick to the same part. He had always known this, experience was superfluous. *His* ambition was to persist stubbornly in the same manner of existence. Not for a mere month, not for a year, but for the whole of his life, he would be true to himself. Character, if you had a character, determined your outward appearance. Ever since he had been able to think, he had been tall and too thin. He knew his face only casually, from its reflection in bookshop windows. He had no mirror in his house, there was no room for it among the books. But he knew that his face was narrow, stern and bony; that was enough.

Since he felt not the slightest desire to notice anyone, he kept his eyes lowered or raised above their heads. He sensed where the book shops were without looking. He simply relied on instinct. The same force which guides a horse home to the stable, served as well for him. He went out walking to breathe the air of alien books, they aroused his antagonism, they stimulated him. In his library everything went by clockwork. But between seven and eight he allowed himself a few of those liberties which constitute the entire life of other beings.

Although he savoured this hour to the full, he did all by rote. Before crossing a busy street, he hesitated a little. He preferred to walk at a regular pace; so as not to hasten his steps, he waited for a favourable moment to cross. Suddenly he heard someone shouting loudly at someone else: 'Can you tell me where Mut Strasse is?'

There was no reply. Kien was surprised: so there were other silent people besides himself to be found in the busy streets. Without looking up he listened for more. How would the questioner behave in the face of this silence? 'Excuse me please, could you perhaps tell me where Mut Strasse is?' So; he grew more polite; he had no better luck. The other man still made no reply. 'I don't think you heard me. I'm asking you the way. Will you be so kind as to tell me how I get to Mut Strasse?' Kien's appetite for knowledge was whetted; idle curiosity he did not know. He decided to observe this silent man, on condition of course that he still remained silent. Not a doubt of it, the man was deep in thought and determined to avoid any interruption. Still he said nothing. Kien applauded him. Here was one among thousands, a man whose character was proof against all chances. 'Here, are you deaf?' shouted the first man. Now he will have to answer back, thought Kien, and began to lose his pleasure in his protégé. Who can control his tongue when he is insulted? He turned towards the street; the favourable moment for crossing it had come. Astonished at the continued silence, he hesitated. Still the second man said nothing. All the more violent would be the outburst of anger to come. Kien hoped for a fight. If the second man appeared after all to be a mere vulgarian, Kien would be confirmed in his own estimation of himself as the sole and only person of character walking in this street. He was already considering whether he should look round. The incident was taking place on his right hand. The first man was now yelling: 'You've no manners! I spoke to you civil. Who do you think you are? You lout. Are you dumb?' The second man was still silent. 'I demand an apology! Do you hear?' The other did not hear. He rose even higher in the estimation of the listener. 'I'll fetch the police! What do you take me for! You rag and bone man! Call yourself a gentleman! Where did you get those clothes? Out of the rag bag? That's what they look like! What have you got under your arm! I'll show you! Go and boil your head! Who do you think you are?'

Then Kien felt a nasty jolt. Someone had grabbed his brief-case and was pulling at it. With a movement far exceeding his usual effort, he liberated the books from the alien clutch and turned sharply to the right. His glance was directed to his brief-case, but it fell instead on a small fat man who was bawling up at him. 'You lout! You lout! You lout!' The other man, the silent one, the man of character, who controlled his tongue even in anger, was Kien himself. Calmly he turned his back on the gesticulating illiterate. With this small knife, he sliced his clamour in two. A loutish creature whose courtesy changed in so many seconds to insolence had no power to hurt him. Nevertheless he walked along the streets a little faster than was his usual custom. A man who carries books with him must seek to avoid physical violence. He always had books with him.

There is after all no obligation to answer every passing fool according to his folly. The greatest danger which threatens a man of learning, is to lose himself in talk. Kien preferred to express himself in the written rather than the spoken word. He knew more than a dozen oriental languages. A few of the western ones did not even need to be learnt. No branch of human literature was unfamiliar to him. He thought in quotations and wrote in carefully considered sentences. Countless texts owed their restoration to him. When he came to misreadings or imperfections in ancient Chinese, Indian or Japanese manuscripts, as many alternative readings suggested themselves for his selection as he could wish. Other textual critics envied him; he for his part had to guard against a superfluity of ideas. Meticulously cautious, he weighed up the alternatives month after month, was slow to the point of exasperation; applying his severest standards to his own conclusions, he took no decision, on a single letter, a word or an entire sentence, until he was convinced that it was unassailable. The papers which he had hitherto published, few in number, yet each one the starting point for a hundred others, had gained for him the reputation of being the greatest living authority on sinology. They were known in every detail to his colleagues, indeed almost word for word. A sentence once set down by him was decisive and binding. In controversial questions he was the ultimate appeal, the leading authority even in related branches of knowledge. A few only he honoured with his letters. That man, however, whom he chose so to honour would receive in a single letter enough stimuli to set him off on years of study, the results of which—in the view of the mind whence they had sprung—were foregone conclusions. Personally he had no dealings with anyone. He refused all invitations. Whenever any chair of oriental philology fell vacant, it was offered first to him. Polite but contemptuous, he invariably declined.

He had not, he averred, been born to be an orator. Payment for his work would give him a distaste for it. In his own humble opinion, those unproductive popularizers to whom instruction in the grammar schools was entrusted, should occupy the university chairs also; then genuine, creative research workers would be able to devote themselves exclusively to their own work. As it was there was no shortage of mediocre intelligences. Should he give lectures, the high demands which he would necessarily make upon an audience would naturally very much reduce its numbers. As for examinations, not a single candidate, as far as he could see, would be able to pass them. He would make it a point of honour to fail these young immature students at least until their thirtieth year, by which time, either through very boredom or through a dawning of real seriousness, they must have learnt something, if only a very little. He regarded the acceptance of candidates whose memories had not been most carefully tested in the lecture halls of the faculty as a totally useless, if not indeed a questionable, practice. Ten students, selected by the most strenuous preliminary tests, would, provided they remained together, achieve far more than they could do when permitted to mingle with a hundred beer-swilling dullards, the general run of university students. His doubts were therefore of the most serious and fundamental nature. He could only request the faculty to withdraw an offer which, although intended no doubt to show the high esteem in which they held him, was not one which he could accept in that spirit.

At scholastic conferences, where there is usually a great deal of talk, Kien was a much-discussed personality. The learned gentlemen, who for the greater part of their lives were silent, timid and myopic mice, on these occasions, every two years or so, came right out of themselves; they welcomed each other, stuck the most inapposite heads together, whispered nonsense in corners and toasted each other clumsily at the dinner table. Deeply moved and profoundly gratified, they raised aloft the banner of learning and upheld the integrity of their aims. Over and over again in all languages they repeated their vows. They would have kept them even without taking them. In the intervals they made bets. Would Kien really come this time? He was more spoken of than a merely famous colleague; his behaviour excited curiosity. But he would not trade on his fame; for the last ten years he had stubbornly refused invitations to banquets and congresses where, in spite of his youth, he would have been warmly acclaimed; he announced for every conference an important paper, which was then read for him from his own manuscript by another scholar: all this his colleagues regarded as mere postponement. The time would come—perhaps this was the time—when he would suddenly make his appearance, would graciously accept the applause which his long retirement had made only the more vociferous, and would permit himself to be acclaimed president of the assembly, an office which was only his due, and which indeed he arrogated to himself after his own fashion even by his absence. But his learned colleagues were mistaken. Kien did not appear. The more credulous of them lost their bets.

At the last minute he refused. Sending the paper he had written to a privileged person, he would add some ironical expressions of regret. In the event of his colleagues finding time for serious study in the intervals of a programme so rich in entertainment—an eventuality which in the interests of their general satisfaction he could hardly desire—he asked leave to lay before the conference this small contribution to knowledge, the result of two years' work. He would carefully save up any new and surprising conclusions to which his researches might have brought him for moments such as these. Their effects and the discussions to which they gave rise, he would follow from a distance, suspiciously and in detail, as though probing their textual accuracy. The gatherings were ready enough to accept his contempt. Eighty out of every hundred present relied entirely on his judgment. His services to science were inestimable. Long might he live. To most of them indeed his death would have been a severe shock.

Those few who had known him in his earlier years had forgotten what his face was like. Repeatedly he received letters asking for his photograph. He had none, he would answer, nor did he intend to have one taken. Both statements were true. But he had willingly agreed to a different sort of concession. As a young man of thirty he had, without however making any other testamentary dispositions, bequeathed his skull with all its contents to an institute for cranial research. He justified this step by considering the advantage to be gained if it could be scientifically proved that his truly phenomenal memory was the result of a particular structure, or perhaps even a heavier weight, of brain. Not indeed that he considered—so he wrote to the head of the institute—that memory and genius were the same thing, a theory all too widely accepted of recent years. He himself was no genius. Yet it would be unscholarly to deny that the almost terrifying memory at his disposal had been remarkably useful in his learned researches. He did indeed carry in his head a library as well-provided and as reliable as his actual library, which he understood was so much discussed.. He could sit at his writing desk and sketch out a treatise down to the minutest detail without turning over a single page, except in his head. Naturally he would check quotations and sources later out of the books themselves; but only because he was a man of conscience. He could not remember any single occasion on which his memory had been found at fault. His very dreams were more precisely defined than those of most people. Blurred images without form or colour were unknown in any of the dreams which he had hitherto recollected. In his case night had no power to turn things topsy turvy; the noises he heard could be exactly referred to their cause of origin; conversations into which he entered were entirely reasonable; everything retained its normal meaning. It was outside his sphere to examine the probable connection between the accuracy of his memory and the lucidity of his dreams. In all humility he drew attention to the facts alone, and hoped that the personal data which he had taken the liberty of recording would be regarded as a sign neither of pretentiousness nor garrulity.

Kien called to mind one or two more facts from his daily life, which showed his retiring, untalkative and wholly unpresumptuous nature in its true light. But his irritation at the insolent and insufferable fellow who had first asked him the way and then abused him, grew greater with every step. There is nothing else I can do, he said at last; he stepped aside into the porch of a house, looked round—nobody was watching him—and drew a long narrow notebook from his pocket. On the title page, in tall, angular letters was written the word: STUPIDITIES. His eyes rested at first on this. Then he turned over the pages; more than half the note-book was full. Everything he would have preferred to forget he put down in this book. Date, time and place came first. Then followed the incident which was supposed to illustrate the stupidity of mankind. An apt quotation, a new one for each occasion, formed the conclusion. He never read these collected examples of stupidity; a glance at the title page sufficed. Later on he thought of publishing them under the title 'Morning Walks of a Sinologist.'

He drew out a sharply pointed pencil and wrote down on the first empty page: 'September 23rd, 7:45 a.m. In Mut Strasse a person crossed my path and asked me the way to Mut Strasse. In order not to put him to shame, I made no answer. He was not to be put off and asked again, several times; his bearing was courteous. Suddenly his eye fell upon the street sign. He became aware of his stupidity. Instead of withdrawing as fast as he could—as I should have done in his place—he gave way to the most unmeasured rage and abused me in the vulgarest fashion. Had I not spared him in the first place, I would have spared myself this painful scene. Which of us was the stupider?'

With that last sentence he proved that he did not draw the line even at his *own* failings. He was pitiless towards everyone. Gratified, he put away his notebook and forgot the man in the Mut Strasse. While he was writing, his books had slipped into an uncomfortable position. He shifted them into their right place. At the next street corner he was startled by an Alsatian. Swift and surefooted the dog cleared itself a path through the crowd. At the extremity of a tautened lead it tugged a blind man. His infirmity—for anyone who failed to notice the dog—was further emphasized by the white stick which he carried in his right hand. Even those passers-by who were in too much of a hurry to stare at the blind man, cast an admiring glance at the dog. He pushed them gently to one side with his patient muzzle. As he was a fine, handsome dog they bore with him gladly. Suddenly the blind man pulled his cap off his head and, clutching it in the same hand as his white stick, held it out towards the crowd. 'To buy my dog bones!' he begged. Coins showered into it. In the middle of the street a crowd gathered round the two of them. The traffic was held up: luckily there was no policeman at this corner to direct it. Kien observed the beggar from close at hand. He was dressed with studied poverty and his face seemed educated. The muscles round his eyes twitched continually—he winked, raised his eyebrows and wrinkled his forehead—so that Kien mistrusted him and decided to regard him as a fraud. At that moment a boy of about twelve came up, hurriedly pushed the dog to one side and threw into the cap a large heavy button. The blind man stared in front of him and thanked him, per-

haps in the slightest degree more warmly than before. The clink of
the button as it fell into the cap had sounded like the ring of gold.
Kien felt a pang in his heart. He caught the boy by the scruff of the
neck and cuffed him over the head with his brief-case. 'For shame,'
he said, 'deceiving a blind man!' Only after he had done it did he
recollect what was in the brief-case: books. He was horrified. Never
before had he taken so great a risk. The boy ran off howling. To
restore his normal and far less exalted level of compassion, Kien
emptied his entire stock of small change into the blind man's cap.
The bystanders approved aloud; to himself the action seemed more
petty and cautious than the preceding one. The dog set off again.
Immediately after, just as a policeman appeared on the scene, both
leader and led had resumed their brisk progress.

Kien took a private vow that if he should ever be threatened by
blindness, he would die of his own free will. Whenever he met a
blind man this same cruel fear clutched at him. Mutes he loved: the
deaf, the lame and other kinds of cripples meant nothing to him;
the blind disturbed him. He could not understand why they did not
make an end of themselves. Even if they could read braille, their
opportunities for reading were limited. Eratosthenes, the great librarian of Alexandria, a scholar of universal significance who
flourished in the third century of the pre-Christian era and held
sway over more than half a million manuscript scrolls, made in his
eightieth year a terrible discovery. His eyes began to refuse their office. He could still see but he could not read. Another man might
have waited until he was completely blind. He felt that to take leave
of his books was blindness enough. Friends and pupils implored
him to stay with them. He smiled wisely, thanked them, and in a
few days starved himself to death.

Should the time come this great example could easily be followed
even by the lesser Kien, whose library comprised a mere twenty-five
thousand volumes.

The remaining distance to his own house he completed at a
quickened pace. It must be past eight o'clock. At eight o'clock his
work began; unpunctuality caused him acute irritation. Now and
again, surreptitiously he felt his eyes. They focused correctly; they
felt comfortable and unthreatened.

His library was situated on the fourth and topmost floor of No.
24 Ehrlich Strasse. The door of the flat was secured by three highly

complicated locks. He unlocked them, strode across the hall, which
contained nothing except an umbrella and coat-stand, and entered
his study. Carefully he set down the brief-case on an armchair. Then
once and again he paced the entire length of the four lofty, spacious
communicating rooms which formed his library. The entire wall-
space up to the ceiling was clothed with books. Slowly he lifted his
eyes towards them. Skylights had been let into the ceiling. He was
proud of his roof-lighting. The windows had been walled up several
years before after a determined struggle with his landlord. In this
way he had gained in every room a fourth wall-space: accommoda-
tion for more books. Moreover illumination from above, which lit
up all the shelves equally, seemed to him more just and more suited
to his relations with his books. The temptation to watch what went
on in the street—an immoral and time-wasting habit—disappeared
with the side windows. Daily, before he sat down to his writing
desk, he blessed both the idea and its results, since he owed to them
the fulfilment of his dearest wish: the possession of a well-stocked
library, in perfect order and enclosed on all sides, in which no single
superfluous article of furniture, no single superfluous person could
lure him from his serious thoughts.

The first of the four rooms served for his study. A huge old writing desk, an armchair in front of it, a second armchair in the opposite corner were its only furniture. There crouched besides an
unobtrusive divan, willingly overlooked by its master: he only slept
on it. A movable pair of steps was propped against the wall. It was
more important than the divan, and travelled in the course of a day
from room to room. The emptiness of the three remaining rooms
was not disturbed by so much as a chair. Nowhere did a table, a
cupboard, a fireplace interrupt the multi-coloured monotony of the
bookshelves. Handsome deep-pile carpets, the uniform covering of
the floor, softened the harsh twilight which, mingling through wide-
open communicating doors, made of the four separate rooms one
single lofty hall.

Kien walked with a stiff and deliberate step. He set his feet down
with particular firmness on the carpets; it pleased him that even a
footfall such as his waked not the faintest echo. In his library it
would have been beyond the power even of an elephant to pound
the slightest noise out of that floor. For this reason he set great store
by his carpets. He satisfied himself that the books were still in the

order in which he had been forced to leave them an hour before. Then he began to relieve his brief-case of its contents. When he came in, it was his habit to lay it down on the chair in front of the writing desk. Otherwise he might perhaps have forgotten it and have sat down to his work before he had tidied away its contents; for at eight o'clock he felt a very strong compulsion to begin his work. With the help of the ladder he distributed the volumes to their appointed places. In spite of all his care—since it was already late, he was hurrying rather more than usual—the last of the books fell from the third bookshelf, a shelf for which he did not even have to use the ladder. It was no other than Mencius beloved above all the rest. 'Idiot!' he shrieked at himself. 'Barbarian! Illiterate!' tenderly lifted the book and went quickly to the door. Before he had reached it an important thought struck him. He turned back and pushed the ladder as softly as he could to the site of the accident. Mencius he laid gently down with both hands on the carpet at the foot of the ladder. Now he could go to the door. He opened it and called into the hall:

'Your best duster, please!'

Almost at once the housekeeper knocked at the door which he had lightly pushed to. He made no answer. She inserted her head modestly through the crack and asked:

'Has something happened?'

'No, give it to me.'

She thought she could detect a complaint in this answer. He had not intended her to. She was too curious to leave the matter where it was. 'Excuse me, Professor!' she said reproachfully, stepped into the room and saw at once what had happened. She glided over to the book. Below her blue starched skirt, which reached to the floor, her feet were invisible. Her head was askew. Her ears were large, flabby and prominent. Since her right ear touched her shoulder and was partly concealed by it, the left looked all the bigger. When she talked or walked her head waggled to and fro. Her shoulders waggled too, in accompaniment. She stooped, lifted up the book and passed the duster over it carefully at least a dozen times. Kien did not attempt to forestall her. Courtesy was abhorrent to him. He stood by and observed whether she performed her work seriously.

'Excuse me, a thing like that can happen, standing up on a ladder.'

Then she handed the book to him, like a plate newly polished. She would very gladly have begun a conversation with him. But she did not succeed. He said briefly, 'Thank you' and turned his back on her. She understood and went. She had already placed her hand on the door knob when he turned round suddenly and asked with simulated friendliness:

'Then this has often happened to you?'

She saw through him and was genuinely indignant: 'Excuse me, Professor.' Her 'Excuse me' struck through her unctuous tones, sharp as a thorn. She will give notice, he thought; and to appease her explained himself:

'I only meant to impress on you what these books represent in terms of money.'

She had not been prepared for so affable a speech. She did not know how to reply and left the room pacified. As soon as she had gone, he reproached himself. He had spoken about books like the vilest tradesman. Yet in what other way could he enforce the respectful handling of books on a person of her kind? Their real value would have no meaning for her. She must believe that the library was a speculation of his. What people! What people!

He bowed involuntarily in the direction of the Japanese manuscripts, and, at last, sat down at his writing desk.

The Secret

Eight years earlier Kien had put the following advertisement in the paper:

> A man of learning who owns an exceptionally large library wants a responsibly-minded housekeeper. Only applicants of the highest character need apply. Unsuitable persons will be shown the door. Money no object.

Therese Krumbholz was at that time in a good position in which she had hitherto been satisfied. She read exhaustively every morning, before getting breakfast for her employers, the advertisement columns of the daily paper, to know what went on in the world. She had no intention of ending her life in the service of a vulgar family. She was still a young person, the right side of fifty, and hoped for a place with a single gentleman. Then she could have things just so; with women in the house it's not the same. But you couldn't expect her to give up here good place for nothing. She'd know who she had to do with before she gave in her notice. You didn't catch her with putting things in the papers, promising the earth to respectable women. You hardly get inside the door and they start taking liberties. Alone in the world now for thirty-three years and such a thing had never happened to her yet. She'd take care it never did, what's more.

This time the advertisement hit her right in the eye. The phrase 'Money no object' made her pause; then she read the sentences, all of which stood out in heavy type, several times backwards and forwards. The tone impressed her: here was a man. It flattered her to think of herself as an applicant of the highest character. She saw the unsuitable persons being shown the door and took a righteous pleasure in their fate. Not for one second did it occur to her that she herself might be treated as an unsuitable person.

On the following morning she presented herself before Kien at the earliest possible moment, seven o'clock. He let her into the hall and immediately declared: 'I must emphatically forbid any stranger whatsoever to enter my house. Are you in a position to take over the custody of the books?'

He observed her narrowly and with suspicion. Before she gave her answer to his question, he would not make up his mind about her. 'Excuse me please,' she said, 'what do you take me for?'

Her stupefaction at his rudeness made her give an answer in which he could find no fault.

'You have a right to know,' he said, 'the reason why I gave notice to my last housekeeper. A book out of my library was missing. I had the whole house searched. It did not come to light. I was thus compelled to give her notice on the spot.' Choked with indignation, he was silent. 'You will understand the necessity,' he added as an afterthought, as though he had made too heavy a demand on her intelligence.

'Everything in its right place,' she answered promptly. He was disarmed. With an ample gesture he invited her into the library. She stepped delicately into the first of the rooms and stood waiting.

'This is the sphere of your duties,' he said in a dry, serious tone of voice. 'Every day one of these rooms must be dusted from floor to ceiling. On the fourth day your work is completed. On the fifth you start again with the first room. Can you undertake this?'

'I make so bold.'

He went out again, opened the door of the flat and said: 'Good morning. You will take up your duties to-day.'

She was already on the stairs and still hesitating. Of her wages, he had said nothing. Before she gave up her present place she must ask him. No, better not. One false step. If she said nothing, perhaps he would give more of his own accord. Over the two conflicting forces, caution and greed, a third prevailed: curiosity.

'Yes, and about my wages?' Embarrassed by the mistake which she was perhaps making, she forgot to add her 'excuse me.'

'Whatever you like,' he said indifferently and closed the door.

She informed her horrified employers—they relied entirely on her, an old piece of furniture in the house for twelve years—that she

wouldn't put up with such goings on any more, she'd rather beg her
bread in the street. No arguments could move her from her purpose. She was going at once; when you have been in the same position for twelve years, you can make an exception of the usual
month's notice. The worthy family seized the opportunity of saving
her wages up to the 20th. They refused to pay them since the creature would not stay her month out. Therese thought to herself: I
shall get it out of him, and went.

She fulfilled her duty towards the books to Kien's satisfaction.
He expressed his recognition of the fact by silence. To praise her
openly in her presence seemed to him unnecessary. His meals were
always punctual. Whether she cooked well or badly he did not
know; it was a matter of total indifference to him. During his meals,
which he ate at his writing desk, he was busy with important considerations. As a rule he would not have been able to say what precisely he had in his mouth. He reserved consciousness for real
thoughts; they depend upon it; without consciousness, thoughts are
unthinkable. Chewing and digesting happen of themselves.

Therese had a certain respect for his work, for he paid her a high
salary regularly and was friendly to no one; he never even spoke to
her. Sociable people, from a child up, she had always despised; her
mother had been one of that kind. She performed her own tasks
meticulously. She earned her money. Besides, from the very beginning she had a riddle to solve. She enjoyed that.

Punctually at six the Professor got out of his divan bed. Washing
and dressing were soon done. In the evening, before going to bed,
she turned down his divan and pushed the wash-stand, which was
on wheels, into the middle of the study. It was allowed to stand
there for the night. A screen of four sections in Spanish leather
painted with letters in a foreign language was so arranged as to
spare him the disturbing sight. He could not abide articles of furniture. The wash-trolley, as he called it, was an invention of his own,
so constructed that the loathsome object could be disposed of as
soon as it had performed its office. At a quarter past six he would
open his door and violently expel it; it would trundle all the way
down the long passage. Close to the kitchen door it would crash
into the wall. Therese would wait in the kitchen; her own little
room was immediately adjoining. She would open the door and
call: 'Up already?' He made no answer and bolted himself in again.

Then he stayed at home until seven o'clock. Not a soul knew what he did in the long interval until seven o'clock. At other times he always sat at his writing desk and wrote.

The sombre, weighty colossus of a desk was filled to bursting with manuscripts and heavy laden with books. The most cautious stirring of any drawer elicited a shrill squeak. Although the noise was repulsive to him, Kien left the heirloom desk in this state so that the housekeeper, in the event of his absence from home, would know at once if a burglar had got in. Strange species, they usually look for money before they start on the books. He had explained the mechanism of his invaluable desk to Therese, briefly yet exhaustively, in three sentences. He had added, in a meaning tone, that there was no possibility of silencing the squeak; even he was unable to do so. During the day she could hear every time Kien looked out a manuscript. She wondered how he could put up with the noise. At night he shut all his papers away. Until eight in the morning the writing desk remained mute. When she was tidying up she never found anything on it but books and a few yellow papers. She looked in vain for clean paper covered with his own handwriting. It was clear that from a quarter past six until seven in the morning, three whole quarters of an hour, he did no work whatever.

Was he saying his prayers? No, she couldn't believe that. Nobody says their prayers. She had no use for praying. You didn't catch her going to church. Look at the sort of people who go to church. A fine crowd they are, cluttered up together. She didn't hold with all that begging either. You have to give them something because everyone is watching you. What they do with it, heaven knows. Say one's prayers at home—why? A waste of beautiful time. A respectable person doesn't need that sort of thing. She'd always kept herself respectable. Other people could pray for all she cared. But she'd like to know what went on in that room between a quarter past six and seven o'clock. She was not curious, no one could call her that. She didn't poke her nose into other people's business. Women were all alike nowadays. Poking their noses into everything. She got on with her own work. Prices going up something shocking. Potatoes cost double already. How to make the money go round. He locked all four doors. Or else you could have seen something from the next room. So particular as he was too, never wasting a minute!

During his morning walk Therese examined the rooms entrusted to her care. She suspected a secret vice; its nature remained vague. First of all she decided for a woman's body in a trunk. But there wasn't room for that under the carpets and she renounced a horribly mutilated corpse. There was no cupboard to help her speculations; how gladly she would have welcomed one; one against each wall preferably. Then the hideous crime must be concealed somehow behind one of the books. Where else? She might have satisfied her sense of duty by dusting over their spines only; the immoral secret she was tracking down compelled her to look behind each one. She took each out separately, knocked at it—it might be hollow— inserted her coarse, calloused fingers as far back as the wooden panelling, probed about, and at length withdrew them, dissatisfied, shaking her head. Her interest never misled her into overstepping the exact time laid down for her work. Five minutes before Kien unlocked the door, she was already in the kitchen. Calmly and without haste she searched one section of the shelves after another, never missing anything and never quite giving up hope.

During these months of indefatigable research, she couldn't think of taking her money to the post-office. She wouldn't lay a finger on it; who knew what sort of money it might be? She placed the notes, in the order in which he gave them to her, in a large clean envelope, which contained, still in its entirety, the stock of notepaper she had bought twenty years before. Overcoming serious scruples she put the whole into her trunk, with the trousseau, specially selected and beautifully worked, which had taken her many years and hard-earned money to accumulate.

Little by little she realized that she would not get to the bottom of the mystery as easily as all that. She knew how to wait. She was very well as she was. If something were to come to light one day—no one could blame her. She had been over every corner of that library with a fine-tooth comb. Of course if you had a friend in the police, solid and respectable, who wouldn't forget you were in a good job, you might say something to him. Excuse me, she could put up with a lot, but she'd no one to rely on. The things people do these days. Dancing, bathing, fooling around, nothing sensible, not a stroke of work. Her own gentleman, though he was sensible enough, had his goings on like anyone else. Never went to bed before midnight. The best sleep is the sleep before midnight.

Respectable people go to bed at nine. Very likely it wasn't anything to write home about.

Gradually the horrible crime dwindled into a mere secret. Thick, tough layers of contempt covered it up. But her curiosity remained; between a quarter past six and seven o'clock she was always on the alert. She counted on rare, but not impossible contingencies. A sudden pain in the stomach might bring him out of his room. Then she would hurry in and ask if he wanted anything. Pains do not go away all in a minute. A few seconds, and she would know all she wanted to know. But the temperate and reasonable life which Kien led suited him too well. For the whole eight long years during which he had employed Therese he had never yet had a pain in the stomach.

The very morning on which he had met the blind man and his dog, it happened that Kien urgently wanted to consult certain old treatises. He pulled out all the drawers of the writing desk violently one after the other. A vast accumulation of papers had piled up in them over the years. Rough drafts, corrected scripts, fair copies, anything and everything which had to do with his work, he carefully preserved them all. He found wretched scraps whose contents he had himself long since surpassed and contradicted. The archives went right back to his student days. Merely in order to find a minute detail, which he knew by heart anyway, merely to check a reference, he wasted hours of time. He read over thirty pages and more; one line was all he wanted. Worthless stuff, which had long since served its purpose, came into his hands. He cursed it, why was it there? But once his eye fell upon anything written or printed he could not pass it over. Any other man would have refused to be held up by these digressions. He read every word, from first to last. The ink had faded. He had difficulty in making out the pale outlines. The blind man in the street came into his mind. There was he, playing tricks with his eyes, as if they would last for all eternity. Instead of restricting their hours of service, he increased them wantonly from month to month. Each single paper which he replaced in the drawer cost his eyes a part of their strength. Dogs have short lives and dogs do not read; thus they are able to help out blind men with their eyes. The man who has frittered away the strength of his eyes is a worthy companion of the beast that leads him.

Kien decided to empty his writing desk of rubbish on the following day immediately he got up; at present he was working.

On the following day, at six o'clock precisely, in the very middle of a dream, he started up from his divan bed, flung himself on the crammed giant and pulled out every one of its drawers. Screeching filled the air; it shrilled through the entire library, swelling to a heartrending climax. It was as if each drawer had its own voice and each was vying with its neighbour in a piercing scream for help. They were being robbed, tortured, murdered. They could not know who it was who dared to touch them. They had no eyes; their only organ was a shrill voice. Kien sorted the papers. It took him a long time. He disregarded the noise; what he had begun, he would finish. With a pyramid of waste paper in his lean arms, he stalked across into the fourth room. Here, some distance from the screeching, he tore them, cursing, into small pieces. Someone knocked; he ground his teeth. Again that knock; he stamped his feet. The knocking changed to hammering. 'Quiet!' he ordered and swore. He would willingly have dispensed with the unseemly row. But he was sorry on account of the manuscripts. Rage alone had given him strength to destroy them. At last he stood, a huge lonely stork on guard over a mountain of scraps of paper. Embarrassed and timid, he stroked them with his fingers, softly mourning over them. So as not to injure them unnecessarily, he lifted a cautious leg and cleared them. The graveyard behind him, he breathed again. Outside the door he found the housekeeper. With a weary gesture, he indicated the pyre and said: 'Clear it away!' The screeching had died down; he went back to the writing desk and closed the drawers. They were silent. He had wrenched them open too violently. The mechanism had been broken.

Therese was in the very act of finding her way into the starched skirt which completed her attire, when the screeching had broken loose. Terrified out of her wits, she fastened her skirt provisionally and glided fast to the door of the study. 'For Heaven's sake,' she wailed, flute-like, 'What has happened?' She knocked, discreetly at first, then louder. Receiving no answer, she tried the door, in vain. She glided from door to door. In the last room she heard him, shouting angrily. Here she hammered on the door with all her strength. 'Quiet!' he shouted in a rage, in such a rage as she had never heard him. Half indignant, half resigned, she let her hard hands drop against her hard skirt, and stood stiff as a wooden doll. 'What a calamity!' she murmured, 'what a calamity!' and was still standing there, out of mere habit, when he opened the door.

Slow by nature, this time she grasped in a flash the opportunity which was being offered to her. With difficulty she said 'At once,' and glided away to the kitchen. On the threshold she had an idea: 'Gracious Heaven, he's bolting himself in, just out of habit! Something will happen, at the last minute, that's life! I've no luck, I've no luck!' It was the first time she had said this, for as a rule she regarded herself as a meritorious and therefore as a lucky person. Anxiety made her head jerk to and fro. She sneaked out into the corridor again. She was stooping far forward. Her legs hesitated before she took a step. Her stiff skirt billowed. She would have reached her goal far more quietly by gliding as usual, but that was too ordinary a process. The solemnity of the occasion demanded its own solemnities. The room was open to her. In the middle of the floor the paper was still lying. She pushed a great fold of the carpet between the door and its frame so that it should not be blown to. Then she went back to the kitchen and waited, dustpan and brush in hand, for the familiar rattle of the wash-trolley. She would have preferred to come and fetch it herself, for she had a long time to wait. When at last she heard it crash against the wall, she forgot herself and called, out of habit, 'Up already?' She pushed it into the kitchen and, stooping even lower than before, crept into the library. She set down dustpan and brush on the floor. Slowly she picked her way across the intervening rooms to the threshold of his bedroom. After every step she stood still, and turned her head the other way about so as to listen with her right ear, the ear which was the less worn-out of the two. The thirty yards which she traversed took her ten minutes; she thought herself foolhardy. Her terror and her curiosity grew at the same rate. A thousand times she had thought out how to behave when she reached her goal. She squeezed herself tightly against the door frame. She remembered the crackling of her newly starched skirt too late. With one eye she tried to survey the situation. As long as the other one was in reserve she felt safe. She must not be seen, and she must see everything. Her right arm, which she liked to hold akimbo and which was constantly doubling itself up, she forced into stillness.

Kien was pacing calmly up and down in front of his books, making incomprehensible noises. Under his arm he carried the empty brief-case. He came to a halt, thought for a moment, then fetched the ladder and climbed up it. From the topmost shelf he extracted a book, turned over the pages and placed it in the brief-case. On the ground again, he continued his pacing up and down, stopped, pulled at a book, which was recalcitrant, wrinkled his forehead, and when he had it at last in his hands, gave it a sharp slap. Then it too disappeared into the brief-case. He selected five volumes. Four small ones and one large one. Suddenly he was in a hurry. Carrying the heavy brief-case he clambered up to the highest rung of the ladder and pushed the first volume back into its place. His long legs encumbered him; he had all but fallen down.

If he fell and hurt himself, there'd be an end of this wickedness. Therese's arm could be controlled no longer; it reached for her ear and tugged vigorously at it. Both eyes were fixed, gloating, on her imperilled employer. When his feet at length reached the thick carpet, she could breathe again. So the books were a fraud. Now for the truth. She knew every inch of the library, but secret vices are crafty. There's opium, there's morphia, there's cocaine—who could remember them all? You couldn't fool her. Behind the books, that's it. Why for instance did he never walk straight across the room? He stood by the ladder and what he wanted was on the shelf exactly opposite. He could fetch it as easy as anything, but no, he must always go creeping round by the wall. Carrying that great heavy thing under his arm, he goes all the way round by the wall. Behind the books, that's it. Murderers are drawn to the scene of the crime. Now the brief-case is full. He can't get anything more into it; she knows the brief-case, she dusts it out every day. Now something must happen. It can't be seven yet. If it's seven he'll go out. Where is it seven? It shan't be seven.

Shameless and sure of herself, she stooped forward, pressed her arm to her side, pricked her two large ears and opened her little eyes greedily. He took the brief-case by both ends and laid it firmly on the carpet. His face looked proud. He stooped down and remained stooping. She was running with sweat and trembling in every limb. Tears came into her eyes, under the carpet then, that's it. She'd always said, under the carpet. What a fool! He straightened himself, cracked his joints and spat. Or did he only say 'There!' He took up the brief-case, extracted a volume and slowly replaced it on the shelves. He did the same with all the others.

Therese came over faint. No thank you, indeed! There's nothing more worth looking at. So that's your sensible man, with never a smile or a word! She's sensible herself, and hard-working, but would she demean herself? You could cut her hand off, you don't find her mixed up in such things. He acts stupid in front of his own housekeeper. A creature like that to have money! And so much money, heaps and heaps of money! Ought to be put away. The way he wastes his money! Anyone else in her position now, any of that ragtag and bobtail there is these days, they'd have had the last stitch of clothing off his back long ago. Doesn't even sleep in a decent bed. What does he want with all these books and books? He can't be reading all of them at once. If you ask her, he's nothing but a loony, ought to have his money taken away before he wastes it all, and then let him go his own way. She'll teach him! Enticing a re-spectable woman into his house, indeed. Thinks he can make a fool of anyone, does he? Nobody can make a fool of her. For eight years perhaps, but not a moment longer!

By the time Kien had made his second selection of books for his morning walk, Therese's first anger had evaporated. She saw that he was ready to go out, glided in her normal, self-possessed manner back to the heap of paper and inserted the dustpan underneath it with dignity. She seemed to herself a more interesting and distin-guished person than before.

No, she decided, she would not give up her post. But she's found him out now. Well, that's something to know. If she sees anything, she knows how to make use of it. She doesn't see many things. She hasn't ever been outside the town. She's not one for excursions, a waste of good money. You don't catch her going bathing, it's not respectable. She doesn't care for travelling, you never know where you are. If she didn't have to go shopping, she'd prefer to stay in all day. They all try to do you down. Prices going up all the time, things aren't the same any more.

Confucius the Matchmaker

On the following Sunday Kien came back elated from his morning walk. The streets were empty on Sundays at this early hour. Humankind began each holiday by lying late. Then they fell upon their best clothes. They spent their first wakeful hours in devotions before the looking glass. During the remainder they recovered from their own grimaces by looking at other people's. Each thought himself the finest. To prove it he must go among his fellows. On weekdays: sweat and babble to earn a living. On Sundays: sweat and babble for nothing. The day of rest had been first intended as a day of silence. Kien noted with scorn that this institution, like all others, had degenerated into its exact opposite. He himself had no use for a day of rest. Always he worked and always in silence.

Outside the door of his flat he found the housekeeper. She had evidently been waiting for him some time.

'The Metzger child from the second floor was here. You promised him he could come. He would have it, you were in. The maid saw someone tall coming upstairs. He'll be back in half an hour. He won't disturb you, he's coming for the book.'

Kien had not been listening. Only at the word 'book' did he become attentive and understood in retrospect what the matter was. 'He is lying. I promised nothing. I told him I would show him some pictures from India and China if I ever had time. I have no time. Send him away.'

'Some people have a cheek. Excuse me, such ragtag and bobtail. The father was a common working man. Where they get the money from, I'd like to know. But there you are. Everything for the children, these days. Nobody is strict any more. Cheeky they are; you wouldn't credit it. Playing at their lessons and going for walks with teacher. Excuse me, in my time it was very different. If a child didn't want to learn its parents took it away from school and put it to a trade. With a hard master, so it had to learn. Nothing like that these days. You don't catch people wanting to work now. Don't know their places any more, that's what it is. Look at young people these days, when they go out on Sundays. Every factory girl has to have a new blouse. I ask you, and what do they do with all their fancy stuff? Go off bathing and take it all off again. With boys, too. Whoever heard of such a thing in my time? Let 'em do a job of work, that'd be more like it. I always say, where does the money come from? Prices going up all the time. Potatoes cost double already. It's not surprising, children have a cheek. Parents don't check them at all. In my days, it was a couple of good smacks, left and right, and the child had to do as it was told. There's nothing good left in the world. When they're little they don't learn, when they grow up they don't do a hand's turn.

Kien had been irritated at first because she was holding him up with a long discourse, but soon he found himself yielding to a kind of astonished interest in her words. So this uneducated creature set great value on learning. She must have a sound core. Perhaps the result of her daily contact with his books. Other women in her position might not have taken colour from their surroundings. She was more receptive, perhaps she yearned for education.

'You are quite right,' he said, 'I am happy to find you so sensible. Learning is everything.'

They had entered the flat while they were talking. 'Wait a minute!' he commanded and disappeared into the library. He came back with a small book in his left hand. As he turned over the pages, he thrust his thin, hard lips outwards. 'Listen!' he said and signalled her to stand a little further from him. What he was about to utter called for space. With an abundance of feeling, grotesquely unsuited to the simplicity of the text, he read:

'My master commanded me to learn three thousand characters every day and to write down another thousand each evening. In the short winter days the sun went down early and I had not finished my task. I carried my little tablet on to the veranda which faced the west and finished my writing there. Late in the evening, when I was going through what I had written, I could no longer overcome my weariness. So I placed two buckets of water behind me. When I grew too sleepy, I took off my gown and emptied the first bucket over myself. Naked, I sat down to my work again. Gradually I would grow warmer and sleepy again. Then I would use the second bucket. With the help of two shower baths I was nearly always able to complete my task. In that winter I entered my ninth year.'

Moved and ablaze with admiration, he clapped the book to. 'That was the way they used to learn! A fragment from the childhood recollections of the Japanese scholar Arai Hakuseki.'

During the reading, Therese had drawn closer. Her head waggled in time to his sentences. Her large left ear seemed to reach out of itself towards the words, as he translated freely from the Japanese original. Unintentionally, he was holding the book a little crooked; doubtless she could see the foreign characters and was astonished at the fluency of his rendering. He was reading as if he had a German book in his hands. 'Well I never!' she said. He had finished; she took a deep breath. Her amazement amused him. Was it too late, he thought, how old can she be? It is never too late to learn. But she would have to begin with simple novels.

The bell rang violently. Therese opened the door. The little Metzger boy pushed his head through the crack. 'I may come in!' he shouted, 'the Professor said I could!' 'No books for you!' screamed Therese, and slammed the door. Outside the little boy raged up and down. He yelled threats at the door; he was so angry that they could not understand a word he said. 'Excuse me, he takes a whole fistful in one. They'd be dirty in no time. I've seen him eat his piece of bread and butter on the stairs.'

Kien was on the threshold of the library: the boy had not seen him. He nodded approvingly to his housekeeper. He was happy to find the interests of his books so well defended. She deserved thanks: 'Should you ever wish to read anything, you may always apply to me.'

'I make so bold, I often thought of asking.'

How she jumped on her opportunity, when books were in question! She was not usually like this. Until this moment she had behaved herself very modestly. He had no intention of starting a lending library. To gain time he answered: 'Good. I shall look something out for you to-morrow.'

Then he sat down to his work. His promise made him feel uneasy. It was true that she dusted the books every day and had not yet injured one of them. But dusting and reading are different. Her fingers were coarse and rough. Delicate paper must be delicately handled. A hard binding can naturally stand rougher handling than sensitive pages. And how did he know that she *could* read? She must be more than fifty, she had not made much use of her time. 'An old man who learnt late', Plato called his opponent, the cynic philosopher Antisthenes. To-day we have old women who learn late. She wanted to quench her thirst at the fountain head. Or was she only ashamed of admitting in my presence that she knew nothing? Charity is all very well, but not at other people's expense. Why should the books have to foot the bill? I pay her high wages. I have a right to, it is my own money. But to hand over books to her would be cowardly. They are defenceless against the uneducated. I cannot sit by her all the time she is reading.

That night he saw a man standing, fast bound, on the terrace of a temple, defending himself with wooden clubs from the savage attacks of two upright jaguars on his left and right. Both animals were decked with strange streamers in all colours. They gnashed their teeth, roared and rolled their eyes so wildly that it made the blood run cold. The sky was black and narrow, and had hidden his stars in his pocket. Tears of glass trickled out of the eyes of the prisoner and splintered into a thousand pieces as they reached the pavement. But as nothing further happened, the savage combat grew boring and made the spectator yawn. Then by chance his eye fell on the feet of the jaguars. They had human feet. Aha, thought the spectator—a lanky, learned man—these are sacrificial priests of ancient Mexico. They are performing a sacred comedy. The victim knows well that he must die in the end. The priests are disguised as jaguars but I see through them at once.

The jaguar on the right seized a heavy stone wedge and drove it into the victim's heart. One edge of it clove sharp through the breast bone. Kien closed his eyes, dazzled. He thought, the blood must spirt up to the very sky; he sternly disapproved of this medieval barbarism. He waited until he thought the blood must have ceased to flow, then opened his eyes. Oh horrible: from the cleft victim's wounded breast a book appeared, another, a third, many. There was no end to it, they fell to the ground, they were clutched at by viscous flames. The blood had set fire to the wood, the books were burning. 'Shut your breast!' shouted Kien to the prisoner,

'Shut your breast!' He gesticulated with his hands; 'you must do it like this, quickly, quickly!' The prisoner understood; with a terrific jerk he freed himself of his bonds and clutched both his hands over his heart; Kien breathed again.

Then suddenly the victim tore his bosom wide open. Books poured forth in torrents. Scores, hundreds, they were beyond counting; the flames licked up towards the paper; each one wailed for help; a fearful shrieking rose on all sides. Kien stretched out his arms to the books, now blazing to heaven. The altar was much further off than he had thought. He took a couple of strides and was no nearer. He must run if he was to save them alive. He ran and fell; this cursed shortness of breath; it came of neglecting his physical health; he could tear himself into pieces with rage. A useless creature, when there was need of him he was no use. Those miserable wretches! Human sacrifices he had heard of—but books, books! Now at last he was at the altar. The fire singed his hair and eyebrows. The wood pyre was enormous; from the distance he had thought it quite small. They must be in the very centre of the fire. Into it then, you coward, you swaggerer, you miserable sinner!

But why blame himself? He was in the middle of it. *Where are you? Where are you?* The flames dazzled him. And what the devil was this, wherever he reached out, he could get hold of nothing but shrieking human beings. They clutched hold of him with all their strength. He hurled them from him, they came back to him. They crept to him from below and entwined his knees; from above his head burning torches rained down on him. He was not looking up yet he saw them clearly. They seized on his ears, his hair, his shoulders. They enchained him with their bodies. Bedlam broke loose. 'Let me go,' he shouted, 'I don't know you. What do you want with me! How can I rescue the books!'

But one of them had thrown himself against his mouth, and clung fast to his tightly closed lips. He wanted to speak again, but he could not open his mouth. He implored them in his mind: *I can't save them! I can't save them!* He wanted to cry, but where were his tears? His eyes too were fast closed; human beings were pressing against them too. He tried to step free of them, he lifted his right leg high in the air; in vain, it was dragged back again, dragged down by a burden of burning human kind, dragged down by a leaden weight. He abhorred them, these greedy creatures; could they not be satisfied with the life they had had? He loathed them. He would have liked to hurt them, torment them, reproach them; he could do nothing, nothing! Not for one moment did he forget why he was there. They might hold his eyes forcibly shut, but in his spirit he could see mightily. He saw a book growing in every direction at once until it filled the sky and the earth and the whole of space to the very horizon. At its edges a reddish glow, slowly, quietly, devoured it. Proud, silent, uncomplaining, it endured a martyr's death. Men screamed and shrieked, the book burnt without a word. Martyrs do not cry out, saints do not cry out.

Then a voice spoke; in it was all knowledge, for it was the voice of God: 'There are no books here. All is vanity.' And at once Kien knew that the voice spoke truth. Lightly, he threw off the burning mob and jumped out of the fire. He was saved. Did it hurt then? Terribly, he answered himself, but not so much as people usually think. He was extraordinarily happy about the voice. He could see himself, dancing away from the altar. At a little distance, he turned round. He was tempted to laugh at the empty fire.

Then he stood still, lost in contemplation of Rome. He saw the mass of struggling limbs; the air was thick with the smell of burning flesh. How stupid men are! He forgot his anger. A single step, and they could save themselves.

Suddenly, he did not know how it could have happened, the men were changed into books. He gave a great cry and rushed, beside himself, in the direction of the fire. He ran, panted, scolded himself, leaped into the flames and was again surrounded by those imploring human bodies. Again the terror seized him, again God's voice set him free, again he escaped and watched again from the same place the same scene. Four times he let himself be fooled. The speed with which events succeeded each other increased each time. He knew that he was bathed in sweat. Secretly he began to long for the breathing space allowed him between one excitement and the next. In the fourth pause, he was overtaken by the Last Judgment. Gigantic wagons, high as houses, as mountains, high as the heavens, closed in from two, ten, twenty, from all sides upon the devouring altar. The voice, harsh and destructive, mocked him: 'Now come the books!' Kien cried out and woke.

This dream, the worst dream he could remember, weighed upon his spirit for half an hour afterwards. An ill-extinguished match dropped while he was enjoying himself in the street—and his library would be lost! He had insured it more than once. But he doubted if he would have the strength to go on living after the destruction of twenty-five thousand books, let alone see about the payment of the insurance. He had taken out the policies in a contemptible frame of mind; later he was ashamed of them. He would have liked to cancel them. Indeed he only paid the necessary fees so as not to have to reenter the office in which books and cattle were subject to the same laws, and to be spared the visits of the companies' representatives who would doubtless be sent to call on him at home.

Divided into its elements a dream loses its terrors. He had been looking at Mexican pictorial writings only yesterday. One of them represented the sacrifice of a prisoner by two priests disguised as jaguars. His chance meeting with a blind man a few days before had made him think of Eratosthenes the aged librarian of Alexandria.

The name of Alexandria would naturally provoke the recollection of the burning of the famous library. A certain medieval woodcut, whose ingenuousness always made him smile, depicted about thirty Jews on a burning pyre flaming to heaven yet obstinately screeching their prayers. He was a great admirer of Michelangelo; above all he admired his Last Judgment. In that picture sinners are being dragged to Hell by pitiless devils. One of the damned, the picture of terror and anguish, covers his cowardly flaccid face with his hands; devils are clutching at his legs but he has never seen the woes of other people and dare not look at his own now. On the height stands Christ, very un-Christlike, condemning the damned with muscular and mighty arm. From all these recollections sleep had concocted a dream.

When Kien pushed the wash-trolley out of his bedroom he heard on an unexpectedly high note the exclamation: 'Up already!' Why did the creature speak so loud early in the morning when he was still almost asleep? Very true he had promised to lend her a book. A novel was the only thing worth considering for her. But no mind ever grew fat on a diet of novels. The pleasure which they occasionally offer is far too heavily paid for: they undermine the finest characters. They teach us to think ourselves into other men's places. Thus we acquire a taste for change. The personality becomes dissolved in pleasing figments of imagination. The reader learns to understand every point of view. Willingly he yields himself to the pursuit of other people's goals and loses sight of his own. Novels are so many wedges which the novelist, an actor with his pen, inserts into the closed personality of the reader. The better he calculates the size of the wedge and the strength of the resistance, so much the more completely does he crack open the personality of his victim. Novels should be prohibited by the State.

At seven o'clock Kien once again opened his door. Therese was standing in front of it, as trusting and modest as always, her prominent left ear perhaps a trifle more crooked.

'I make so bold,' she reminded him impertinently.

What little blood Kien had rushed to his head. So she would stick to it, this cursed creature in her starched skirt, and exact what had once been thoughtlessly promised. 'You want that book,' he cried and his voice cracked. 'You shall have it.'

He slammed the door in her face, strode with quivering steps into the third room, inserted one finger into the shelves and extracted *The Trousers of Herr von Bredow*. He had possessed this book from his earliest schooldays, had then lent it to all his classmates, and on account of the deplorable condition in which it had been ever since could not bear the sight of it. He looked with malice at its grease-spotted binding and sticky pages. Calm now, he went back to Therese and held the book close to her eyes.

'That was unnecessary,' she said and pulled out from under her arm a thick bundle of paper, packing paper, as he now noticed for the first time. With some ceremony she selected a suitable piece and wrapped it round the book like a shawl round a baby. Then she selected a second piece of paper and said, 'A stitch in time saves nine.' When the second piece of paper did not lie smoothly enough, she tore it off and tried a third one.

Kien followed her movements as though he were seeing her for the first time. He had underestimated her. She knew how to handle a book better than he did. This old thing was loathsome to him, but she wrapped it carefully up in two layers of paper. She kept the palms of her hands clear of the binding. She worked with her finger tips alone. Her fingers were not so coarse after all. He felt ashamed of himself and pleased with her. Should he fetch her something else? She deserved something less shabby. Still, for a beginning she could make do with this one. Even without encouragement she would soon be asking for another. For eight long years his library had been safe in her care; he had not known it.

'I have to leave to-morrow,' he said suddenly, as she was smoothing down the paper cover with her knuckles. 'For some months.'

'Then I shall be able to dust properly for once. Is an hour long enough?'

'What would you do if a fire broke out?'

She was horrified. She dropped the paper to the ground. The book remained in her hand. 'Gracious Heavens, save the books!"'

'But I am not really going away: I was only joking,' Kien smiled. Carried away by this picture of extreme devotion—himself absent and the books alone—he came closer to her and patted her on the shoulder with his bony fingers, saying in a tone almost friendly, 'You're a good creature.'

'I must have a look what you've chosen for me,' she said, and the corners of her mouth seemed to reach out almost to her ears. She opened the book and read aloud, *'The Trousers'*—she interrupted herself but did not blush. Her face was bedewed with a light sweat.

'Excuse me, Professor,' she exclaimed, and glided away, swiftly triumphant, towards the kitchen.

During the ensuing days Kien exerted himself to recover his old power of concentration. He too knew moments when he was tired of his services to the written word and felt a secret desire for more of the company of human kind than his strength of character normally permitted. When he entered into open conflict with such temptations he wasted much time; they tended to grow stronger if he fought them. He had contrived a more ingenious method: he outmanœuvred them. He did not pillow his head on the writing desk and lose himself in idle desires. He did not walk up and down the streets and enter into trivial conversations with fools. On the contrary he filled the library with the distinguished friends he had read. Mostly he inclined to the ancient Chinese. He commanded them to step out of the volume and the shelf to which they belonged, beckoned to them, offered them chairs, greeted them, threatened them, and according to his taste put their own words into their mouths and defended his own opinions against them until at length he had silenced them. When he entered into written controversy he found his words acquired from this practice an unexpected force. In this way he practiced speaking Chinese and took pride in the clever phrases which flowed from his lips so easily and so emphatically. If I go to the theatre (he thought) I hear a conversation in double-Dutch which is entertaining but not instructive, and in the end not even entertaining, only boring. Two or even three whole valuable hours must I sacrifice only to go to bed feeling irritated. My own dialogues do not go on so long and have meaning and balance. In this way he justified to himself the harmless game which might have seemed odd to a spectator.

Sometimes Kien would meet, either in the street or in a book-shop, a barbarous fellow who amazed him by uttering a reasonable sentiment. In order to obliterate any impression which contradicted his contempt for the mass of mankind he would in such cases perform a small arithmetical calculation. How many words does this fellow speak in a single day? At a conservative reckoning ten thousand. Three of them are not without sense. By chance I overheard those three. The other words which whirl through his head at a rate of several hundred thousand per day, which he thinks but does not even speak—one imbecility after another—are to be guessed merely by looking at his features; fortunately one does not have to listen to them.

His housekeeper, however, spoke little, since she was always alone. At a flash, they seemed to have something in common; his thoughts recurred to it hourly. Whenever he saw her, he remembered at once how carefully she had wrapped up *The Trousers of Herr von Bredow*. The book had been in his library for years. Every time he passed it the sight of its back alone smote his heart. Yet he had left it, just as it was. Why had it not occurred to him to care for its improvement by providing it with a handsome wrapper? He had lamentably failed in his duty. And now came a simple housekeeper and taught him what was right and seemly.

Or was she play-acting for his benefit? Perhaps she was merely flattering him into a sense of false security. His library was famous. Dealers had often besieged him for unique editions. Perhaps she was planning some vast robbery. He must find out how she acted when she was alone with the book.

One day he surprised her in the kitchen. His doubts tormented him; he longed for certainty. Once unmasked, he would throw her out. He wanted a glass of water; she had evidently not heard him calling. While she made haste to satisfy his wishes, he examined the table at which she had been sitting. On a small embroidered velvet cushion lay his book. Open at page 20. She had not yet read very far. She offered him the glass on a plate. It was then he saw that she had white kid gloves on her hands. He forgot to close his fingers round the glass; it fell to the floor, the plate after it. Noise and diversion were welcome to him. He could not have brought a word to his lips. Ever since he was five years old, for thirty-five years, he had been reading. And the thought had never once crossed his mind, to put on gloves for the purpose. His embarrassment seemed ridiculous, even to himself. He pulled himself together and asked casually: 'You have not got very far yet?'

'I read every page a dozen times, otherwise you can't get the best out of it.'

'Do you like it?' He had to force himself to go on speaking, or he would have fallen to the ground as easily as the glass of water.

'A book is always beautiful. You need to understand it. There were grease spots on it, I've tried everything but I can't get them out. What shall I do now?'

'They were there before.'

'All the same, it's a pity. Excuse me, a book like this is a treasure.'

She did not say 'must cost a lot,' she said 'is a treasure.' She meant its intrinsic value, not its price. And he had babbled to her of the capital which was locked up in his library! This woman must despise him. Hers was a generous spirit. She sat up night after night trying to remove old grease spots from a book, instead of sleeping. He gave her his shabbiest, most dog-eared and worn-out book out of sheer distaste, and she took it into loving care. She had compassion, not for men (there was nothing in that) but for books. The weary and heavy-laden could come to her. The meanest, the most forsaken and forgotten creature on the face of God's earth, she would take to her heart.

Kien left the kitchen in the deepest perturbation. Not one word more did he say to the saint.

In the lofty halls of his library he paced up and down and called on Confucius. He came towards him from the opposite wall, calm and self-possessed—it is easy to be self-possessed when you have been dead for centuries. With long strides Kien went to meet him. He forgot to make any obeisance. His excitement contrasted strangely with the bearing of the Chinese sage.

'I think that I am not wholly without education!' he shouted from a distance of five paces, 'I think I am not wholly without tact. People have tried to persuade me that education and tact are the same thing, that one is impossible without the other. Who tried to persuade me of this? You!' He was not shy of Confucious; he called him 'you' straight out. 'Here comes a person without a spark of education and she has more sensibility, more heart, more dignity, more humanity than I or you and all your learned disciples put together!'

Confucius was not to be put out of countenance. He did not even forget to make his bow before he was spoken to. In spite of these incredible accusations, he did not even raise his eyebrows. Beneath them, his eyes, very ancient and black, were wise as those of an ape. Deliberately he opened his mouth and uttered the following saying:

'At fifteen my inclination was to learning, at thirty I was fixed in that path, at forty I had no more doubts—but only when I was sixty were my ears opened.'

Kien had this sentence firmly fixed in his head. But as an answer to his violent attack, it disturbed him greatly. Quickly he compared the dates to see if they fitted. When he was fifteen he had been secretly devouring book after book, much against his mother's will, by day at school, and by night under the bedclothes, with a tiny pocket torch for sole wretched illumination. When his younger brother George, set to watch by his mother, woke up by chance during the night, he never failed to pull the bedclothes off him, experimentally. The fate of his reading programme for the ensuing nights depended on the speed with which he could conceal torch and book underneath his body. At thirty he was fixed in the path of knowledge. Professorial chairs he rejected with contempt. He might have lived comfortably on the income from his paternal inheritance. He preferred to spend the capital on books. In a few more years, three perhaps, it would all be spent. He never even dreamed of the threatening future, he did not fear it. He was forty. Until this day he had never known a doubt. But he could not get over *The Trousers of Herr von Bredow*. He was not yet sixty, otherwise his ears would have been opened. But to whom should he open them?

Confucius came a step closer to him, as if he had guessed the question, bowed, although Kien was at least two heads taller, and gave him the following confidential advice:

'Observe the manner of men's behaviour, observe the motives of their actions, examine those things in which they find pleasure. How can anyone conceal himself! How can anyone conceal himself!'

Then Kien grew very sad. What had it availed him to know these words by heart? They should be applied, proved, confirmed. For eight long years he had had a human being in the closest proximity, and all for nothing. I knew how she behaved, he thought, I never thought of her motives. I knew what she did for my books. I had the evidence of it daily before my eyes. I thought, she did it for money. Now that I know what she takes pleasure in, I know her motives better. She takes the grease spots off wretched and rejected books for which no one else has a good word to say. That is her recreation, that is her rest. Had I not surprised her in the kitchen, out of shameful mistrust, her deeds would never have come to light. In her solitude she had embroidered a pillow for her foster-child and laid it softly to rest. For eight long years she never wore gloves. Before she could bring herself to open a book, and *this* book, she went out and bought with her hard-earned money a pair of gloves. She is not a fool, in other things she is a practical woman, she knows that for the price of the gloves she could have bought the book, new, three times over. I have committed a great sin, I was blind for eight years.

Confucius gave him no time to think again. 'To err without making amendment is to err indeed. If you have erred, be not ashamed to make the fault good.'

It shall be made good, cried Kien. I will give her back her eight lost years! I will marry her! She is the heaven-sent instrument for preserving my library. If there is a fire I can trust in her. Had I constructed a human being according to my own designs, the result could not have been more apt for the purpose. She has all the elements necessary. She is a born foster-mother. Her heart is in the right place. There is room for no illiterate fools in her heart. She could have had a lover, a baker, a butcher, a tailor, some kind of barbarian, some kind of an ape. But she cannot bring herself to it. Her heart belongs to the books. What is simpler than to marry her?

188 · Elias Canetti

He took no more notice of Confucius. When he chanced to look in his direction, he had dissolved into air. Only his voice could still be heard, saying faintly but clearly: 'To see the right and not to do it is to lack courage.'

Kien had no time to thank him for this last encouragement. He flung himself towards the kitchen, and seized violently upon the door. The handle came off in his hand. Therese was seated in front of the cushion and made as if she were reading. When she sensed that he was already behind her, she got up, so that he could see what she had been reading. The impression of his last conversation had not been lost on her. She had gone back to page 3. He hesitated a moment, did not know what to say, and looked down at his hands. Then he saw the broken door handle; in a rage he threw it to the ground. He took his place stiffly in front of her and said: 'Give me your hand!' 'Excuse me,' breathed Therese and stretched it out to him. Now for the seduction, she thought and began to sweat all over. 'No,' said Kien; he had not meant her hand in that sense. 'I want to marry you!' So sudden a decision had been beyond Therese's expectations. She twisted her astonished head round in the opposite direction and replied proudly, though with an effort not to stammer: 'I make so bold!'

The Survivor

The moment of *survival* is the moment of power. Horror at the sight of death turns into satisfaction that it is someone else who is dead. The dead man lies on the ground while the survivor stands. It is as though there had been a fight and the one had struck down the other. In survival, each man is the enemy of every other, and all grief is insignificant measured against this elemental triumph. Whether the survivor is confronted by one dead man or by many, the essence of the situation is that he feels *unique*. He sees himself standing there alone and exults in it; and when we speak of the power which this moment gives him, we should never forget that it derives from his sense of uniqueness and from nothing else.

All man's designs on immortality contain something of this desire for survival. He does not only want to exist for always, but to exist when others are no longer there. He wants to live longer than everyone else, and to *know* it; and when he is no longer there himself, then his name must continue.

The lowest form of survival is killing. As a man kills an animal for food, and cuts bits from it as it lies defenceless on the ground and divides it for himself and his kin to devour, so also, and in the same manner, he seeks to kill anyone who stands in his way, or sets himself up against him as an enemy. He wants to strike him down so that he can feel that he still stands while the other lies prostrate. But this other must not disappear completely; his physical presence as a corpse is indispensable for the feeling of triumph. Now the victor can do whatever he wants with him, and he cannot retaliate, but must lie there, never to stand upright again. His weapon can be taken away and pieces cut from his body and kept forever as trophies. This moment of confronting the man he has killed fills the survivor with a special kind of strength. There is nothing that can be compared with it, and there is no moment which more demands repetition.

For the survivor knows of many deaths. If he has been in battle he has seen those around him fall. He went into battle with the conscious intention of maintaining his ground against the enemy. His declared aim was to despatch as many of them as possible and he can only conquer if he succeeds. Victory and survival are one and the same to him. But a victor also has a price to pay. Many of his own people lie among the dead. Friend and foe share the battlefield; their dead are heaped together and often, indeed, can no longer be distinguished; a common grave awaits them.

Fortunate and favoured, the survivor stands in the midst of the fallen. For him there is one tremendous fact; while countless others have died, many of them his comrades, he is still alive. The dead lie helpless; he stands upright amongst them, and it is as though the battle had been fought in order for him to survive it. Death has been deflected from him to those others. Not that he has avoided danger; he, with his friends, stood in the path of death. They fell; he stands exulting.

This feeling of superiority to the dead is known to everyone who has fought in a war. It may be masked by grief for comrades, but these are few and the dead are always many. The feeling of strength, of standing alone against the dead, is in the end stronger than any grief. It is a feeling of being chosen from amongst the many who manifestly shared the same fate. Simply because he is still there, the survivor feels that he is *better* than they are. He has proved himself, for he is alive. He has proved himself among many others, for the fallen are not alive. The man who achieves this often is a *hero*. He is stronger. There is more life in him. He is the favoured of the gods.

Survival and Invulnerability

Man's body is naked and vulnerable, exposed in its softness to every assault. With care and cunning he may be able to fend off things which come near, but it is easy to reach him from a distance; spears and arrows can transfix him. He has invented shields and armour, and built walls and whole fortresses round himself;

what he most desires from all these precautions is a feeling of invulnerability.

There are two different ways by which he has sought to acquire this. They are exactly opposite to each other and their results, therefore, are also quite different. At times he has sought to keep danger at a distance. He has set large spaces between danger and himself, which can be watched and guarded. He has as it were, hidden from danger; he has banished it.

But the other way is the one on which he has always prided himself. He has sought out danger and confronted it. He has allowed it to approach as closely as possible and staked everything on the issue. Out of all possible situations, he has chosen the one involving risk and the enhanced that risk. He has made an enemy and challenged him—the man may have been his enemy already, or he himself may first have chosen him as one, but here, as always, his movement is towards the greatest danger and an ineluctable decision.

This is the way of the *hero*. What does the hero really want? What is his true aim? The glory which all peoples accord their heroes—a tough and enduring glory if their deeds offer sufficient variety in quick succession—tends to mask their deeper motives. It is assumed that glory is their sole motive, but it is more likely that they were originally seeking for something different: for the ever-growing sense of invulnerability which can be won in this way.

The concrete situation in which the hero finds himself when he has overcome a danger is that of survivor. His enemy wanted his life as he his enemy's; this was the declared and fixed intent with which they met. The enemy succumbs, but the hero comes through the fighting unhurt and, filled with the consciousness of this prodigious fact, plunges into the next fight. No harm came to him, and no harm will, for each victory, each enemy killed, makes him feel more secure; his invulnerability armours him more and more completely.

There is no other way in which this feeling can be won. The man who hides from danger, or who banishes it, simply postpones the moment of decision. The man who faces it, and truly survives it; who then faces the next one; who piles up the moments of survival—he is the man who attains the feeling of invulnerability. Only when he has attained it does he actually become a hero, able to take any risk, for by then there is nothing that he fears. We might perhaps admire him more if he acted *in spite of* fear, but that is the point of view of a spectator, of someone who stands outside events. The people want their hero invulnerable.

A hero's deeds, however, are by no means confined to single combats. He may take on a whole pack of enemies and not only escape alive from the fight, but succeed in killing them, thus, as if at one blow, establishing his conviction of invulnerability.

Genghis Khan was once asked by one of his oldest and most faithful companions: "You are the ruler and you are called a hero. What marks of conquest and victory do you carry on you?" Genghis Khan replied: "Once, before I ascended the throne, I was riding along a road and I came on six men who lay in ambush by a bridge, waiting to attempt my life. When I got near, I drew my sword and attacked them. They showered me with a hail of arrows, but the arrows all went astray and none of them touched me. I killed all the men with my sword and rode on unharmed. On my way back, I passed the place where I had killed the six men. Their horses were straying riderless and I drove them home before me."

It was his invulnerability while fighting six enemies at once that Genghis Khan considered the certain mark of victory and conquest.

Survival as a Passion

The satisfaction in survival, which is a kind of pleasure, can become a dangerous and insatiable passion. It feeds on its occasions. The larger and more frequent the heaps of dead which a survivor confronts, the stronger and more insistent becomes his need for them. The careers of heroes and soldiers suggest that a kind of addiction ensues, which in the end becomes incurable. The usual explanation of this is that such men can only breathe in danger; to them an existence without danger is stale and flat; they find no savour in a peaceful life. The attraction of danger should not be underestimated, but what we tend to forget is that such men do not set out on their adventures alone. There are others with them who succumb to the danger and this affords them the continually repeated pleasure of survival, which is what they really need and what they can no longer do without.

In order to satisfy this craving it is not always necessary to expose oneself to danger. No one man can himself kill enough other men. On a battlefield, however, there are thousands all acting in the same way, and, if a man is their commander, if he controls their movements, if the very battle springs from his decision, then he can appropriate to himself all the dead bodies which result from it, for he is responsible for them. It is not for nothing that the commander in the field bears his proud title. He commands; he sends his men against the enemy, and to their death. If he is victorious, all the dead on the battlefield belong to him, both those who fought for him and those who fought against him. In victory after victory he survives them all. And this is what he wants; the triumph he celebrates later leaves no doubt of it. The significance of his victories is measured by the number of the dead. A triumph is ludicrous when the enemy has surrendered without a proper fight and there are only a few dead. It is glorious when the enemy has defended himself bravely, when the victory was strongly contested and cost many lives.

"Caesar surpassed all other commanders in the fact that he fought more battles than any of them and killed greater numbers of the enemy. For, though his campaigns in Gaul did not last for as much as ten complete years, in this time he took by storm more than 800 cities, subdued 300 nations and fought pitched battles at various times with three million men, of whom he destroyed one million in the actual fighting and took another million prisoners."

This is the opinion of Plutarch, one of the humanest spirits mankind has produced, who cannot be reproached with war-lust or blood-thirstiness. It is worth considering for that reason, and because of the exactness of the reckoning. Caesar fought three million enemies, of whom he killed one million and made another million prisoners. The numbers were surpassed by later commanders, both Mongols and non-Mongols, but this judgment is significant for the naïvety with which everything that happened is ascribed to the commander alone: the towns taken by storm, the subjugated nations, the millions fought and captured, all belong to Caesar. But it is not Plutarch who is naïve; it is history. Ever since the Pharaohs described their battles, such reports have been customary, and to this day they have scarcely altered.

Caesar was fortunate and survived many enemies. It is considered tactless in such circumstances to reckon the victor's own losses. They are known, but one does not reproach the great man with them. In Caesar's case they were not excessive compared with the number of the enemy fallen. He did, none the less, survive several thousand of his allies and fellow Romans. Here, too, he was not entirely unsuccessful.

These proud balance sheets are handed down from generation to generation and each generation contains potential warrior-heroes whose passion to survive great crowds of fellow human beings is fanned to fury by them. History seemed to vindicate their purpose even before they had achieved it. Those who are most skilled in this kind of survival have the largest and securest place in it. Their fame depends in the end less on victory or defeat than on the monstrous number of their victims. Nobody knows what Napoleon's real feelings were during the retreat from Moscow.

The Ruler as Survivor

The paranoiac type of ruler may be defined as one who uses every means to keep danger away from his person. Instead of challenging and confronting it and abiding the issue of a fight which might go against him, he seeks by circumspection and cunning to block its approach to him. He creates empty space all round him which he can survey, and he observes and assesses every sign of approaching danger. He does this on all sides, for he knows that he is dealing with many who may simultaneously advance against him, and this keeps awake in him the fear of being surrounded. Danger is everywhere, not only in front of him; it threatens especially from behind, where he might not notice it quickly enough. He has eyes all round him and not the slightest sound must escape his attention, for it might conceal a hostile intent.

The essence of all danger is naturally death and it is important to discover what is his special attitude to this. The first and decisive attribute of the autocrat is his power over life and death. No-one may come near him; a messenger, or anyone who has to approach him, is searched for weapons. Death is systematically kept away from him, but he himself may and must decree it. He may decree it as and when he wills and his sentence will always be executed; it is the seal of his power, and his power is only absolute so long as his right to decree death remains uncontested.

For the autocrat's only true subject is the man who will let himself be killed by him. This is the final proof of obedience and it is always the same. His soldiers are trained in a kind of double preparedness: they are sent to kill his enemies and they are ready to die for him. But all his other subjects too, who are not soldiers, know that he can pounce on them at any time. The terror that he spreads around him is part of him; it is his right, and it is for this right that he is most honoured: in extreme cases he will be worshipped for it. God himself has suspended the sentence of death over all living men, and over all who are yet to live. *When* the sentence is carried out depends on his whim. No one thinks of opposing it, for this would be fruitless.

Earthly rulers, however, are less fortunate than God, for they do not live for ever and their subjects know that to their days, too, an end is set; and that this end, like any other, can be hastened by violence. Any man who refuses obedience to his ruler, challenges him. No ruler can be permanently certain of the obedience of his subjects. As long as they allow themselves to be killed by him he can sleep in peace, but as soon as anyone evades his sentence he is endangered.

The sense of this danger is always alert in a ruler. Later, when the nature of command is discussed, it will be shown that his fears *must* increase the more often his commands are carried out. He can only calm his fears by making an example of someone. He will order an execution for its own sake, the victim's guilt being almost irrelevant. He *needs* executions from time to time and, the more his fears increase, the more he needs them. His most dependable, one might say his truest, subjects are those he has sent to their deaths.

For, from every execution for which he is responsible, some strength accrues to him. It is the strength of *survival* which he gains from it. His victims need not actually have challenged him, but they might have, and his fear transforms them—perhaps only retrospectively—into enemies who have fought against him. He condemns them; they are struck down and he survives them. The right to pronounce sentence of death becomes in his hands a weapon like any other, only far more effective. Many barbarian and oriental rulers have set great store on this heaping up of victims round them, where they can actually see them all the time; but, even where custom has been against such accumulation, the thoughts of rulers have been busy with it. The Emperor Domitian is reported to have contrived a macabre game of this kind. The banquet he arranged, which has certainly never been repeated in the same form, gives a clear picture of the inmost nature of the paranoiac ruler. The description of it by Dio Cassius runs as follows:

"On another occasion he entertained the foremost men among the senators and knights in the following fashion. He prepared a room that was pitch black on every side, ceiling, walls and floor, and had made ready bare couches of the same colour resting on the uncovered floor; then he invited in his guests, alone at night, without their attendants. And first he set beside each of them a slab shaped like a gravestone, bearing the guest's name, and also a small lamp, such as hangs in tombs. Next comely naked boys, likewise painted black, entered like phantoms, and after encircling the guests in an awe-inspiring dance took up their stations at their feet. After this all the things that are commonly offered at the sacrifices to departed spirits were likewise set before the guests, all of them black and in dishes of similar colour. Consequently, every single one of the guests feared and trembled and was kept in constant expectation of having his throat cut the next moment, the more so as on the part of everybody except Domitian there was dead silence, as if they were already in the realms of the dead, and the emperor himself conversed only upon topics relating to death and slaughter. Finally he dismissed them; but he first removed their slaves, who had stood in the vestibule, and now gave his guests in charge of other slaves whom they did not know, to be conveyed either in carriages or litters; and by this procedure he filled them with far greater fear. And scarcely had each guest reached his home and was beginning to get his breath again, as one might say, when word was brought him that a messenger from the Augustus had come. While they were accordingly expecting to perish this time in any case, one person brought in the slab, which was of silver, and the others in turn brought in various articles, including the dishes which had been set before them at the dinner, which were constructed of very costly material; and last of all came that particular boy who had been each guest's familiar spirit, now washed and adorned. Thus, after having passed the entire night in terror, they received the gifts."

Such was the Funeral Banquet of Domitian, as people called it.

The continuous state of terror in which Domitian kept his guests rendered them speechless. He alone spoke, and he spoke of death and killing. It was as though they were all dead and he alone lived. He had gathered together at this banquet all his victims—for victims they must have seemed to themselves—and as such, though disguised as guests, he addressed them. He himself was disguised as host, but in reality was the survivor. His situation as a survivor was not only reaffirmed in relation to each guest, but was also subtly enhanced. The guests are as if dead, but he is still in a position to kill them. Thus the very *process* of survival is caught. In releasing them, he pardons them; but they tremble again when he hands them over to unknown slaves. They reach their homes and he again sends messengers of death to them; but these bring gifts and, amongst them, the greatest of all—the gift of life. He is able, as it were, to despatch them from life to death and then to bring them back to life again. It was a game which gave him the most intense sensation of power imaginable and he enjoyed it to the full.

The Escape of Josephus

Among the stories of the war between the Jews and the Romans, which took place during Domitian's youth, there is an account of an incident which perfectly illustrates the nature of the survivor. The Roman forces were commanded by Vespasian, the father of Domitian, and it was during this war that the Flavii achieved imperial power.

The Jews had been chafing under Roman rule for some time. When they finally rose against it in earnest, they appointed commanders in each district of the country, to collect troops and to prepare the defence of the towns so that there would be some chance of their being able to repel the inevitable attack of the Roman legions. Josephus, then barely thirty years old, was appointed commander in Galilee and he set to work zealously to accomplish his task. In his *History of the Jewish War* he describes the obstacles he had to contend with: dissensions among the townspeople; rivals who intrigued against him and collected troops on their own account; towns which refused to acknowledge his leadership, or later denied it again. But, with astonishing energy, he got together an army—though it was badly equipped—and fortified strongholds against the coming of the Romans.

And, in due course, they came. They were under the command of Vespasian, who had with him his son, Titus, a young man the same age as Josephus. (Nero was then still emperor in Rome.) Vespasian had distinguished himself in many theatres of war and was known as a general of long experience. He advanced into Galilee and surrounded Josephus and his army in the town of Jotapata. The Jews defended it stubbornly and bravely. Josephus was full of resource and knew how every attack should be met. The siege lasted for forty-seven days and the Romans suffered heavy losses in the course of it. When at last, and then only by treachery and at night, they succeeded in forcing their way in, the defenders were all asleep and did not realize that the Romans were among them until daybreak. Then they fell into terrible despair and many of them killed themselves.

Josephus escaped. I shall give in his own words his story of what happened to him after the capture of the town, for, as far as I know, there is in all literature no other comparable account of a survivor. With curious self-awareness and with an insight into the very nature of survival, he describes everything that he did in order to save his life. It was comparatively easy for him to be honest, for he did not write his account until later, when he already stood high in the favour of the Romans.

"After the fall of Jotapata, the Romans searched everywhere for Josephus—among the dead and in all the secret hiding places of the city—partly because the soldiers themselves were incensed against him, and partly because their commander was set on his capture, thinking that it might determine the whole course of the war. Josephus, however, as if helped by divine providence, had managed to slip through the enemy during the fighting and had jumped down into an underground cistern which opened on one side into a large cave, invisible from above. In this cave he found forty men of importance concealed, who had provided themselves with food for several days, and here he lay hid in the daytime, for the enemy were all around, but emerged at night to search for a way of escape and to see where sentries were posted. But the whole neighbourhood was so closely guarded on his account that there was no possibility of escape, and so he retreated into the cave again. For two days he eluded his pursuers in this way, but on the third day a woman who had been among those in the cave was captured, and she betrayed him. Vespasian immediately despatched two Tribunes with instructions to promise Josephus his safety and to persuade him to come out of the cave.

"The Tribunes arrived and spoke courteously to him and guaranteed his life; but to no purpose, for he knew, or thought he knew, what he had to expect in return for all the injuries the Romans had suffered at his hands. The gentle bearing of those who spoke to him in no way altered his estimate of the fate that awaited him. He could not rid himself of the fear that the Romans were only trying to entice him out of the cave in order to execute him. Finally, Vespasian sent a third messenger, the Tribune Nicanor, who was well known to Josephus; in fact, they had formerly been friends. Nicanor described the leniency with which the Romans treated their vanquished foes. He explained, too, that the generals admired Josephus for his courage more than they hated him, and that Vespasian had no intention of having him executed. If he wished, he could kill him without his leaving the cave; but, in fact, what he wanted was to save the life of a brave man. He added that it was unthinkable that Vespasian should maliciously send Josephus's friend to him to trap him, covering a breach of faith with the mask of friendship; nor would he, Nicanor, ever have lent himself to such a betrayal of friendship.

"As even Nicanor, however, failed to bring Josephus to a decision, the soldiers in their fury prepared to set fire to the cave; but Nicanor held them back, for he was determined to take Josephus alive. Surrounded thus by hostile, threatening soldiers, and with Nicanor still urging him to surrender, Josephus remembered suddenly the terrible dreams in which God had revealed to him the impending disasters of the Jewish people and the fates of the Roman Emperors; for he was skilled in the interpretation of dreams. A priest himself, and the son of a priest, he was familiar with the prophecies of the Holy Scriptures and could expound those that were obscure. At this very moment he was filled with inspiration, the terrors of those dreams rose up before him and silently he prayed to God, thus: 'Since Thou art resolved to humble the Jewish people, whom Thou didst create; since all good fortune is passed to the Romans; and since Thou hast chosen my spirit to make known the things that are to come, I yield myself to the Romans; but Thou art my witness that I go, not as a traitor, but as Thy servant.'

"After he had prayed, he told Nicanor he would go with him. When the Jews who had been with him in hiding saw that he had decided to yield to the enemy's persuasion, they crowded round him and reproached him vehemently. They reminded him of all who, on his persuasion, had died for freedom; of his own reputation for courage, which had been so great, yet now he wanted to live a slave. They asked what mercy he, supposed to be so wise, thought he would obtain from those he had fought so stubbornly. They said he had wholly forgotten himself and that his care for his own life was an outrage to God and to the Laws of their fathers. *He* might be dazzled by the good fortune of the Romans; *they* were still mindful of the honour of their people; their right hands and their swords were his to command if he died willingly as leader of the Jews; if he refused, the should die unwillingly as a traitor. They drew their swords and threatened to cut him down if he gave himself up to the Romans.

"Josephus was very frightened, but it seemed to him that he would be betraying the commands of God if he died before proclaiming them, and in his urgent need he began to reason with his companions. He said that it was indeed noble to die in war, but then it must be according to the custom of war, that is, by the hand of the victor. It was cowardly in the extreme to kill oneself. Suicide was both repugnant to the very nature of all living beings and an outrage against God the Creator. God gave men life and to God must men commit their end. Those who turned their hands against themselves were hateful to God, and he would punish both them and their descendants. To all that they had suffered in this life, they must not now add sin against their Creator. If deliverance should come, they should not refuse it. It would not be shameful in them to accept their lives, for they had sufficiently proved their courage by their deeds. But if they had to die, then they should die at the hands of their conquerors. He had no thought of going over to the Romans and so becoming a traitor himself; he hoped rather for treachery on *their* part. If, in spite of their given word they killed him, he would die joyfully. Their broken faith, which God would punish, would be to him a greater consolation than victory itself.

"Thus Josephus put forward every possible argument to dissuade his companions from suicide. But despair had made them deaf. They had long dedicated themselves to death and his words served only to increase their frenzy. They accused him of cowardice and pressed round him with drawn swords, as if ready to strike him down. In danger of his life, and torn by conflicting emotions, Josephus called one man by name, fixed another with a stare of command, took a third by the arm, pleaded with a fourth and so, in each case, succeeded in averting the sword of death. He was like a wild animal at bay, turning to face each successive assailant; and as they still, even in this last extremity, respected him as their commander, their arms were as if paralysed, their daggers slipped from their hands, and many who had drawn their swords against him sheathed them again of their own free will.

"In spite of his desperate position, Josephus's presence of mind did not fail him. On the contrary, putting his trust in God, he staked his life on a gamble and addressed his companions thus: 'Since we are resolved to die, and will not be turned from it, let us draw lots and kill each other accordingly. The first man on whom the lot falls shall be killed by the second, and he, in turn, by the third; and so on, as chance decides. In this way, all shall die, but no-one will have been compelled to take his own life, except the last man. It would be unfair if he, after the death of his companions, changed his mind and did not kill himself.'

"With this proposal Josephus won their confidence again, and when they had all declared their agreement, he drew lots with the rest and each man on whom the lot fell offered himself to be killed by the next, for each imagined that a moment later his general would die too; and death with Josephus seemed sweeter than life. At last—let us say that it was either by chance or by divine providence—only Josephus was left with one other man. Since he did not want to risk the lot falling on him, nor, supposing he escaped it, to stain his hands with the blood of a fellow Jew, he persuaded this man that they should both give themselves up to the Romans and so save their lives.

"Having thus come safely through two wars—one with the Romans and one with his own people—Josephus was brought by Nicanor before Vespasian. All the Romans crowded to see the commander of the Jews and pressed shouting round him, some exulting in his capture, some threatening him, and others thrusting their way forwards to see him close. Those at the back clamoured for his execution; those nearer him remembered his deeds and marvelled at the change in his fortunes. Among the officers, though, there were none who, in spite of their former hatred, were not moved by the sight of him. Titus, in particular, was impressed by his steadfast bearing in misfortune, and moved by fellow feeling for his youth—he was the same age as Josephus. He wanted to save his life and pleaded strenuously for him with his father. Vespasian, however, put Josephus under strict guard, proposing to send him immediately to Nero.

"When Josephus heard this, he asked to speak to Vespasian alone. Vespasian ordered everyone to withdraw, except his son, Titus, and two close friends, and Josephus then spoke thus:

"'You think, Vespasian, that I am simply a prisoner of war who has fallen into your hands. But you are mistaken: I stand before you as harbinger of great events. I, Josephus, am sent by God to declare this message to you. Were this not so, I would not be here, for I know the Jewish law and how a general should die. You want to send me to Nero. Why? He and his successors who will ascend the throne before you will not rule for long. You yourself, Vespasian, shall be Caesar and Emperor, you and your son here. Fetter me more securely and guard me for yourself till that time comes. For you will be Caesar and master, not only over me, but over land and sea and the whole human race. Let me be closely watched and, if I have taken the Name of God in vain, then kill me as I shall have deserved.'

"At first Vespasian did not really trust Josephus; he thought he was lying to save his life. Gradually, however, he began to believe what he said, for God Himself had already awoken in him imperial ambitions, and he had also received other signs of future power. He discovered, too, that Josephus had prophesied truly on other occasions. One of those who had been present at his private interview with Vespasian expressed surprise that he had not predicted either the fall of Jotapata or his own capture, and suggested that what he put forward now was a fable to ingratiate himself with his enemies. But Josephus replied that he had predicted to the people of Jotapata that the town would fall after forty-seven days and that he himself would be taken alive by the Romans. Vespasian had secret enquiries made among the other prisoners, and when they confirmed what Josephus had said, he began to believe the predictions about himself. It is true that he still kept Josephus fettered and in prison, but he gave him a splendid robe and other valuable presents and, from then on, thanks to Titus, treated him with kindness and consideration."

Josephus's struggle falls into three distinct acts. First, he escapes the slaughter after the fall of Jotapata. The defenders of the town either kill themselves or are killed by the Romans; a few are taken prisoner. Josephus escapes by hiding in the cave by the cistern. Here he finds forty men, whom he expressly describes as "important." They, like himself, are all survivors. They have provided themselves with food and hope to remain hidden from the Romans until some way of escape offers.

But the presence of Josephus, who is the man the Romans are actually searching for, is betrayed to them by a woman. Thereupon, the situation changes radically and the second, and by far the most interesting act, begins; one may say that it is unique in the frankness with which events are described by the chief actor.

The Romans promise Josephus his life. As soon as he believes them, they cease to be enemies. It is, in the deepest sense, a question of faith. At precisely the right moment, he remembers a prophetic dream he once had. In it he had been warned that the Jews would be conquered. They are conquered, though at first, it is true, only in the fortress of Jotapata which he had commanded. Fortune is on the side of the Romans. The vision in which this had been revealed to him came from God and God would also help him to find the way to the Romans. He commends himself to God and turns to his new enemies, the Jews who are with him in the cave. They want to commit suicide, so as not to fall into the hands of the Romans. He, their leader, who had spurred them on to fight, should be the first to welcome this form of annihilation. But he is determined to live. He pleads with them and with a hundred arguments seeks to take from them their desire for death. But he does not succeed. Everything he says against death increases their blind passion for it, and also their anger against himself, who shuns it. He sees that he can only escape if they all kill each other and he is the last to remain alive. He therefore makes a show of agreeing with them and hits upon the notion of drawing lots.

The reader will have his own ideas about the way in which these lots were drawn; it is difficult not to suspect fraud. It is the one point in his narrative where Josephus is obscure. He ascribes the extraordinary outcome of this gamble on death either to God or to chance, but he also, as it were, leaves it open to the reader to guess the real course of events. For what follows is monstrous: his companions butcher each other before his eyes. But not simultaneously. Each killing follows the other in due order, and between each the lots are drawn again. Each man has with his own hand to kill one of his comrades and then himself be killed by the next on whom the lot falls. The religious scruples that Josephus advanced against self-murder evidently do not apply to murder. As each man falls, his own hope of deliverance grows. Individually and collectively, he wants them all dead. For himself he wants nothing but to live. They die gladly, believing that their commander dies with them. They cannot suppose that he will be the last left alive. It is unlikely that they even envisage the possibility. But since one of them has to be the last, Josephus forearms himself against this thought too. He tells them that it would be very unfair if the last man changed his mind after the death of his companions, and so saved his life. This, precisely, is what he intends to do. What could least be done after the death of comrades is what he himself wants to do. Pretending in this last hour to be wholly with them, to be one of them, he sends them all to their deaths and, by doing so, saves his own life. They are all caught in the same fate and believe him caught too. But he stands outside it, and destines it only for them. They die so that he may live.

The deception is complete. It is the deception of all leaders. They pretend that they will be the first to die, but, in reality, they send their people to death, so that they themselves may stay alive longer. The trick is always the same. The leader wants to survive, for with each survival he grows stronger. If he has enemies, so much the better; he survives *them*. If not, he has his own people. In any event he uses both, whether successively or together. Enemies he can use openly; that is why he has enemies. His own people must be used secretly.

In Josephus's cave the trick is made manifest. Outside are the enemy, but their former threats have turned to a promise. Inside the cave are his friends. They still hold firmly to their leader's old convictions, convictions with which he himself had imbued them, and they refuse to take advantage of this new hope. Thus the cave which Josephus had intended as his refuge becomes the place of his greatest danger. He dupes the friends who want to lay violent hands both on him and on themselves, and consigns them to a common death. From the very beginning, he has had no thought of sharing it; nor does he share it when it comes. He is left in the end with one sole companion and since, as he says, he has no wish to stain his hands with the blood of a fellow Jew, he persuades this man to surrender. One man alone he can persuade to live. Forty had been too many for him. The two of them give themselves up to the Romans.

Thus he emerges safely from the war against his own people. This is precisely what he brings the Romans: the enhanced sense of his own life, feeding on the deaths of those he had led. The transmission of this newly won power to Vespasian is the third act of the struggle. It is embodied in a prophetic promise. The Romans were perfectly familiar with the Jews' stubborn belief in God. They knew that the last thing a Jew would do was to take the name of God in vain. Josephus had strong reasons for wanting to see Vespasian emperor in place of Nero. Nero, to whom Vespasian proposed sending him, had not promised him his life; Vespasian had. He knew, too, that Nero despised Vespasian, who was much older than himself, and fell asleep in public when he sang. He had often treated him harshly and had only called again on his military experience when the insurrection of the Jews had begun to assume dangerous proportions. Vespasian thus had every reason to mistrust Nero. A promise of future power must have been welcome to him.

Josephus may himself have believed that the message he gave Vespasian was from God. Prophecy was in his blood; he believed that he was a true prophet and, in prophesying, he brought the Romans something that they themselves lacked. He did not take the gods of the Romans seriously; to him they were superstition. But he knew that he had to convince Vespasian of the importance and authenticity of his message; and Vespasian, like every other Roman, despised the Jews and their religion. He was one man alone among enemies on whom he had inflicted terrible injuries, enemies who but lately had been cursing him, yet he faced them confidently, he expressed himself with force, and he believed in himself more strongly than in anything else. This belief he owed to the fact that he had survived his own people. The power which he had achieved in the underground cave he transmitted to Vespasian, so that the latter survived not only Nero, his junior by thirty years, but also no less than three of Nero's successors. Each of these died, in effect, by the hand of the other, and Vespasian became Emperor of the Romans.

The Despot's Hostility to Survivors. Rulers and Their Successors

Muhammad Tughlak, the Sultan of Delhi, had various schemes even more grandiose than those of Napoleon and Alexander. Among them was the conquest of China from across the Himalayas. An army of 100,000 horsemen was collected, which set out in the year 1337. Of this whole army, all but ten men perished cruelly in the mountains. These ten returned to Delhi with the news of the disaster and there, at the command of the Sultan, were all executed.

This hostility to survivors is common to despotic rulers, all of whom regard survival as their prerogative; it is their real wealth and their most precious possession. Anyone who presumes to make himself conspicuous by surviving great danger, and especially anyone who survives large numbers of other people, trespasses upon their province and their hatred is accordingly directed against him.

Wherever government was absolute and unquestioned, as in the Islamic East for example, the rage that survivors aroused in the ruler could be shown openly. Even if he felt obliged to find pretexts for their destruction, these barely disguised the naked passion which filled him.

By secession from Delhi, another Islamic empire arose in the Deccan. One Sultan of the new dynasty, Muhammad Shah, spent his whole reign in fierce wars against the neighbouring Hindu kings. One day the Hindus succeeded in capturing the important town of Mudkal, and all its inhabitants, men, women and children, were put to the sword. *One* man only escaped and carried the news to the capitals of the Sultan. "On hearing it," says the chronicler, "Muhammad Shah was seized with a transport of grief and rage, in which he commanded the unfortunate messenger to be instantly put to death; exclaiming that he could never bear in his presence a wretch who could survive the sight of the slaughter of so many brave companions."

Here it is still possible to speak of a pretext, and it is probable that the Sultan did not really know why he could not bear the sight of the only survivor. Hakim, the Khalif of Egypt who ruled about A.D. 1000, was much clearer-headed about the games which could be played with power and enjoyed them in a manner reminiscent of the Emperor Domitian. He liked to wander around at night disguised in various ways. During one of these nocturnal wanderings, on a hill near Cairo, he came across ten well-armed men, who recognised him and begged him for money. He said to them, "Divide into two groups and fight each other. The winner shall be given money." They obeyed him and fought so fiercely that nine of them were killed. To the tenth, the man who was left, Hakim threw a large number of gold coins which he had in his sleeve. But as the man stooped to pick them up, Hakim had him cut to pieces by his guards. In all this he showed a clear insight into the *process* of survival. He also enjoyed it as a kind of performance which he himself had conjured up. He finished by adding to it the pleasure of destroying the survivor.

Strangest of all is the relationship between the despotic ruler and his successor. Where succession is hereditary, the ruler being succeeded by his own son, the relationship is doubly difficult. It is natural for a ruler, as for any other man, to be survived by his son, and since in this case the son is himself a future ruler, it is natural that he too, from an early age, should have harboured a mounting passion for survival. Thus both father and son have every reason to hate each other. Their rivalry originates in the disparity of their positions and, for this very reason, is particularly acrimonious. The one who has present power knows that he will die before the other. The one who as yet has no power, feels certain that he will outlive the other. On the one side is an ardent desire for the death of an older man—one who, of all men, least wants to die, for otherwise he would not be a ruler; on the other is a determination to delay by all possible means the accession to power of a younger man. It is a conflict for which there is no real solution. History is full of the rebellions of sons against their fathers. Some succeed in bringing about their fathers' downfall; others are defeated by them and then either pardoned or killed.

It is not surprising that, with a dynasty of long-lived absolute rulers, it should become a kind of institution for sons to rebel against their fathers. The history of the Mogul emperors illustrates this point very clearly. Prince Salim, the eldest son of the Emperor Akbar, "impatient to take the reins of government into his hands, and chafing at the long life of his father, which kept him from the enjoyments of the dignities he so much desired, resolved to usurp the same, and on his own authority began to assume the name and exercise the prerogatives of a king." This statement appears in a contemporary chronicle of the Jesuits, who knew both father and son well, since they strove for the favour of both. Prince Salim formed his own court. He hired assassins who ambushed and murdered his father's most intimate friend and counsellor. His rebellion lasted for three years, during which period there was one feigned reconciliation. Finally Akbar threatened to nominate another successor to the throne and, under this pressure, Salim accepted an invitation to his father's court. He was received with apparent cordiality, then his father drew him into an inner chamber, boxed his ears and locked him into a bathroom. Then he handed him over to a physician and two servants, as though he were mad; and wine, of which he was very fond, was forbidden him. The prince was then in his 36th year. After a few days Akbar released him and reinstated him as his successor. The following year Akbar died from dysentery. It was said that he had been poisoned by his son, but there is now no means of finding out what really happened. "After the death of his father, which he had so much desired," Salim became Emperor at last, taking the name Jahangir.

Akbar ruled for forty-five years; Jahangir for twenty-two. But though the latter's reign was only half as long as his father's, exactly the same experience befell him. His favourite son, Shah Jehan, whom he himself had nominated as his successor, rebelled and fought against him for three years. Finally he was defeated and sued his father for peace. He was pardoned, but on one hard condition: he had to send his two sons as hostages to the imperial court. He himself waited for his father's death, taking good care never to appear in his presence again. Two years after the conclusion of peace Jahangir died and Shah Jehan became emperor.

Shah Jehan ruled for thirty years. What he had done to his father was now done to him, but *his* son was luckier. Aurangzeb, the younger of the two princes who had been kept as hostages at their grandfather's court, rebelled against his father and his elder brother. The famous "War of Secession" which started then was described by European eye-witnesses. It ended with the victory of Aurangzeb, who had his brother executed and kept his father prisoner for the eight years until his death.

Soon after his victory Aurangzeb made himself Emperor and reigned for half a century. His own favourite son lost patience long before the expiry of that time, and rebelled against his father. The old man, however, was much more cunning than his son and managed to estrange the latter's allies. The son had to flee to Persia and died in exile before his father.

From the dynastic history of the Mogul Empire as a whole a remarkably uniform picture emerges. Its age of splendour lasted for 150 years and, during this time, only four emperors ruled, each the son of the preceding one and each tenacious, long-lived and clinging to power with all his might. Their reigns are all strikingly long; Akbar's lasted forty-five years, his son's twenty-two, his grandson's thirty and his great-grandson's fifty. Beginning with Akbar himself, none of the sons could endure waiting; each who later became emperor rose against his father. Their rebellions ended differently. Jahangir and Shah Jehan were defeated and afterwards pardoned by their fathers; Aurangzeb took his father prisoner and then deposed him; his own son died, a failure, in exile. With Aurangzeb's death the power of the Mogul Empire came to an end.

In this long-lived dynasty each son rebelled against his father and each father waged war on his son.

The intensest feeling for power is that found in a ruler who *wants no son*. The best known case is that of Shaka, the early nineteenth century founder of the nation and empire of the Zulus in South Africa. He was a great general, who has been compared with Napoleon, and never has there been a more naked despot. He refused to marry, because he did not want a legitimate heir. Even the urgent entreaties of his mother, whom he always greatly honoured, did not move him. She wanted a grandson more than anything else, but he was obdurate. His harem consisted of hundreds of women— ultimately there were 1,200 of them—whose official title was "sis-ters." They were forbidden to be with child and were strictly watched. Any "sister" found pregnant was punished with death. With his own hands Shaka killed the child of one of these women which had been concealed from him. He flattered himself on his skill and self-control and therefore believed that no woman could ever become pregnant by him. Thus he avoided being put in the position of having a growing son to fear. He was murdered at the age of forty-one by two of his brothers.

If it is permissible to turn from human to divine rulers we might remember here the God of Mohammed, whose autocracy is the least disputed of any god's. He is there from the very beginning in the plenitude of his power and, únlike the God of the Old Testament, never has serious rivals to contend with. Again and again in the Koran it is vehemently affirmed that no-one begot him, and also that he begot no-one. This affirmation, and the disputatious attitude to Christianity which it expresses, derives from the sense of the unity and indivisibility of God's power.

Contrasted with this, there are cases of oriental rulers with hundreds of sons, all compelled to fight each other for the succession. One can assume that knowledge of the hostility between them does something to lessen the bitterness their father feels about the succession of any one of them.

The deeper significance of hereditary succession, its real purpose and advantage, will be discussed in another context. Here I have only wished to show that the hostility between a ruler and his successor is of a particular kind which must increase side by side with the increase of the specific passion of power, the passion for survival.

Forms of Survival

There are many different forms of survival and it is worth while seeing that we leave no important one out of account.

The earliest event in every man's life, occurring long before birth and of even greater importance, is his conception; and this has never yet been considered in relation to the concept of survival. We already know a great deal, and may soon know everything, about what happens once the spermatozoon has actually penetrated into the egg cell. Scarcely any thought, however, has been given to the fact that there are an overwhelming number of spermatozoa which do not reach their goal, although they play an active part in the process of generation as a whole. It is not a single spermatozoon which sets out for the egg cell, but about 200 million, all of which are all released together in *one* ejaculation and then, in a dense mass, move together towards *one* goal.

They are present in enormous numbers and, since they come into existence through partition, they are all equal; their density could not be greater, and they all have the same goal. These four traits, it will be remembered, are what I have described as the essential attributes of the crowd.

It is unnecessary to point out that a crowd of spermatozoa cannot be the same as a crowd of people. But there is undoubtedly an analogy between the two phenomena, and perhaps more than an analogy.

All the spermatozoa except one *perish,* either on the way to, or in the immediate vicinity of, the goal. One single seed alone penetrates the egg cell, and this seed can very well be called the survivor. It is, as it were, the leader of all the others and succeeds in achieving what every leader, either secretly or openly, hopes for, which is to *survive* those he leads. It is to such a survivor, one out of 200 million, that every human being owes his existence.

From this we pass on to other, more familiar forms of survival. In the preceding chapters there has been frequent mention of *killing*. A man is confronted by the enemy. It may be a single enemy, whom he can ambush or fight an open duel with; it may be a pack which he feels closing in on him; or it may be a whole crowd. In this last case he will not be fighting alone, but together with his own people. The higher his rank, however, the more he will feel that survival is his sole right: it is generals who "win." But, since many of his own people as well as of the enemy will have fallen, the heap of the dead is a mixed one, consisting of friends and enemies alike; in this respect battles are "neutral," like epidemics.

At this point we pass from *killing* to *dying,* dying on the most colossal scale known, that is, in epidemics and other natural catastrophes. In these anyone who survives, survives *all* who are mortal, friend and foe alike. All normal ties are dissolved, and dying becomes so universal that no-one even knows who it is that is being buried. Of great significance in this context are the continually re-curring stories of people who come back to life in the midst of a heap of the dead, who wake amongst the dead. Such people tend to think of themselves as invulnerable, plague-heroes as it were.

The satisfaction which follows individual deaths is more moder-ate and more concealed. The victims may be friends or relatives and there is no question of active killing and no sense of being attacked. Nothing is done to hasten death, but it is waited for. The young survive the old; sons their fathers.

A son finds it natural that his father should die before him. Filial duty hurries him to the death-bed, to close his father's eyes and carry him to his grave. During this period, which may last for days, he has his father lying dead before him. The man who, more than anyone else, could once order him about is now reduced to silence and, helpless, must endure everything which is done to his body. And it is his son, for many years wholly at his mercy, who directs and arranges all this.

Here the satisfaction in survival results from the relationship be-tween the two protagonists. One who was once all-powerful is now impotent, his strength extinguished and his lifeless remains at the disposal of the very being who was for many years weak, helpless and entirely in his power.

Everything the father leaves strengthens the son; the inheritance is the son's booty. He can do the opposite of everything the father would have done. If the father was thrifty, the son can be wasteful, reckless where he was prudent. It is as though a new régime had been proclaimed and the breach between the old and the new is im-mense and irreparable. The breach results from survival and is also the most intimate and personal expression of it.

Among people of the same age survival is very different. Since it is a question of one's own group the urge to survive is concealed by milder forms of rivalry. Young men of the same age are grouped together as a class and then, on the fulfillment of certain rites in-volving severe and often cruel ordeals, are promoted to the next class. It may happen that some of them perish during these ordeals, but that is the exception.

The old, that is those men who are still alive after the lapse of a certain number of years, enjoy great authority, especially among primitive peoples, who, on the whole tend to die earlier than we do, for they undergo greater perils and are more vulnerable to disease. For them it is a real achievement to reach a certain age, and one which brings its reward. Not only do the old know more, having gained experience in a great variety of situations, but the fact that they are still alive shows that they have proved themselves. To emerge unscathed from all the dangers of war, hunting and accident they must have been lucky; and with every escape their prestige will have grown. They have trophies proving their victories over their enemies. The group they belong to is of necessity small and therefore very much aware of their long-continued membership in it. They have experienced many occasions for lament, but they are still alive and every death of a contemporary increases their prestige. The group may not be fully conscious of this and may well attach greater importance to victories over enemies, but one thing is certain: the most elementary and obvious form of success is to remain alive. The old are not only alive, but are *still* alive. Old men can take as many young wives as they want, whilst young men may have to content themselves with old ones. They have the right of deciding where the group shall migrate, whom it shall make war on and with whom ally itself. In so far as one can speak of government in such conditions, it is the old men together who govern.

The desire for a long life which plays such a large part in most cultures really means that most people want to survive their contemporaries. They know that many die early and they want a different fate for themselves. Whey they pray to the gods for long life they differentiate themselves from their companions. It is true that the latter are not mentioned in the prayer, but what the supplicant visualizes is himself living longer than others. The most wholesome embodiment of longevity is the *Patriarch,* one who can survey many generations of his descendants, but is always imagined alone in his own generation. It is as though a new race began with him. As long as he has grandsons and great-grandsons alive it does not matter if some of his sons have died before him. Indeed, the fact that his life has proved tougher than theirs increases his authority.

Within the class of old men there is always one who in the end is left solitary, the very oldest of them all. The Etruscans fixed the length of the century by the duration of his life. It is worth saying a little more about this.

The "century" of the Etruscans varied, being sometimes shorter and sometimes longer, its duration in each case being decided afresh. In every generation there is one man who lives to be older than the rest. The Etruscans believed that when this man died, who was the very oldest of all, the one who had survived all his contemporaries, the gods gave men certain signs, and they then adjusted the length of the century to coincide with the length of his life. If he lived to the age of 110, the century was counted as 110 years; if he died at 105, the century was that much shorter. The survivor *was* the century; the years of his life constituted it.

Each city and each people were thought to have a predestined number of such centuries, starting from the foundation of the city. Ten were allotted to the nation of the Etruscans. If the survivor of each generation had an unusually long life, the nation as a whole lived to be so much older. The connection between the two is remarkable and, as a religious institution, unique.

Only survival at a distance in time is wholly innocent. A man cannot have killed people who lived long before him and whom he did not know; he cannot have wished for their death, nor even have waited for it. He learns of their existence only when they exist no longer. In fact, by his awareness of their lives, however insubstantial the form of survival it assists them to, he serves them more than they serve him. It can, however, be shown that they do contribute something to his own sense of survival.

We survive the ancestors we have not known personally and we also survive preceding humanity as a whole. It is in graveyards and cemeteries that the second of these experiences is brought home to us, and we see then how closely it resembles survival in epidemics. Instead of plague, it is the general epidemic of death which confronts us, whose victims over the years lie gathered together in this one place.

At this point it may be objected that the concept of survival, as I have described it, has long been known under a different name: that of the instinct of self-preservation.

But are the two really identical? Do the words express the same thing? It seems to me that they do not, and, if we ask ourselves what kind of activity we imagine when we speak of self-preservation and if we look at the word itself, the reasons for the inadequacy of the concept become apparent. First there is the stress on *self*: every human being is postulated as solitary and self-sufficient. But the second half of the word is even more important; by "preservation" we actually mean two things: first, that every creature must *eat* in order to stay alive and, second, that, in some way or other, every creature defends itself against attack. We see it before us rather as if it were a statue, with one hand reaching for food and with the other fending off its enemies. A peaceful creature indeed! Left to itself, it would eat a handful of grass and never do anyone the slightest harm.

Is there any conception less appropriate to man, more misleading and more ridiculous? It is true that man does eat, but not the same food as a cow; nor is he led to pasture. His way of procuring his prey is cunning, bloodthirsty and strenuous; there is certainly nothing passive about it. He does not mildly defend himself, but attacks his enemies as soon as he senses them in the distance; and his weapons of attack are far better developed than his weapons of defence. True, he wants to "preserve" himself, but he also simultaneously wants other things which are inseparable from this. He wants to kill so that he can survive others; he wants to stay alive so as not to have others surviving him.

If "self-preservation" included these two desires then the concept would have a meaning, but, as it is, there is no reason why we should retain it when another is so much more accurate.

All the forms of survival I have enumerated are of great antiquity and, as will be shown, are found even amongst primitive peoples.

The Survivor in Primitive Belief

Mana is the name given in the Pacific to a kind of supernatural and impersonal power, which can pass from one man to another. It is something which is much desired, and an individual can increase his own measure of it. A brave warrior can acquire it to a high degree, but he does not owe it to his skill in fighting or to his bodily strength; it passes into him as the *mana* of his slain enemy.

"In the Marquesas it was through personal prowess that a tribesman became a war chief. The warrior was thought to embody the *mana* of all those whom he had killed, his own *mana* increasing in proportion with his prowess. In the mind of the native, the prowess was the result, however, not the cause of his *mana*. The *mana* of the warrior's spear was likewise increased with each death he inflicted. As the sign of his assumption of his defeated enemy's power, the victor in a hand-to-hand combat assumed his slain foe's name; with a view to absorbing directly his *mana*, he ate some of his flesh; and to bind the presence of the empowering influence in battle, to insure his intimate rapport with the captured *mana*, he wore as a part of his war dress some physical relic of his vanquished foe—a bone, a dried hand, sometimes a whole skull."

The effect of victory on the survivor could not be more clearly conceived. By killing his opponent the survivor becomes stronger and the addition of *mana* makes him capable of new victories. It is a kind of blessing which he wrests from his enemy, but he only obtains it if the latter is killed. The physical presence of the enemy, first alive and then dead, is essential. There must have been fighting and killing, and the personal act of killing is crucial. The manageable parts of the corpse which the victor removes and either embodies into himself, or wears as trophies, serve as continual reminders of the increase of his power.

Immortality

Consideration of literary or any other private immortality can best start with a man like Stendhal. It would be hard to find a man less sympathetic to religion and more completely unaffected by its promises and obligations. His thoughts and feelings were directed wholly to this life and he experienced it with exactness and depth. He gave himself up to it, enjoying what could give him pleasure; but he did not become shallow or stale in doing so, because he allowed everything that was separate to remain separate, instead of trying to construct spurious unities. He thought much, but his thoughts were never cold. He was suspicious of everything that did not move him. All that he recorded and all that he shaped remained close to the fiery moment of genesis. He loved many things and believed in some, but all of them remained miraculously concrete for him. They were all there in him and he could find them at once without resort to specious tricks of arrangement.

This man, who took nothing for granted, who wanted to discover everything for himself; who, as far as life is feeling and spirit, was life itself; who was in the heart of every situation and therefore had a right to look at it from outside; with whom word and substance were so intuitively one that it was as though he had taken it on himself to purify language single-handed—this rare and truly free man had, none the less, one article of faith, which he spoke of as simply and naturally as of a mistress.

Without pitying himself, he was content to write for a few, but he was certain that in a hundred years he would be read by many. Nowhere in modern times is a belief in literary immortality to be found in a clearer, purer and less pretentious form. What does a man mean who holds this belief? He means that he will still be here when everyone else who lived at the same time is no longer here. It is not that he feels any animosity towards the living as such; he does not try to get rid of them, nor harm them in any way. He does not even see them as opponents. He despises those who acquire false fame and would despise himself too if he fought them with their own weapons. He bears them no malice, for he knows how completely mistaken they are, but he chooses the company of those to whom he himself will one day belong, men of earlier times whose work still lives, who speak to him and *feed* him. The gratitude he feels to them is gratitude for life itself.

Killing in order to survive is meaningless to such a man, for it is not now that he wants to survive. It is only in a hundred years that he will enter the lists, when he is no longer alive and thus cannot kill. Then it will be a question of work contending against work, with nothing that he himself can do. The true rivalry, the one that matters, begins when the rivals are no longer there. Thus he cannot even watch the fight. But the *work* must be there and, if it is to be there, it must contain the greatest and purest measure of life. Not only does he abjure killing, but he takes with him into immortality all who were alive with him here, and it is then that all these, the least as well as the greatest, are most truly alive.

He is the exact opposite of those rulers whose whole entourage must die when they die, so that they may find among the dead all they have been used to on earth. In nothing is their ultimate powerlessness more terribly revealed. They kill in death as they have killed in life; a retinue of the slain accompanies them from one world to the other.

But whoever opens Stendhal will find him and also everything which surrounded him; and he finds it *here*, in this life. Thus the dead offer themselves as food to the living; their immortality profits them. It is a reversal of sacrifice to the dead, which profits both dead and living. There is no more rancour between them and the sting has been taken from survival.

.

The silent house and the empty rooftops

In order to feel at home in a strange city you need to have a secluded room to which you have a certain title and in which you can be alone when the tumult of new and incomprehensible voices becomes too great. The room should be quiet; no one should see you make your escape there, no one see you leave. The best thing is when you can slip into a cul-de-sac, stop at a door to which you have the key in your pocket, and unlock it without a soul hearing.

You step into the coolness of the house and close the door behind you. It is dark, and for a moment you can see nothing. You are like one of the blind men in the squares and passages you have just left. But you very soon have your eyesight back. You see a stone stairway leading to the first floor, and at the top you find a cat. The cat embodies the noiselessness you have been longing for. You are grateful to it for being alive: a quiet life is possible, then. It is fed without crying 'Allah' a thousand times a day. It is not mutilated, nor is it obliged to bow to a terrible fate. Cruel it may be, but it does not say so.

You walk up and down and breathe in the silence. What has become of the atrocious bustle? The harsh light and the harsh sounds? The hundreds upon hundreds of faces? Few windows in these houses look onto the street, sometimes none at all; everything opens onto the courtyard, and this lies open to the sky. Only through the courtyard do you retain a mellow, tempered link with the world around you.

But you can also go up on the roof and see all the flat roofs of the city at once. The impression is one of levelness, of everything being built in a series of broad terraces. You feel you could walk all over the city up there. The narrow streets present no obstacle; you cannot see them, you forget that there are streets. The Atlas gleam close and you would take them for the Alps were the light on them not brighter and were there not so many palm trees between them and the city.

The minarets that rise here and there are not like church spires. They are slender, but they do not taper; they are the same width top and bottom, and what matters is the platform in the sky from which the faithful are called to prayer. A minaret is more like a lighthouse, but with a voice for a light.

The space above the rooftops is peopled with swallows. It is like a second city, except that here things happen as fast as they happen slowly in the human streets below. They never rest, those swallows, you wonder if they ever sleep; idleness, moderation, and dignity are qualities they lack. They snatch their prey in flight; maybe the roofs in their emptiness look like a conquered land to them.

You see, you do not show yourself on the roof. Up there, I had thought, I shall feast my eyes on the women of fable; from there I shall overlook the neighbours' courtyards and overhear their goings-on. The first time I went up on the roof of my friend's house I was full of expectations, and as long as I continued to gaze into the distance, at the mountains and out over the city, he was content and I could sense his pride at being able to show me something so beautiful. But he started to fidget when, tiring of the far off, I became curious as to the near at hand. He caught me glancing down into the courtyard of the house next door, where to my delight I had become aware of women's voices speaking Spanish.

'That's not done here,' he said. 'You mustn't do that. I've often been warned against it. It's considered indelicate to take any notice of what goes on next door. It's considered bad manners. In fact one oughtn't to show oneself on the roof at all, and a man certainly not. Sometimes the womenfolk go up on the roofs, and they want to feel undisturbed.'

'But there aren't any women up here at all.'

'We may have been seen,' said my friend. 'One gets a bad name. One doesn't address a veiled woman on the street, either.'

'What if I want to ask the way?'

'You must wait till a man comes along.'

'But surely you can sit up on your own roof, can't you? If you see someone on the next roof it's not your fault.'

'Then I must look away. I must show how uninterested I am. A woman's just come up on the roof behind us, an old servant. She has no idea I've seen her, but she's already going down again.'

She was gone before I could turn round.

'But then one's less free on the roof than one is on the street,' I protested.

'Certainly,' he said. 'One wants to avoid getting a bad name with one's neighbours.'

I watched the swallows and envied the way they went swooping at their ease over three, five, ten roofs at a time.

The donkey's concupiscence

I liked to return from my evening strolls through the streets of the city by way of the Djema el Fna. It was strange, crossing that great square as it lay almost empty. There were no acrobats any more and no dancers; no snake-charmers and no fire-eaters. A little man squatted forlornly on the ground, a basket of very small eggs before him and nothing and no one else anywhere near him. Acetylene lamps burned here and there; the square smelled of them. In the cookshops one or two men still sat over their soup. They looked lonely, as if they had nowhere to go. Around the edges of the square people were settling down to sleep. Some lay, though most squatted, and they had all pulled the hoods of their cloaks over their heads. Their sleep was motionless; you would never have suspected anything breathing beneath those dark hoods.

One night I saw a large, dense circle of people in the middle of the square, acetylene lamps illuminating them in the strangest way. They were all standing. The dark shadows on faces and figures, edged by the harsh light thrown on them by the lamps, gave them a cruel, sinister look. I could hear two native instruments playing and a man's voice addressing someone in vehement terms. I went up closer and found a gap through which I could see inside the circle. What I saw was a man, standing in the middle with a stick in his hand, urgently interrogating a donkey.

Of all the city's miserable donkeys, this was the most pitiful. His bones stuck out, he was completely starved, his coat was worn off, and he was clearly no longer capable of bearing the least little burden. One wondered how his legs still held him up. The man was engaged in a comic dialogue with him. He was trying to cajole him into something. The donkey remaining stubborn, he asked him questions; and when he refused to answer, the illuminated onlookers burst out laughing. Possibly it was a story in which a donkey played a part, because after a lengthy palaver the wretched animal began to turn very slowly to the music. The stick was still being brandished above him. The man was talking faster and faster, fairly ranting now in order to keep the donkey going, but it sounded to me from his words as if he too represented a figure of fun. The music played on and on and the men, who now never stopped laughing, had the look of man-eating or donkey-eating savages.

I stayed only a short time and so cannot say what happened subsequently. My repulsion outweighed my curiosity. I had long before conceived an affection for the donkeys of the city. Every step offered me occasion to feel indignant at the way they were treated, though of course there was nothing I could do. But never had quite such a lamentable specimen as this crossed my path, and on my way home I sought to console myself with the thought that he would certainly not last the night.

The next day was a Saturday and I went to the Djema el Fna early in the morning. Saturday was one of its busiest days. Onlookers, performers, baskets, and booths thronged the square; it was a job to make one's way through the crowd. I came to the place where the donkey had stood the evening before. I looked, and I could hardly believe my eyes: there he was again. He was standing all by himself. I examined him closely and there was no mistaking him; it was he. His master was nearby, chatting quietly with a few people. No circle had formed round them yet. The musicians were not there; the performance had not yet begun. The donkey was standing exactly as he had the night before. In the bright sunshine his coat looked even shabbier than at night. I found him older, more famished, and altogether more wretched.

Suddenly I became aware of someone behind me and of angry words in my ear, words I did not understand. Turning, I lost sight of the donkey for a moment. The man I had heard was pressed right up against me in the crowd, but it became apparent that he had been threatening someone else and not me. I turned back to the donkey.

He had not budged, but it was no longer the same donkey. Because between his back legs, slanting forwards and down, there hung all of a sudden a prodigious member. It was stouter than the stick the man had been threatening him with the night before. In the tiny space of time in which I had had my back turned an overwhelming change had come over him. I do not know what he had seen, heard, or smelled. But that pitiful, aged, feeble creature, who was on the verge of collapse and quite useless for anything any more except as the butt of comic dialogue, who was treated worse than a donkey in Marrakesh, that being, less than nothing, with no meat on his bones, no strength, no proper coat, still had so much lust in him that the mere sight absolved me of the impression caused by his misery. I often think of him. I remind myself how much of him was still there when I saw nothing left. I wish all the tormented his concupiscence in misery.

Robert Walser
Translated by Christopher Middleton

Jakob von Gunten

One learns very little here, there is a shortage of teachers, and none of us boys of the Benjamenta Institute will come to anything, that is to say, we shall all be something very small and subordinate later in life. The instruction that we enjoy consists mainly in impressing patience and obedience upon ourselves, two qualities that promise little success, or none at all. Inward successes, yes. But what does one get from such as these? Do inward acquisitions give one food to eat? I would like to be rich, to ride in coaches and squander money. I have discussed this with Kraus, my school-friend, but he only shrugged his shoulders in scorn and did not honor me with a single word of reply. Kraus has principles, he sits firmly in the saddle, he rides satisfaction, and that is a horse which people should not mount if they want to do some galloping. Since I have been at the Benjamenta Institute I have already contrived to become a mystery to myself. Even I have been infected by a quite remarkable feeling of satisfaction, which I never knew before. I obey tolerably well, not so well as Kraus, who has a masterly understanding of how to rush forward helterskelter for commands to obey. In one thing we pupils are all similar, Kraus, Schacht, Schilinski, Fuchs, Beanpole Peter, and me, all of us—and that is in our complete poverty and dependence. We are small, small all the way down the scale to utter worthlessness. If anyone owns a single mark in pocket money, he is regarded as a privileged prince. If anyone

smokes cigarettes, as I do, he arouses concern about the wasteful-
ness in which he is indulging. We wear uniforms. Now, the wearing
of uniforms simultaneously humiliates and exalts us. We look like
unfree people, and that is possibly a disgrace, but we also look nice
in our uniforms, and that sets us apart from the deep disgrace of
those people who walk around in their very own clothes but in torn
and dirty ones. To me, for instance, wearing a uniform is very pleasant because I never did know, before, what clothes to put on. But
in this, too, I am a mystery to myself for the time being. Perhaps
there is a very very commonplace person inside me. But perhaps I
have aristocratic blood in my veins. I don't know. But one thing I
do know for certain: in later life I shall be a charming, utterly spher-
ical zero. As an old man I shall have to serve young and confident
and badly educated ruffians, or I shall be a beggar, or I shall perish.

We pupils, or cadets, have really very little to do, we are given
hardly any assignments. We learn the rules by heart. Or we read in
the book *What Is the Aim of Benjamenta's Boys' School?* Kraus is
also studying French, on his own, for there are no foreign languages
or suchlike things on our timetable. There is only a single class, and
that is always repeated: "How Should a Boy Behave?" Basically, all
our instruction is centered on this question. We are not taught anything. There is a shortage, as I said before, of teachers, that is to
say, the educators and teachers are asleep, or they are dead, or
seemingly dead, or they are fossilized, no matter, in any case we get
nothing from them. Instead of the teachers, who for some strange
reason really are lying around like dead men, and sleeping, a young
lady instructs and rules us, Fräulein Lisa Benjamenta, the sister of
the Principal. She comes, with a small white cane in her hand, into
the classroom and the class. We all stand up at our desks when she
appears. Once she has sat down, we are allowed to sit down also.
She gives three sharp and imperious knocks on the edge of her desk,
and the instruction begins. What instruction! But I would be telling
lies if I found it curious. No. I find the things that Fräulein Benjamenta teaches us adorable. It is little, and we are always revising,
but perhaps there is some mystery hidden behind all these nothings
and laughable things. Laughable? We boys of the Benjamenta Institute never feel like laughing. Our faces and our manners are very
serious. Even Schilinski, who is still a complete child, laughs very
seldom. Kraus never laughs, or, when he is carried away, he gives a

very short laugh only, and then he is angry that he let himself be drawn into adopting such a prohibited tone. Generally, we pupils do not like to laugh, that is to say, we are hardly able to any more. We lack the requisite jolliness and airiness. Am I wrong? God knows, sometimes my whole stay here seems like an incomprehensible dream.

The youngest and smallest of us pupils is Heinrich. One can't help feeling gentle toward this young man, without thinking anything of it. He stands quietly in front of shop-windows, quite absorbed by the sight of the goods and of the tasty things in there. Then he usually goes in and buys some sweets for six groschen. Heinrich is still a complete child, but he already talks and behaves like a grown person, with good manners. His hair is always faultlessly combed and parted, which compels me at once to realize that, in this important detail, I am very slovenly. His voice is as thin as a delicate twittering of birds. One involuntarily puts an arm around his shoulders when one goes for a walk with him, or when one speaks with him. He has no character, for he still has no idea at all what that is. Certainly he has not thought about life yet, and why should he think about it? He is very polite, ready to serve, and well-mannered, but without knowing it. Yes, he is like a bird. Cosiness comes out all over him. A bird gives one its hand when he does so, a bird walks like that and stands like that. Everything about Heinrich is innocent, peaceful, and happy. He wants to be a page, he says. But he says it without any indelicate wistfulness, and indeed the profession of page is thoroughly right and apt for him. The tenderness of his behavior and feeling aspires in some direction or other, and look, it reaches the right goal. What sort of experiences will he have? Will any experiences and any knowledge venture to approach this boy at all? Will not life's raw disappointments be too shy to upset him, him, with his pixie delicateness? I also observe that he is a little cold, there is nothing tempestuous and challenging about him. Perhaps he will not even notice many things that might have struck him low, and will not feel many things that might have robbed him of his blitheness. Who knows if I'm right! But I like, very very much, to make such observations. Heinrich is, to a certain extent, mindless. That is his good fortune, and one must allow him it. It he were a prince, I would be the first to bow my knee before him and make obeisance. What a pity!

How stupidly I behaved when I arrived here! Mainly I was shocked at the shabbiness of the front steps. Well, all right, they were just the stairs to an ordinary big-city backstreet building. Then I rang the bell and a monkey-like being opened the door. It was Kraus. But at that time I simply thought of him as a monkey, whereas today I have a high opinion of him, because of the very personal quality which adorns him. I asked if I could speak to Herr Benjamenta. Kraus said: "Yes, sir!" and bowed to me, deeply and stupidly. This bow infused me with strange terror, for I told myself at once that there must be something wrong with the place. And from that moment, I regarded the Benjamenta school as a swindle. I went to the Principal's office. How I laugh when I think back on the scene that followed! Herr Benjamenta asked me what I wanted. I told him quietly that I wanted to become his pupil. At this, he fell silent and read newspapers. The office, the Principal, the monkey who led me in, the doors, the way of falling silent and reading newspapers, everything, everything seemed deeply suspicious to me, a promise of destruction. Suddenly I was asked for my name and where I came from. Now I thought I was lost, for suddenly I felt that I would never escape from the place. I stuttered out the information, I even ventured to emphasize that I came from a very good family. Among other things, I said that my father was an alderman, and that I had run away from him because I was afraid of being suffocated by his excellence. Again the Principal fell silent for a while. My fear that I had been deceived grew most intense. I even thought of secret murder, of being slowly strangled. Then the Principal inquired, in his imperious voice, if I had any money with me, and I said that I had. "Give it to me, then, Quickly!" he commanded, and, strange to relate, I obeyed at once, although I was shaking with misery. I was now quite certain that I had fallen into the clutches of a robber and swindler, and all the same I obediently laid the school fees down. How laughable my feelings at that time now seem to me! Then I found the heroic courage to ask, quietly, for a receipt, but I was given the following answer; "Rascals like you don't get receipts!" I almost fainted. The Principal rang a bell. Immediately the silly monkey Kraus rushed into the room. Silly monkey? Oh, not at all. Kraus is a dear, dear person. Only I understood no better at that time. "This is Jakob, the new pupil. Take him to the classroom." The Principal had hardly spoken when

Kraus grabbed me and thrust me into the presence of the instructress. How childish one is when one is frightened! There is no worse behavior than that which comes from distrust and ignorance. That is how I became a pupil.

My school-friend Schacht is a strange person. He dreams of becoming a musician. He tells me that he plays the violin marvelously, with the help of his imagination, and I quite believe him. He likes to laugh, but then he lapses suddenly into wistful melancholy, which suits his face and bearing incredibly well. Schacht has a completely white face and long slender hands, which express a nameless suffering of soul. Being slight, as to the build of his body, he is easily all a-fidget, it is difficult for him to stand, or to sit, still. He is like a sickly, obstinate girl, he also likes grumbling, which makes him even more like a young and somewhat warped female being. He and I, we often lie together in my room on the bed, in our clothes, without taking our shoes off, and smoke cigarettes, which is against the rules. Schacht likes to offend against the rules and I, to be candid, unfortunately no less. We tell each other whole stories, when we are lying thus, stories from our lives, that is, experiences, but even more often invented stories, with the facts plucked from the air. When we do so, it seems to us that a soft music plays all up and down the walls. The narrow dark room expands, streets appear, palatial rooms, cities, châteaux, unknown people and landscapes, there are thunders and whisperings, voices speak and weep, et cetera. It is nice to talk to this slightly dreamy Schacht. He seems to understand everything that one tells him, and from time to time he says something significant himself. And then he often complains, and that is what I like about our conversation. I like hearing people complain. Then one can look just so at the person speaking, and have deep, intimate sympathy with him, and Schacht has something about him that rouses sympathy, even when he does not say depressing things. If there dwells in any man a delicate-minded dissatisfaction, that is, the yearning for something beautiful and lofty, it has made itself at home in Schacht. Schacht has a soul. Who knows, perhaps he has the disposition of an artist. He has confided to me that he is sick, and, since it is a question of a rather improper sickness, he has asked me urgently not to speak about it, which I have naturally promised, on my word of honor, in order to put his mind at rest. Then I asked him to show me the object of his malaise, but at that point he became a little angry and he turned to the wall. "You're terrible," he told me. Once I ventured to take his hand gently in mine, but he withdrew it and said: "What silliness are you up to now? Stop it." Schacht prefers to go about with me, this in particular I notice clearly, but in such matters clarity is not at all necessary. As a matter of fact, I like him enormously and regard him as an enrichment of my existence. Naturally I never told him such things. We say stupid things to each other, often serious things too, but avoiding big words. Fine words are much too boring. Ah, the meetings with Schacht in my room make me realize it: we pupils at the Benjamenta Institute are condemned to a strange idleness, often lasting half the day. We always crouch, sit, stand, or lie around somewhere. Schacht and I often light candles in my room, for our enjoyment. It is strictly forbidden. But that is why it is so much fun. Whatever may be said in the rules: candlelight is so beautiful, so mysterious. And how my friend's face looks when the small red flame illuminates it! When I see candles burning, I always feel that I am wealthy. The next moment, in comes the janitor and gives me a scolding. That is all very senseless, but this senselessness has a pretty mouth, and it smiles. Actually Schacht has coarse features, but the pallor which suffuses his face refines them. His nose is too big, so are his ears. His mouth is tight shut. Sometimes when I see Schacht in this way I feel that this person will have a bitterly hard time one day. How I love people who evoke this mournful impression! Is that brotherly love? Yes, perhaps.

On the first day my behavior was enormously prim, I was like mother's little boy. I was shown the room in which I was to sleep together with the others, i.e., with Kraus, Schacht, and Schilinski. A fourth to make up the party, as it were. Everyone was there, my comrades, the Principal, who was looking at me grimly, and his sister. Well, and then I simply threw myself at the maiden's feet and exclaimed: "No, I can't sleep in that room, it's impossible! I can't breathe in there. I'd rather spend the night on the street." While I was speaking, I clung to the young lady's legs. She seemed to be annoyed and told me to stand up. I said: "I won't stand up until you promise to give me a decent room to sleep in. I ask you, Fräulein, I implore you, put me somewhere else, in a hole, for all I care, but not in here. I can't be here. I certainly won't offend my fellow-pupils, and if I've already done so I'm sorry, but to sleep together with three people, as a fourth person, and in such a small room, too? It won't do. Ah, Fräulein!" She was smiling now, I noticed it, and so I quickly added, clinging even more tightly to her: "I'll be good, I promise you. I'll obey all your commands. You'll never, never have to complain of my behavior." Fräulein Benjamenta asked: "Is that so? Shall I never have to complain?" "No, it certainly isn't so, Fräulein," I replied. She exchanged a meaningful look with her brother, the Principal, and said to me: "Do please first stand up. Good heavens, what insistency and what a fuss! And now come along. You can sleep somewhere else, for all I care." She took me to the room in which I live now, showed it to me, and asked: "Do you like this room?" I was cheeky enough to say: "It's small. At home the windows had curtains. And the sun shone into the rooms there. Here there's only a narrow bed and a washstand. At home there were completely furnished rooms. But don't be angry Fräulein Benjamenta. I like it, and thank you. At home it was much more refined, friendlier and more elegant, but it's very nice here too. Forgive me for coming at you with the comparisons with how it was at home, and heaven knows what else besides. But I find the room very very charming. To be sure, the window up there in the wall can hardly be called a window. And the whole thing is definitely rather like a rat's hole, or a dog-kennel. But I like it. And I'm impertinent and ungrateful to talk to you like this, aren't I? Perhaps the best thing would be for you to take the room away from me again, though I have a really high opinion of it, and give me strict orders to sleep with the others. My comrades certainly feel offended. And you, Fräulein, are angry. I see it. It makes me very sad." She said to me: "You're a silly boy, and now you be quiet." And yet she was smiling. How silly it all was, on that first day. I was ashamed of myself, and I'm ashamed, to this day, when I think how improperly I behaved. I slept very restlessly the first night. I dreamed of the instructress. And as regards my own room, I would to this day be quite happy to share it with one or two other people. One is always half mad when one is shy of people.

Herr Benjamenta is a giant, and we pupils are dwarfs beside this giant, who is always rather gruff. As guide and commander of a crowd of such tiny, insignificant creatures as we boys are, he is certainly obliged, it is most natural, to be peevish, for this can never be a task that matches his powers: just ruling over us. No, Herr

Benjamenta could do quite different things. Such a Hercules cannot help falling asleep, that is, growling and musing as he reads his newspapers, when he confronts such a petty exercise as that of educating us. What can the man have been thinking of when he decided to found the Institute? In a certain sense, it hurts me, and this feeling increases still more the respect that I have for him. Between him and me, at the beginning of my time here, I think it was during the morning of my second day, there was a small scene, but a violent one. I went into his office, but I couldn't manage to open my mouth. "Go outside again! See if it's possible for you to enter the room like a decent human being," he said austerely. I went out and then I knocked on the door, which I had quite forgotten to do before. "Come in," said a voice, and then I went in and stood there. "Well, aren't you going to make your bow? And what does one say on entering?" I bowed and said, in a feeble tone of voice: "Good day, Principal." Today I am so well trained that I positively trumpet out this "Good day, Principal." In those days, I hated this servile and polite way of behaving, it was just that I knew no better. What seemed to me laughable and dimwitted then, now seems apt and beautiful. "Speak louder, you rascal," exclaimed Herr Benjamenta. I had to repeat the greeting "Good day, Principal" five times. Only then did he ask what I wanted. I had got furious, and said: "One learns absolutely nothing here and I don't want to stay. Please give me my money back, and then I'll get out of the place. Where are the teachers here? Is there any plan, any idea to what we do? There's nothing. And I'm leaving. Nobody, whoever he is, will stop me from leaving this place of darkness and mystification. I come from much too good a family to let myself be plagued by your silly rules. To be sure, I don't mean to run back to my father and mother, never, but I'll take to the streets and sell myself as a slave. There's no harm in that." Well, I had said it. Today I almost have to double up with laughing when I recall this silly behavior. At that time, I felt altogether serious. But the Principal didn't say a word. I was on the verge of saying something rude and offensive to his face. Then he quietly spoke: "Sums of money, once paid in, are not paid back. As for your foolish opinion that you can learn nothing here, you are wrong, for you can learn. Learn, first of all, to know your surroundings. Your comrades are worth the attempt to get to know them. Talk with them. I advise you, keep calm. Nice and calm."

This "nice and calm" he uttered as if in deep thought, without a care in the world for me. He kept his eyes downcast, as if he wanted me to understand how well and how gently he meant it. He gave me clear proofs of his being absent in thought, and was silent again. What could I do? Herr Benjamenta was already busy reading his newspapers again. I felt as if a terrible, incomprehensible storm was creeping up on me. I bowed deeply, almost to the ground, to him who was paying no more attention to me, said, as the rules required, "Adieu, Principal," clicked my heels, stood at attention, turned about, that is, no, I groped for the door handle, still kept looking at the Principal's face, and thrust myself, without turning around, through the door and out again. Thus ended my attempt at revolution. Since then, there have been no wilful scenes. My God, and I have been defeated. He defeated me, he, to whom I attribute a truly great heart, and I didn't move, didn't bat an eyelid, and he didn't even insult me. Only it hurt me, and not for my own sake, but for the Principal's. Actually, I am always thinking of him, of both of them, of him and Fräulein, the way they go on living here with us boys. What are they always doing in there, in their apartment? How do they keep themselves busy? Are they poor? Are the Benjamentas poor? There are "Inner Chambers" here. I have never been in them to this day. Kraus has, he is privileged, because he is so loyal. But Kraus doesn't want to give any information about the way the Principal's apartment is. He only goggles at me, when I ask him questions on this point, and says nothing. Oh, Kraus can really be silent. If I were a master, I would take Kraus into my service at once. But perhaps one day I shall penetrate into these inner chambers. And what will my eyes discover then? Perhaps nothing special at all? Oh, yes, something special. I know it, somewhere here there are marvelous things.

One thing is true, there is no nature here. That's just it, this is the big city, after all. At home there were views everywhere, near and far. I think I always heard the songbirds twittering up and down the streets. The streams were always murmuring. The woody mountain gazed down majestically upon the neat town. On the nearby lake one traveled, evenings, in a gondola. Cliffs and woods, hills and fields could be reached with a short walk. There were always voices and fragrances. And the streets of the town were like garden paths, they looked so soft and clean. Nice white houses peeped roguishly from green gardens. One saw well-known ladies, for example Frau Haag, out for a walk on the other side of the park fence. Silly it is, really, anyway nature, the mountain, the lake, the river, the foaming waterfall, the green foliage, and all sorts of songs and sounds were simply near at hand. If one went for a walk, it was like walking in the sky, for one saw blue sky everywhere. If one stood still, one could lie down straightaway and dream quietly up into the air, for there was grass or moss under one. And the pine trees that smell so wonderfully of spicy power. Shall I never see a mountain pine again? Really that would be no misfortune. To forgo something: that also has its fragrance and its power. Our alderman's house had no garden, but everything around was a neat, sweet, and pretty garden. I hope I am not yearning. Nonsense. It's good being here, too.

Although there's nothing much that merits a scrape, I run to the barber from time to time, for the sake of the excursion on the street, and have myself shaved. The barber's assistant asks if I am a Swede. An American? Not that either. A Russian? Well, then, what are you? I love to answer such nationalistically tinted questions with a steely silence, and to leave people who ask me about my patriotic feelings in the dark. Or I tell lies and say that I'm Danish. Some kinds of frankness are only hurtful and boring. Sometimes the sun shines like mad in these lively streets. Or everything is shrouded in rain, which I also very much like. The people are friendly, although I am unspeakably cheeky sometimes. Often in the lunch hour I sit idly on a bench. The trees in the park are quite colorless. The leaves hang down unnaturally, like lead. Sometimes, it is as if everything here were made of metal and thin iron. Then the rain descends and wets it all. Umbrellas are opened, coaches rumble over the asphalt, people hurry, the girls lift their skirts up. To see legs protruding from a skirt has something peculiarly homey about it. A female leg like that, tightly stockinged, one never sees, and now suddenly one sees it. The shoes cling so beautifully to the shape of the beautiful soft feet. Then the sun is shining again. A little wind blows, and then one thinks of home. Yes, I think of Mamma. She will be crying. Why don't I ever write to her? I can't tell why, can't understand it, and yet I can't decide to write. That's it: I don't want to tell anything. It's too silly. A pity, I shouldn't have parents who love me. I don't want to be loved and desired at all. They will have to get used to not having a son any more.

To be of service to somebody whom one does not know, and who has nothing to do with one, that is charming, it gives one a glimpse into divine and misty paradises. Even then: all people, or almost all, have something to do with one. The people passing by, they have something to do with me, that's for sure. Of course, it's really a private affair. I walk along, the sun is shining, then suddenly I see a puppy whimpering at my feet. At once I observe that this little animal extravagance has got his small legs caught up in his muzzle. He can't walk any more. I stoop and this great big misfortune is a thing of the past. Now the dog's mistress comes marching along. She sees what has happened, and thanks me. Fleetingly I doff my hat to the lady and I go on my way. Ah, that lady back there is now thinking that there are still polite young men in the world. Well and good. I have been of service to young people in general. And how this woman (she was not unpretty) smiled at me. "Thank you, sir." Ah, she made me a Sir. Yes, when one knows how to behave, one is a Sir. And when one says thank you, one respects the person whom one is thanking. The person who smiles is pretty. All women deserve politeness. Every woman has something refined about her. I have seen washerwomen who moved like queens. That is all comical, oh, so comical. And how the sun shone, and then how I ran off!—off into the shop: I'm getting myself photographed there. Herr Benjamenta wants a photograph of me. And then I must write a short and true account of my life. That means paper. So I have the added pleasure of walking into a stationer's.

Comrade Schilinski comes from a Polish family. He speaks an attractive broken German. Everything that is foreign sounds noble, I don't know why. Schilinski's great pride is an electric tiepin that he got hold of somehow. He also likes, very much indeed, striking wax matches. Remarkably often one sees him cleaning his suit, polishing his boots and brushing his cap. He likes to look at himself in a cheap pocket mirror. Of course, we pupils have all got pocket mirrors, although we really do not know the meaning of vanity. Schilinski is slim and has an attractive face and curly hair, which he tirelessly combs and tends during the day. He says he would like to have a pony. To comb and groom a horse, and then go out on it, is his fondest dream. His mental gifts are few and far between. He is not quick-witted at all, one should not, in his case, speak of subtlety of mind. And yet he is not at all stupid, limited perhaps, but I don't like to use this word when thinking of my school-friends. That I am the cleverest of them all is perhaps not altogether so very delightful. What is the use of thoughts and ideas if one feels, as I do, that one doesn't know what to do with them? Anyway. No, no, I'll try to see things clearly and I don't want to be hoitytoity, I never want to feel superior to my surroundings. Schilinski will have good luck in life. Women will prefer him, that is how he looks, altogether the future darling of women. His face and hands have a light-brownish complexion, which reminds one of something distinguished, and his eyes are bashful as a doe's. They are charming eyes. He could be the perfect young country nobleman. His behavior reminds one of a country estate, where city and peasant life, the refined and the rough, commingle in graceful and strong human culture. He likes especially to stroll idly around, and in the liveliest streets, where I sometimes accompany him, to the horror of Kraus, who hates idleness and persecutes and scorns it. "So you two have been out having fun again, have you?"—that's how Kraus welcomes us when we come back home. I shall have much to say about Kraus. He is the most honest and efficient of us pupils, and efficiency and honesty are inexhaustible and immeasurable domains. Nothing can excite me so deeply as the sight and smell of what is good and just. You soon reach the end of feeling about vulgar and evil things, but to get wise to something good and noble is so difficult, and yet also so alluring. No, vices do not interest me much, much less than the virtues. Now I shall have to describe Kraus and I'm positively scared of doing so. Pruderies? Since when? I hope not.

I now go every day to the shop and ask if my photographs will not be ready soon. Each time, I can go up to the top floor in the elevator. I find that rather nice, and it matches my many other inanities. When I travel in an elevator, I really do feel that I am a child of my times. Do other people find it so? I haven't written the account of my life yet. It embarrasses me a little to tell the simple truth about my past. Kraus looks at me more and more reproachfully every day. That suits me very well. I like to see people I love getting a little angry. Nothing pleases me more than to give a completely false image of myself to people for whom I have made a place in my heart. Perhaps that's unjust, but it is audacious, so it is right. Of course, it is a little morbid, in my case. Thus, for example, I imagine that it would be unspeakably lovely to die with the terrible knowledge that I have offended whomsoever I love the most and have filled them with bad opinions of me. Nobody will understand that, or only someone who can sense tremblings of beauty in defiance. To die miserably, because of some mischief, some silliness. Isn't that desirable? No, certainly not. But these are all sillinesses of the crassest kind. At this point something occurs to me and I see myself compelled, for some unknown reason, to say it. A week or more ago I still had ten marks. Well, now these ten marks are gone. One day I walked into a restaurant, one with hostesses. I was quite irresistibly drawn into the place. A girl leaped toward me and forced me to sit down on a sofa. I half knew how it would end. I resisted, but without the slightest emphasis. I just didn't care, and yet I did. It was pleasure beyond compare to play to the girl the role of the refined and condescending gentleman. We were quite alone, and we did the nicest of silly things. We drank. She kept running to the bar, to fetch new drinks. She showed me her charming garter and I caressed it with my lips. Ah, how silly one is. She kept standing up and fetching new things to drink. And so quickly. It was just that she wanted to earn a nice little sum of money from the silly boy. I know this perfectly well, but it was precisely this that I liked—her thinking me silly. Such a peculiar vice: to be secretly pleased to be allowed to observe that one is being slightly robbed. But how enchanting it all seemed to me. All around me, everything was fading out in fluting, caressing music. The girl was Polish, slim and supple, and so deliciously sinful. I thought: "There go my ten marks." So I kissed her. She said: "Tell me, what are you? You behave like a nobleman." I was gulping my fill of the fragrance that flowed from her. She noticed it and thought it was refined. And in fact: what sort of a scoundrel would go, without any feeling for love and beauty, to places where only delight forgives what depravity has undertaken? I lied and said that I was a stableboy. She said: "Oh, no, you behave much too beautifully to be that. Now say Hello." And so I did what they call Saying Hello in such places, that is, she explained it to me, laughing and joking and kissing me, and then I did it. A moment later I found myself on the evening street, cleaned out, down to the last penny. How do I feel about that now? I don't know. But one thing I do know: I must get hold of some money. But how shall I do that?

Almost every early morning there begins a duel of whisperings between Kraus and me. Kraus always believes that he must spur me on to work. Perhaps he's not entirely wrong in supposing that I do not like to get up early. I certainly do like getting up early, but I also find it quite delicious to lie in bed a little longer than I should. To be supposed not to do something is so alluring sometimes that one cannot help doing it. Therefore I love so deeply every kind of compulsion, because it allows me to take joy in what is illicit. If there were no commandments, no duties in the world, I would die, starve, be crippled by boredom. I only have to be spurred on, compelled, regimented. It suits me entirely. Ultimately it is I who decides, only I. I provoke the frowning law to anger a little, afterwards I make the effort to pacify it. Kraus is the embodiment of all the rules here in the Benjamenta Institute, consequently I am always challenging the best of all my fellow-pupils to somewhat of a struggle. I would get ill if I could not quarrel, and Kraus is wonderfully well-suited for quarreling and teasing. He is always right: "Now it really is time you got up, you lazy rat!" And I am always wrong: "Yes, yes, patience, I'm coming." A person in the wrong is cheeky enough always to challenge the patience of a person in the right. Being right is heated, being wrong always makes a show of proud, frivolous composure. The one who is so passionately well-meaning (Kraus) is always defeated by the one (me) who is not so outspokenly intent on what is good and requisite. I triumph, because I carry on lying in bed, and Kraus quakes with wrath, because he has to keep knocking vainly on the door, stamping his foot and saying: "Get up now, Jakob! Do it now! God, what a lazybones." Ah, I do like people who can get angry. Kraus gets angry on the slightest pretext. That is so beautiful, so humorous, so noble. And we two suit one another so well. The sinner must always be faced with the person outraged, or else something would be missing. Then once I have finally got up, I act as if I were standing idly around. "There he is now, standing and gaping, the ninny, instead of doing something," he says then. How splendid that sort of thing is. The mumbling of a grumbler is lovelier to me than the murmuring of a woodland stream, with the loveliest of Sunday morning sunshine sparkling on it. People, people, nothing but people! Yes, I feel it most strongly: I

love people. Their follies and sudden excitements are more dear and
valuable to me than the subtlest wonders of nature.—We pupils
have to sweep and clean the classroom and the office early in the
morning, before our superiors wake up. Two of us do it, in turns.
"Get up now. Are you ready yet?" Or: "You won't be so satisfied
with yourself for long." Or: "Get up, get up. It's time. You should
have had the broom in your hand long ago." How amusing this is!
And Kraus, eternally angry Kraus, how fond of him I am.

Once again I must go back to the very beginning, to the first day.
In the break, Schacht and Schilinski, whom I did not know at that
time, ran into the kitchen and brought breakfast, laid on plates,
into the classroom. I also was given something to eat, but I wasn't
hungry, I didn't want to touch any of it. "You must eat," Schacht
said to me, and Kraus added: "Everything on the plate has to be
eaten up, everything. Do you understand?" I still remember how
repulsive I found those words. I tried to eat, but disgustedly left
most of it. Kraus came through the crowed to me and clapped me
dignifiedly on the shoulder and said: "You're new here, but you
must understand that the rules insist on all food being eaten up.
You're proud, but wait a while, you'll soon lose your pride. Can
you pick buttered bread and slices of sausage off the street? Can
you? Wait a while and see, perhaps you'll get an appetite. Anyway,
you must eat up all this here, that's for certain. In the Benjamenta
Institute no leftovers are tolerated. Get on with it, eat. Quickly.
What anxious hesitation, I suppose you think you're so refined!
You'll soon lose your refinements, I can tell you. You've no appetite, you say? But I advise you to have one. It's because of pride that
you haven't got one, that's what it is. Give it here! This time I'll
help you to eat it up, though it's all against the rules. Right. Now
you see how one can eat it? And this? And that? That was clever, I
can tell you." How embarrassed I was. I felt a violent aversion to
this eating boy, and today? Today I eat everything up as tidily as
any of the pupils. I even look forward every time to the nicely prepared and modest meals, and it would never occur to me to disdain
them. Yes, I was vain and proud at the start, offended by I don't
know what, humiliated I no longer know how. Everything, everything was still simply new to me, and, consequently, hostile, and
besides, I was a wholly outstanding fool. I am a fool to this day, but
in a way that is finer and friendlier. And everything depends on the

way a thing is. A person can be utterly foolish and unknowing: as
long as he knows the way to adapt, to be flexible, and how to move
about, he is still not lost, but will come through life better perhaps
than someone who is clever and stuffed with knowledge. The way:
yes, yes.

Kraus has had a hard life, even before he came here. He and his
father, who is a boatman, traveled up and down the Elbe, on heavy
coal barges. He had to work hard, hard, until one day he fell ill.
Now he wants to be a servant, a real servant, to some master, and
it's as if he was born for it, with all his good-hearted qualities. He
will be a quite wonderful servant, for not only does his appearance
suit this profession of humility and obligingness, no, also his soul,
his whole nature, the whole human character of my friend has, in
the best sense, something servant-like about it. To serve! If only
Kraus can find a decent master, I wish that for him. There certainly
are gentlemen, or lords, in brief, superiors, who do not like or wish
to be served perfectly, who do not know how to accept real achievements of service. Kraus has style and he definitely belongs to a
Count, that is, to an entirely distinguished gentleman. One should
not let Kraus work like an ordinary laborer or worker. He can be a
representative. His face is perfect for indicating a certain tone, a
manner, and anyone hiring him can be proud of his bearing and his
behavior. Hire him! Yes, that is the expression people use. And one
day Kraus will be hired out to somebody, or hired by somebody.
And he is looking forward to it, and that is why he is so zealously
stowing French away in his somewhat slow head. There's something about his head that troubles him. At the barber's, so he says,
he acquired a rather horrid mark of distinction, a garland of small
reddish plants, or briefly, points, or, even more briefly, and unmer-
cifully, spots. Anyway, that's bad, of course, especially since he
wants to go to a fine and really decent master. What's to be done?
Poor Kraus! The points that disfigure him would not prevent me,
for example, from kissing him if it came to such a pass, not at all.
Seriously: they really would not, for I don't notice such things any
more, I no longer see that it looks unbeautiful. I see his beautiful
soul in his face, and it is the soul that most deserves to be caressed.
But the future lord and master will, of course, think quite differently, and that is also why Kraus puts ointments on his inelegant
wounds, which disfigure him. Also he often uses the mirror to ob-

serve the progress of the treatment, not out of empty vanity. If he didn't have these blemishes, he would never look into a mirror, for the earth cannot produce anything more unvain, uninflated, than him. Herr Benjamenta, who has a lively interest in Kraus, often inquires about the evil and its hoped-for disappearance. For Kraus will soon be going out into life and into a job. I'm afraid of the moment when he will leave the school. But it won't come all that soon. He can still spend quite a long time doctoring his face, I believe, which I don't wish to be the case, and yet I do wish it. He will come to his master quite soon enough, to one who will know how to prize his qualities, and soon enough I shall have to do without a person whom I love, without his knowing it.

I write all these lines mostly in the evening, by the lamplight, at the big school table, at which, obtusely or not obtusely, we pupils so often have to sit. Kraus is sometimes very inquisitive and looks over my shoulder. Once I corrected him: "But Kraus, tell me, since when have you been bothering about things that don't concern you?" He was very annoyed, as all people are when they are caught on the secret pathways of stealthy curiosity. Sometimes I sit idly quite alone until late in the night on a bench in the public garden. The streetlights are on, the garish electric light descends, liquid and burning, among the leaves of the trees. Everything is hot and promises strange intimacies. People walk back and forth. Whisperings come from the hidden paths of the park. Then I go home and find the door closed. "Schacht," I call softly, and my comrade, as arranged, throws me the key down into the courtyard. I creep on tiptoe, since it is forbidden to stay out for long, into my room, and go to bed. And then I dream. I often dream terrible things. Thus one night I dreamed that I struck my mother in the face, my dear mother, far away. What a scream I gave, and how suddenly I woke up. Pain at the dreadfulness of what I had done chased me out of bed. I had seized the holy one by her respect-arousing hair and had thrown her to the ground. Oh, not to think of such things. The tears shot like sharp jets from the motherly eyes. I still clearly remember how the misery cut and tore her mouth, and how engulfed in sorrow she was, and how her head then sank back. But why recall these images again? Tomorrow I shall finally have to write the account of my life, or I shall be in peril of a severe reproof. In the evenings, at about nine o'clock, we boys always sing a short goodnight song. We stand in a semicircle by the door that leads to the inner chambers, and then the door opens, Fräulein Benjamenta appears on the threshold, clad all in wholesomely flowing white robes, and says to us, "Good night, boys," orders us to go to sleep now, and warns us to be quiet. Then, each time, Kraus puts out the lamp in the schoolroom, and from this moment not the slightest sound may be made. Everyone has to go on tiptoe to his bed. It is all quite peculiar. And where do the Benjamentas sleep? The Fräulein looks like an angel when she says goodnight to us. How I revere her! In the evening the Principal is never to be seen. Whether that is peculiar or not, it is certainly conspicuous.

It seems that the Benjamenta Institute once had more of a reputation and more customers than now. On one of the four walls of our classroom hangs a large photograph, with portraits of a great number of boys who attended the school during a previous year. Apart from that, our classroom is very sparsely equipped. Apart from the longish table, about ten or twelve chairs, a big wall-cupboard, an old traveling trunk, and a few other negligible objects, it has no furniture. Over the door which leads into the secret, unknown world of inner chambers, there hangs as a wall decoration a rather tedious-looking policeman's saber with an equally tedious-looking sheath laid across it. The helmet is enthroned above them. This decoration is like a sign, or like delicate evidence, of the rules that prevail here. As for me, I wouldn't accept these adornments if I were made a present of them; probably they were bought from an old junk-dealer. Every fortnight saber and helmet are taken down to be cleaned, which, it must be said, is a very nice but certainly altogether stupid job. Beside these ornaments there hang in the classroom the pictures of the late Emperor and Empress. The old Emperor looks unbelievably peaceful, and the Empress has a simple, motherly look. Often we pupils wash out the classroom with soap and hot water, so that afterwards everything smells and shines with cleanliness. We have to do everything ourselves, and each of us has for this housemaid's work an apron around his waist, in which garment, with its redolence of femininity, we all without exception look comical. But we have a merry time on such cleaning days. The floor is gaily polished, the objects, also those in the kitchen, are rubbed until they shine, for which purpose there are dusters and cleaning powders in plenty. Tables and chairs are smothered in water, door handles are polished till they gleam, windowpanes are breathed on and rubbed clean, each of us has his little task, each of us does something. On such days of cleaning, rubbing, and washing, we are like the elves in fairy tales, who, as is known, used to do all their rough and laborious tasks out of pure, supernatural goodness of heart. What we pupils do, we do because we have to, but why we have to, nobody quite knows. We obey, without considering what will one day come of all this thoughtless obedience, and we work without thinking if it is right and good to do our work. On one such cleaning day, Tremala, the oldest of us all, came up to me and tried an ugly trick. He stood quietly behind me and reached with his disgusting hand (hands that do this are crude and disgusting) for my intimate member, with the intention of doing me a loathsome favor, almost like tickling an animal. I turn around quickly and knock the villain to the floor. Usually I'm not so strong, Tremala is much stronger. But anger gave me irresistible strength. Tremala drags himself to his feet and hurls himself at me, then the door opens and Herr Benjamenta is standing in the doorway. "Jakob, you rascal!" he calls, "come here!" I go to my Principal and he doesn't ask at all who started the fight, but gives me a slap on the head and walks off. I'm about to run after him and shout at him how unjust he is, but I control myself, think, look over at the whole crowd of boys, and go back to my work. Since then I haven't spoken a word to Tremala, and he also avoids me, he knows why. But whether he's sorry, or anything like that, doesn't matter to me. The indelicate incident has long been, how shall I say, forgotten. In earlier times, Tremala has been to sea in ships. He's a depraved person, and rejoices in his vile tendencies. Also he is frantically uncultivated, therefore he doesn't interest me. Sly, and at the same time incredibly stupid: how uninteresting! But Tremala has taught me one thing: one must always be somewhat on the lookout for all kinds of assaults and injuries.

Often I go out onto the street, and there I seem to be living in an altogether wild fairy tale. What a crush and a crowd, what rattlings and patterings! What shoutings, whizzings, and hummings! And everything so tightly penned in. Right up close to the wheels of cars people are walking, children, girls, men, and elegant women; old men and cripples and people with bandaged heads, one sees all these in the crowd. And always fresh bevies of people and vehicles.

The coaches of the electric trolleys look like boxfuls of figures. The buses go galumphing past like clumsy great beetles. Then there are wagons that look like traveling watchtowers. People sit on the seats high up and travel over the heads of whatever is walking, jumping, and running below. Fresh crowds thrust in among the existing ones, and all at the same time there's a going and a coming, an appearing and a vanishing. Horses trample. Wonderful hats with ornamental feathers nod from open, swiftly-passing rich folks' coaches. All Europe sends its human specimens here. Gentility walks cheek by jowl with the menial and the bad, people are going who knows where, and here they come again and they are quite different people and who knows where they are coming from. One thinks that one can untangle it all a little, and one is glad to be taking the trouble to do so. And the sun sparkles down on it all. It shines on one person's nose, on another's toecap. Lacework pokes from the hems of skirts in a glittering confusion. Small dogs go riding on the laps of genteel old women in coaches. Breasts bounce toward one, female breasts pressed into clothes and shapes. And then again there are the many silly cigars in the many slits of masculine mouthparts. And one thinks of undreamed-of streets, invisible new regions, equally swarming with people. Evenings, between six and eight, the swarming is most graceful and dense. At this hour the best society goes promenading. What is one, really, in this flood, in this various, never-ending river of people? Sometimes all these mobile faces are reddishly tinted and painted by the glow of the setting sun. And when it is grey and raining? Then all these figures, and myself among them, walk quietly along like images in a dream under the dark gauze, looking for something and, it seems, almost never finding anything that is beautiful and right. Everyone is looking for something here, everyone is longing to be rich and to possess the fabulous goods of fortune. One walks quickly. No, they all restrain themselves, but the haste, the longing, the torment, and the restlessness gleam out of their greedy eyes. Then again everything swims in the hot noonday sun. Everything seems to be asleep, even the vehicles, the horses, the wheels, the noises. And the people look so blank. The tall, apparently collapsing houses seem to be dreaming. Girls hurry along, parcels are carried. One would like to fling one's arms around somebody. When I come home, Kraus sits there and makes fun of me. I tell him that one really must get to know the world a little. "Know the world?" he says, as if immersed in deep thought. And he smiles scornfully.

About a fortnight after my arrival at the school, Hans appeared among us. Hans is a regular peasant boy, like the ones in the Grimms' fairy tales. He comes from deepest Mecklenburg, and he smells of flowery, luxuriant meadows, of cow barn and farmyard. He is slim, rough, and bony, and he speaks a strange, goodhearted peasant language, which I like, as a matter of fact, if I take the trouble to hold my nose. Not that Hans gives off bad smells or anything. And yet one does not hold some kind of a nose, perhaps a mental one, a cultural nose or soul nose, and one can't help doing so, without even wanting to offend the good Hans. And he doesn't notice such things at all, this country person sees and hears and feels in far too healthy and plain a way for that. Something like the earth itself and earth-furrows and curves confronts one, when one looks deeply into this boy, but there's no need to look deeply. Hans doesn't demand pensiveness. Not that he doesn't matter to me, not that at all, but, how shall I say, he is a little remote and lightweight. One takes him quite lightly, because nothing about him gives serious cause for emotion. The Grimms' Fairy Tale Peasant Boy. Old-fashioned and agreeable, understandable and essential at the first fleeting glance. Very worthwhile to be a good friend to the fellow. In later life, Hans will work hard, without sighing. He will hardly notice the exertions, worries, and adversities. He is bursting with strength and health. And yet he's not bad-looking. Altogether: I can't help laughing at myself: I find something slightly nice in everything and about everything. I like them all so much, my pupils here, my school-friends.

Am I a born city dweller? It's quite possible. I hardly ever get stunned or surprised. There's something unspeakably cool about me, in spite of the excitements that can attack me. I have shed provincial habits in six days. Of course, I did grow up in a very very small metropolis. I drank in city life and city feeling with my mother's milk. As a child I saw yowling drunken workers reeling about. Even when I was very small, nature seemed to me a remote heaven. So I can do without nature. Doesn't one then have to do without God, too? To know that goodness, pure and sublime, is hidden somewhere, somewhere in the mists, and to revere and adore it very very quietly, with an ardor that is, as it were, totally cool and shadowy: I'm accustomed to that. One day as a child I saw an Italian workman lying dead against a wall, in a pool of blood, and pierced by numerous knifewounds. And another time, it was in the days of Ravachol, we young people told each other that bombs would soon be getting thrown in our part of the world as well, et cetera. Old times, those. I meant to talk of something quite different, that is, of comrade Peter, Beanpole Peter. This exceedingly tall boy is too funny, he comes from Teplitz in Bohemia and can speak Slavic and German. His father is a policeman, and Peter was trained as a clerk in a rope works, but he seems to have played being ignorant, unusable, and unsuccessful, which I, privately, find very endearing. He says that he can also speak Hungarian and Polish, if it is asked of him. But here nobody asks any such thing of him. What extensive knowledge of languages! Peter is quite decidedly the silliest and the clumsiest of us pupils, and that heaps him and wreathes him with distinctions in my inconsiderable eyes, for I am unbelievably fond of silly people. I hate the kind of person who pretends he understands everything and beamingly parades knowledge and wit. Sly and knowing people are to me an unspeakable abomination. How nice Peter is, in precisely this point. His being tall, so tall that he could crack in two, is good, but even better is the goodness of heart which keeps whispering to him that he is a cavalier and has the looks of a noble and elegant rake. It's a great laugh. He's always talking of adventures he has had, but probably hasn't had. Anyway, one thing is true: Peter owns the finest and most delicate walking stick in the world. And now he is always going out and walking the liveliest streets with this stick in his hand. Once I met him in the F—— Street. F—— Street is the fascinating focus of cosmopolitan life in this big city. Still a long way off, he was waving his hand to me nodding and brandishing his walking stick. Then, when I was close to him, he looked paternally and anxiously at me, as if to say: "What? You here too? Jakob, Jakob, this is no place for you." And then he took his leave, like one of the great men of the world, like the editor of an internationally famous newspaper who can't spare a moment of his highly valuable time. And then I saw his round, silly, nice little hat vanishing in the mass of other heads and hats. He melted, as they say, into the crowd. Peter learns absolutely nothing, although in his so humorous way he really needs to, and it seems that he only came to the Benjamenta Institute in order to distinguish himself with the most delightful sillinesses. Perhaps he's even becoming a few considerable degrees sillier than he was, and why, indeed, shouldn't his silliness be allowed to develop? I, for instance, am convinced that Peter will have a shameful amount of success in life, and, strange to say, I grant him this. Yes, I even go further. I have the feeling, and it is a very comforting one, tingling and pleasant, that I shall one day obtain a master, lord, and superior such as Peter would be, for such silly people are made for promotion, advancement, good living, and the giving of commands, and such people as I am, to some extent intelligent, should let the good impulses which they possess blossom and exhaust themselves in the service of others. Me, I shall be something very lowly and small. The feeling that tells me this is like a complete and inviolable fact. My God, and do I have, all the same, so much, so much zest for life? What is it with me? Often I'm a little frightened of myself, but not for long. No, no, I have confidence in myself. But isn't that altogether comic?

For my fellow-pupil Fuchs I have only one single expression: Fuchs is crosswise, Fuchs is askew. He speaks like a flopped somersault and behaves like a big improbability pummeled into human shape. Everything about him is unpleasant, therefore unlovable. To know something about Fuchs is an abuse, a coarse and bothersome superfluity. One only knows such rascals in order to despise them; but since one doesn't want in the least to despise anything, one forgets and overlooks it. It, yes. For an it is what he is, a thing. O God, why must I talk angrily today? I could almost hate myself for it. Away to something better.—I see Herr Benjamenta very rarely. Sometimes I go into the office, bow to the ground, say, "Good day, Principal," and ask this kingly man if I may go out. "Have you written the account of your life, eh?" I am asked. I reply: "Not yet. But I shall do so." Herr Benjamenta comes up to me, that is, up to the counter at which I'm standing, and pushes his gigantic fist up to my nose. "You'll be on time with it, boy, or else—you know what comes of that." I understand him, I bow again and disappear. Curious, the pleasure it gives me to annoy practicers of force. Do I actually want this Herr Benjamenta to punish me? Do I have reckless instincts? Everything is possible, everything, even the most sordid and undignified things. Very well, then, soon I shall write the account of my life. I find Herr Benjamenta very handsome indeed. A glorious brown beard—what? Glorious brown beard? I'm a fool. No, there's nothing handsome about the Principal, nothing glorious, but behind this man one senses difficult paths of destiny and heavy blows of fate, and it is this human thing, this almost divine thing, that makes him handsome. True people and true men are never visibly handsome. A man who has a really handsome beard is an opera singer or a well-paid departmental chief in a big store. Surface people are handsome, as a rule. However, there may be exceptions and specimens of masculine handsomeness that are authentic. Herr Benjamenta's face and hands (I have already felt his hand) are like knotty roots, roots which at some sad moment have had to withstand a few unmerciful ax-blows. If I were a lady of noblesse and intelligence, I would know absolutely how to bestow distinction on men like this apparently so impecunious principal of an institute, but, as I suppose, Herr Benjamenta doesn't mix with society on the worldly stage. Actually he is always at home, doubtless he keeps sort of hidden away, he creeps away, "into the solitude," and, indeed, this noble and clever man must live a horribly lonely life. Something must have happened to make on this character a deep and perhaps even destructive impression, but who knows? A pupil at the Benjamenta Institute, whatever can such a person know? But at least I am always investigating. In order to investigate, I often go to the office for no other reason than to ask the man just such fiddling questions as this "May I go out, Principal?" Yes, this man has a fascination for me, he interests me. The instructress also arouses my most intense interest. Yes, and for this reason, to get something out of all this mystery, I irritate him so that something like an incautious remark may escape from him. What's the harm if he hits me? My desire for experiences is growing into a domineering passion, and the pain which this strange man's annoyance causes me is small in comparison with my trembling wish to lead him on into saying something a little revealing. Oh, I dream— glorious, glorious—of winning the confidence which this man is just beginning to show. It may take a long time, but I think, I think I shall manage to penetrate at last the mystery of the Benjamentas. Mysteries make one dream of unendurable bewitchments, they have the fragrance of something quite, quite unspeakably beautiful. Who knows, who knows. Ah—

I love the noise and restless movement of the city. Perpetual motion compels morality. A thief, for example, when he sees all the bustling people, would not be able to help thinking what a scoun-

drel he is, and then the blithe and brisk sight of it all can feed better-
ment into his crumbling, ruin-like character. The braggart will
perhaps become more modest and thoughtful when he catches sight
of all the forces at work here, and this unseemly fellow may tell
himself, when the supple throngs catch his attention, that he must
be a dreadful rogue to set himself up, stupidly and vainly, with such
conceit and arrogance. The city educates, it cultivates, and by examples, what's more, not by arid precepts from books. There is
nothing professorial about it, and that is flattering, for the towering
gravity of knowledge discourages one. And then there is so much
here that fosters, sustains, and helps. One can hardly express it.
How difficult it is to give living expression to that which is fine and
good! One is grateful, here, for one's morsel of life, one is always a
little grateful, while it is urging one on, while one is in a hurry. A
person with time to waste doesn't know what time means, and he
is the natural stupid ingrate. In the city, there isn't a messenger boy
who doesn't know the value of his time, there isn't a newsboy who
trifles his time away. And then how dreamlike it is, picturesque and
poetic! People keep scuttling and shoving by. Well, now, that's important, that is stimulating, that gives the mind a more zestful
rhythm. While one is standing hesitantly around, a hundred people
and a hundred things have passed through one's head and before
one's eyes, which proves very clearly what a dawdler and a sluggard
one is. There is such a general hurry here because people think every
moment how nice it is to go struggling and grasping for things. The
breath of life becomes more bewitching. The wounds and pains go
deeper, joy jubilates more joyously and for longer than elsewhere,
because anyone who is joyous here always seems to have bitterly
and justly earned it by hard toil. Then again there are the gardens
that lie behind the delicate fencings, so quiet and lost, like secret
corners in English parklands. Right beside them the business traffic
rushes by and clatters past, as if landscapes or dreams had ever ex-
isted. The railway trains thunder over the quivering bridges. Evenings, the fabulous rich and elegant shop-windows shine, and
streams, serpents, and billows of people roll past the allures of in-
dustrial riches on display. Yes, that all seems grand and good to me.
One profits from being in the midst of the whirling and bubbling.
One has a good feeling in the legs, the arms, and the chest while
making the effort to wriggle cleverly and without much fuss

through all the living stuff. In the morning everything comes to life anew, and in the evening everything sinks into the wildly embracing arms of a new and unknown dream. That's very poetic. Fräulein Benjamenta would quite rightly admonish me if she were to read what I am writing here. Not to speak of Kraus, who makes no such passionate distinction between village and city. Kraus sees, firstly, people, second, duties, and third, at the most, savings which he will put aside, he thinks, to send to his mother. Kraus always writes home. He has an education that is as simple as it is purely human. The turmoil of the big city with all its many foolish, glittering promises leaves him completely cold. What an upright, tender, solid human soul!

At last my photographs are finished. The portrait, a really good one, shows me looking out very very energetically into the world. Kraus tries to annoy me and says that I look like a Jew. At last, at last he laughs a bit. "Kraus," I say, "please realize, even Jews are people." We quarrel about the worth and worthlessness of Jews and it is splendid entertainment. I wonder what good opinions he has: "The Jews have all the money," he thinks. I nod, I agree and say: "It's money that makes people Jews. A poor Jew isn't a Jew, and rich Christians, they're dreadful, they're the worst Jews of all." He nods. At last, at last I have found this person's approval. But now he's angry again and says very gravely: "Stop this gabbling! What's all this about Jews and Christians? Such people don't exist. There are mean people and good ones. That's all. And what do you think about that, Jakob? Which sort are you?" And now a really long discussion starts. Oh, Kraus likes to talk with me very much, I know it. The good, fine soul. Only he doesn't want to admit it. How I love people who don't like making admissions! Kraus has character: how clearly one feels that.—Of course, I've written the account of my life, but I tore it up. Fräulein Benjamenta warned me yesterday to be more attentive and obedient. I have the loveliest ideas about obedience and attentiveness, and it's strange: they escape me. I am virtuous in my imagination, but when it comes to practicing virtue? What then? You see, then it's quite another matter, then one fails, then one is reluctant. Also I am impolite. I long very much to be courtly and polite, but when it's a question of speeding ahead of the instructress and opening the door for her respectfully, who's that scoundrel there, sitting at the table? And who springs up like a gale to show his manners? Aha, it's Kraus. Kraus is a knight from head to toe. Truly, he belongs in the Middle Ages, and it really is a pity that he hasn't got a Twelfth Century at his disposal. He is fidelity in person, ardent service and unobtrusive, selfless obligingness. He has no judgment about women, he merely respects them. Who lifts from the floor what has fallen there, and hands it quick as a squirrel to the lady? Who leaps from the house on errands? Who carries the shopping bag when the instructress goes to market? Who scrubs the stairs and the kitchen without being told? Who does all this and doesn't ask for thanks? Who is so gloriously, so powerfully happy in himself? What is his name? Ah, I know who it is. Sometimes I'd like this Kraus to punch me. But people like him, how could they punch? Kraus only wants what is right and good. That is no exaggeration at all. He never has bad intentions. His eyes are frighteningly kind. This person, what is he really doing in a world that is meant and built for empty words, lies, and vanity? When one looks at Kraus, one can't help feeling how hopelessly lost in the world modesty is.

I have sold my watch, so as to buy tobacco for cigarettes. I can live without a watch, but not without cigarettes, that is shameful, but a necessity. Somehow I must get some money or I shan't have any clean clothes to wear. Clean collars are things I can't do without. A person's happiness depends, yet does not depend, on such things. Happiness? No. But one should be proper. Cleanliness alone is a joy. I'm just talking. How I hate all the right words! Today the Fräulein cried. Why? Halfway through the class, tears suddenly poured from her eyes. It strangely moves me. Anyway, I shall have to keep my eyes peeled. I like listening for something that doesn't want to make a sound. I pay attention, and that makes life more beautiful, for if we don't have to pay attention there really is no life. It is clear, Fräulein Benjamenta is grieving and it must be a violent grief, because usually our instructress is very self-controlled. I must get some money. And another thing: I've written the account of my life. This is how it goes:

My Life

The undersigned, Jakob von Gunten, son of honorable parents, born on such and such a day, raised in such and such a place, entered the

Benjamenta Institute as a pupil in order to acquire knowledge of the few things necessary for entering someone's service. The same has no high hopes of life. He wishes to be treated strictly, so that he may know what it means to pull himself together. Jakob von Gunten is not very promising, but he proposes to behave well and honestly. The von Guntens are an old family. In earlier times they were warriors, but their pugnacity has diminished and today they are aldermen and tradesmen, and the youngest of the house, subject of this report, has resolved to lapse from every proud tradition. He wants life to educate him, not inherited or noble principles. Of course, he is proud, for it is impossible for him to deny his inborn nature, but by pride he means something quite new, something that corresponds, in some degree, to the times in which he is living. He hopes that he is modern, to some extent suitable for the performance of services, and not altogether stupid and useless, but that is a lie, he does not only hope this, he affirms it, and he knows it. He is defiant, the untamed spirit of his ancestors is still alive in him a little, but he asks to be admonished when he acts defiantly, and, if that does not work, to be punished, for then he believes it will work. In general, it will be necessary to know how to deal with him. The undersigned believes that he is adaptable to all circumstances, therefore it is a matter of indifference to him what he is ordered to do, he is firmly convinced that any carefully executed work will be for him a greater honor than sitting idly and timidly in a cosy corner at home. A von Gunten does not sit in a cosy corner. If the ancestors of the obedient undersigned bore the knightly sword, their descendant acts in the same tradition by desiring ardently to make himself useful somehow. His modesty knows no limits, as long as one flatters his spirit, and his zeal to serve is like his ambition, which commands him to disdain obstructive and harmful feelings of honor. At home, the same undersigned always used to give his history teacher, the esteemed Dr. Merz, a drubbing, which was shameful, and which he regrets. Today he longs to be allowed to shatter his arrogance and conceit, which perhaps still animate him in part, against the merciless rock of hard work. He is reticent of speech and will never divulge confidences. He believes neither in heaven nor in hell. The satisfaction of that person who engages him will be his heaven, and the sorrowful opposite will be his annihilating hell, but he is convinced that he will give satisfaction in himself and in what he does. This firm belief gives him the courage to be the person he is,

Jakob von Gunten.

I handed the account of my life to the Principal. He read it through, I think, twice, and he seemed to like what I had written, for the shimmering ghost of a smile crossed his lips. Oh, certainly, I was watching my man very closely. He did smile a little, that is and remains a fact. At last, then, a sign of something human. What cavortings does one have to perform in order to stir people up, people whose hands one would like to kiss, even to get from them a quite fleeting friendly gesture! Intentionally, intentionally I wrote the account of my life with such pride and cheek: "Now read it. Well? Doesn't it make you want to fling it back in my face?" Those were my thoughts. And then he gave a fine and crafty smile, this fine and crafty Principal whom I unfortunately, unfortunately revere above all others. And I noticed it. A vanguard skirmish has been won. Today I absolutely must get up to one more little piece of mischief. Or I shall die of rejoicing and laughing. But the Fräulein is crying? What is all this? Why am I so strangely happy? Am I mad?

I must now report a matter which will perhaps raise a few doubts. And yet what I say is quite true. There is a brother of mine living in this immense city, my only brother, in my opinion an extraordinary person, his name is Johann, and he's something like a quite famous painter. I know nothing definite about his present situation in the world, since I have avoided visiting him. I shall not go to see him. If we should happen to meet on the street, and if he should recognize me and walk up to me, well and good, then I shall be pleased to give his brotherly hand a strong shake. But I shall never provoke such a meeting, never in my life. What am I, and what is he? I know what a pupil at the Benjamenta Institute is, it's obvious. Such a pupil is a good round zero, nothing more. But what my brother is at the moment I cannot know. Perhaps he's surrounded by fine, cultivated people and by God knows what formalities, and I respect formalities, therefore I don't visit my brother, for possibly a well-groomed gentleman, giving a forced smile, might come toward me. I know Johann von Gunten from earlier times, of course. He's just as cool and calculating as me and all the Guntens, but he's much older, and differences of age between people and brothers are insuperable barriers. In any case, I don't allow him to give me any pieces of good advice, and that is precisely what he will do, I fear, when he sees me, for if he sees me looking so poor and unimportant he will certainly feel provoked, as a well-situated person must, to make me feel the lowliness of my position all up and down the line, and I wouldn't be able to put up with that, I would show my von Gunten pride and become decidedly rude, for which I would later be sorry. No, a thousand times no. What? Accept charity from my brother, my own flesh and blood? I'm sorry, it's impossible. I imagine that he is very refined, smoking the world's best cigar, and lying among cushions and rugs of bourgeois snugness. And why so? Yes, there's something unbourgeois in me now, something utterly opposite to well-being, and perhaps my brother is reposing right in the midst of the loveliest, most splendid worldly well-being. It's definite: we shall not see one another, perhaps we never shall. And it isn't even necessary. Not necessary? Good, let's leave it at that. Mutton-head that I am, talking about "we" like a very dignified schoolteacher.—My brother must be surrounded, certainly, by the best and most exclusive salon behavior. Merci. Oh, thank you. Women will be there, poking their heads out the door and asking pertly: "Now who's here again today? Oh, I say. Is he a beggar?" Thanks a lot for the welcome. I'm too kind to be pitied. Sweetly smelling flowers in the room. Oh, I don't like flowers at all. And cool cosmopolitan people? Ghastly. Yes, I'd like to see him, I'd like very much to see him. But if I saw him like this, in splendor and all snug: bang would go the feeling that this was a brother, I'd only be able to pretend happiness, and so would he. So I won't see him.

During the class, we pupils sit there, gazing rigidly to the fore, motionless. I think one isn't even allowed to blow one's personal nose. Our hands rest on our knees and are invisible during the class. Hands are the five-fingered evidence of human vanity and rapacity, therefore they stay nicely hidden under the desk. Our schoolboy noses have the greatest spiritual similarity, they all seem to strive more or less aloft, to where insight into the confusion of life floats and glows. Pupils' noses should look blunt and downcurved, that is what the rules demand, the rules which think of everything, and indeed, all our instruments of smell are humbly and meekly bent. It's as if they had been trimmed with sharp knives. Our eyes always gaze into the thoughtless emptiness, the rules demand this too. Actually one shouldn't have any eyes, for eyes are cheeky and inquisitive, and cheek and inquisitiveness are to be condemned from almost every healthy standpoint. Fairly delightful are the ears of us pupils. They hardly venture to listen, for sheer intensity of listening.

They always quiver a little, as if they were frightened of being suddenly pulled in admonishment from behind, and hauled out side-
ways. Poor ears, having to put up with such terrors. If the sound of
a call or command strikes these ears, they vibrate and tremble like
harps that have been touched and disturbed. Well, now, it also happens that pupils' ears like to sleep a little, and how they are aroused!
It's a joy. The best-trained part of us, though, is the mouth, it is
always obediently and devoutly shut. And it's only too true: an
open mouth is a yawning fact, the fact that its owner is dwelling
with his few thoughts in some other place than the domain and
pleasure-garden of attentiveness. A firmly shut mouth indicates
open, eager ears, therefore the gates down there below the nostrils
must be always carefully bolted. An open mouth is just a gob, and
each of us knows that perfectly well. Lips aren't allowed to parade
themselves and bloom voluptuously in the comfortable natural
position, they must be folded and pressed as a sign of energetic self-
denial and expectation. We pupils all do this, we treat our lips, according to the existing rules, very strictly and cruelly, and therefore
we all look as grim as sergeants giving commands. A noncom wants
his men, as is well known, to look as snarling and grim as he does,
that suits him, for he has a sense of humor, as a rule. Seriously: people obeying usually look just like the people giving orders. A servant can't help putting on the masks and allures of his master, in
order faithfully to propagate them, as it were. Now, of course, our
esteemed Fräulein isn't a sergeant, on the contrary, she very often
laughs, yes, she sometimes allows herself simply to laugh at us rule-
obeying beaverboys, but she reckons that we shall quietly let her
laugh, without changing our expressions, and that is just what we
do, we act as if we didn't hear the sweet silver tones of her laughter
at all. What singular oddities we are. Our hair is always neatly and
smoothly combed and brushed, and everyone has to cut his own
parting up there in the world on his head, a canal incised into the
deep black or blond hair-earth. That's how it should be. Partings
are also in the rulebook. And because we all look so charmingly
barbered and parted, we all look alike, which would be a huge joke
for any writer, for example, if he came on a visit to study us in our
glory and littleness. This writer had better stay at home. Writers are
just windbags who only want to study, make pictures and observations. To live is what matters, then the observation happens of its

own accord. Our Fräulein Benjamenta would in any case let fly at such a wandering writer, blown in upon us by rain or snow, with such force that he would fall to the floor at the unfriendliness of the welcome. Then the instructress, who loves to be an autocrat, would say to us, perhaps: "Boys, help the gentleman to pick himself up." And then we pupils of the Benjamenta Institute would show the un-invited guest the whereabouts of the door. And the morsel of in-quisitive authordom would disappear again. No, these are just imaginings. Our visitors are gentlemen who want to engage us boys in their service, not people with skills behind their ears.

Either the teachers in our institute do not exist, or they are still asleep, or they seem to have forgotten their profession. Or perhaps they are on strike, because nobody pays them their monthly wages? Strange feelings seize me when I think of the poor slumberers and absent minds. There they all sit, or slump, against the walls in a room specially arranged for their repose. Herr Wälchli is there, the supposed Natural History teacher. Even asleep he keeps his pipe stuck in his mouth. A pity, he would have done better as a bee-keeper. How red his face still is, and how fat his oldish, softish hand. And here beside him, isn't that Herr Blösch, the much-respected French teacher? Ah, yes, it really is he, and he's telling lies when he supposes he's asleep, he's a quite terrible liar. His classes, too, consisted entirely of lies, a paper mask. How pale he looks, and how angry! He has a bad face, thick hard lips, coarse merciless fea-tures: "Are you asleep, Blösch?" He doesn't hear. He's really repul-sive. And that one, who is he? Parson Strecker? Tall thin Parson Strecker, who teaches Scripture? the devil yes, it's he. "Are you asleep, Parson? All right, sleep, then, there's no harm in your sleep-ing. You only waste time teaching Scripture. Religion, you see, means nothing today. Sleep is more religious than all your religion. When one is asleep, one is perhaps closest to God. What do you think?" He doesn't hear. I'll go somewhere else. Ha, now who's this, choosing such a comfortable position? Is it Merz, Doctor Merz, who teaches the History of Rome? Yes, it's he, I know his pointed beard. "You seem to be angry with me Doctor Merz. Well, carry on sleeping and forget the improper scenes we had, stop scolding into your pointed beard. It's a good thing for you to sleep. For some time past, the world has been revolving around money, not around history. All the ancient heroic virtues you unpack have lost their importance long ago, you know it yourself. Thanks for some wonderful impressions. Sleep well." But here now, as I see, Herr von Bergen seems to have snuggled down, the boy-torturer von Bergen. Looks like he's dreaming, and he likes so much to bestow, with such tickling-heavenly partiality, "smacks." Or he commands: "Bend over!" and then it is such a delight for him to patch up the poor boy's backside with his meerschaum cane. A very elegant Parisian phenomenon, but cruel. And who is this here? Headmaster Wyss? Very nice. One needn't spend long on legitimate people. And who's here? Bur? Schoolmaster Bur? "I'm delighted to see you." Bur is the biggest genius of an ex-mathematics master on the continent. Only for the Benjamenta Institute he is too broadminded and intelligent. Kraus and the others are not the right pupils for him. He is too outstanding and his demands are too high. Here in the Institute no excessive pre-conditions exist. But am I dreaming of my schoolteachers at home? In my other school there was plenty of knowledge, here there is something quite different. Something quite different to us pupils here.

Shall I get a job soon? I hope so. My photographs and my applications make, as I presume, a favorable impression. Recently I went with Schilinski to a top-class concert-café. How Schilinski trembled all over with timorousness. I behaved approximately like his kind father. The waiter ventured, after giving us a good look up and down, to ignore us; but when I requested him, with an enormously austere expression on my face, kindly to wait upon us, he at once became polite and brought us some light beer in tall, delicately cut goblets. Ah, one must play the part. A person who can throw his chest out is treated like a gentleman. One must learn to dominate situations. I know excellently well how to throw my head back, as if I were outraged by something, no, only surprised by it. I look around, as if to say: "What's this? What did you say? Is this a madhouse?" It works. I have also acquired a bearing in the Benjamenta Institute. Oh, I sometimes feel that it's within my power to play with the world and all things in it just as I please. Suddenly I understand the sweet character of women. Their coquetries amuse me and I discern profundity in their trivial gestures and manners of speaking. If one doesn't understand how it is when they raise a cup to their lips or snatch in their skirts, one will never understand them at all. Their souls go tripping along with the high-swelling heels of their sweet little boots, and their smiling is both things: a foolish habit and a piece of world history. Their conceit and their small intelligence are charming, more charming than the works of the classic authors. Often their vices are the most virtuous thing under the sun, and when they get furious and scold us? Only women know how to scold. But quiet now! I'm thinking of Mamma. How holy to me is the memory of the moments when she scolded. Quiet now, be still! What can a pupil at the Benjamenta Institute know about all these things?

I couldn't restrain myself, I've been to the office, have as usual bowed deeply, and I said to Herr Benjamenta the following words: "I have arms, legs, and hands, Herr Benjamenta, and I would like to work, and so I permit myself to ask you to obtain for me soon a job of work with pay. I know that you have all sorts of connections. To you come the most refined gentlefolk, people with crowns on their lapels of their overcoats, officers rattling sharp sabers, ladies whose robes ripple like tittering waves in their wake, older women with enormous amounts of money, old men who give a million for half a smile, people of rank, but not of intellect, people who ride about in automobiles, in a word, Principal, the world comes to you." "Now don't you be impertinent," he warned me, but, I don't know why, I no longer feel at all afraid of his fists, and I went on speaking, the words positively flew out of me: "Obtain for me at once some exciting activity. Actually my view is this: all activity is exciting. I've already learned so much from you, Principal." He said calmly: "You haven't learned anything yet." Then I took up the thread again and said: "God himself commands me to go out into life. But what is God? You are my God, Principal, if you allow me to go and earn money and respect." He was silent for a while, then he said: "Get out of this office, this instant!" That annoyed me terribly. I shouted: "In you I see an outstanding person, but I'm wrong. You're as common as the age you live in. I shall go out on the street and hold somebody up, I'm being forced to become a criminal." I knew what peril I was in. The moment I said these words I leaped for the door and then shrieked in a rage: "Adieu, Principal!" and slid out through it, wonderfully nimbly. In the corridor I stopped and listened at the keyhole. Everything in the office was as quiet as a mouse. I went into the classroom and immersed myself in the book *What Is the Aim of the Boys' School?*

Our instruction has two sides, one theoretical and the other practical. But both sections seem to me still like a dream, like a fairy tale that is at once meaningless and rich in meaning. Learning by heart, that's one of our main tasks. I learn by heart very easily, Kraus with great difficulty, therefore he's always busy learning. The difficulties that he has to overcome are the secret of his industry, and the solution to it. He has a slow memory, and yet he impresses everything on his mind, even if it takes great effort. What he knows is then, so to speak, engraved in metal and he can never forget it again. In his case there can be no talk of forgetting. In a school where little is taught, Kraus is quite at home, therefore he's completely at home in the Benjamenta Institute. One of the maxims of our school is: "A little, but thoroughly." Well, now, Kraus stands firm on this principle, with the somewhat thick skull that is his in the world. To learn a little! The same thing over and over! Gradually I too am beginning to understand what a large world is hidden behind these words. To imprint something firmly, firmly on one's mind! I understand how important that is above all things, how good and how dignified it is. The practical or physical part of our instruction is a kind of perpetually repeated gymnastics or dancing, or whatever you want to call it. The salutation, the entrance into a room, behavior toward women or whatever, is practiced, and the practice is very long drawn out, often boring, but here too, as I now observe, and feel, there lies a deeply hidden meaning. We pupils are to be trained and shaped, as I observe, not stuffed with sciences. We are educated by being compelled to learn exactly the character of our own soul and body. We are given clearly to understand that mere discipline and sacrifice are educative, and that more blessings and more genuine knowledge are to be found in a very simple, as it were stupid, exercise than in the learning of a variety of ideas and meanings. We grasp one thing after another, and when we have grasped a thing, it is as if it possessesd us. Not we possess it, but the opposite: whatever we have apparently acquired rules over us then. It is impressed upon us that a beneficent effect is to be had from acquiring a little that is firm and definite, that is to say, from growing accustomed and shaping oneself to laws and commands that prescribe a strict external discipline. Perhaps we're being stupefied, certainly we're being made small. But that doesn't make us timid, not at all. We pupils all know, one as well as the next, that timidity is a punishable offence. Whoever stutters and shows fear is exposed to the scorn of our Fräulein, but we must be small, and we must know, know precisely, that we are nothing big. The law which commands, the discipline which compels, and the many unmerciful rules which give us a direction and give us good taste: that is the big thing, not us pupils. Well, everyone feels this, even I do, that we are small, poor dependent dwarfs, obliged to be continuously obedient. And so that's how we behave: humbly, but with the utmost confidence. We are all, without exception, a little energetic, for the smallness and deprivation which are our conditions cause us to believe firmly in the few achievements that we have made. Our belief in ourselves is our modesty. If we didn't believe in anything, we wouldn't know how little we are. Nonetheless, we small young people are something. We may not be extravagant, we may not have imaginings, it is forbidden for us to look about us, and this makes us satisfied and makes us useful for any quick task. We know the world very badly, but we shall come to know it, for we shall be exposed to life and its storms. The Benjamenta school is the antechamber to the drawing rooms and palatial halls of life at large. Here we learn to feel respect, and to act as all those must act who have something to look up to. I, for one, am a little above all this, which is good, because all these impressions are so much the better for me. Precisely I have need to learn to feel esteem and respect for the objects of this world, for where would I end up if I was disrespectful to old age, if I denied God, mocked laws, and was allowed to stick my juvenile nose into everything sublime, important, and big? In my view, the present young generation is sick for precisely this reason, bellowing hell and blue murder and then miaowing for daddy and mummy when they're obliged to give in a little to duties and commandments and limitations. No, no, here the Benjamentas are my dear shining lodestars, the brother as well as the Fräulein, his sister. I will think of them as long as I live.

I have seen my brother; we met, what's more, in the thick of the city crowd. Our meeting turned out to be a very friendly one. It was unforced and affectionate. Johann behaved very nicely, and probably I did, too. We went to a small, reticent restaurant and had a talk there. "Just as you go on being yourself, brother," Johann said to me, "begin from all the way down, that's fine. If you need help . . ." I made a gesture of refusal. He went on: "For look, you see, it's hardly worth it, up there at the top. If you see what I mean. Don't misunderstand me, brother." I gave a lively nod, for I knew in advance what he was saying, but I asked him to go on, and he said: "It's the atmosphere up there. I mean, they've all got an air of having done enough, and that stops things, it's cramping. I hope you don't quite understand me, for, if you did understand me, brother, you'd be a dreadful person." We laughed. Oh, to be able to laugh with my brother, I like that. He said: "You are now, so to speak, a zero, my good brother. But when one is young, one should be a zero, for nothing is more ruinous than being a bit important early on, too early on. Certainly: you're a bit important to yourself. That's fine. Excellent. But for the world you're still nothing, and that's almost just as excellent. I keep hoping you won't quite understand me, for if you understood me completely . . ." "I'd be a dreadful person," I broke in. We laughed again. It was very jolly. A strange fire began to animate me. My eyes were burning. I like it very much, by the way, when I feel so burned up. My face gets quite red. And then thoughts full of purity and loftiness usually assail me. Johann went on, he said: "Brother, please, don't always interrupt me. That silly young laughter of yours has a stifling effect on ideas. Listen! Pay close attention now. What I'm telling you may be useful to you one day. Above all: never think of yourself as an outcast. There are no outcasts, brother, for perhaps there's nothing in this world that's worth aspiring to. And yet you must aspire, even passionately so. But so as to become not too full of longings: realize that there is nothing, nothing worth aspiring to. Everything is rotten. Do you understand that? Look, I keep hoping that you can't quite understand all this. It worries me." I said: "Unfortunately I'm too intelligent to misunderstand you, as you hope I might. But don't worry. Your revelations don't frighten me at all." We smiled at one another. Then we ordered some more drinks, and Johann, who, by the way, did look uncommonly elegant, went on talking: "Of course there's progress on earth, so called, but that's only one of the many lies which the business people put out, so that they can squeeze money out of the crowd more blatantly and mercilessly. The masses are the slaves of today, and the individual is the slave of the vast mass-ideas. There's nothing beautiful and excellent left. You must dream up beauty and goodness and justice. Tell me, do you know how to dream?" I contented myself with a nod, two nods, and let Johann carry on while I listened intently: "Try to earn lots and lots of money. Everything else has gone wrong, but not money. Everything, everything is spoiled, halved, robbed of grace and splendor. Our cities are vanishing relentlessly from the face of the earth. Big chunks of nothing are taking up the space once occupied by dwellings and princely palaces. The piano, dear brother, and the tinkling that goes with it. Concerts and theaters are going down and down, the standpoint sinks lower and lower. There is, to be sure, still something like a society that sets the tone, but it no longer has the capacity for striking the notes of dignity and subtlety of mind. There are books—in a word, don't ever despair. Keep on being poor and despised, dear friend. Give up the money-idea, too. It's the most lovely and triumphant thing, it makes one a very poor devil. Rich people, Jakob, are very unsatisfied and unhappy. The rich today: they've got nothing left. They are the really starving people." I nodded again. It's true, I say yes to everything very easily. But I liked what Johann said, and it suited me. There was pride in what he said, and sorrow. And, well, these two together, pride and sorrow, have a good sound. We ordered some more beer and my opposite number said: "You must hope and yet hope for nothing. Look up to something, yes, do that, because that is right for you, you're young, terribly young, Jakob, but always admit to yourself that you despise it, the thing that you're looking up to with respect. Nodding again, are you? Lord, what an intelligent listener you are. You're like a tree hung with understanding. Be content, dear brother, strive, learn, do whatever good and kind things you can do for people. Look, I've got to go. When shall we meet again? Frankly, you interest me—" We went out and on the street we said goodbye. For a long time I watched my dear brother as he walked away. Yes, he's my brother. How glad I am that he is.

My father has a coach and horses and a servant, old Fehlmann. Mamma has her own box at the theater. How she is envied by the women of the town, with its 28,000 inhabitants! Despite her age, my mother is still a pretty woman, even a beautiful one. I remember a light-blue, tightly fitting dress that she once wore. She was holding up a delicately white sunshade. The sun was shining. It was splendid Spring weather. In the streets there was a smell of violets. People were out for a stroll and beneath the green foliage of the trees in the park the band was playing. How sweet and bright everything was! A fountain was splashing, and children in light-colored clothes were laughing and playing. And a soft caressing breeze was blowing, with fragrances in it, awakening desire for inexpressible things. From the windows of houses on the Neuquartierplatz people were looking out. Mother was wearing long pale-yellow gloves over her slender hands and sweet arms. Johann had at that time already left home. But father was there. No, never shall I accept help (money) from the parents whom I so tenderly respect. My injured pride would fling me onto a sickbed and bang would go all my dreams of an independent life, destroyed forever these ardently cherished plans for self-education. That's the point: to educate myself, or prepare myself for a future education, that is why I became a pupil at the Benjamenta Institute, for here one readies oneself for some darkly approaching arduous task. And that is also why I don't write home, for even writing about it would make me have doubts about myself, would completely ruin my plan for starting from all the way down. Something great and audacious must happen in secrecy and silence, or it perishes and falls away, and the fire that was awakened dies again. I know how I want it, that's enough. —Ah, yes, that was it. I have a merry tale in store, about our old servant Fehlmann, who is still alive and in service. It was like this: Fehlmann did something very wrong one day and he was going to be dismissed. "Fehlmann," said Mamma, "you can go. We do not need you any more." Thereupon the poor old man, who shortly before this had buried a son of his who had died of cancer (that isn't funny), threw himself at my mother's feet and begged for mercy, yes, actually for mercy. The poor devil, he had tears in his old eyes. Mamma forgives him. I recount the scene next day to my friends, the Weibel brothers, and they laugh me to scorn. They stop being my friends, because they think that my family is too royalistic. They find this falling at someone's feet suspicious, and they go along and slander me and Mamma in the most tasteless way. Like regular little boys, yes, but also like regular little republicans, for whom the dispensing of personal and autocratic mercy or displeasure is a monstrosity and an object of revulsion. How comical it seems to me now! And yet how significant this small incident is for the tendency of the times. The whole world today judges as the Weibel brothers did. Yes, that's how it is: nothing lordly or ladylike is tolerated any more. There are no more masters who can do as they please, and there haven't been any mistresses for ages. Should I be sad about this? It wouldn't even cross my mind. Am I responsible for the spirit of the age? I take the times as they come and only reserve the right to make my own quiet observations. Good old Fehlmann: he was pardoned, in the patriarchal way. Tears of loyalty and dependence, how beautiful that is!

From three o'clock in the afternoon we pupils are left almost to our own devices. Nobody bothers with us any more. The Benjamentas are secluded in the inner chambers and in the classroom there's an emptiness, an emptiness that almost sickens one. All noise is forbidden. One is only allowed to scurry and creep about and to talk in whispers. Schilinski looks at himself in his mirror, Schacht looks out of the window or he gesticulates to the kitchen maids on the other side of the street, and Kraus is learning things by heart, murmuring the lessons to himself. It's as quiet as the grave. The courtyard out there lies deserted, like a foursquare eternity, and I usually practice standing on one leg. Often, for a change, I see how long I can hold my breath. That is an exercise, too, and it is even supposed to be good for the health, as a doctor once told me. Or I write. Or I close my untired eyes, so as to see nothing any more. The eyes transmit thoughts, therefore I shut them from time to time, in order to stop having to think. When one is just there like this and doing nothing, one suddenly feels how painful existence can be. To do nothing and yet maintain one's bearing, that requires energy, a person doing something has an easy time in comparison. We pupils are masters of this kind of propriety. Ordinarily, do-nothings start something out of boredom, lounge about, fidget, yawn broadly or sigh. We pupils do nothing like this. We close our lips firmly and are motionless. Over our heads the grumpy rules are always floating. Sometimes, when we are sitting or standing there, the door opens and the Fräulein walks slowly through the schoolroom, giving us a strange look. She always seems like a ghost to me. It's as if it were someone coming from far far away. "What are you doing, boys?" she may ask then, but she doesn't wait for an answer, she walks on. How beautiful she is! What a luxuriance of raven hair! Mostly one sees her with her eyes downcast. She has eyes that are wonderfully apt for being downcast. Her eyelids (oh, I observe all these things very sharply) are richly curved and are curiously capable of quick movement. These eyes! If one ever sees them, one looks down into something frighteningly abyssal and profound. These eyes, with their shining darkness, seem to say nothing and yet to say everything unspeakable, they are so familiar and yet so unknown. The eyebrows are thin to breaking and are drawn in rounded arches over the eyes. If you look at them, you have a prickly feeling. They are like crescent moons in a morbidly pallid evening sky, like fine wounds, but all the more sharp, inwardly cutting wounds. And her cheeks! Silent yearning and swooning seem to celebrate festivities on them. There is a weeping on them, up and down, of delicacy and tenderness that nobody has understood. Sometimes there appears on the shimmering snow of these cheeks a soft imploring red, a reddish timid life, a sun, no, not that, only the faint reflection of such a sun. Then it's as if the cheeks were suddenly smiling, or a little feverish. When one looks at Fräulein Benjamenta's cheeks, one has no more joy in living, for one has the feeling that life must be a turbulent hell full of vile crudities. Such delicacy as this almost forces one to look deep into such hardness and peril. And her teeth, which one sees shimmering when she parts her full and kindly lips in a smile. And when she weeps. One thinks that the earth must drop away from every footfall of hers, in shame and sorrow to be seeing her weep. And when one only hears her weeping? Oh, then one swoons away. Recently we heard her, right there in the schoolroom. We were all trembling like aspens. Yes, all of us, we love her. She is our instructress, our higher being. And something is making her suffer, that is obvious. Is she unwell?

Fräulein Benjamenta has spoken a few words with me, in the kitchen. I was just going up to my room, and she asked me, without honoring me with a look: "How are you getting on, Jakob? Is everything all right?" I at once stood at attention, as is required, and said in a submissive voice: "Oh, yes, certainly, Fräulein Benjamenta. Things just couldn't go wrong for me." She smiled faintly and asked: "What does that mean?" She said it over her shoulder. I replied: "I have everything I need." She looked at me for a moment and was silent. After a while she said: "You can go, Jakob. You're excused now. You needn't stand there." I did her the honor prescribed, bowing, and rushed to my room. Hardly five minutes had passed when there was a knock. I leaped to the door. I knew the knock. She stood there before me. "Jakob," she said, "tell me, how do you get on with the other boys? They're nice people, don't you find?" My answer was that I felt I liked and respected them all, without exception. The instructress looked at me cunningly, with her beautiful eyes, and said: "Well, well. And yet you do quarrel with Kraus. Is quarreling for you a sign of love and respect?" I replied without hesitating: "Yes, to some extent, Fräulein. This quarreling isn't meant so seriously, you see. If Kraus were clever, he would notice that I like him better than any of the others. I respect Kraus very very much. It would hurt me to think that you didn't believe that." She took my hand and pressed it lightly and said: "All right, now, don't get excited. You must watch out, when you get heated. You hothead. If things are as you say, then I must be content with you. I shall be content, too, if you go on being well-behaved. Yes, remember this: Kraus is a splendid boy and it offends me when you don't behave well with him. Be nice to him. That is my special wish. But don't be sad, now. Look, I'm not reproaching you. What a coddled and pampered little aristocrat you are! Kraus is such a good person. Isn't it so, isn't Kraus a good person, Jakob?" I said: "Yes." Nothing more than Yes and then suddenly I couldn't help giving a rather stupid laugh, I don't know why. She shook her head and went away. Why did I have to laugh? I still don't know. But it's not a matter of any importance. When shall I get some money? This question seems important. Money, as I see it, has a completely ideal value at the moment. When I imagine the clink of a gold coin, I go practically frantic. I have food to eat: so what. I would like to be rich and smash my head in. Soon I shan't like eating any more.

If I were rich, I wouldn't travel around the world. To be sure, that would not be so bad. But I can see nothing wildly exciting about getting a fugitive acquaintance with foreign places. In general I would decline to educate myself, as they say, any further. I would be attracted by deep things and by the soul, rather than by distances and things far off. It would fascinate me to investigate what is near at hand. And I wouldn't buy anything, either. I would make no acquisitions. Elegant clothes, fine underwear, a top hat, modest gold cufflinks, long patent leather shoes, that would be about all, and with these things I would start out. No house, no garden, no servant, yes, a servant, I would engage a good, dignified Kraus. And then I could begin. Then I would walk out into the swirling mist on the street. Winter with its melancholy cold would match my gold coins excellently. I would carry the banknotes in a simple briefcase.

I would walk about on foot, just as usual, with the consciously secret intention of not letting people notice very much how regally rich I am. Perhaps, too, it would be snowing. All the same to me, on the contrary, that would suit me fine. Soft snowfall among the evening glow of streetlamps. It would be glittering, fascinating. It would never occur to me to take a cab. Only people who are in a hurry or want to put on noble airs do that. But I wouldn't want to put on noble airs, and I would be in no hurry whatever. Thoughts would occur to me as I strolled along. Suddenly I would greet someone, very politely, and look, it's a man. Very politely, then, I would look at the man, then I would see that he's having hard times. I would notice this, not see it, one notices such things, even if one hardly sees them, but there's something about it that one sees. Well, now, anyway, this man would ask me what I want, and his question would be a cultivated one. This question would be asked very gently and simply, and I would be very deeply moved by it. For I would have been quite expecting something harsh. "This man must have been deeply wounded," I would at once say to myself, "otherwise he would have got annoyed." And then I would say nothing, absolutely nothing, but it would be enough to keep looking at him, more and more. Not a sharp look, no, a very simple look, perhaps even rather a blithe one. And then I would know who he was. I would open my briefcase, would extract from it ten thousand marks in ten separate notes, and would give this sum to the man. Then I would doff my hat, as politely as ever, say goodnight, and walk away. And it would go on snowing. As I walked along I would not be thinking any more thoughts, I wouldn't be able to, I would be feeling far too good for anything like that. The man was a horribly destitute artist, I knew it for certain, it was to him that I had given the money. Yes, I knew it, for I wouldn't have let myself be deceived. Oh, there would be one great passionate worry less in the world. Well, now, the next night I would perhaps have some quite different ideas. In any case I wouldn't travel around the world, but would prefer to get up to some crazy and foolish tricks. For example, I could give a madly rich and joyous banquet and arrange orgies such as the world has never seen. I would like it to cost one hundred thousand marks. Quite definitely the money would have to be spent in an utterly wild way, for only genuinely wasted money would be—would have been—beautiful money. And one day I would be a beggar and the sun would be shining and I would be so happy, and I wouldn't ever want to know why. And then Mamma would come and hug me—what nice imaginings these are!

Kraus's face and nature have something old about them, and this oldness he radiates takes anyone who looks at him away to Palestine. The times of Abraham come to life again in the face of my fellow-pupil. The old patriarchal epoch, with its mysterious customs and landscapes, rises to the surface and gazes at one paternally. I feel as if all people in that time were fathers with ancient faces and long brown complicated beards, which is nonsense, of course, and yet perhaps there is something in this very simple-minded notion that corresponds to facts. Yes, in that time! Even this phrase, "in that time": how parental and domestic it sounds! In the old Israelite time there could very well be, now and again, a Papa Isaac or Abraham, he enjoyed respect and lived out the days of his old age in natural wealth, which consisted in landed property. In those days something like majesty surrounded grey old age. Old men were in those days like kings, and the years they have lived meant the same as the same number of acquired titles of nobility. And how young these old men kept! They were still begetting sons and daughters at the age of a hundred. In those days there were still no dentists, so one must assume that there were absolutely no decayed teeth either. And how beautiful, for example, Joseph in Egypt is. Kraus has about him something of Joseph in Potiphar's house. He has been sold into the house as a young slave, and look, they are bringing him into the presence of an immensely rich, honest, and fine man. There he is now, a household slave, but he has a pleasant time of it. The laws in those days were perhaps inhuman, certainly, but the customs and usages and ideas were correspondingly more delicate and refined. Today a slave would have a much harder time, God help him. Of course, too, there are very very many slaves in the midst of us arrogantly ready-made modern people. Perhaps all we present-day people are something like slaves, ruled by an angry, whip-wielding, unrefined idea of the world.— Well and good, now one day the lady of the house demands of Joseph that he do what she desires. How peculiar that such backstairs stories are still very well known today, they live on, from mouth to mouth, through all ages. In all primary schools the story is taught, and do people still object to Joseph's pedantry? I despise people who underestimate the beauty of pedantry, they are thoroughly mindless people, weak in judgment. Good, and then Kraus, I mean Joseph, refuses. But it could very well be Kraus, because there is something very like Joseph in Egypt about him. "No, my lady, I wouldn't do a thing like that, I owe loyalty to my liege lord." Then the lady, who is, incidentally, charming, goes and accuses the young servant of committing a base deed and of trying to seduce his lady into an error. But I don't know any more. Peculiar that I don't know what Potiphar said and did next. I can still see the Nile quite clearly. Yes, Kraus could be Joseph, or anything, for that matter. His bearing, figure, face, haircut, and gestures are imcomparably suitable. Even his unfortunately still-uncured skin feature. Spots are Biblical, oriental. And his morality, character, the firm possession of a chaste young man's virtues? They are wonderfully suitable. Joseph in Egypt, too, must be a good all-around little pedant, or else he would have obeyed the wanton woman and have been disloyal to his lord. Kraus would act precisely as his ancient Egyptian likeness did. He would raise his hands in protest, and say with a half-imploring, half-chastising look on his face: "No, no, I wouldn't do a thing like that," et cetera.

Dear Kraus! My thoughts keep returning to him. In him one can see what the word "culture" really means. Later in life, wherever he goes, Kraus will be regarded as a useful but uncultivated person, but for me he is thoroughly cultivated, and mainly because he is the embodiment of good, steadfast wholeness. One can even call him a culture in human form. Around Kraus there are no flutterings of winged and whispered knowledge, but something in him is at rest, and he himself, he rests and reposes on something. One can safely entrust one's very soul to his keeping. He will never deceive or slander anybody, and, well, this above all, this non-talkativeness, that's what I call culture. Anyone who chatters is a deceiver, he may be a very nice person, but this talking about everything that enters his head makes him a common fellow and a bad one. Kraus is guarded, he always keeps something back, he thinks that it is unnecessary just to talk, and this has the same effect as goodness and a lively leniency. That's what I call culture. Kraus is unkind and often fairly rough to people of his own age and sex, and precisely this is why I like him, for it proves to me that he would be incapable of brutal and thoughtless betrayal. He is loyal and decent to everybody. For that's the trouble: out of common kindness one usually just goes along and desecrates in the most terrible way the reputations and lives of neighbors, friends, even brothers. Kraus doesn't know much, but he is never, never thoughtless, he always subjects himself to certain commands of his own making, and that's what I call culture. Whatever is kind and thoughtful about a person is culture. And there's so much else besides. To be so far removed from any and every self-seeking, even in a small way, and to be so close to self-discipline as Kraus, that is what I think made Fräulein Benjamenta say: "Isn't it so, Jakob, Kraus is good?" Yes, he's good. When I lose this friend, I lose a kingdom of heaven, I know it. And I'm almost afraid to quarrel freely with Kraus. I only want to contemplate him, always to contemplate him, for later I shall have to content myself with his image, because rampageous life is certain to separate the two of us.

I now understand also why Kraus has no outward advantages, no physical graces, why nature has so dwarfishly squashed and disfigured him. She wants something from him, she has plans for him, or she had plans for him from the start. Perhaps this person was, for nature, too pure, and that's why she threw him into an insignificant, small, unbeautiful body, in order to preserve him against pernicious outward successes. Or perhaps it wasn't so, and nature was annoyed and malicious when she made Kraus. But how sorry she must be now, to have treated him like a wicked stepmother! And who knows. Perhaps she rejoices in this graceless masterpiece of hers, and indeed she would have cause to rejoice, for this graceless Kraus is more beautiful than the most graceful and beautiful people. He doesn't shine with talents, but with the radiance of a good and unspoiled heart, and his plain bad manners, despite the woodenness attaching to them, are perhaps the most beautiful kind of motion and manners that there can be in human society. No, Kraus will never have any successes, either with women, who will find him dry and ugly, or otherwise in the world, which will pass him heedlessly by. Heedlessly? Yes, nobody will ever pay any attention to Kraus, and precisely this, his going on living without enjoying attention, that is the wonderful thing, which seems to be part of a plan, the sign of the Creator. God gives a Kraus to this world, in order to entrust to it, as it were, a deep, insoluble riddle. And the riddle will never be understood, for look: people don't even try to solve it, and for this very reason the Kraus riddle is such a glorious and deep one: because nobody wants to solve it, because there isn't a person living who'll suppose there is some task, some riddle, or a more delicate meaning, at the back of this nameless, inconspicuous Kraus. Kraus is a genuine work of God, a nothing, a servant. To everyone he will seem uncultivated, just about good enough to do the roughest work, and it is strange: people won't be wrong in this either, but they'll be perfectly right, for it is true: Kraus, modesty itself, the crown, the palace of humility, he will do menial work, he can do it and he will do it. He has no thought but to help, to obey and to serve, and people will at once notice and exploit this, and in this exploiting of him lies such a radiant, golden, divine justice, shimmering with goodness and splendor. Yes, Kraus is the image of legitimate being, utterly monotonous, monosyllabic, and unambiguous being. Nobody will mistake this person's plainness, and therefore nobody will notice him, and he will be thoroughly unsuccessful. Charming, charming, three times charming I find this. Oh, the creations of God are so full of grace, of charm, beribboned with charms and thoughts. People will think that this is a very excessive way of putting it. Well, I must confess it's not by any means the most excessive thing. No, for Kraus no success will ever flower, no fame, no love, that is very good, for successes go inseparably with fickleness and a few cheap ideas about life. One notices it at once, when people have successes and recognition to display, they grow fat with satiating complacency, and the power of vanity blows them up like balloons, so that they become unrecognizable. God preserves a good person from being recognized by the crowd. If it doesn't make him bad, it merely confuses and weakens him. Gratitude, yes. Gratitude is something quite different. But nobody will ever be grateful to Kraus, and that too isn't necessary. Once every ten years somebody will perhaps say to Kraus: "Thanks, Kraus," and then give a stupid, cruelly stupid smile. My Kraus will never go to ruin, because there will always be great and loveless difficulties confronting him. I think that I, I am one of the very few people, perhaps the only person, or perhaps there are two or three, who will know what they have in Kraus, or have had in him. The Fräulein, yes, she knows. Also the Principal, perhaps. Yes, certainly he knows. Herr Benjamenta is certainly penetrating enough to know what Kraus is worth. I must stop writing for today. It excites me too much. I'm getting confused. And the letters are flickering and dancing in front of my eyes.

Behind our house there is an old, neglected garden. When I see it in the early morning from the office window (every other morning I have to tidy the office, together with Kraus), I am sorry for it, lying there untended, and each time I want to go down and look after it. But those are sentimental ideas. The devil take such misleading dreamy softness. There are quite other gardens with us in the Benjamenta Institute. To go into the real garden is forbidden. No pupils are allowed in there. I don't really know why. But, as I said, we have another garden, perhaps more beautiful than the actual one. In our primer, *What Is the Aim of the Boys' School?*, it says on page 8: "Good behavior is a garden full of flowers." It's in such gardens of spirit and sentiment that we pupils are allowed to leap around. Not bad. If one of us is badly behaved, he walks of his own accord in a horrible dark hell. If he is good, he can't help going out for his reward among shady green leaves flecked with sunlight. How seductive! And in my poor boyish opinion, there is some truth in that nice dogma. If a person behaves stupidly, he must be ashamed and angry with himself, and that is the painful hell in which he sweats. But if he has been attentive and compliant, then something invisible takes him by the hand, something friendly, like a little spirit, and that is the garden, the kind dispensation, and then he really does go strolling of his own accord over friendly green meadows. If ever a pupil at the Benjamenta Institute is allowed to be satisfied with himself, which seldom occurs, since the rules are always storming at us, with hail, snow, lightning, and rain, then there is a fragrance all around him, and it is the sweet fragrance of modest but staunchly fought-for praise. If Fräulein Benjamenta utters a word of praise, the fragrance comes, and if she scolds, then the schoolroom goes dark. What a peculiar world, our school. If a pupil has been well behaved and seemly, there is suddenly a vault overhead, and it is the blue irreplaceable heaven above the imaginary garden. If we pupils have been very patient, and if we have maintained our exertions well, if we have been able, as they say, to stand and wait, then suddenly before our somewhat weary eyes the air turns gold, and we know that it is the heavenly sun. Anyone with a right and title to fatigue finds the sun shining down upon him. And if there has been no need for us to catch ourselves having impure wishes, which always make one so unhappy, then we listen and, aha! what is that? Birds are singing! Well, it must have been the happy and fine-feathered songsters of our garden who were singing and making their graceful clamor. Now admit: do we pupils of the Benjamenta Institute need any other gardens than those which we create for ourselves? We are rich lords, if we conduct ourselves with delicacy and good manners. Whenever, for example, I wish to possess money, which unfortunately is all too often the case, then I sink into the deep gulfs of hopeless, raging desire, oh, then I suffer and swoon, and doubt if I shall ever be rescued. And then, if I look at Kraus, a deep, murmuring, springlike, wonderful comfort takes hold of me. That is the peaceful spring of modesty, which rises in our garden, splashing up and down, and then I am so happy, in such a good mood, so attuned to goodness. Ah, and they say I don't love Kraus? If one of us is, that is to say, were to have been, a hero, if he had done something brave in peril of his life (that's what it says in the primer), then he would be allowed to enter the pillared marble house with its wall paintings that is hidden among the greenery of our garden, and there a mouth would kiss him. The primer doesn't say what sort of a mouth. And of course we aren't heroes. And why should we be? First, we have no chance to behave like heroes, and second: I doubt if Schilinski, for example, or Beanpole Peter, could be unveigled into making sacrifices. Even without kisses, heroes, and pillared pavilions, our garden is a nice arrangement, I think. Talking of heroes gives me the shivers. I'd rather not say anything on that.

Recently I asked Kraus if he too didn't sometimes feel something like boredom. He gave me a reproving and corrective look, thought for a moment, and said: "Boredom? That's not very clever of you, Jakob. And, let me tell you, your questions are as naive as they are sinful. Whoever can be bored in this world? You, perhaps. Not me, I can tell you. I'm learning things by heart from this book here. Well? Have I got time to be bored? What foolish questions. Noble folk get bored, perhaps, not Kraus, and you get bored, or you wouldn't think of the idea, and wouldn't come to me asking such a thing. One can always be doing something, if not outside, then at least inside, one can murmur, Jakob. I know you've often laughed at me on account of my murmuring, but listen and tell me, do you know what I murmur? Words, Jakob. I always murmur and repeat words. It does one good, I can tell you. Get away with you and your boredom. People who get bored are ones who always reckon that something amusing ought to come at them from outside. Boredom is where bad moods are, and where people want things. Go away now, don't bother me, let me learn, go away and do some work. Bother yourself with something, then you certainly won't feel bored any more. And in the future please avoid such almost exasperating, utterly silly questions." I asked: "Is that all you had to say, Kraus?" and laughed. But he just looked at me pityingly. No, Kraus can never be bored, never. I knew that perfectly well, I only wanted to tease him again. How nasty of me that is, and how empty headed. I definitely must improve. How bad it is, always to be wanting to ape and annoy Kraus! And yet: how delightful! His reproaches sound so funny. There is something of old father Abraham in his admonitions.

What a terrible dream I had a few days ago. In the dream I had become a very bad man indeed. I couldn't make out how. I was crude, from top to toe, a dressed-up, crass, and cruel bit of human flesh. I was fat, things were going splendidly for me, it seemed. Rings glittered on the fingers of my coarse hands, and I had a belly with flabby hundredweights of fleshy dignity hanging down it. I felt so completely that I could give commands and let fly with moods. Beside me, on a table richly spread, shone the objects of an insatiable appetite for food and drink, bottles of wine and liqueurs, and the most exquisite cold dishes. I had only to reach out a hand, and from time to time I did so. To the knives and forks clung the tears of enemies I destroyed, and the glasses sang with the sighs of many poor people, but the tear-stains only made me want to laugh, while the hopeless sighs sounded to me like music. I needed banquet music and had it. Evidently I had been extremely successful in business at the expense of the well-being of others, and that put joy into my very guts. Oh, oh, how I reveled in the knowledge of having pulled the ground from under the feet of a few fellow-men! And I reached for the bell and rang. An old man walked in, no, excuse me, crawled in, it was Wisdom, and the fellow crawled up to my boots, to kiss them. And I let him do this, in his humiliation. Just think: experience itself, the good and noble precept: it kissed my feet. That's what I call being rich. Because I felt like it, I rang again, for I had an itch, I don't recall where it was, for an ingenious change, and in came a young girl, a real delicacy for a libertine like me. Childish Innocence, that's what she called herself, and she began with a glance at the whip at my side, to kiss me, which was incredibly refreshing. Fear and her precocious depravity fluttered in the child's beautiful deer-like eyes. When I had had enough of her, I rang again and in came Seriousness, a handsome, slim, but poor young man. He was one of my lackeys, and I ordered him, with a scowl, to fetch that thingummy, what's its name, can't remember, now I've got it, Joy-in-Work. Soon after this, in came Zeal and I took the pleasure of giving him, the complete man, this splendidly built Working Man, a lash with the whip, right in the middle of his quietly waiting face, it was a tremendous laugh. And he didn't mind, native creative energy himself, he didn't mind. Then, of course, with an indolent condescending gesture I invited him to have a glass of wine, and the foolish idiot drank up this wine of his disgrace. "Off you go now, work for me," I said, and he left. Then Virtue came in, a female figure of overwhelming beauty for anyone not frozen rigid, and weeping. I took her on my knee and fooled around with her. When I had robbed her of her unspeakable treasure, the Ideal, I chased her out with derision, and then I whistled and God himself appeared. I shouted: "What? You too?" And I woke up, dripping with sweat—how glad I was that it was only a bad dream. My God, I do hope that I shall make something of myself one day. How close to the edge of madness everything is in dreams! Kraus would goggle at me like anything if I were to tell him all this.

The way we revere the Fräulein really is comic. But I, for one, am all in favor of comedy, it certainly has its magic. The class always begins at eight. But we pupils sit there for ten minutes beforehand, in our seats, full of excitement and expectation, and we gaze fixedly at the door through which the Principaless will appear. For this kind of anticipatory display of respect, we also have exact rules. It's as good as law that we should listen for her, to tell when she is coming, she who will certainly enter at a particular time. For ten silly-boy-like minutes, we pupils have to be getting ready to stand up in our places. All these petty requirements are slightly humiliating, actually they're ridiculous, but it's a question not of our personal honor but of the honor of the Benjamenta Institute, and that is possibly just as it should be, for does the pupil have any

honor at all? Not a scrap. To be well and truly regimented and har-
rassed, that's the highest of honors for us. To be drilled is an honor
for pupils, that's as clear as day. But we don't rebel, either. It would
never cross our minds. We have, collectively, so few thoughts. I
have perhaps the most thoughts, that's quite possible, but at root I
despise my capacity for thinking. I value only experiences, and
these, as a rule, are quite independent of all thinking and compar-
ing. Thus I value the way in which I open a door. There is more
hidden life in opening a door than in asking a question. Yet everything does provoke one to question and compare and remember.
Certainly one must think, one must even think a great deal. But to
comply, that is much more refined, much more than thinking. If one
thinks, one resists, and that is always so ugly and ruinous to things.
Thinkers, if only they knew what harm they do. Anyone who indus-
triously does not think, does something, he certainly does, and that
is more necessary. There are ten thousand superfluous heads at
work in the world. It's clear, clear as day. The generations of men
are losing the joy of life with all their treatises and understandings
and knowledge. If, for example, a pupil of the Benjamenta Institute
doesn't know that he's being polite, then polite is what he's being.
If he knows it, then all his unconscious grace and politeness disappear, and he makes some mistake or other. I like running down
stairs. What a lot of talk!

It's nice to be a bit prosperous and to have one's worldly affairs
somewhat in order. I've been to my brother Johann's apartment,
and I must say it was a pleasant surprise, it's quite an old-fashioned
von Guntenish place. The mere fact that the floor is covered with a
soft, dull-blue carpet, I found extraordinarily imposing. All the
rooms show taste, not ostentatious taste, but a definite and fine
choiceness. The furniture is placed gracefully, which has the effect
of greeting you politely and gently when you come in. There are
mirrors on the walls. There's even one big mirror that reaches from
floor to ceiling. The particular objects are old, yet not old, elegant,
yet not elegant. There's warmth and carefulness in the rooms, one
feels this, and it's pleasant. A free and solicitous will hung the mirrors up and showed the delicately curved sofa to its place. I
wouldn't be a von Gunten if I didn't notice that. Everything is clean
and without dust, and yet it doesn't all shine, but everything looks
at one calmly and serenely. Nothing strikes the eye sharply. The

whole combination has a significant kindly look. A beautiful black cat was lying on the dark red plush chair, like black, soft easefulness bedded in red. Very pretty. If I were a painter, I'd paint the intimacy of such an animal image. My brother came toward me in a very friendly way and we stood facing one another like measured men of the world who know how enjoyable the properties can be. We talked of this and that. Then a large and slender snow-white dog ran up to us, with graceful joyous movements. Well, naturally I stroked the animal. Everything about Johann's apartment is good. He took the trouble to discover, with love, each of the objects and pieces of furniture in antique shops, until he had collected together the cosiest and most graceful ones. He has managed to make something simple but perfect within modest limits, so that convenient and useful objects join with beautiful and graceful ones and make his apartment look like a painting. Soon, as we sat there, a young lady appeared and Johann introduced me to her. Later, we drank tea and were very happy. The cat miaowed for milk and the beautiful large dog wanted to eat some of the biscuits that were on the table. Both animals also had their wishes gratified. Evening came and I had to go home.

Here in the Benjamenta Institute one learns to suffer and endure losses, and that is in my view a craft, an exercise without which any person will always remain a big child, a sort of crybaby, however important he may be. We pupils have no hopes, it is even forbidden to us to nourish hopes for life in our hearts, and yet we are completely calm and happy. How can that be? Do we feel that guardian angels, or something similar, are flying back and forth over our smoothly combed heads? I can't say. Perhaps we are happy and carefree from being so restricted. That's quite possible. But does that make the happiness and freshness of our hearts any less valuable? Are we really stupid? We have our vibrations. Unconsciously or consciously we take thought for many things, we are with the spirits here and there, and we send out our feelings in all directions, gathering experiences and observations. There's so much that comforts us, because we are, in general, very zealous and inquiring people, and because we set little value on ourselves. A person who sets a high value on himself is never safe from discouragements and humiliations, for confronting a self-conscious person there is always something hostile to consciousness. And yet we pupils aren't by any

means without dignity, but the dignity we have is a very very mobile, small, pliant, and supple dignity. Also we put it on and off,
according to the requirements. Are we products of a higher culture,
or are we nature-boys? I don't know that either. One thing I do
know for certain: we are waiting! That's our value. Yes, we're waiting, and we are, as it were, listening to life, listening out into that
plateau which people call the world, out across the sea with its
storms. Fuchs, by the way, has left. I was very glad of that. I
couldn't get along with him.

I have spoken with Herr Benjamenta, that's to say, he has spoken
with me. "Jakob," he said to me, "tell me, don't you find the life
here sterile, sterile? Eh? I'd like to know your opinion. Be quite
frank with me." I preferred not to say anything, but not out of defiance. My defiance disappeared long ago. But I said nothing, and
roughly in such a way that my answer would have been: "Sir, allow
me not to say anything. In reply to such a question, the most I could
say would be something unseemly." Herr Benjamenta looked at me
closely, and I thought he understood my silence. And it really was
so, for he smiled and said: "You're wondering, aren't you, Jakob,
why I spend my life here in the Institute so lethargically, so absent-
mindedly, as it were? Isn't that so? Have you noticed it? But the last
thing I want is to lead you astray into giving outrageous answers.
I must confess something to you, Jakob. Listen, I think you're an
intelligent and decent young person. Now, please, be cheeky. And I
feel that I must confess something else to you: I, your Principal,
think well of you. And a third confession: I have begun to feel a
strange, a quite peculiar and now no longer repressible peference
for you. You'll be cheeky with me now, won't you, Jakob? You will,
won't you?—now that I've revealed something of myself to you,
young man, you'll dare to treat me with disdain? And you'll defy
me now? Is it so, tell me, is it so?" We two, the bearded man and I,
the boy, looked one another in the eye. It was like an inner combat.
I was about to open my mouth and say something submissive, but
I managed to control myself and said nothing. And now I noticed
that the Principal, this gigantic man, was trembling slightly. From
this moment, some common bond was between us. I felt it, yes, I
didn't only feel it, I knew it. "Herr Benjamenta respects me," I told
myself, and as a result of this realization, which came down on me
like a flash of lightning, I found it right, even imperative, not to say

anything. All the worse for me if I had said a single word. A single word would have made me into an insignificant little pupil again, and I had just risen to the most unpupil-like human heights. I felt all this deeply, and, as I now know, I behaved quite correctly during that moment. The Principal, who had come close to me, then said as follows: "There's something important about you, Jakob." He stopped, and at once I felt why. He doubtless wanted to see how I would now behave. I noticed this and therefore I didn't move a muscle in my face, but looked ahead, rigidly, mindlessly. Then we looked at one another again. I stared austerely and sternly at my Principal. I managed to sham coldness, superficiality, while in fact I'd have liked best to laugh in his face for joy. But at the same time I saw that he was satisfied with my bearing, and finally he said: "My boy, go back to your work! Get busy with something. Or go and talk to Kraus. Go now!" I bowed deeply, just as usual, and went out. In the corridor I stopped, as once before, but actually also as usual, and listened at the keyhole, to hear if anything was going on in there. But everything was quiet. I couldn't help laughing softly and happily, a very silly laugh, and then I went into the classroom, where I saw Kraus sitting in the twilight, a brownish light seemed to surround him. I stood there for a long time. Really, I stood there a long time, for there was something, something that I couldn't quite understand. I felt as if I were at home. No, it was as if I hadn't yet been born, as if I were swimming in some element before birth. I felt hot and before my eyes there was a sea-like vagueness. I went to Kraus and said to him: "Kraus, I love you." He growled what's-all-this-about. Quickly I went up to my room. And now? Are we friends? Are Herr Benjamenta and I friends? In any case there's a relationship between us, but of what kind? I forbid myself to try to explain it. I want to keep bright, light, and happy. Away with thoughts!

I still haven't found a position. Herr Benjamenta says he's looking for one. He says so in a peremptory tone, and adds: "What? Impatient? All in good time. Wait!" The pupils are saying that Kraus will soon be departing. Departing, that sounds comically professional. Is Kraus going away soon? I hope these are only empty rumors, institutional excitements. Even among us pupils there's a kind of newspaper gossip, snatched out of air and emptiness. The words, I notice, are everywhere the same. Also I have visited my brother again, and this fellow had the courage to introduce me to people. I sat at the tables of the rich, and I'll never forget the way I behaved. I was wearing an old, but still rather grand, frock coat. Frock coats make one old and important. So it was, and I acted like a man with an income of at least twenty thousand. I have talked with people who would have turned their backs on me if they could have guessed who I am. Women who would have despised me completely if I had told them that I'm only a pupil have smiled at me and have, as it were, made gestures of encouragement to me. And I was amazed at my appetite. How placidly one helps oneself at other people's tables! I saw how they all did it, and I copied them, with great talent. How vulgar that is. I feel something like shame to have shown my happy eating and drinking face there, in those particular circles. I didn't notice much in the way of refined manners. But I did notice that people thought of me as a timorous boy, whereas (in my own eyes) I was bursting with impudence. Johann behaves well in society. He has the light and pleasant manner of a man who is of some importance and who knows it. His behavior is a delight for the eyes that behold it. Do I speak too well of Johann? Oh, no. I'm not enamoured of my brother at all, but I try to see him whole, not only half. Of course, that may be love. No matter. It was very nice in the theater, too, but I don't want to enlarge on that. Then I took off the fine frock coat again. Oh, it's nice to walk and whizz around in the clothes of a person one esteems! Yes, whizz! One chirps and whizzes around there, in cultivated circles. Then I crept back to the Institute again and into my school clothes. I like it here and I shall probably have a foolish yearning for the Benjamentas later on, when I've become something grand, but I shall never, never be anything grand, and I tremble with a peculiar satisfaction that I should know this for certain in advance. One day I shall be laid low by a stroke, and then everything, all these confusions, this longing, this unknowing, all this, the gratitude and ingratitude, this telling lies and self-deception, this thinking that one knows and yet never knowing anything, will come to an end. But I want to live, no matter how.

Something incomprehensible has happened. Perhaps it's of no significance at all. I'm not much inclined to let myself be overcome by mysteries. I was sitting all alone in the schoolroom, it was almost nightfall. Suddenly Fräulein Benjamenta was standing behind me. I hadn't heard her come in, so she must have opened the door very quietly. She asked me what I was doing, but in a tone of voice that made an answer unnecessary. She said, as it were, even in asking, that she already knew. When that happens, one naturally doesn't answer. She placed a hand on my shoulder, as if she were tired and needed a support. Then I felt strongly that I belonged to her, that's to say, or is it, that I *did* belong to her? Yes, simply belonged to her. I always distrust feelings. But here my sort of belonging to her, to the Fräulein, was a true feeling. We belonged together. Naturally there was a difference. But suddenly we were close. Always, always, the difference. I really hate feeling little or no difference. To sense that Fräulein Benjamenta and I were two different kinds of being, in different situations, this was a joy for me. I usually despise deceiving myself. I consider distinctions and advantages as my enemies, unless they are completely genuine. So there was this big difference. Now what's all this? Can't I get over certain differences? But then the Fräulein said: "Come with me! Stand up and come with me. I want to show you something." We walked along together. Before our eyes, at least before mine (not hers, perhaps), everything was veiled in impenetrable darkness. "It's the inner chambers," I thought, and I wasn't wrong, either. That's how it was, and my dear instructress seemed to be resolved to show me a world that had been hidden until now. But I must pause for breath.

It was, as I said, completely dark at first. The Fräulein took me by the hand and said in a friendly voice: "Look, Jakob, there will be darkness all around you. And then someone will take you by the hand. And you will be glad of this and you will feel deep gratitude for the first time. Don't be disheartened. There will be brightnesses too." She had hardly said this when a white dazzling light shone toward us. A door appeared and we went, she in front and me close behind, through the opening, into the glorious fire of the light. Never had I seen anything so radiant and promising, so I was really quite stunned. The Fräulein spoke with a smile, in an even more friendly voice: "Does the light dazzle you? Then make every effort to endure it. It means joy and one must know how to feel and endure it. You can also think, if you like, that it means your future happiness, but look what's happening? It's disappearing. The light is falling to pieces. So, Jakob, you'll have no long-enduring happiness. Does my frankness hurt you? No. Come further now. We must hurry a little, for we must walk and tremble through several other apparitions. Tell me, Jakob, do you understand my words? But don't say anything. You're not allowed to talk here. Do you think that I'm an enchantress? No, I'm not an enchantress. To be sure, I know how to enchant a little, to seduce, I know that much. Every girl knows how to do that. But come on now." With these words the admirable girl opened a trap door in the floor, I had to help her, and we climbed together, she as ever in front, down into a deep cellar. At length, as the stone stairs came to an end, we were walking over moist, soft earth. I felt that we were standing in the middle of the earth's sphere, so deep and lonely was the place. We walked along a dark, lengthy corridor. Fräulein Benjamenta said: "We are now in the vaults of poverty and deprivation, and since you, dear Jakob, will probably be poor all your life, please try now to get a little accustomed to the darkness and to the cold, penetrating odor of the place. Don't be afraid, and don't be angry. God is here, too, he's everywhere. One must learn to love and nourish necessity. Kiss the wet earth of the cellar. I ask you, yes, do it. Thus you give the token of your willing submission to the heaviness and darkness which will, it seems, make up the greatest part of your life." I obeyed her, threw myself down on the cold earth and kissed it ardently, whereupon a hot and cold shudder ran through me. We walked on. Ah, these corridors of compulsory suffering and of terrible deprivation seemed endless to me, and perhaps they really were endless. The seconds were like whole lifetimes, and the minutes took on the size of anguished centuries. Enough, at last we reached a mournful wall, the Fräulein said: "Go and fondle the wall. It is the Wall of Worries. It will always stand before your eyes, and you'll be unwise to hate it. Ah, one must simply know how to avoid rigidity and whatever yields to no conciliation. Go and try it." I went quickly, as if in a passionate hurry, up to the wall and flung myself against its breast. Yes, against the stony breast, and I spoke to it a few kindly, almost joking words. And it remained unmoved, as was to be expected. I play-acted, to please my instructress, certainly, and yet again it was anything but play-acting that I was doing. And yet we both smiled, she, the instructress, as well as I, her callow pupil. "Come on," she said, "let's treat ourselves to a little freedom now, a little movement." And with her small white familiar cane she touched the wall, and the whole horrible cellar disappeared and we found ourselves on a smooth, spacious, narrow track of ice or glass. We floated along it, as if on marvelous skates, and we were dancing, too, for like a wave the track rose and fell beneath us. It was delightful. I had never seen anything like it and I shouted for joy: "How glorious!" And overhead the stars were shimmering, in a sky that was strangely all pale blue and yet dark, and the moon with its unearthly light was staring down upon us skaters. "This is freedom," said the instructress, "it's something very wintry, and cannot be borne for long. One must always keep moving, as we are doing here, one must dance in freedom. It is cold and beautiful. Never fall in love with it! That would only make you sad afterwards, for one can only be in the realm of freedom for a moment, no longer. Look how the wonderful track we are floating on is slowly melting away. Now you can watch freedom dying, if you open your eyes. You will have your full share of this agonizing sight later in life." Hardly had she spoken when we sank from our summit of happiness down into a place that was tired and cosy, it was a small bedchamber, chockfull of sophisticated comforts, tapestried with all kinds of wanton scenes and pictures. It was a proper pillowy boudoir. Often I had dreamed of real boudoirs. And now I was inside one of them. Music was rippling down around the walls like a graceful snowfall, one could even see the music being made, the notes like magical flakes of snow. "Here," said the Fräulein, "you can rest. You must decide for yourself how long." We both smiled at these mysterious words, and although an unspeakably slight fear stole up on me, I wasted no time in making myself comfortable in this chamber on one of the rugs that lay around. An uncommonly good-tasting cigarette flew down from above into my involuntarily opened mouth, and I smoked. A novel fluttered into my hands and I could read it undisturbed. "That's not the right thing for you. Don't read such books. Stand up. It's better we move on. Softness seduces one to thoughtlessness and cruelty. Listen, can't you hear their angry thunder, they're coming. This room is the chamber of calamity. You have had your repose in it. Now calamity will rain down on you and doubt and restlessness will drench you through. Come on! One must go out and meet the inevitable, bravely." Thus spoke the instructress and she had hardly finished when I was swimming in a gluey and most unpleasant river of doubt. Thoroughly disheartened, I didn't dare to look around to see

284 · Robert Walser

if she was still near to me. No, the instructress, the enchantress who had conjured up all these visions and states, had disappeared. I was swimming all alone. I tried to scream, but the water only started to flow into my mouth. Oh, these calamities, I wept, and I bitterly regretted my surrender to the wanton pleasures of easefulness. Then suddenly I was sitting in the Benjamenta Institute again, in the dark classroom, and Fräulein Benjamenta was still standing behind me, and she stroked my cheeks, but as if she needed to comfort herself, not me. "She's unhappy," I thought. Then Kraus, Schacht, and Schilinski, who had been out together, came back. Quickly the girl drew her hand away from me and went into the kitchen to get supper. Had I been dreaming? But why ask myself this, now that it's time for supper? There are times when I simply love to eat. I can bite into the silliest foods then, just like a hungry young apprentice, then I am living in a fairy tale and am no longer a cultured being in an age of culture.

Sometimes our gymnastic and dancing classes are very amusing. To have to show skill is not without its dangers. What a fool one can make of oneself. To be sure, we pupils don't make fun of each other. We don't? Oh, yes, we do. One laughs with one's ears, if one isn't allowed to laugh with one's mouth. And with one's eyes. Eyes are very fond of laughing. And to make rules for the eyes, that's quite possible, to be sure, but pretty difficult. Thus, for example, we aren't allowed to wink, winking is mocking and therefore to be spurned, but one certainly does wink sometimes. To repress nature completely can't be done. And yet it can. But even if one has shed nature entirely, there's always a breath of it left, a remnant, and it shows. Beanpole Peter, for example, finds it very difficult to shed his own most personal nature. Sometimes when he's supposed to be dancing, moving gracefully and showing how graceful he is, he consists entirely of wood, and wood is Peter's natural state, like a gift of God. Yet one can't help laughing at a rafter when it appears in the form of a tall person, one has a glorious inside laugh. Laughter is the opposite of a piece of wood, it's something inflammatory, something that strikes matches inside you. Matches giggle, exactly like a repressed laugh. I very much like stopping the outburst of laughter. It tickles, marvelously: not letting it go, the thing that so much wants to come shooting out, I like things that aren't allowed to be, things that have to go down into my inside. It makes these

repressed things more awkward, but at the same time more valuable. Yes, yes, I admit I like being repressed. To be sure. No, not
always to be sure. On your way, Toby Shaw! What I mean is: if you
aren't allowed to do something, you do it twice as much somewhere
else. Nothing's more insipid than an indifferent, quick, cheap bit of
permission. I like earning everything, experiencing everything, and
a laugh, for example, also needs to be thoroughly experienced.
When inside me I'm bursting with laughter, when I hardly know
what to do with all this hissing gunpowder, then I know what
laughing is, then I have laughed most laughishly, then I have a complete idea of what was shaking me. So I must firmly suppose and
keep it as my strong conviction that rules do gild existence, or at
least they silver it, in a word, they make it delectable. For certainly
it's the same with almost all other things and pleasures as it is with
the forbidden delectable laugh. Not being allowed to cry, for example, well, that makes crying larger. Doing without love, yes, that
means loving. If I oughtn't to love, I love ten times as much. Everything that's forbidden lives a hundred times over; thus, if something
is supposed to be dead, its life is all the livelier. As in small things,
so in big ones. Nicely put, in everyday words, but in everyday
things the true truths are found. I'm gabbling somewhat again,
aren't I? I admit that I'm gabbling, but the lines have got to be filled
with something. Forbidden fruits, how delectable, how delectable
they are!

Perhaps now between Herr Benjamenta and me, visible to us
both, a sort of forbidden fruit is hanging. But neither of us says anything openly, and that is certainly to be approved of. To me, for
instance, friendly treatment is unpleasant. I mean generally. Certain
people who feel affection for me are repulsive to me, I can't emphasize this overmuch. Naturally, I'm not averse to gentleness, and to
warmth of heart. Who could be so crude as to shun completely all
intimacy, all warmish feelings? But I'm always cautious about coming close to people, and I don't know, but I must have some sort of
gift for convincing others, silently, that a closer approach would be
unwise, at least I think it's difficult for anyone to steal into my confidence. And my warmth is precious to me, and anyone who wants
to have it must be extremely cautious, and it's this that the Principal
wants now. This Herr Benjamenta, it seems, wants to possess my
heart and make friends with me. But for the present I'm treating

him very coldly indeed, and who knows: perhaps I don't want to have anything to do with him.

"You're young," the Principal says to me, "you're bursting with prospects. Wait a moment, was there something else I forgot to say? You must realize, Jakob, that I've got a lot of things to say to you, and yet you can have forgotten the best and deepest things before you know where you are. And you yourself, you look like good fresh memory itself, whereas my memory is getting old now. My mind, Jakob, is dying. Forgive me if I'm saying things that are too weak, too intimate. It's a laugh. So I ask you to forgive me, whereas I could give you a good beating if I thought it necessary. What stern looks you're giving me. Well, well, I could throw you against the wall there, so hard you'd never see or hear anything again. I don't know what's happened to make me lose all my authority over you. Probably you laugh at me, secretly. But between ourselves: watch out. You must realize that wild feelings seize me sometimes and before I can stop myself I forget what I'm doing. O my little lad, no, don't be afraid. It would be so completely impossible, completely, to do you any harm, but—well, now, what was it I meant to say to you? Tell me, are you just a little frightened? And you're young and you've got hopes, and soon you want to find a position. Isn't that so? Yes, that's it. Yes, that's it and I'm sorry, for just think, sometimes I feel that you're my young brother or something near as nature to me, you seem so related to me, with your gestures, talk, mouth, everything, in short, yourself. I'm a king who's been deposed. You're smiling? I find it simply delightful, you know, that precisely when I'm talking about kings deposed and deprived of their thrones a smile escapes you, such a mischievous smile. You have intelligence, Jakob. Oh, it's so nice to be talking to you. It's a delightful prickly feeling to behave with you in a rather weak sort of way and more softly than usual. Yes, you really do provoke easy going, loosening up, the sacrifice of dignity. One attributes to you—do you believe me?—a nobility of mind, and this tempts one very strongly to indulge, when you are there, in fine and helpful explanations and confessions, as I do, for example, your master, confessing to you, my poor young worm, whom I could utterly crush if I chose to. Give me your hand. Good! Let me tell you that you've managed to make me feel respect for you. I respect you highly, and—I—don't mind—telling you. And now I want to ask you something: will you be my friend, the small sharer of my confidences? I ask you, please do. But I'll give you time to think it over, you may go now. Please go, leave me alone." That's the way my Principal speaks to me, the man who, as he says himself, could utterly crush me just when he chooses. I don't bow to him any more, it would hurt his feelings. What was that he was saying about deposed kings? I'll waste no time thinking about all this, as he recommends, but I shall simply carry on maintaining the formalities. In any case, it means I must watch out. He talks about wildness? Well, I must say, that's very disturbing. I'm much too good to be squashed against a wall. Shall I tell the Fräulein? Good heavens, no. I've got enough courage to keep silent about something that's strange, and enough intelligence to cope with something dubious alone. Perhaps Herr Benjamenta is mad. In any case, he's like the lion, but I'm the mouse. A nice state of affairs in the Institute now. Only I mustn't tell anyone. Sometimes a thing that's kept hidden is an advantage gained. It's all quite silly. Basta!

What strange imaginings I sometimes have! They're almost quite absurd. Suddenly, without my being able to stop it, I had become a commander in the war around the year 1400, no, a bit later, at the time of the Milan campaigns. I and my officers, we were having dinner. It was after a victory in battle, and our fame would be spreading throughout Europe during the next few days. We were drinking and making merry. We were dining not in a room, no, but out of doors. The sun was just setting, then before my eyes, whose ray meant the start of battle and victory in arms, a creature was brought, a poor devil, a captured traitor. The unhappy man bowed his head and was trembling, knowing that he had no right to look at the commander-in-chief. I looked at him, quite fleetingly, then I looked just as lightly and fleetingly at the men who had brought him along, then I devoted myself to the full glass of wine before me, and these three movements meant: "Take him away and hang him!" At once the people seized him, and then the poor fellow screamed in desperation, worse, as if he was being torn apart, torn apart already by a thousand dreadful martyrs' deaths. My ears had heard all kinds of sounds in the fights and battles that filled my life, and my eyes were more than accustomed to the sight of terrible and painful things, but strangely enough, this was something I couldn't endure. Once more I turned to the condemned man, also I gestured

to the soldiers. "Let him go," I said, the glass at my lips, to make it
short. Then something at once moving and repulsive happened. The
man to whom I had given back his life, his criminal's and traitor's
life, plunged madly to my feet and kissed the dust on my shoes. I
thrust him away. I was overcome with disgust and horror. I was
stirred by the power at my command, the power with which I could
freely play, as the gale plays with leaves, stirred so that it hurt, so I
laughed and ordered the man to go away. He was almost out of his
mind. A bestial joy gushed from eyes and mouth, he babbled
thanks, thanks, and crawled away. Until late in the night we others
gave ourselves up to wild drinking and revelry, and early in the
morning, as we still sat at the table, I received with a dignity, a grandeur that nearly made even me smile, the emissaries of the Pope. I
was the hero, the master of the day. On my whim, my satisfaction,
depended the peace of half of Europe. Yet for the diplomatic gentlemen I played the fool, the kind fool, it suited me that way, I was a
bit tired, I wanted to go home. I allowed the advantages won in war
to be taken away from me. Naturally I was later made a Count,
then I got married, and now I have sunk so low that I'm not troubled at all to be a humble little pupil at the Benjamenta Institute,
and to have friends like Kraus, Schacht, and Schilinski. Throw me
naked on the cold street and perhaps I'll imagine that I'm the all-
embracing Lord God. It's time I laid down my pen.

For such small and humble people as us pupils there is nothing
comic. Without dignity, one takes everything in a serious way, but
also lightly, almost frivolously. For me our classes in dancing, propriety, gymnastics, seem like public life itself, large, important, and
then before my eyes the schoolroom is transformed into a splendid
drawing room, into a street full of people, into a castle with old
long corridors, into an official chamber, into a scholar's study, into
a lady's reception room, it just depends, it can be anything. We
must enter, make formal greeting, bow, speak, deal with imaginary
business matters or tasks, carry out orders, then suddenly we're at
table and dining in a metropolitan manner and servants are waiting
on us. Schacht, or perhaps even Kraus, pretends to be a lady of the
high aristocracy, and I undertake to entertain her. Then we are all
cavaliers, not excluding Beanpole Peter, who always feels that he's
a cavalier anyway. Then we dance. We hop around, followed by the
laughing gaze of the instructress, and suddenly we rush to the aid

of a casualty. He has been run over on the street. We give some small charity to a beggar, write letters, bellow at our valets, go to meetings, visit places where French is spoken, practice doffing our hats, talk about hunting, finance, and art, submissively kiss the five outstretched pretty fingers of ladies whom we want to feel fond of us, loaf like lay-abouts, quaff coffee, eat hams cooked in Burgundy, sleep in imaginary beds, get up again apparently early in the morning, say, "Good day, Judge," fight with one another, for that happens in life too, and simply do all the things that occur in life. If we get tired of all of these follies, the Fräulein taps her cane on the edge of her desk and says: "*Allons,* come on, boys! Work!" Then we work at it again. We cruise around the room like wasps. It's quite hard to describe, and if we get tired again, the instructress calls: "What? Are you sick of public life already? Get on with it! Show how life is. It's easy, but you must be brisk, or life will tread on you." And briskly off we go again. We travel, and our servants do silly things. We sit in libraries and study. We are soldiers, genuine recruits, and we must lie down and shoot. We walk into shops, to buy things, into swimming places, to swim, into churches, to pray: "Lord, lead us not into temptation." And the next moment we are slap in the middle of the crassest error, and committing sins. "Stop. Enough for today," the instructress then says, when it's time. Then life is extinguished and the dream called human life takes another course. Usually then I go for half an hour's walk. A girl always meets me in the park, where I sit on a bench. She seems to be a shopgirl. She always cranes her neck around and gives me a long look. She's always swooning. It happens that she thinks I'm a gentleman earning a monthly salary. I look so good, like the right sort of thing. She's wrong, and that's why I ignore her.

Now and again we also act plays, comedies, to be precise, which deteriorate into farce, until the instructress signals us to stop. The Mother: "I cannot give you my daughter for a wife, you are too poor." The Hero: "Poverty is no disgrace." The Mother: "Fiddlesticks! That's empty talk. What are your prospects?" The Loving Girl: "Mamma, I must ask you, with all due respect, to speak more politely to the man whom I love." The Mother: "Silence! One day you'll be grateful to me for treating him with ruthless severity. Now, sir, tell me, where did you do your studies?" The Hero (he is Polish, and is played by Schilinski): "I graduated at the Benjamenta

Institute, gracious lady. Forgive me for the pride with which I speak these words." The Daughter: "Ah, Mamma, just see how well he behaves. What refined matters." The Mother (severely): "Don't talk to me about manners. Aristocratic behavior doesn't matter a fig nowadays. You, sir please would you tell me this: What did you learn at the Bagnamenta Institute?" The Hero: "Forgive me, but the Institute is called Benjamenta, not Bagnamenta. What did I learn? Well, of course, I must confess that I learned very little there. But learning a lot doesn't matter a fig nowadays. You yourself must admit that." The Daughter: "You heard what he said, Mamma dear?" The Mother: "Don't talk to me, you little wretch, about hearing such nonsense or even taking it seriously. Now, my pretty young gentleman, you would do me a favor if you removed yourself from my sight, once and for all." The Hero: "What's this you venture from my sight, once and for all." The Hero: "What's this you venture to offer me? Oh, well, so be it. Adieu, I'm going." Exit, et cetera. The content of our little dramas always relates to the school and the pupils. A pupil experiences all kinds of mixed and various fates, bad and good. He has success in the world, or total failure. A play always ends with a glorification and tableau of humble service. Happiness serves: that is the lesson of our dramatic literature. Our Fräulein usually represents, during the performance, the world of the spectators. She sits, as it were, in her box and gazes through her eyeglasses down upon the stage, that's to say, upon us actors. Kraus is the worst actor. Acting doesn't suit him at all. The best is definitely Beanpole Peter. Heinrich, too, is charming on the stage.

I have the somewhat unpleasant feeling that I shall always have something to eat in the world. I'm healthy, and shall remain so, and people will always be able to make use of me somehow. I shall never be a burden to my nation, or my community. To think this, that's to say, to think that as a humble person one will always have one's daily bread to eat, would deeply wound me if I were the earlier Jakob von Gunten, if I were still the descendant, scion of the house, but I have become a quite quite different person, I have become an ordinary person, and I have to thank the Benjamentas for my becoming ordinary, and this fills me with a confidence beyond words, that shines with the dew of contentment. I've changed my pride, my kinds of honor. How have I come to be degenerate so young? But is this degeneration? To some extent it is, in other ways it's the preservation of my kind of being. Perhaps I shall remain, lost and forgotten somewhere else in life, a purer and prouder von Gunten than if I were to have stayed at home, pecking at the family tree, rotting, heartless, ossified. Well, be that as it may. I have made the choice and there it is. There's a strange energy in me, an urge to learn life from the roots, and an irrepressible desire to provoke people and things into revealing themselves to me. This makes me think of Herr Benjamenta. But I want to think of something else, that's to say, I don't want to think of anything.

I have met quite a number of people, thanks to Johann's friendliness. There are artists among them, and they seem to be pleasant people. Well, what can one say after such fleeting contact? Actually, people who make efforts to be successful are terribly like each other. They all have the same face. Not really, and yet they do. They're all alike in their rapid kindness, which just comes and goes, and I think this is because of the fear which these people feel. They deal with persons and objects, one after the other, only so that they can cope again with some new thing that also seems to be demanding attention. They don't despise anyone, these good people, and yet perhaps they despise everything, but they aren't allowed to show it, because they're frightened of being suddenly incautious. They're kind out of *Weltschmerz* and pleasant out of fear. And then everyone wants to be respected. These people are cavaliers. And they seem never to feel quite right. Whoever can feel right if he places value on the tokens of respect and the distinctions conferred by the world? And then I think that these people, who are, after all, society people and not living in a state of nature, are always feeling that some successor is pursuing them. Everyone senses the awful ambush, the secret thief, who comes creeping up with some new gift or other, spreading damage and humiliations of every kind all around, and therefore in these circles the completely new person is the most sought-after and most preferred, and woe to the older ones if this new one is somehow distinguished by intelligence, talent, or natural genius. I'm expressing myself rather too simply. There's something quite different about it all. In these circles of progressive culture there's a fairly obvious and unmistakable fatigue. Not the formal blasé-ness, say, of an aristocracy of birth, no, but a genuine, a completely authentic fatigue that dwells in higher and more lively feelings, the fatigue of the healthy-unhealthy person.

They're all cultivated, but do they respect one another? They are, if they think about it honestly, content with their positions in life, but are they really contented people? Of course, there are rich people among them. I'm not talking about them here, for the money a man has forces one to assume wholly different things when judging him. Yet they're all well-mannered people and, in their own way, important ones, and I must be extremely grateful to my brother for acquainting me with this bit of the world. Already in those circles people like to call me the little von Gunten, in contrast to Johann, whom they have christened the big von Gunten. These are jokes, the world just likes jokes. I don't, but it doesn't matter, all this. I feel how little it concerns me, everything that's called "the world," and how grand and exciting what I privately call the world is to me. My brother has tried to introduce me to people, and it's my duty to make much of this. And it is much, too. Even the smallest of things is much to me. To know a few people perfectly takes a lifetime. That's another of the Benjamenta precepts, and how unlike the world the Benjamentas are. I'm going to bed now.

I never forget that I'm a descendant beginning from all the way down, without having the qualities which one needs if one is going to rise to the top. Perhaps I have. Everything is possible, but I put no trust in the idle moments when I imagine happiness for myself, combined with splendor. I have none of the virtues of an upstart. I'm cheeky sometimes, but only as a passing mood. The upstart's cheekiness is a permanent shamming of modesty, or his gesture is that of cheeky, permanently cheeky insignificance. And there are many upstarts, and stupidly they cling to what they have attained, and that is excellent. They may also be nervous, indignant, peevish, and fed up with "all those things," but the fed-upness of the genuine upstart is nothing deep. Upstarts are masters, and perhaps as a descendant of my family, or whatever I am, I shall serve a master, perhaps a somewhat pompous master, and serve him honorably, loyally, reliably, steadfastly, without thinking, without the least concern for personal advantage, for only in this way, that is, with every decency, shall I be able to serve anyone at all, and now I notice that I've got something in common with Kraus, and I'm almost a little ashamed. Feelings like those with which I confront the world will never lead to great things, unless one snaps one's fingers at the sparkling grandeurs and calls that great which is quite grey, quiet, hard and humble. Yes, I shall serve and I shall always accept duties whose fulfillment is anything but a glitter, this will happen over and over again, and I shall blush with utter stupid joy if anyone says a flippant word of thanks. That is stupid but completely true, and I'm incapable of being sad about it. I must confess: I'm never sad, and I never feel lonely, never, and that is also stupid, for with sentimentality, with the thing that people call the cry from the heart, the best and most upstartish and topping business is done. But thanks very much for the trouble, for the indelicate effort it takes to reach an honorable status in such a way. At home, with father and mother, the whole house smelled of tact. Well, I don't mean literally. Things were genteel with us at home. And so bright. The entire household was like a gracious, kindly smile. Mamma is so refined. All right, then. I'm from that family and am condemned to be a servant and play a sixth-rate role in the world. In my view this is apt, for—oh, what did Johann say?—"The people with the power, they are the really starving people." I don't like to think that this is so. And do I need to console myself at all? Can anyone console a Jakob von Gunten? As long as I have a healthy body, there can be no question of it.

If I want to, if I tell myself to, I can revere everything, even bad behavior, but it must have the color of money. The bad manners would have to drop twenty-mark gold pieces behind them, then I'd bow to them, and behind them as well. Herr Benjamenta is of the same opinion. He says it's wrong to despise money and the advantages that fall from unlovely hands. A pupil at the Benjamenta Institute is supposed to respect most things, not to despise them.—Let's change the subject. Gymnastics, I like that. I love it passionately, and of course I'm good at it. To make friends with a noble person and to do gymnastics, these are probably the best things in the world. To dance and to find a person who engages my respect is one and the same thing for me. I like so much to set minds and limbs in motion. Just to kick up one's legs, how nice that is! Gymnastics is silly, too, and leads to nothing. Does everything I love and prefer have to lead to nothing? But listen! What's that? Someone's calling for me. I must stop.

"Are you still making honest endeavors, Jakob?" the instructress asked me. It was toward evening. Somewhere there was a reddish light, like the glow of an immense and lovely sunset. We were standing by the door to my room. I'd gone there a moment before, to ponder my dreams and forebodings a little. "Fräulein Benjamenta," I said, "do you doubt the seriousness and honesty of my endeavors? Am I, in your eyes, a swindler and a cheat?" I think I was looking positively tragic as I said this. She turned her beautiful face to me and said: "Heaven forbid. You're a nice boy. You're impetuous, but you're decent and pleasant, I like you, just as you are. Are you content? Are you? Well? Do you make your bed properly every morning? Yes? And you stopped obeying the rules long ago? You didn't? Or did you? Oh, you're a very good boy, I believe you. And no praise could be fulsome enough for you. Never. Whole buckets full of flattering praise, just think, whole pitchers and pannikins full. One would have to use a broom to sweep them all up. The many fine words of recognition for your behavior. No. Jakob, quite seriously now, listen. I must whisper something to you. Do you want to hear it or would you rather slip away into your room here?" "Tell me what it is, Fräulein, I'm listening," I said, full of anxious expectation. Suddenly the instructress gave a great shudder. But quickly she controlled herself and said: "I must go, Jakob, I must go. And it will go with me. I just can't tell it to you. Perhaps another time. Yes? Yes, perhaps tomorrow, or in a week. It still won't be too late to tell you then. Tell me, Jakob, do you love me a little? Do I mean anything to you, to your young heart?" She stood there in front of me, her lips pressed angrily together. I quickly stooped to her hand, which hung unspeakably sadly down against her dress, and kissed it. I was so happy to be allowed to tell her now what I had always felt for her. "Do you think highly of me?" she asked, the pitch of her voice rising till it was almost stifled and died away. I said: "How could you be in any doubt? I am unhappy." But I felt so outraged that I could have wept. I abruptly let go of her hand and stood there respectfully. And she went away, with an almost imploring look. How everything has changed in this once so tyrannical Benjamenta Institute! Everything's collapsing, the classes, the effort, the rules. Is this a morgue, or is it a celestial house of joy? Something is going on and I don't understand it yet.

I ventured to make a remark to Kraus about the Benjamentas. I said that I thought the old splendor of the Institute was clouding over. I asked what it meant, and if Kraus knew anything about it. He got angry and said: "You, you've got yourself pregnant with silly ideas. What a notion. Do something! Work, then you won't notice anything. You snooper. Snooping around for opinions and thoughts. Go away. I'm beginning to hate the sight of you." "You're getting a bit rude, aren't you?" I said, but I thought it better to leave him alone. During the day I had a chance to talk to Fräulein Benjamenta about Kraus. She said to me: "Yes, Kraus isn't like other people. He sits there till one needs him, if one calls him he gets moving and rushes up. One doesn't make much fuss about people like him. Actually, one never praises Kraus, and one is hardly grateful to him. One only asks of him, Do this or Do that. And one hardly notices that he's been of service, and how excellently so, his service is that perfect. As a person, Kraus is nothing, Kraus is something as a doer, as a person for a job, but he doesn't make himself noticeable at all. You, for instance, Jakob, one praises you, it's a joy to make you feel good. One hasn't a word for Kraus, one feels no fondness for him. You're very nasty to Kraus, Jakob. You're nicer than he is, though. I won't put it any other way, for you wouldn't understand. And Kraus will be leaving us soon. That will be a loss, Jakob. Oh, that's a loss. If Kraus isn't there any more, who is there left? You, yes. That's true, and now you're angry with me, aren't you? Yes, you're angry with me, because I'm sad about Kraus leaving. Are you jealous?" "Not at all. I'm very sorry, too, about Kraus leaving us," I said. I spoke intentionally in a formal sort of way. I had begun to feel sad, too, but I found it proper to be a little cold. Later I tried to have a talk with Kraus, but he was still incredibly stand-offish. He sat glumly at the table and said nothing to anybody. He is also feeling that something's not quite right here, only he doesn't say anything, except to himself.

Often the feeling of a great inner defeat comes over me. When it does so, I position myself in the middle of the classroom and do silly things, quite childish silly things. I put Kraus's cap on my head, or a glass of water, et cetera. Or Hans is there. With Hans one can throw hats, trying to make them land on the other person's head and stick there. How Kraus despises us for this. Schacht has had a job for three days, but he has come back, very depressed and with all kinds of angry, painful excuses. Didn't I say earlier that things would go badly for Schacht out in the world? He will always wriggle into functions, tasks, and jobs and he won't like it anywhere. Now he says he had to work too hard, and he talks about cunning, malicious, and lazy halfway superiors who began to heap unfair duties on him mischievously the moment he arrived, and to torment him utterly and to cheat him. Ah, I believe Schacht. Only too willingly; that's to say, I think what he says is absolutely true, for the world is incomprehensibly crass, tyrannical, moody, and cruel to sickly and sensitive people. Well, Schacht will stay here for the time being. We laughed at him at bit, when he arrived, that can't be helped either, Schacht is young and after all he can't be allowed to think that there are special degrees, advantages, methods, and considerations for him. He has now had his first disappointment, and I'm convinced that he'll have twenty disappointments, one after the other. Life with its savage laws is in any case for certain people a succession of discouragements and terrifying bad impressions. People like Schacht are born to feel and suffer a continuous sense of aversion. He would like to admit and welcome things, but he just can't. Hardness and lack of compassion strike him with tenfold force, he just feels them more acutely. Poor Schacht. He's a child and he should be able to revel in melodies and bed himself in kind, soft, carefree things. For him there should be secret splashings and birdsong. Pale and delicate evening clouds should waft him away into the kingdom of Ah, What's Happening to Me? His hands are made for light gestures, not for work. Before him breezes should blow, and behind him sweet, friendly voices should be whispering. His eyes should be allowed to go quietly to sleep again, after being wakened in the morning in the warm, sensuous cushions. For him there is, at root, no proper activity, for every activity is for him, the way he is, improper, unnatural, and unsuitable. Compared with Schacht I'm the trueblue rawboned laborer. Ah, he'll be crushed, and one day he'll die in a hospital, or he'll perish, ruined in body and soul, inside one of our modern prisons. Now he crouches around in the corners of the classroom, is ashamed of himself and trembling with dread of the repulsive unknown future. The Fräulein looks at him anxiously, but she's at present much too concerned with her very own peculiar affairs to be much troubled about Schacht. Anyway, she couldn't help him. A God would have to do that, and could do it perhaps, only there are no gods, only one, and he's too sublime to help. To help and to alleviate, that wouldn't be proper for the Almighty, at least that's how I feel.

Fräulein Benjamenta now says a few words to me every day, either in the kitchen or in the sometimes very quiet and empty classroom. Kraus is acting as if he reckoned on spending another decade here in the Institute. Dryly and fretfully he learns his lessons, yes, he really is fretful about it, but he always did look that way, it doesn't mean anything special. This person isn't capable of any overhastiness, or any impatience. "Wait for It" is written almost majestically on his tranquil brow. Yes, the Fräulein said this once, she said that Kraus has majesty, and it's true, the unassumingness of his character has something of an invisible emperor about it. To my Fräulein I ventured to say yesterday: "If my attitude to you has ever been a single time, for a tiny, shrinking, single moment, more self-possessed than swayed by feelings and bonds of the purest respect, I will hate myself, persecute myself, hang myself with a rope, poison myself with the deadliest poisons, cut my throat with knives, no matter of what sort. No, it's quite impossible, Fräulein. I could never do you any injury! Your very eyes. How they have always been for me the command to obey, the inviolable and beautiful commandment. No, no, I'm not telling lies. Your appearance in the doorway! I have never needed a heaven here, never needed moon, sun, and stars. You, yes, you, have been for me the higher presence. I'm speaking the truth, Fräulein, and I must assume that you can feel how far these words are from any kind of flattery. I hate all future success, I find life repugnant. Yes, yes, and yet soon I too must leave, like Kraus, and go out into hateful life. You have been my body's health. Whenever I have read a book, it was you I was reading, not the book, you were the book. You were, you were. Often I've behaved badly. Several times you had to warn me against the pride that was eating me up and trying to bury me under the ruins of improper imaginings. How it subsided then, as quick as lightning. How attentively I listened to what Fräulein Benjamenta was saying. You smile? Yes, your smile has always been a spur to goodness, courage, and truth. You have always been too kind to me! Much, much too kind for such a pig-head. And at the sight of you my many failings fell at your feet, imploring forgiveness. No, I don't want to go out into life, into the world. I despise everything that the future may hold in store. When you walked into the classroom, I was happy, and then I always scolded myself for being such a fool. Often—just think, yes, I must confess it—often, secretly, I thought to rob you of your dignity and grandeur, but I found in my raging spirit not a word, not a single little word with which to revile and reduce what it was I wanted to injure a little. And my punishment, every time, was my remorse and my restlessness. Yes, always, always I have had to revere you, Fräulein. Are you angry that I should speak to you so? I, I am happy to be speaking so." She looked at me with twinkling eyes and smiled. She was a bit scornful, but she was quite content. Moreover, she was preoccupied, I noticed, with some faraway thoughts. In spirit she was somewhere else, and therefore, only for that reason, did I dare to speak to her in this way. I shall take care not to do so again.

It's not my concern, I know, but it's a noticeable fact that no new pupils are entering the Institute. Is the reputation which Herr Benjamenta enjoyed in the world as an educator on the wane or even near to vanishing? That would be sad. But perhaps it's only because I'm over-sensitive. I've become a little nervous here, if that's what one can call it when one's powers of observation are at once excited and tired. Everything has become so fragile here, and it's as if one were standing in midair, not on firm ground. And then this being permanently prepared and alert, that does something too. It's quite possible. One's always waiting for something, well, that tends to weaken one. And, again, one forbids oneself to listen and wait for things, because it's not permissible. Well, that makes claims on one's powers as well. Often the Fräulein stands at the window and looks out for a long time, as if she were living somewhere else already. Yes, that's it, that's the somewhat unhealthy and unnatural way in which things are moving here: we're all, superiors and pupils, all nearly living somewhere else. It's as if we had only a little time left to breathe, sleep, wake up, and give and enjoy instruction here. There's something like a rushing, ruthless energy beating its wings and fluttering about the place. Are we all listening for what's to come? For some future happening? Also possible. And what if we present pupils all leave and no new ones arrive? What then? Will the Benjamentas be poor and forsaken? When I imagine this, I feel ill, simply ill. No, never, never! It shall never be allowed to happen. Yet it has to be. Has to be?

To be robust means not spending time on thought but quickly and quietly entering into what has to be done. To be wet with the rains of exertion, hard and strong from the knocks and rubs of what necessity demands. I hate such clever turns of phrase. I was intending to think of something quite different. Aha, yes, that's what it was, it's about Herr Benjamenta. I've been with him in the office again. I keep teasing him about the job I am to get, and soon. So this time I asked again how things stood now, if I could reckon . . . et cetera. He started to get furious. Oh, he keeps getting furious now, and I'm always very daring when I excite him. I asked in a very loud voice, abruptly and shamelessly. The Principal got very embarrassed, he even began to rub behind his big ears. Of course he hasn't got what people call big ears, his ears are relatively not big at all, it's just that everything about the man is big, consequently his ears are big too. At length he came up to me, gave a very kind-hearted laugh, and said: "You want to go out to work, Jakob? But I tell you, you'll do better to stay here. It's very nice here for you and people like you. Or isn't it? Stay on a little longer. I would even like to advise you to be a little torpid, forgetful, lazy-minded. For you see, what people call the vices play such a large role in human life, they're important, I might even say they're necessary. If there were no vices and failings, there'd be a shortage of warmth, charm, and richness in the world. Half of the world, and perhaps it is at root the better half, would perish along with the indolence and the weaknesses. No, be lazy. Well, well, now, don't misunderstand me, be just as you are, just as you have come to be, but please play at being a little remiss. Will you do it? Yes? It would please me to see you given to dreaming a little. Hang your head, be pensive, look gloomy, won't you? Because for my taste you're a little bit too full of will power, too full of character. And you're proud, Jakob! What's your attitude, really? Do you think you'll attain and achieve great things out there in the world? That you have to do so? Do you seriously intend to do something important? You almost give me this unfortunately somewhat vehement impression. Or do you perhaps, perhaps out of defiance, want to remain very small? I can believe that of you as well. You're in rather a too festive, too violent, too triumphal state. But none of that matters, you'll stay for a while, Jakob. I'm not going to find a job for you, I won't do any such thing for you, not for a long time. Do you know, what I want is to keep you. I've hardly got you for myself and you want to run away? That can't be done. Get bored here in the Institute as well as you can. Oh, you little world-conqueror, out in the world, out there, in a profession, endeavoring, achieving things, whole seas of boredom, emptiness, loneliness will yawn at you. Stay here. Go on yearning for a bit longer. You've no idea what bliss, what grandeur there is in yearning, in waiting. So wait. Let it press on you inside, all the same. But not too much. Listen, if you left it would hurt me, it would wound me, quite incurably, it would almost kill me. Kill me? Now you have a good laugh at me, go on. Laugh me utterly to scorn, Jakob. You have my permission. Yet, tell me, what is there that I can order or permit you to do in future? I, who have just convinced you that I'm almost, almost dependent on you? I've started something that makes me shudder, that outrages me and at the same time makes me happy, Jakob. But, for the first time, I love somebody. But you don't understand that. Go away now! Be off with you. You insolent fellow, remember that I can still punish. Watch out!" Well, there it was, suddenly he got furious again. I quickly disappeared from under his dark, penetrating gaze. What eyes he has! The Principal's eyes. I must here observe that I have incredible skill in fitting out of places. I positively flew out of the office, no, I whistled out of it, as the wind whistles, when the gentleman said to me: "Watch out!" Oh, yes, one sometimes can't help feeling frightened of him. I'd find it improper if I weren't frightened, for then I'd have no courage, since courage is precisely the thing that comes of conquering fear. Once more, out in the corridor, I listened at the keyhole, and again it was all quiet in there. I even stuck out my tongue, in a quite childish and schoolboyish way, and then I couldn't help laughing. I think I've never laughed so much in all my life. Very quietly, of course. It was the purest repressed laugh imaginable. When I laugh like that, well, then there's nothing more that's above me. Then I'm the unbeatable embracer and ruler of all things. At such moments I'm simply grand.

Yes, that is how it is: I'm still at the Benjamenta Institute, I must still go in fear of of the existing statutes, lessons are still being given, questions are asked and answered, we still fly to commands, Kraus still knocks in the mornings on my door, with his peevish "Get up, Jakob" and his angrily raised forefinger, we pupils still say "Good day, Fräulein" when she appears and "Good night" when she retires in the evening. We're still caught in the iron talons of the numerous rules and indulge in didactic, monotonous repetitions. Also I've been, at last, in the authentic inner chambers, and I must say, they don't exist. There are two rooms, but these two rooms don't look chamber-like at all. The furniture is frugal and ordinary in the extreme, and there's nothing mysterious about them at all. Strange. How did I get the mad idea that the Benjamentas live in chambers? Or was I dreaming, and is the dream over now? As a matter of fact, there are goldfish there and Kraus and I regularly have to empty and clean the tank in which these animals swim and live, and then fill it with fresh water. But is there anything remotely magical about that? Goldfish can occur in any middling Prussian official's family, and there's nothing incomprehensible and unusual about the families of officials. Wonderful! And I believed in the inner chambers so steadfastly. I thought that beyond the door through which the Fräulein passes to and fro there would be hundreds of castle rooms and apartments. In my mind I saw delicately coiling spiral stairways and other broad stone staircases laid with carpets, behind that simple door. Also an ancient library was there, and corridors, long and serene corridors with floor mats, ran in my imagination from one end of the building to the other. With all my ideas and follies I could one day found a corporate company for the propagation of beautiful but unreliable imaginings. The capital's there, it seems to me, there will be funds enough, and buyers of such shares are to be found wherever the idea of beauty and belief in it have not quite perished. What things I imagined! A park, of course. I can't live without a park. Also a chapel, only, strangely enough, not a romantically ruined one, but a smartly restored one, a small Protestant house of God. The parson was having breakfast. And all that sort of thing. People dined, and arranged hunts. Evenings they danced in the baronial hall, on whose high walls of dark wood hung the portraits of family ancestors. What family? I stammer that word, for in fact I can't say it. No, I deeply regret having dreamed up these fantasies. I saw snow flying too, into the castle courtyard. There were large wet snowflakes, and it was early in the morning, the time was always early on a dark winter morning. Ah, and there was something else beautiful, a hall, yes, I saw a hall. Fascinating! Three noble old dames were sitting beside a tittering and crackling fire. They were doing crochet work. What kind of a fantasy is that, not to be able to see further than where people are knitting and crocheting! But it was just this that enraptured me. If I had enemies, they'd say that it was morbid, and they'd think they had reason to shun

me along with the dear cosy crochet work as well. Then there was
a wonderful nocturnal feast, with candles shining down from silver
candelabra. The joyous table sparkled and dazzled and talked. I
thought that was really beautiful. And women, what women. One
looked like a veritable princess, and she was one, too. There was
an Englishman there. How the feminine garments rustled, how the
breasts, naked, rose and fell! The diningroom was crisscrossed with
perfumes in snakelike lines. The splendor was allied with modesty,
the tact with pleasure, the joy with refinement, and the elegance
was festooned with nobility of birth. Then it all swam away, the
other things came, new things. Yes, the inner chambers, they were
alive, and now it's as if they've been stolen away from me. Bare reality: what a crook it sometimes is. It steals things, and afterwards
it has no idea what to do with them. It just seems to spread sorrow
for fun. Of course, I like sorrow very much as well, it's very valuable, very. It shapes one.

Heinrich and Schilinski have left. Shaken hands and said adieu.
And gone. Probably forever. How short these leave-takings are!
One means to say something, but has forgotten precisely the right
thing to say, and so one says nothing, or something silly. To say
goodbye, and to have it said to me, is terrible. At such moments
something gives human life a shake, and one feels vividly how nothing one is. Quick goodbyes are loveless, and long ones are un-
bearable. What can one do? Well, one just says something
goofish.—Fräulein Benjamenta said something very peculiar to me.
"Jakob," she said, "I am dying. Don't be afraid. Let me talk to you
quite calmly. Tell me, why have you become my confidant like this?
From the start, when you arrived here, I thought you were nice, and
sensitive. Please don't make any falsely honest objections. You're
vain. Are you vain? Listen, soon it will be over with me. Can you
keep a secret? You must say nothing about what I'm going to tell
you. Above all, your Principal, my brother, mustn't know anything,
make a point of remembering that. But I'm quite calm, and so are
you, and you'll keep your word and keep your mouth shut, I know.
Something is gnawing at me, and I'm sinking down into something,
and I know what that means. It's so sad, my dear young friend, so
sad. I think you're strong, don't I, Jakob? But I know it, I know
you're strong. You have a heart. Kraus wouldn't listen to everything
I had to say. I find it so nice that you aren't crying. Oh, I'd find it

repulsive if just now your eyes were to moisten over. That can wait. And you listen so nicely. You listen to my miserable tale as if it were something small, fine, and ordinary, something that attracts attention only, but no more, that's how you're listening. You can behave immensely well, if you take the trouble. Of course, you're arrogant, we know that, don't we? Quiet, now, not a murmur. Yes, Jakob, death (oh, what a word) is standing behind me. Look, like this, the way I breathe on you, that's how he's breathing his cold, horrible death at me from behind, and I'm sinking, sinking because of this breath. My breast is pressing it out of me. Have I made you feel sad? Tell me. Is this sad for you? A little, isn't it? But now you must forget it all, do you hear? Forget it! I'll come to you again, like today, and then I'll tell you how I am. You'll try to forget it, won't you? But come here. Let me touch your forehead. You're a good boy."—She drew me gently toward her and pressed something like a breath on my forehead. It was nothing like the touch that she spoke of. Then she quietly went away and I surrendered to my thoughts. Thoughts? Not really. I thought once more of my not having any money. That was my thought. That's how I am, so crude, and so thoughtless. And it's like this: heartfelt emotions put something like any icy coldness into my soul. If there's immediate cause for sadness, the feeling of sadness entirely escapes me. I don't like to tell lies. And to tell them to myself: what point would that have? I tell lies somewhere else, but not here, not in front of myself. No, it beats me, but here I am, alive, and Fräulein Benjamenta says such a terrifying thing, and I, who worship here, I can't shed a single tear? I'm mean, that's what it is. But stop. I don't intend to disparage myself too much. I'm puzzled, and therefore—. It's lies, all lies. Actually I knew it all along. Knew it? That's another lie. It's not possible for me to tell myself the truth. Anyway, I shall obey the Fräulein and say nothing about this. To be allowed to obey her! As long as I obey her, she will live.

Assuming I were a soldier (and by nature I'm an excellent soldier), an ordinary infantryman, and serving under the banners of Napoleon, then one day I would march off to Russia. I would get on well with my comrades, because the misery, the deprivations, and our many rough deeds would forgive us into something like a mass of iron. Grimly we would stare ahead. Yes, grimness, dull, unconscious anger, would unite us. And we would march, always with our rifles slung on our shoulders. In the cities through which we passed, an idle, drooping crowd of people would gape at us, demoralized by the tramp of our feet. And then there would be no more cities, or just very seldom, only unending stretches of country would crawl away to the horizon before our eyes and legs. The country would positively crawl and creep. And now the snow would come and snow us in, but we would always go on marching. Legs, that would be everything now. For hours on end my gaze would be fixed on the wet earth. I would have time for remorse, for endless self-accusations. But I would always keep in step, swing my legs back and forth, and go on marching. Also, our marching would by now be more like a trot. Now and again, very far off, a mocking ridge of hills would appear, thin as the blade of a pocket knife, a sort of forest. And then we'd know that beyond this forest, whose edge we would reach after many hours, other endless plains extended. From time to time there would be shots. These scattered shots would remind us of what was coming, the battle which would one day have to be fought. And we would march. The officers would ride around with mournful expressions on their faces, adjutants would whip their horses past the column, as if they were being harried by fearful forebodings. One would think of the Emperor, the Commander-in-Chief, quite remotely, but, all the same, one would imagine him, and that would be consoling. And we would keep on marching. Countless small but terrible interruptions would hinder the march for short periods. Yet we would hardly notice them, but would go on marching. Then memories would come to me, not clear ones, and yet excessively clear ones. They would gobble at my heart like buzzards at a welcome prey, they would transport me to a cosy and homely place, to the golden, roundish vineyard hills wreathed with delicate mists. I would hear cowbells ringing and clamoring against my heart. A caressing sky would be curving with watery colors and full of sounds over my head. The ache would nearly madden me, but I would go on marching. My comrades to left and right, before and behind, that would be all that mattered. The legs would work like an old but still willing machine. Burning villages would be a daily sight for the eyes, no longer even interesting, and one would not be surprised by cruelties of an inhuman sort. Then one evening, in the ever-increasing bitter cold, my comrade, his name could be Tscharner, would drop to the ground.

I would try to help him up, but the officer would give the command: "Let him lie there!" And we would go on marching. Then, one noon, we would see our Emperor, his face. But he would smile, he would enchant us. Yes, it wouldn't occur to this man to unnerve and discourage his soldiers by having a gloomy look on his face. Sure of victory, future battles won in advance, we would go on marching through the snow. And then, after endless marches, it would at last come to blows, and it is possible that I would remain alive and have gone on marching again. "Now we're off to Moscow, pal!" someone in our rank would say. I would decline to answer him, though I would not know why. I would be only a little cog in the machine of a great design, not a person any more. I would know nothing of parents any more, of relatives, songs, personal troubles or hopes, nothing of the meaning and magic of home any more. Soldierly discipline and patience would have made me into a firm and impenetrable, almost empty lump of body. And so the march would go on, toward Moscow. I wouldn't curse life, it would have long since become too abominable for cursing. I would feel no more pain, I would have finished with feeling pain and all its sudden tremors. That is roughly what it would be like, I think, as a soldier under Napoleon.

"You're a fine one," Kraus said to me, actually quite without reason, "you're one of those worthless fellows who think they're above the rules. I know. You needn't say anything. You think I'm a grumpy pedagogue and dogmatist. Well, I'm not. And what do you and your sort, big mouths, what do you suppose it really means to be serious and attentive? You imagine you're king, just because you can leap and dance around, definitely and quite rightfully, without a doubt, don't you? Oh, I can see through you, you dancer. Always laughing at what's right and proper, you can do that well enough, yes, yes, you're quite the master in that, you and your lot. But watch out, watch out. The storms and lightning and thunder and blows of fate certainly haven't yet been done away with, so as to save you the trouble. Just because of your gracefulness, you artists, for that's what you are, there certainly hasn't been any dropping-off in the difficulties facing anyone who really does something, who's really alive. Learn by heart the lesson in front of you, instead of trying to prove that you can look down on me and laugh. What a little gentleman! He wants to show me that he can act big if it happens to suit him. Let me tell you, Kraus simply despises such pitiful play-acting! Do something! That's the message for you, my lad, and telling you a dozen times over wouldn't stop you from turning up your noble nose. Do you know something, Jakob, lord of life: let me be. Go and make your conquests! I'm certain a few will fall at your feet, and they'll be there for the picking. Everything's soft on you, everything comes your way, you mop-maker. What? Still got your hands in your pockets? I see the point, yes. If the roast pigeons come flitting into a fellow's mouth, why ever should he take the trouble to look like someone who's ready for doing something, for work, for using his hands? Yawn a little, won't you? That makes it easier. As things are, you're looking too self-possessed, controlled, and modest. Or do you want to read me a few rules? Go ahead. It would be very exciting. Oh, go away. Your silly presence confuses me, you old—I nearly said something there. Makes me say sinful things, gets my dander up, that's what he does. Make yourself invisible, or get busy with something. And you lose all your manners, yes, you do, when you're up before the Principal and the Fräulein. I've seen it. But what's the use of talking to a goof like you? Admit it, you'd be very nice if you weren't a fool. If you admit that, I'll hug you." "O Kraus, dearest friend," I said, "are you, of all people, scoffing and jeering at me? Can Kraus do that? Is it possible?" I laughed aloud and sauntered to my room. Soon there'll be nothing here in the Benjamenta Institute but sauntering. It looks as if the "days are numbered" here. But people are wrong. Perhaps Fräulein Benjamenta is also wrong. Perhaps the Principal, too. Perhaps all of us are wrong.

I am a Croesus. The money, well, as for that—quiet, not a word about money. I'm leading a strange double life, a life that is regular and irregular, controlled and uncontrolled, simple and highly complicated. What does Herr Benjamenta mean when he says that he has never loved anyone? What does it mean when he says this to me, his pupil and slave? Yes, of course, pupils are slaves, young leaves, torn from branches and trunks, given up to the merciless gale, and already a little yellow as well. Is Herr Benjamenta a gale? It's quite conceivable, for I've often had occasion to feel the roarings and rages and dark explosions of this gale. And also he's so ominpotent, and I, a pupil, how tiny I am. Quiet now, not a word about omnipotence. One is always wrong when one takes up with big words. Herr Benjamenta is so prone to excitement and frailty, so very prone, that it almost makes me laugh, perhaps even grin. I think that everything, everything is frail, everything must needs tremble like worms. Yes, of course, and this illumination, this certainty, makes me a Croesus, that's to say, it makes me a Kraus. Kraus loves and hates nothing, therefore he is a Croesus, something in him verges on the inviolable. He's like a rock, and life, the stormy wave, breaks against his virtues. His nature, his character, is positively festooned with virtues. One can hardly love him, to hate him is unthinkable. One likes anything that is pretty and attractive, and that's why beauty and prettiness are so much exposed to being eaten up or abused. No consuming, guzzling fondnesses dare come anywhere near Kraus. How forsakenly he stands there, and yet how steadfastly, how unapproachably! Like a demigod. But nobody understands that, I don't either—sometimes I say and think things that surpass my own understanding. Perhaps, therefore, I should have been a parson, the founder of a religious sect or movement. Well, that could still happen. I can make anything of myself. But Benjamenta?—I'm certain that he'll soon tell me the story of his life. He's going to feel the urge to reveal things, to tell stories. Very probably. And oddly enough: sometimes I feel that I should never leave this man, this giant, never, as if we were fused into one. But one is always mistaken. I want to keep my self-possession, to some extent. Not too much, no. To be too self-possessed makes one cheeky. Why reckon on anything important in life? Must it be so? I'm so small. That's what I'll loosely hang on to, my smallness, smallness and worthlessness. And Fräulein Benjamenta? Will she really die? I daren't think of that, and I'm not allowed to, either. A higher sort of sentiment forbids me. No, I'm not a Croesus. And as for the double life, everybody lives one, actually. Why boast about it? Ah, all these thoughts, all this peculiar yearning, this seeking, this stretching out of hands toward a meaning. Let it all dream, let it all sleep. I'll simply let it come. Let it come.

I'm writing this in a hurry. I'm trembling all over. There are lights dancing and flickering before my eyes. Something terrible has happened, seems to have happened, I hardly know what it was. Herr Benjamenta has had a fit and tried to—strangle me. Is this true? I can't think straight, I can't say if what happened is true. But I'm so upset, it must be true. The Principal got so angry, it was indescribable. He was like a Samson, that man in the history of Palestine who shook the pillars of a tall house full of people till the festive, wanton palace, till the stone triumph, till naughtiness itself came tumbling down. Here, to be sure, that's to say less than an hour ago, there was nothing naughty, nothing vile, to be cast down, and there were also no pillars and columns, but it looked exactly the same, exactly, and I was frightened as never before, like a rabbit, terribly frightened. Yes, I was a rabbit, and indeed I had reason to run like a rabbit, I really would have been in trouble otherwise. I escaped with—I must say—marvelous agility from his throttling fists, and I think that I even bit Herr Benjamenta's, this Goliath's, finger. Perhaps that quick, energetic bite saved my life, for quite possibly the pain which the wound caused reminded him suddenly of good manners, reason, and humanity, so that conceivably I owe my life to a blatant offense against the rules of conduct for pupils. Certainly there was a danger of my being choked, but how did it all come about, how was it possible? He attacked me like a madman. He threw himself at me, his powerful body, like a dark lump of mad anger; it was coming at me like a wave, to batter me against hard sea walls. I'm inventing the water. That's nonsense, to be sure, but I'm still quite stunned, quite confused and shaken. "What are you doing, dear and honored Principal, hey?" I shrieked, and ran through the office door like a thing possessed. And there I listened again. As I stood, safe and sound, in the corridor, I put, trembling all over, of course, my ear to the keyhole, and listened. And I heard him quietly laughing in there. I ran all the way to the classroom table and here I am, and I don't know if I dreamed it or if it really did happen to me. No, no, it's real, it's a fact. If only Kraus would come! I'm still a bit scared. How nice it would be if dear Kraus would come and give me a scolding, as he often does, out of his Book of Commandments. I'd like to be scolded a little, told off, condemned and sentenced, that would do me no end of good. Am I childish?

I was never really a child, and therefore something in the nature of childhood will cling to me always, I'm certain. I have simply grown, become older, but my nature never changed. I enjoy mischief just as I did years ago, but that's just the point, actually I never played mischievous tricks. Once, very early on, I gave my brother a knock on the head. That just happened, it wasn't mischief. Certainly there was plenty of mischief and boyishness, but the idea always interested me more than the thing itself. I began, early on, to look for deep things everywhere, even in mischief. I don't develop. At least, that's what I claim. Perhaps I shall never put out twigs and branches. One day some fragrance or other will issue from my nature and my originating, I shall flower, and the fragrance will shed itself around a little, then I shall bow my head, which Kraus calls my stupid arrogant pig-head. My arms and legs will strangely sag, my mind, pride, and character, everything will crack and fade, and I shall be dead, not really dead, only dead in a certain sort of way, and then I shall vegetate and die for perhaps another sixty years. I shall grow old. But I'm not afraid of myself. I couldn't possibly inspire myself with dread. For I don't respect my ego at all, I merely see it, and it leaves me cold. Oh, to come in from the cold! How glorious! I shall be able to come into the warmth, over and over again, for nothing personal or selfish will ever stop me from becoming warm and catching fire and taking part. How fortunate I am, not to be able to see in myself anything worth respecting and watching! To be small and to stay small. And if a hand, a situation, a wave were ever to raise me up and carry me to where I could command power and influence, I would destroy the circumstances that had favored me, and I would hurl myself down into the humble, speechless, insignificant darkness. I can only breathe in the lower regions.

I quite agree with the rules which are—still—valid here, when they say that the eyes of the pupil and of the apprentice to life must shine with gaiety and good will. Yes, eyes must radiate steadfastness of soul. I despise tears, and yet I have been crying. More inwardly than outwardly, of course, but that is perhaps the most dreadful thing about it. Fräulein Benjamenta said to me: "Jakob, I am dying, because I have found no love. The heart which no deserving person deserved to possess and to wound, it is dying now. Adieu, Jakob, it's already time to say adieu. You boys, Kraus, you, and the others, you will sing a song by the bed in which I shall lie. You will mourn for me, softly. And each of you will lay a flower, perhaps still moist with nature's dew, upon my shroud. I want to take your young human heart into my sisterly and smiling confidence now. Yes, Jakob, to confide in you is so natural, for when you look as you are looking now, it's as if you must have ears, a hearing heart, and eyes, a soul, a compassionate understanding and fellow-feeling for every-thing and for each particular thing, even for what cannot be said and cannot be heard. I am dying of the incomprehension of those who could have seen me and held me, dying of the emptiness of cau-tious and clever people, and of the lovelessness of hesitancy and not-much-liking. Someone thought he would love me one day, thought he wanted to have me, but he hesitated, left me waiting, and I hesitated too, but then I'm a girl, I had to be hesitant, it was allowed and expected of me. Ah, how deceived I have been by dis-loyalty, tormented by the vacancy and unfeeling of a heart in which I believed, because I believed it was full of genuine and insistent feelings. If a thing can reflect and choose, it's not a feeling. I'm speaking to you of a man in whom my sweet and graceful dreams made me believe, believe without any hesitation. I can't tell you ev-erything. I'd rather be silent. Oh, the annihilating thing that's kill-ing me, Jakob! All the desolations that are crushing me!—but that's enough. Tell me, do you love me, as young brothers love their sis-ters? Good. Everything is good, just the way it is, don't you think, Jakob? We shan't grumble, shan't despair, the two of us, shall we? And it is beautiful, isn't it, not to want anything any more? Or isn't it? Yes, it is beautiful. Come, let me kiss you, just once, a kiss in innocence. Be soft. I know that you don't like to cry, but let's have a little cry together. And quietly now, quietly." She didn't say any more. It was as if she wanted to say many other things, but could find no more words for what she was feeling. Outside in the court-yard big wet snowflakes were falling. The inner chambers! And I had always thought of Fräulein Benjamenta as the mistress of these inner chambers. I have always thought of her as a tender princess. And now? Fräulein Benjamenta is suffering, tender, feminine per-son. Not a princess. So one day she will lie in there on the bed. Her mouth will be rigid, and around her lifeless brow the curls will be deceptively playing. But why picture this? I'm going to see the Prin-cipal now. He has sent for me. On one side of me the lament and the corpse of a girl, on the other side her brother, who seems never to have lived. Yes, Benjamenta seems to me like a starved and im-prisoned tiger. And now? Now I'm going into his gaping jaws? On-ward! I hope his courage will cool down at the sight of a defenseless pupil. I am at his disposal. I am afraid of him, but at the same time something in me laughs him to scorn. Moreover, he still owes me his life-story. He gave me a firm promise of it and I shall be sure to remind him. Yes, that is how he seems: he has never yet lived. Does he want to live through me now? Does he think living is fuller if you commit crimes? That would be stupid, very stupid, and dangerous. But I must! I must go to this man. Some soul-force that I don't understand is compelling me to go and listen to him, again and again, and to find out all about him. Let the Principal eat me if he wants to, in other words, let him do me any harm he likes. In any case I shall have perished in a big way. Now to the office. Poor Fräulein Benjamenta!—

A little scornfully, I must say, but otherwise very confidingly (yes, thus confiding because scornfully), the Principal slapped me on the shoulder and laughed with his wide but well-shaped mouth. This made his teeth show. "Principal," I said, "I must ask you to treat me with somewhat less offensive friendliness. I am still your pupil. Moreover, I decline, and the word is not strong enough, your favors. You should be condescending and generous to such a menial fellow. My name is Jakob von Gunten, and he is a young person, but still conscious of his dignity. I am unforgivable, that I see, but also I am not to be humiliated, that I forbid."—And with these quite ridiculously arrogant words, with these words that were so little suited to the present age, I thrust away the Principal's hand. Then Herr Benjamenta laughed again, even more merrily, and said: "I have to contain myself, I can't help laughing at you, Jakob, and I shall kiss you if I'm not careful, you splendid boy." I exclaimed: "Kiss me? Are you mad, Principal? I hope not." I was myself amazed how easily I said that, and involuntarily I took a step backward, as if to avoid a blow. But Herr Benjamenta, all kindness and reticence, his lips trembling with strange gratification, said: "You, boy, are quite delectable. I would like to live with you in deserts or on icy mountains in the northern seas, it's most enticing. Come here! Ah, now, don't be afraid, please don't be afraid of me. I won't do anything to you. What could I do, whatever would I want to do to you? I can't help finding you estimable and rare, I do that, but it needn't frighten you. Besides, Jakob, and now in all seriousness, listen. Will you stay with me for keeps? You don't understand what I mean, really, so let me make it all quite plain. This place is finished, do you understand that?" I suddenly burst out with: "Ah, Principal, it's just as I suspected." He laughed and said: "Well, then, you suspected that the Benjamenta Institute is here today but will be gone tomorrow. Yes, that's for sure. You are the last pupil here. I'm not accepting any more. Look at me! I am so immensely pleased, you understand, that there was still time to get to know you, young Jakob, such a right sort of person, before I shut up shop forever. And now I'm asking you, you scamp, who have bound me with such peculiar and happy chains, will you go along with me, shall we stay together, start something together, do and dare and achieve something, shall we both, you the little one and I the big one, try to stand up to life together? Please answer me at once." I replied: "In my view, my answer to this question needs time, Principal. But what you say interests me, and I shall think over the matter between now and tomorrow. But I think my answer will be yes." Herr Benjamenta, it seemed, could hardly restrain himself, and he said: "You are enchanting." After a pause, he began again: "For look, together with you one could survive something like danger, like a daring and adventurous voyage of discovery. But we could also easily do something refined and polite. You have both kinds of blood: gentle and fearless. Together with you, one can venture either something courageous or something very delicate." "Principal," I said, "don't flatter me, that is horrid and suspicious. And stop! Where is the story of your life, which you promised to tell me, as you will surely remember?" At this moment somebody tore open the door. Kraus, it was he, rushed breathless and pale, and unable to deliver the message which he had, obviously, on his lips, into the room. He only made a rapid gesture, telling us to come. We all three went into the darkening classroom. What we saw here froze us in our tracks.

On the floor lay the lifeless Fräulein. The Principal took her hand, but let it go again, as if a snake had bitten him, and moved back, shuddering with horror. Then he returned to the dead girl, looked at her, went away again, only to return once more. Kraus was kneeling at her feet. I was holding the instructress's head in both hands, so that it would not need to touch the hard floor. Her eyes were still open, not very wide, but as if she were smiling. Herr Benjamenta closed them. He, too, was kneeling on the floor. None of us said anything, and we weren't "plunged in thought." I, at least, could think of nothing definite at all. But I was quite calm. I even felt, vain as it may sound, good and beautiful. From somewhere I heard a very thin trickling of melody. Lines and rays were moving and crisscrossing before my eyes. "Take hold of her," said the Principal quietly, "come! Carry her into the livingroom. Take her gently, oh, gently. Careful, Kraus. For God's sake, not so rough. Jakob, be careful now, will you? Don't knock her against anything. I'll help you. Forward now, very slowly. That's right. And someone reach out and open the door. That's it, that's it. We can do it. Only careful now." His words were unnecessary, in my opinion. We carried Fräulein Benjamenta to the bed, the Principal quickly pulling away the cover, and now she lay there, just as she had told me she would, in advance, as it were. And then the pupils came in and they all saw it, and then we all stood there, by the bed. The Principal gave us a sign, which we understood, and we pupils and boys began to sing softly in chorus. It was the lament which the girl had wanted to hear when she lay on the bed. And now, so I imagined, she heard the quiet song. I think we all felt as if it were a class and we were singing as the instructress told us to, whose commands we were always so quick to obey. When we had finished the song, Kraus stepped from the semicircle we had formed and spoke as follows, a little slowly, but giving all the more weight to his words: "Sleep, rest sweetly, dear and honored Fräulein. Thou art free from the difficulties, from the fears, from the troubles and events of life. (He addressed her as "Thou." I liked that.) We have sung at thy bedside, as thou hast commanded. Are we, thy pupils, now all forsaken? That is how it seems, and it is so. Yet thou who hast died before thy time, will never disappear, never, from our memories. Thou shalt remain alive in our hearts. We, thy boys, whom thou has commanded and ruled, we shall be scattered abroad into restless and wearisome life, seeking gain and seeking a home, and perhaps we shall never find and see one another again. But we shall all think of thee, our instructress, because the thoughts which thou has planted in our minds, the teachings and knowledge which thou hast secured in us, will always remind us of thee, creator of goodness. Quite of their own accord. When we eat, the fork will tell us how thou has desired us to handle and manage it, and we shall sit decently at table, and the knowledge that we are doing so will make us think of thee. In us, thy guidance, thy commands, thy life, thy teachings, thy questions, and thy voice's sound shall continue. If one of us pupils gets further in life than the others, he will perhaps no longer wish to know those whom he has left behind, if ever they should meet again. Certainly. But then he will be sure to remember the Benjamenta Institute and its lady, and he will be ashamed to have so quickly and arrogantly denied and forgotten thy precepts. Then without hesitation he will stretch out his hand in greeting to his friend, his brother, this other person. What were thy teachings, O dear departed one? Thou hast always told us that we should be modest and willing. Ah, we shall never forget this, as little as we shall be able to surpass and forget the dear person who told us this. Sleep well! Dream! Lovely imaginings may be floating and whispering around thee. May Loyalty, who is near to thee, bow to thee its knee, and Graceful Devotion and Memory, wanton with unending tender remembrances, scatter blossoms, branches, flowers, and words of love around thy brow and hands. We, thy pupils, would like now to sing one more song, and then we shall be certain that we have prayed at thy deathbed, which will be for us a bed of joy, of happy and devoted memory. For thou hast taught us to pray. Thou hast said: Singing is praying. And thou shalt hear us, and we shall imagine that thou art smiling. It is such grief for our hearts to see thee lying here, for thy movements were to us as refreshing spring-water to a man who thirsts. Yet, it is a grievous sorrow. But we are masters of ourselves, and certainly thou wouldst have wished for that as well. Thus we are tranquil. Thus we obey thee and sing." Kraus stepped back from the bed and we sang another song, with sounds coming and going as softly as those of the first. Then we walked, in turn, to the bed, and each of us pressed a kiss on the hand of the dead girl. And each of us pupils said something. Hans said: "I shall tell Schilinski. And Heinrich must be told, too." Schacht said: "Goodbye, thou wast always so kind." Peter said: "I shall do thy commands." Then we went back to the classroom, leaving the brother alone with the sister, the Principal with the Principaless, the living man with the dead girl, the lonely man with the lonely girl, the man bowed by sorrows, Herr Benjamenta, alone with Fräulein Benjamenta, blessed, dead and gone.

I have had to say goodbye to Kraus. Kraus has gone. A light, a sun, has disappeared. I feel that from now on it could only be evening in the world and all around me. Before a sun sets, it casts reddish rays across the darkening present, so did Kraus. Before he went, he gave me one more quick scolding, and as he did so the whole veritable Kraus was radiantly manifest for the last time.

"Adieu, Jakob, improve yourself, change yourself," he said to me as he held out his hand, almost annoyed at having to do so. "I'm going now, out into the world, into service. I hope you will have to do this soon too. It certainly won't do you any harm. I hope your incomprehension gets a few hard knocks. Someone ought to take you by your naughty ears. Don't laugh now that we're saying good-bye. Though it suits you. And who knows, perhaps things in this world are so foolish that they'll haul you up to the heights. Then you can quietly and cheekily carry on with your shameless ways, your defiance, your arrogance and smiling indolence, with your mockery and all kinds of mischief, and keep youself carefree, as you are. Then you'll be able to boast until you burst about all the bad habits that they haven't been able to rid you of here in the Benja-menta Institute. But I hope that worry and toil will take you into their hard, vice-breaking school. Look, Kraus is saying hard words. But perhaps I mean it better for you, Brother Funny, than people who would wish you good luck to your gaping face. Work more, wish less, and something else: please forget all about me. I would only be annoyed if I felt that you might have one of your shabby old cast-off, dancing, here-today-and-gone-tomorrow thoughts left over for me. No, pal, realize this, Kraus doesn't need any of your von Guntenish jokes." "You dear, loveless friend," I exclaimed, full of frightened farewell thoughts and feelings. And I wanted to hug him. But he stopped that in the simplest way in the world, just by quickly going, and forever. "The Benjamenta Institute is here today and will be gone tomorrow," I said to myself. I went to see the Prin-cipal. I felt as if the world had been rent apart by a glowing, fiery, yawning gulf between one spatial possibility and the diametrically opposite one. With Kraus, the half of life was gone. "From now on, a different life!" I murmured. Besides, it's quite simple: I was sad and a little stunned. Why go off into big words? To the Principal I bowed more ceremoniously than ever, and it seemed appropriate to say: "Good day, Principal." "Are you mad, my boy?" he shouted. He came toward me and would have embraced me, but I stopped him with a knock on his outstretched arm. "Kraus has gone," I said, very gravely. We were silent and contented ourselves with looking at one another for a fairly long time.

Then Herr Benjamenta said in a quiet manly voice: "I have found jobs today for all the others, your comrades. Now only we three are left here, you, me, and her lying on the bed. She (why not talk of the dead? They're alive, aren't they?) will be taken away tomorrow. That's an ugly thought, but a necessary one. And we shall sit up all night. We two shall have a talk by her bedside. And when I think how one day you arrived with your request, demand, and question, wanting to be admitted to the school, I'm seized by a terrific zest for life and for laughter. I'm over forty years old. Is that old? It was, but now that you're here, Jakob, it means youth, all green and budding, this being forty. With you, you heart of a boy, fresh life, life itself for the first time, came over me and into me. Here in this office, you see, I was desperate, I was drying up, I had positively buried myself. I hated the world, hated it, hated it. All this being and moving and living, I hated it unspeakably and avoided it. Then you came in, fresh, silly, impolite, cheeky, and blossoming, fragrant with unspoilt feelings, and quite naturally I gave you a mighty ticking-off, but I knew, the moment I saw you, that you were a magnificent fellow, flown down, I felt, from heaven for me, sent to me and given to me by an all-knowing God. Yes, it was you I needed, and I always smiled secretly when you came in from time to time, to pester me with your delightful cheek and clumsiness, which looked to me like successful works of art. Oh, no, not to pester, but to infatuate me. Stop it, Benjamenta, stop it. —Tell me, didn't you ever notice that we two were friends? Don't say anything. And when I kept my dignity, I would have liked to tear it to shreds. And even today that bow you gave was quite insanely ceremonious! But listen, how about my attack of rage recently? Did I want to hurt you? Did I want to play a deadly trick on myself? Perhaps you know, Jakob? Yes? Then tell me, please, at once. At once, do you understand? What's happening to me? What is it? What do you say?" "I don't know, I thought you were mad, Principal," I said. Cold shudders ran through me as I saw the tenderness and zest for life showing all over his face. We said nothing for a while. Suddenly it occurred to me to remind Herr Benjamenta about the story of his life. That was very good. That might distract him, restrain him from fresh murderous attacks. I was at this moment firmly convinced that I was in the clutches of a semi-lunatic, and so I quickly said, with the sweat running down my forehead: "Yes, your life story, Principal, how about it? Do you know that I don't like hints? You gave me a dark hint that you were a dethroned ruler. Now then. Please express yourself clearly. I'm very much looking forward to it." He scratched behind his ear, quite embarrassed. Then suddenly he became really angry, pettily angry, and he shouted at me with a sergeant's voice: "Dismissed! Leave me alone!" Well, I didn't need telling twice, but vanished immediately. Was he ashamed, was he tormented by something, this King Benjamenta, this lion in his cage? Anyway I was very glad to be able to stand outside in the corridor and listen. It was deathly quiet in there. I went to my room, lit the stump of a candle, and sat gazing at the picture of Mamma, which I had always carefully kept. Later, there was a knock at the door. It was the Principal, he was dressed all in black. "Come," he ordered, with iron severity. We went into the livingroom, to keep vigil by the body of Fräulein Benjamenta. Herr Benjamenta showed me, with gestures, to my seat. We sat down. Thank heavens, at least I didn't feel at all tired. I was very glad of that. The dead girl's face was still beautiful, yes, it even seemed to have become more graceful, and another thing: as the moments passed more and more beauty, feeling, and grace seemed to descend upon it. Something like a smiling forgiveness for mistakes of every kind seemed to float around and echo softly around the room. There was a sort of chirping. And it was so light, a bright seriousness in the room. Nothing dismal, nothing at all. I had a good feeling, because simply to be watching made me feel the pleasant peace that comes from quietly doing what it is one's duty to do.

"Later, Jakob," the Principal started to say, as we sat there, "later I'll tell you everything. For we shall stay together. I am certain, quite certain, that you'll agree to do this. Tomorrow, when I ask you for your decision, you won't say no, I'm certain. For today, I must tell you that I'm not really a dethroned king, I only put it that way for the sake of the image. Of course, there were times when this Benjamenta, who is sitting beside you, felt himself a lord, a conqueror, a king, when life lay before me to be seized on, when I believed with all my senses in the future and in greatness, when my footsteps carried me elastically along as over carpet-like meadows and encouragements, when I possessed all I saw, enjoyed everything I fleetingly thought of, when everything was ready to crown me with satisfaction, to anoint me with successes and achievements, when I was king without really noticing it, great without needing consciously to take account of it. In this sense, Jakob, I have been exalted, that's to say, simply young and promising, and in this sense the deposing and dethronement also occurred. I collapsed. And I doubted myself and everything. When one despairs and is sad, dear Jakob, one is so miserably small, and more and more small things hurl themselves over one, like greedy, fast-moving vermin eating us, very slowly, managing to choke us, to unman us, very slowly. But that bit about the king was just a figure of speech. I apologize, little listener, if I made you believe in a scepter and purple robes. But I think you really knew what was meant by these kingdoms in stammerings and sighs. I seem a bit more cosy to you now, don't I? Now that I'm not a king? For even you will admit that rulers who are compelled to give lessons, et cetera, and to found institutes, must certainly be pretty dismal characters. No, no, I was proud and happy only for the future: those were my estates and royal revenues. Then for long years I was discouraged and humiliated. And now I am again, that is, I am beginning again, to be myself, and I feel as if I had inherited a fortune, good heavens no, not that, no, I feel as if I—had been raised up and crowned ruler. Of course the dark moments, the cruelly dark moments still come, when there's blackness all around me and around my burnt and charred heart, as it were, don't misunderstand me, everything is detestable, and at such moments I have an urge to destroy, to kill. O my soul, you, would you stay with me still, now that you know this? Could you, perhaps out of a simple liking for me, or out of any other feeling that appeals to you, decide to defy the danger of being together with a monster like me? Can you be defiant with a high heart? Are you that sort of a defiant person? And will you or won't you hold all this against me? Against me? Ah, how silly. Besides, Jakob, I know that we shall live together. It is decided. Why still question you? Look, I do know my former pupil. You aren't my pupil any more now, Jakob. I don't want to educate and teach you any more, I want to live and, living, to shoulder some burden, carry it, and do something. Oh, it would be glorious, so glorious, to suffer with such a heart for one's friend. I have what I wanted to have and so I feel as if I could do everything, could endure and gladly suffer everything. No more thoughts, no more words. Please don't say anything. Tell me tomorrow, after this life there on the bed has been carried away, after I've been able to shed the purely external ceremony and turn it into an inward one, then tell me your opinion.

You'll say yes, or you'll say no. Realize, you're completely free now. You can say or do whatever you like." Very quietly I said, trembling with a desire to give this all too confident person a bit of a fright: "But how shall I eat, Principal? You get homes for the others, and not for me? I find that strange. It isn't right. And I insist on it. It's your duty to find me a decent job. All I want is a job." Ah, he shuddered. He jumped. How I giggled, inside. Devilment is the nicest thing in life. Herr Benjamenta said sadly: "You're right. The correct thing is to get you a position, on the basis of your leaving-certificate. Certainly, you're quite right. Only I thought, only—I thought—that you might make an exception." I exclaimed in a blaze of dismay: "Exception? I make no exceptions. That is not fitting for the son of an alderman. My modesty, my birth, all my feelings forbid me to wish for more than what my fellow-pupils have received." From then on, he spoke not another word. I liked leaving Herr Benjamenta in a state of visible, and for me flattering, uncertainty. We spent the rest of the night in silence.

But sleep did overcome me as I sat there at our vigil. Not for long, for half an hour, or perhaps a little longer, I was rapt away from reality. I dreamed (the dream, I remember, shot down upon me from above, violently, showering me with rays of light) that I was in a meadow on a mountainside. It was a dark, velvety green. And it was embroidered all over with flowers, like kisses in the shapes of flowers. It was nature, and yet not so, image and body at the same time. A wonderfully beautiful girl lay on the meadow, I told myself it must be the instructress, but quickly I said: "No, it can't be. We haven't got an instructress any more." Well, then, it must have been somebody else, and I positively saw how I was consoling myself, and I heard the consoling. It said: "Bah! Stop all this interpreting!" The girl was naked, undulant and shining. On one of her beautiful legs there was a garter, softly fluttering in the wind that was caressing everything. It seemed as if the whole dream was fluttering, the whole sweet dream, clear as a mirror. How happy I was! For a fleeting moment I thought of "This Person." Naturally it was the Principal of whom I was thinking. Suddenly I saw him, mounted on a high horse and clad in a shimmering, black, noble, and serious suit of armor. The long sword hung down at his side and the horse whinnied pugnaciously. "Well, just look now. There's the Principal on horseback," I thought, and I shouted, as loud as I could, so that the echoes rang in the gorges and ravines: "I have made my decision." But he didn't hear me. Agonized, I shouted: "Hey! Principal! Listen!" But no, he turned his back on me. He was looking into the distance, out and down into life. And he didn't even turn his head. For my benefit, it seems, the dream now rolled on, bit by bit, like a wagon, and then we found ourselves, I and "This Person," naturally no other than Herr Benjamenta, in the middle of the desert. We were traveling and doing business with the desert dwellers, and we were quite peculiarly animated by a cool, I might say splendid, contentment. It looked as if we had both escaped forever, or at least for a very long time, from what people call European culture. "Aha," I thought, involuntarily, and, it seemed to me, rather foolishly, "so that was it, that was it!" But what it was, the thing I thought, I couldn't puzzle out. We wandered on. Then a throng of hostile people appeared, but we dispersed them, though I really don't know how it happened. The regions of the earth shot like lightning past us on our days of wandering. I knew the experience of entire long decades of tribulation, signaling as they passed us by. How peculiar that was. The particular weeks eyed one another like small, glittering gems. It was ridiculous and it was glorious too. "Getting away from culture, Jakob, you know, it's wonderful," said the Principal from time to time, looking like an Arab. We were riding camels. And the customs of the people we saw delighted us. There was something mysterious, gentle, and delicate in the movements of these countries. Yes, it was as if they were marching along, no, flying along. The sea extended majestically like a great blue wet world of thought. One moment I heard the wingbeats of birds, then animals bellowing, then trees rustling overhead. "So you did come along, then. I knew you would," said Herr Benjamenta, whom the Indians had made a Prince. How crazy! As cruelly exciting as it may sound: the fact was, we were organizing a revolution in India. And apparently the trick worked. It was delicious to be alive, I felt it in every limb. Life was flourishing before our farseeing gaze, like a tree with branches and twigs. And how steadfast we were! And through dangers and experiences we waded as through icy waters that were a balm to our heat. I was always the Squire and the Principal was the Knight. "Well and good," I suddenly thought. And as I was thinking this, I woke up and looked around in the living-room. Herr Benjamenta had fallen asleep too.

I woke him up by telling him: "How can you sleep, Principal! But permit me to tell you that I've decided to go with you, wherever you want to go." We shook hands, and that meant a great deal.

I'm packing. Yes, we two, the Principal and I, we are busy packing, really packing everything up, leaving, clearing out, tearing things apart, pushing and shoving. We shall travel. Well and good. This person suits me and I'm not asking myself why any more. I feel that life demands impulses, not considerations. Today I shall say adieu to my brother. I shall leave nothing here. Nothing's keeping me, nothing obliges me to say: "How would it be if . . ." No, there's nothing left to be woulding and iffing about. Fräulein Benjamenta is under the ground. The pupils, my friends, are scattered in all kinds of jobs. And if I am smashed to pieces and go to ruin, what is being smashed and ruined? A zero. The individual me is only a zero. But now I'll throw away my pen! Away with the life of thought! I'm going with Herr Benjamenta into the desert. I just want to see if one can live and breathe and be in the wilderness too, willing good things and doing them, and sleeping and dreaming at night. What's all this. I don't want to think of anything more now. Not even of God? No! God will be with me. What should I need to think of Him? God goes with thoughtless people. So now adieu, Benjamenta Institute.

Translated by Christopher Middleton

Acknowledgments

Works by Karl Kraus originally published by Frederick Ungar, Inc.

"The Anarchist," "Studienrat Zacharias" and "Zerline's Tale" from THE GUILTLESS by Hermann Broch, translated by Ralph Manheim. Copyright © 1974 by Little, Brown and Company, Inc. Originally published in German under the title DIE SCHULD-LOSEN © 1950 by Rhein-Verlag AG, Zürich. Reprinted by permission of Farrar, Straus and Giroux, LLC.

"The Morning Walk," "The Secret," and "Confucius the Matchmaker" from AUTO-DA-FE by Elias Canetti, translated by C.V. Wedgwood. Translation copyright © 1947, renewed 1974 by Elias Canetti.

"The Survivor" from CROWDS AND POWER by Elias Canetti, translated by Carol Stewart. Translation copyright © 1962, 1973 by Victor Gollancz, Ltd.

Excerpt of Robert Walser, *Jakob von Gunten*. Ein Tagebuch. © Helmut Kossodo Verlag 1996. Alle Rechte vorbehalten Suhrkamp Verlag Zurich. Mit Genehmigung der inhaberin der Rechte, der Carl Seelig-Stiftung Zurich.